THE CHILEAN

ROAD TO SOCIALISM

Ex Libris

Hugh & Georgie O'Shaughnessy

THE CHILEAN ROAD TO SOCIALISM

Proceedings of an ODEPLAN—IDS Round Table March 1972

Edited by J. Ann Zammit

with co-operation from Gabriel Palma

Institute of Development Studies
at the University of Sussex, England

A Spanish edition of this book is being published in Chile under the title "La Via Chilena al Socialismo".

Edited by Gabriel Palma

with the cooperation of J. Ann Zammit.

Published in 1973 by the Institute of Development Studies at the University of Sussex, England.

ISBN 0 903354 06 3

ISBN 0 903354 05 5

Printed in Great Britain by The Kensington Press, Brighton.

CONTENTS

SECTION ONE

SECTION TWO

OFFICIAL CHILEAN DOCUMENTS AND BACKGROUND PAPERS

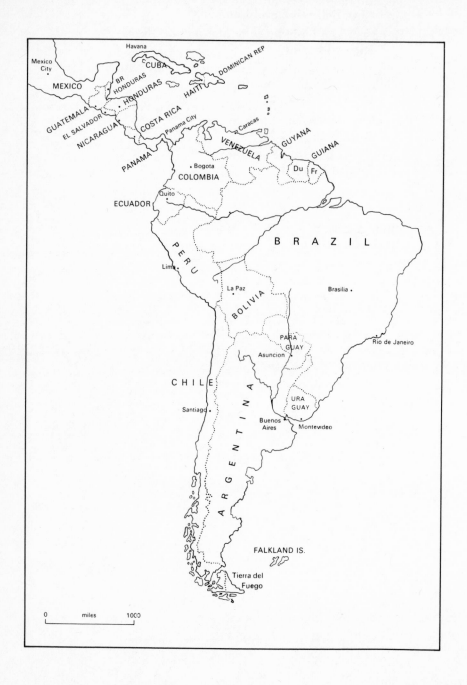

SECTION ONE

PREFACE TO THE ENGLISH EDITION

In March 1972 the Chilean National Planning Office (ODEPLAN) and the Institute of Development Studies (I.D.S.) at Sussex University organized an international Round Table in Santiago, Chile, to discuss the first phase of the Chilean Road to Socialism and its future prospects.

The Round Table was, perhaps, unique. Planned in discussions in 1971 between the Chilean Ministers of Economics (Pedro Vuskovic) and Planning (Gonzalo Martner) and the Director of I.D.S. (Dudley Seers), it brought together social scientists from widely varying backgrounds to discuss the country's current political strategy and socio-economic policies, not just with Chilean social scientists and politicians from different Chilean political parties, but also with Government officials involved in formulating and implementing policy. Discussions between economists, sociologists and political scientists from both socialist and capitalist, 'developed' and 'developing', countries are not frequent,[1] but it is even less usual for such a group to discuss acute policy problems with a government actually in power. The multi-disciplinary approach was essential since it is impossible to discuss the political aspects of the Chilean Road to Socialism without understanding the Chilean social and economic situation. Conversely, analysis of the Popular Unity's economic policy cannot be divorced from social and political aspects. While the occasion provided participants with an opportunity to voice their doubts and criticisms concerning the Popular Unity's policies and gave the Government an opportunity to explain and clarify its plans and policies to an international audience, it's main purpose and result was to provide participants with the opportunity to study the many problems involved in an exceedingly interesting experiment.

In addition to numerous discussion sessions, a day and a half was set aside for field visits in the agricultural, industrial and social sectors, covering both private and socially-owned enterprises, enabling participants to discuss problems and Popular Unity policies at first hand with different sections of the public.

---

[1] See list of participants on pages 463-465.

Although ODEPLAN and I.D.S., as joint sponsors, were responsible for initiating, organizing and financing the Round Table, the travel of the non-Latin American participants was made possible by contributions from the Swedish International Development Authority, the Royal Institute of International Affairs (London), and the Ford Foundation.

Thanks are due to ODEPLAN for its preparatory work for the Round Table and for the facilities with which it provided me while helping to organize the Round Table, and particularly to Adriana Peric of ODEPLAN, a colleague who gave so much of her time and energy to ensure its success. It would be wrong to mention only the more obvious efforts and contributions — the secretarial staff of both ODEPLAN and I.D.S. deserve special thanks for their vital contribution to both the Round Table preparations and the edited proceedings. The efforts of Gonzalo Martner, Dudley Seers and Emanuel de Kadt, as Chairmen, successfully steered the Round Table through ten days of wide-ranging debate.

The electoral victory of the Popular Unity Government and its attempt to effect a peaceful and constitutional transition to socialism have made Chile a centre of interest for political observers and activists, social scientists and the well-informed layman. However, to date no book has been published in English which describes and analyses this important political experiment. These Round Table proceedings are an attempt to bridge the gap. But they do have their limitations.

First, a conference summary is limited to the material provided in the discussions. Additional chapters which could have described the Chilean political and socio-economic situation prior to the Popular Unity's access to power, or analysed events since March 1972, are ruled out by the need to avoid lengthy delays in publication, during which the bulk of the material would have become out-of-date.

Second, there are inherent difficulties in trying to provide a succinct but lively account in reported speech of nine days of discussion mainly in Spanish and English, especially since, in order to facilitate a free discussion, we had assured participants that speakers would not be named. It was no easy task drawing together the many strands of argument spread over nine days into a useful framework. The structure of the book and each section does not follow the chronological sequence of the Round Table nor the ordering of the debate. Instead, in each chapter, I have drawn on material from several different sessions and tried to integrate them into my own view of a logical scheme. Naturally this adds one more subjective element to the editor's usual task but I hope that my presentation does not do injustice to the wide range of contributions.

In spite of these shortcomings I hope that this book will stimulate readers into reading more about the Chilean Road to Socialism;[2] and that it will provoke someone into writing a more substantial assessment in due course. A Spanish version is being published by ODEPLAN, under the supervision of Gabriel Palma.

J.A.Z.

---

[2] See pages 457-461 for a short guide to the bibliography on Chile under the Popular Unity.

INTRODUCTION

The Context of the Round Table and Subsequent Events

In late March 1972, when the ODEPLAN – I.D.S. Round Table took place, the economic and political difficulties facing the Popular Unity Government of President Salvador Allende were already beginning to assume major proportions. In contrast, Allende's first year in office appeared a triumph. Politically, the president had increased his government's support – exemplified by the municipal elections in March 1971. He had secured a unanimous vote from Congress for his copper nationalization project, and a section of the Christian Democrat opposition (the *Izquierda Cristiana* or Christian Left) had joined the Popular Unity coalition. Economically, prices had been stabilized, wages increased, and a start had been made on major structural reform.

By the beginning of 1972, however, some of the euphoria of the first year was beginning to die away. The famous 'march of the saucepans' in December 1971, when the middle class wives of Santiago took to the streets to protest against the Government, had given the first indication of an adverse wind. In January 1972, the Congressional byelections in Colchagua and O'Higgins and in Linares (in which the Christian Democrats and the National Party joined forces) seemed to show that popular support for the Government was certainly not growing. A sustained attack in Congress on the Popular Unity's plans for restructuring the economy – waged by means of a Christian Democrat-sponsored constitutional reform – led to the withdrawal from the Government and from the Popular Unity coalition of the *Partido de Izquierda Radical* (PIR) – the Party of the Radical Left – in April 1972. The PIR had been considered to be the the spokesman of the middle class within the coalition. An analysis of the economic situation seemed to indicate that, if the path towards socialism was to be continued, new and unpopular measures would have to be taken. Yet such measures, arousing strong political opposition, would certainly be inopportune in the run-up to the vital Congressional elections of March 1973. Unless the Popular Unity could

win control of Congress at those elections, its hopes of moving democratically towards socialism would be set back.

The economic strategy of the Popular Unity Government —
mainly devised and carried out till his resignation in June 1972 by
the Economics Minister, Pedro Vuskovic — combined a long-term
programme of structural change with a short-term economic policy
that was designed to broaden the Government's political support by
correcting the country's more glaring socio-economic inequalities.

In 1971 progress was made on both fronts. Copper nationalization was approved unanimously by Congress, land reform was
speeded up under the existing legislation, and banks and factories
were taken over — either by acquiring shares or by applying a law of
1932 that permits government 'intervention' when production is interrupted or when the 'national interest' demands it. Sizeable wage
increases, especially for lower paid workers — on average about 50%
— together with price controls and improved social benefits had involved a substantial measure of income redistribution. Remarkably,
increased income for the working class had not meant a decline in
the level of income and consumption of the upper income groups.
Substantial unused capacity and unemployment permitted a rapid
growth of industrial output. With a modest rise (in Chilean terms) in
retail prices of about 20% the real value of wages had risen substantially. Unemployment had declined from 7% in late 1970 to 4% in
December 1971.

In short, considerable advance towards increased social,
economic and political democracy had been made in the Popular
Unity Government's first year and important structural changes had
been initiated, though these changes and advances were still taking
place within the framework of the capitalist system.

Nevertheless, already in 1971, well-intentioned and necessary
policies had created problems whose seriousness was to become more
apparent later. Higher incomes inevitably raised the demand for food
which could not be satisfied by the very limited expansion of production in the agricultural sector — itself undergoing reform. Chile
has been a net importer of food for many years, but, to cope with
increased demand, the government was forced to step up imports
causing a considerable drain on the foreign exchange reserves.

By March 1972 there appeared to be little that could be done to
change the situation in the short run except by restricting consumption, particularly that of beef which traditionally has been imported
from Argentina. Working class and peasant pressure for higher incomes was bound to continue, and the Government, still intent on

improving the distribution of income, was hardly likely to curb these demands. However, in contrast with the situation in 1971, there was a real danger that increased demand would outstrip industrial production. The ample supply of labour and unused capacity that characterised the industrial situation when Allende took over had all been absorbed. Moreover, the policy of high wage increases and price control had led to a significant profits squeeze in 1971 and to a decline in stocks. Private entrepreneurs, uncertain about their future, had been hesitant in investing. Unless circumstances radically changed, it seemed highly doubtful whether private investment would increase in 1972 and permit a further expansion of output.

The Government had hoped that it would be able to respond to the new structure of demand — and to compensate for the decline in private investment — by incorporating all the large, high profit, monopolistic enterprises into the 'socially-owned' sector. But in February 1972 several constitutional amendments were approved by Congress which would prevent the Government from taking over any more industries by means of the 1932 legislation. The opposition amendments required that each act of nationalization would be authorised by a separate piece of legislation — and they were to be made retroactive to October 1971. Since the Popular Unity coalition lacked a majority in Congress, the opposition was thus challenging the very basis of its economic strategy.

Early in March, President Allende decided that the Christian Democrat bill containing the proposed constitutional amendments would be subjected to a presidential veto. Theoretically Congress could over-rule the veto by voting to oppose it, though there was some dispute as to whether a two-thirds majority, or merely a simple majority, would be sufficient. (After the withdrawal of the PIR from the Government in April, the Government's supporters in the Senate were reduced to an exact third.) If the opposition insisted on a simple majority, the Government announced that it would submit the question to the Constitutional Court — a body within which, it was thought, the Government's view would in all probability prevail. Nevertheless, with or without the blocking tactics of Congress, it was generally recognised — notably by the President's legal adviser, Eduardo Novoa — that the possibilities of further manipulation of the country's legal inheritance were now strictly limited.

The new pattern of demand, generated by higher wages, was also partly responsible for the growing shortages which by March 1972 were beginning to have political implications. Distribution problems and uncertainty were the principal causes, inevitably encouraging hoarding, speculation and the development of a black market. Although overall shortages were not yet prevalent they promised to increase unless measures were taken to affect supply, prices, and the high volume of liquidity. High Government expenditure on public works programmes had contributed to the latter, which in 1971 increased by around 120%.

The balance of payments and the size of the foreign debt were also subjects for considerable concern. Import capacity depends largely on the volume and price of copper exports — both of which are beyond the direct control of the Chilean government. Moreover an increase in consumer imports to satisfy the pressure of increased demand would be detrimental to the import of much needed inputs and capital goods to maintain and expand the level of production, and stocks would need replenishing in 1972 after the 1971 run-down.

The servicing of the foreign debt had reached unprecedented levels, absorbing around $400 million in 1972, or 35% of total export earnings. At the end of 1971, Chile had requested its creditors for a renegotiation of the debt and, in the absence of any clear indication of the outcome of the discussion at the Club of Paris, it was impossible in March 1972 to be optimistic about the future of the balance of payments.

Faced with this growing list of political and economic problems, it seemed then that further progress in achieving the Popular Unity's objectives would depend largely on a change in the Government's short-term economic policy. Continued improvement in the standard of living of the working class would need to be accompanied either by a reduction in the income and consumption of the rich, or by some form of generalised constraint on the consumption of certain items.

Price policy also seemed in need of revision. If the pressure of demand for some products was to be reduced and if surpluses were to be generated for re-investment, a policy of discriminate price increases was clearly called for. There was also a strong case for revising the exchange rates to encourage certain exports and to discourage unnecessary imports, the practice of under-invoicing, and the black market in foreign currency. In view of the difficulties in the way of rapidly building up a dominant state sector, it seemed that the government would have to rely increasingly on fiscal and financial measures to guide the economy coupled with the few instruments of direct control it had at its disposal.

Nevertheless, any change in economic policy was almost bound to exacerbate the political struggle, gathering momentum as the months passed. The continued efforts of the Government to develop the socially-owned sector of the economy — even after the replacement of Pedro Vuskovic as Minister of Economics by Carlos Matus in June 1972[1] — and the pursuit of economic policies which purposely or indirectly affected the interests of the upper middle class, was already leading to an intensified class struggle. Moreover the long campaign for the Congressional elections in March 1973 could not fail to inject a new feeling of intensity into the political struggle.

In the months since March 1972, almost each week has seen new and complicated interactions between politics and economics. Wishing to avoid a major clash on the question of re-structuring the economy, the Popular Unity and the Christian Democrats entered into lengthy discussions in an endeavour to achieve an agreed settlement. The talks caused a considerable crisis both within the ranks of the Popular Unity itself, and between the Christian Democrats and their allies of the traditional Right in the National Party. The Communist Party was the most powerful advocate within the Popular Unity of a rapprochement with the Christian Democrats, whereas the extremes of the political spectrum tended to favour a breakdown in the relationship. In the end the talks came to nothing, though there appears to have been a tacit understanding that the Christian Democrats would not press home their numerical advantage in Congress and the Popular Unity would not accelerate their programme of nationalization.

The breakdown of the talks cleared the way for the establishment of new alignments in preparation for the Congressional elections in March 1973. In 1970 the opponents of Allende lost the presidential election quite simply because they divided their votes between Jorge Alessandri and Radomiro Tomic. Had they fallen in behind a single candidate, as they did in 1964 with Eduardo Frei, Salvador Allende would inevitably have been defeated. Thus the task of the right wing since 1970 has been to construct a permanent alliance capable of defeating the left. The National Party, as the embodiment of Chilean conservatism, has therefore been critical of the efforts made by the left wing of the Christian Democrat party to make common cause with the Popular Unity. By July 1972, however, the Christian Democrats as a whole had decided (for the moment) to join forces with the National Party and to move towards

---

[1] Pedro Vuskovic was appointed Vice-President of CORFO and Executive Secretary of the Economic Coordination Committee, retaining a post in the cabinet.

the Congressional elections as part and parcel of the *Confederación Democratica Unida,* a right-wing coalition that will present a joint list of candidates at the elections. The Popular Unity, for its part, has formed the *Federación de Unidad Popular* which means that it too will be able to put forward a joint list of candidates.[2] The Congressional elections will choose an entire new Chamber of Deputies (150) and half the Senate (25). At present the government has 17 senators and the opposition has 33. In the Chamber of Deputies, the government has 37 seats, the opposition 93.

Although politics within Chile became increasingly polarized during 1972, the principal external problem faced by the Government derived from a decision that had been wholly national, voted on by every party represented in Congress. The unanimously approved copper nationalization legislation included a clause permitting the President of the Republic to deduct excess profits earned by the copper companies when fixing the compensation. Allende's decision to apply this principle and discount the excess profits made by the United States copper companies in the previous fifteen years prompted an appeal by the companies. In August 1972, the Chilean Court declared that it had no cause to review President Allende's decision. The Chilean government then quickly acted to prevent a threatened embargo on its property in the United States. Government funds were transferred from New York to banks in Europe, and, for payments purposes, purchases of American machinery and equipment were not regarded as complete until the goods had reached Chile.

However, in September, the Kennecott Corporation declared that it would pursue all means to get proper compensation. It informed Chile's copper clients that it might well have claims on their Chilean purchases. October is traditionally the month when contracts for the following year are arranged, and Kennecott made an attempt to disrupt Chilean copper sales by getting a French court to embargo payment on a Chilean copper shipment. In mid-October another shipment, diverted from France (where workers made a pro-Chilean gesture in refusing to handle the copper) to Rotterdam, was prevented from being unloaded by the action of a Dutch transport union.

---

[2] A change in the law in May 1972 made this possible. Previously a candidate could only be sponsored by a political party, not by a political alliance or coalition. In practice this means that within each *Federación* each party will be able to run its own candidates. The candidate with the highest vote will be awarded all the *Federación's* votes, and the sum total of these will determine the ultimate winner between the candidates of the two *Federaciónes.* Other changes in the law included giving the vote to illiterates and reducing the voting age to eighteen. The electorate has thus been extended from 3.7 million in 1971 to a probable 4.5 million in 1973. Voting is compulsory in Chile.

Fortunately Chile was able to make a successful appeal against the decision of the French court, and this gives some grounds for optimism concerning future copper sales. Nevertheless, uncertainty about the major source of Chile's foreign exchange caused Dutch and Canadian banks to suspend the loans that had already been negotiated. Allende's government, it should be recalled, has been wholly unsuccessful in raising loans from the World Bank, which has not provided Chile with a single loan since before October 1970.

The continuing low price of copper, at 49 cents a pound compared with a peak price of around 70 cents in 1969, reinforces Western bankers' doubts about Chile's credit-worthiness, and it does reduce the contribution this major industry makes to the rest of the economy. Chile did in fact secure a short-term renegotiation of its debt from the Club of Paris in April 1972, but only at the cost of further indebtedness — providing a necessary though only temporary alleviation of the burden. The current account situation continues in a critical state with many of the normal lines of credit still closed. Food imports are higher than ever, partly as a result of higher world food prices, and partly because the increase in agricultural output has slowed to a bare 1 per cent.

As 1972 drew to a close, it was evident that the foreign exchange bottleneck was as critical as ever. Allende's visit to Moscow in December (as this book was going to press) has generally been seen as an attempt to persuade the Soviet Union to provide a loan to finance food imports and capital investment, and to tide the country over a difficult period.

Towards the middle of the year the economic situation began to deteriorate noticeably, and it could not be long before the Government took the situation in hand. In July the price of cigarettes was doubled — the Government's first step towards restructuring prices. At the beginning of August a series of steep price increases were introduced on a wide range of consumer goods except for food and a specific list of fifteen basic necessities. (Cotton goods went up by 90%, wine by 70%) Then, later in the month, food itself was affected, with price increases ranging from 36% to 117%. Simultaneously, a 100% increase in wages and salaries was announced for October 1. (Normally the next cost-of-living-related increase (the *'reajuste'*) would have been in January 1973.) In addition a 700 *escudo* bonus was to be paid to everyone for September 18 — National Day. At the end of September, the Government announced a price freeze, to remain in effect till after the March elections, a halt in beef and butter imports, and a further reduction in the amount of hard currency allowed to those travelling abroad. According to official figures, prices had increased by 115% in the first ten months of 1972.

Inevitably the sharp price rise and the alleged scarcity of goods sparked off a further series of middle class protests in August, culminating in a 24 hour strike by shopkeepers.[3] Each new protest showed the Chilean bourgeoisie to be reacting more and more strongly in defence of its interests, while the working classes continued to demonstrate support for the Government.

Several other political disturbances followed over a number of issues and a state of emergency was declared on several occasions. In Santiago there were incidents between secondary school youths, young socialists and the right wing parties. In Concepcion there were clashes between right wing and left wing youths. Increasing talk of violence, military interventions and coups d'etat prompted both the church and the military to clarify their position. General Prats, the commander-in-chief, stressed several times in September that the Chilean military would not be sidetracked from its constitutionally defined task of guarding the external defence of Chile and internal peace, and ensuring that the elections of March 1973 would take place freely and peacefully.

Finally in mid-October the Popular Unity Government confronted its worst crisis. Sparked off by a strike of Chilean lorry owners protesting about Government plans to set up a nationalized transport service in the much neglected and sparsely populated south, the event quickly snowballed and became the vehicle of widespread middle class protest and attempts to topple the Government. The Christian Democrat party declared its support for the strikers and middle class professionals and shopkeepers organised sympathy strikes. As essential food supplies were affected, lorries had to be requisitioned and the army was called in to maintain public order.

The crisis lasted for over three weeks, almost bringing the country to a complete standstill. It was finally resolved by a political solution of far-reaching importance.

At the beginning of November, Allende requested the resignation of the entire cabinet. He was under pressure not only from the

---

[3] Following these protests an opinion survey conducted on behalf of the Christian Democrat weekly *Ercilla* revealed that 99% of the upper classes, and 77% of the middle classes claimed it was now difficult to obtain goods. However, 75% of the lower classes said that it was now easier to obtain goods. Asked whether they considered the Government was doing well, 27% of the lower classes replied in the affirmative, 41% thought it was 'doing all right' and 32% thought it was doing badly. On the other hand 72% and 52% of the upper and middle classes respectively thought the government was doing badly.

snowballing effects of the 'bosses' strike but also from Congress, where four of his ministers were under threat of impeachment. The time had clearly come to take a step for which the President had been preparing the ground ever since his election. Rather than allow the army to intervene against him, he was determined that it should come in on his side. Already there had been indications of this in April when General Pedro Palacios was briefly appointed Minister of Mines after the crisis caused by the departure from the government of the PIR. Now in November the President had to make it absolutely clear to the country where power lay, and who controlled it. His new cabinet included General Carlos Prats, his commander-in-chief, in the key post of Minister of Interior — and Acting-President should Allende choose to travel abroad (which he promptly did) — Admiral Ismael Huerta as Minister of Public Works, and Air-Marshal Claudio Sepulveda as Minister of Mines. At the same time, Luis Figueroa, the Communist President of the *Central Unica de Trabajadores* or Trade Union Confederation, was brought in as Minister of Labour, and a Socialist peasant leader, Rolando Calderon, replaced Jacques Chonchol as Minister of Agriculture. There were some misgivings about Allende's decision, both on the extreme right and the extreme left, but the impact on the country was immediate. The strike was promptly solved, the professional classes returned to work, and Allende travelled to the United Nations to denounce the subversive activities of multi-national firms, Chile having particular cause for complaint against the ITT. The smaller parties in the Popular Unity coalition seemed unhappy at the emergence of the military as the Government's chief prop, but the Communists and particularly the Socialists seemed positively to welcome what was widely regarded as Allende's 'auto-golpe'. Shortly before Allende left for his foreign trip in December, the cabinet with its new military members met and reaffirmed its determination to lay the foundations for a 'socialist transformation' of Chile and to maintain the 'anti-imperialist and anti-monopolist' nature of the government. In spite of all the obstacles, the Chilean road to socialism still lay open.

J. Ann Zammit,
December 1972.

Part I

Aspects of the Chilean Road to Socialism

Chapter 1

THE CHILEAN ROAD TO SOCIALISM

**Opening address by the President of the Republic
Dr. Salvador Allende**

Chile's Institutional Development

Our country has been through a long struggle. It has gone further than most other Latin American countries in its bourgeois-democratic evolution. Chile is also noted for its institutional structure, which, with only brief interruptions, has lasted for many years. The Chilean Congress, of which I have been a member for 27 years and in which I was President of the Senate, has had almost 160 years of uninterrupted life. Chile is, I believe, one of the three countries in the world with Parliaments dating back more than 150 years. This indicates a certain degree of stablility in our institutional development. Within the framework of this bourgeois-democratic process, Chile, more than most, has achieved a wide degree of political tolerance; yet from the economical and social point of view, the country's characteristics are more or less comparable with those of the other dependent countries in Latin America and other continents.

The Popular Struggle

The Chilean process, culminating in the Popular victory of 4 September 1970, was no matter of chance, nor was it a transitory alliance of popular parties for one specific election. It had its roots in 1938 when Chile was one of the three countries in the world where the revolutionary forces led by the Socialist and Communist parties united with the small and middle bourgeoisie to form what was then called the Popular Front. We did battle and won, electing Pedro Aguirre Cerda — illustrious teacher and statesman — on 25 October 1938. Our programme in those days was essentially humanitarian, defined in three words; bread, shelter and clothing. This simple programme mobilized the masses and facilitated the Popular victory.

Nevertheless the leaders of that time, myself included — I was Minister of Health in the Popular Front — put forward this programme without realizing the full significance of offering more bread. For the problem of bread is the problem of flour, of wheat — and basically of land. The problem of clothing — the right to be able to clothe oneself, and of shelter — housing — both basic necessities, is closely tied to industrial development which alone can satisfy the basic needs of the population.

Nevertheless positive steps were made during the Popular Front government to develop Chile. We passed a law establishing the Development Corporation (Corfo) which made possible in Chile the development of heavy industry such as steel, petroleum and electricity. From the social point of view, the period marked the incorporation of the middle sectors into the machinery of political power, and the ousting of the old oligarchic groups.

The continuing dialogue between organized workers and politicians from the popular parties indicates that Chile was the only country where the Popular Front successfully completed a significant stage — we all know what happened in France and Spain. The premature death of Pedro Aguirre Cerda left unfinished the task of organizing what today is the Popular Unity. But it was on the basis of the experience acquired then that the possiblility could become reality in 1969.

The governments which followed that of Pedro Aguirre Cerda were essentially representative of the old capitalist outlook. The government which preceded ours was a step forward, but it still operated within the rules of the capitalist system. It could be described as a reformist government within the capitalist system.

Thus there has been a succession of capitalist and reformist governments in our country. Nevertheless, in spite of this process of political evolution, Chile is still a country with all the typical problems of Latin America.

In these circumstances, on the basis of the experience of successive governments in Chile, and with regard to the social ferment, which implies a growing consciousness on the part of the masses — especially the working class — it became possible for the popular parties to group together.

The Present Political Model

Grouped together in the present Chilean political model are the Marxist parties — the Socialists and Communists who have now been working together for 15 years after having had many visible differences — together with the parties of the smaller and middle bourgeoisie, like the Radical Party, the Social Democrat Party, and the independents of the left, grouped in the API (Acción Popular

Independiente). These forces are similar to those that united in 1938, but there is a difference in that the Christian groups are now present, first MAPU (Movement for United Popular Action) and later the Christian Left. Both these groups split from the Christian Democrats. The Popular Unity therefore embraces secular, Marxist, and Christian groups, united around a programme to achieve a common task.

The fundamental difference between the process in 1938 and in 1970 is that in 1938 it was a bourgeois party — the Radical Party — which held the most powerful position, whereas today no single party reigns supreme within the Popular Unity. Even so, it is certainly true that within the existing constellation of forces the working class parties, with the presence of the Socialist and Communist parties, weigh very heavily.

Furthermore, the programme we devised in 1969 to bring about a revolution and a new society on the basis of pluralism, democracy and liberty, was different from the one presented in 1938. Now we have external and internal pluralism in as far as there are six movements and parties which constitute the Popular Unity. Democracy is necessary, but it must be a wider and more effective democracy, for in the past it was essentially the privilege of the restricted group that has always wielded power in our country. We must turn the abstract ideal of liberty into a concrete fact.

People speak of *La Via Chilena* — the *Chilean* Road to Socialism. What the Chilean people are doing has not yet been done in other countries. In our political model, starting from pluralism, democracy, and liberty, we want to use the bourgeois institutional framework to achieve the changes in the political, economic and social field which the country is demanding and needs — and to achieve socialism. In the Chilean case the use of legal institutions is possible because they are open to the possiblility of change. It was by using these bourgeois institutions, skilfully handled by the workers, that we got into government in the first place, and these same institutions have enabled us to achieve certain of the objectives which we set ourselves.

The Principles of Foreign Policy
In the international field, our actions are based essentially on our national independence. We speak of a Second Independence. The first was when we defeated colonialism and achieved political independence. Now we are struggling for our economic independence which will lead to full political independence, something which developing countries unfortunately do not fully enjoy.

With regard to self-determination and non-intervention, we believe that each nation has the right to the government it thinks fit. We respect this right and we reject intervention in the internal affairs of other countries. For this reason we have firmly decided to move away from the hegemonic concept of ideological frontiers. Our ideas have been given life in the 'Southern Cone' of Latin America by the understanding shown to them by the governing groups in such countries as Argentina, Peru and Ecuador. I mention these countries because I have visited them, at the invitation of their governments, yet it is worth recalling that there was a moment when an attempt was made to isolate our country, for the enormous crime of having a Popular Unity government and a socialist President.

We unreservedly support the principle of non-intervention and self-determination in the same way as we are convinced of the necessity of the continent's integration. We have underwritten the commitments already entered into by our country to the Andean Pact and to the Cartagena Agreements. We believe that cultural and commercial interchange between the Latin American peoples is vital. We have common origins. Soldiers from different countries passionately took up the same liberating banner beyond the frontiers of their homeland which gave life and character to the nations of this continent. For this reason we believe it is necessary to identify and intensify those actions which will enable us to increase our degree of economic integration. We are not unaware of the difficulties this creates in the political field. At times they seem even more acute, especially when one takes account of the fact that there is great interest in keeping this continent divided and that efforts have been made to promote the supremacy of certain countries in defence of interests which are not ours. But we are confident that within Latin America consciousness of the problem is growing.

The New Economic Model

From the economic point of view our country, like many others in this and other continents, was a dependent one; its basic resources were controlled by foreign capital. For many years the country lived through a stage of deformed capitalism, producing solely to satisfy the needs of a minority. Our development process was never oriented towards satisfying the needs of the people — a fact proved by statistics on food consumption, education, housing and health. The economy was a dependent one. Some progress was made, but it was based on techniques brought from abroad and often irrationally applied in the local situation.

Economic dependence essentially affected basic resources like nitrate and copper. Chile is the only country in the world which possesses natural nitrate fertilizer. At one time Chile supplied 70% of world nitrate consumption, but world consumption of nitrate has increased as Chilean production has declined. Chile was confronted with synthetic nitrates, but the country's natural nitrates could have formed the basis of a large heavy chemicals industry. It was one of our natural resources which the oligarchy controlled but then allowed to be taken over by foreign capitalists. This clearly marks the beginning of dependence. Nevertheless it was in this industry, in response to this dependence, that the powerful struggle of the working classes began — it was Luis Emilio Recabarren, the leader of the nitrate workers, who came to personify the struggle of all the Chilean workers. In the nitrate industry 140 nitrate plants, with a capacity of 3,200,000 tons, were demolished. Only enterprises in foreign hands survived, with production falling to 1,400,000 tons. By 1970 the industry was only producing 560,000 tons.

The case of nitrates was dramatic and resulted in an international conflict, but the case of copper was even more dramatic and instructive. Chile is estimated to have the largest copper reserves in the world. The open-cast mine — *Chuquicamata* — is the largest copper mine in the world. Our technicians and economists have estimated that 40 years ago foreign capitalists invested $30 million in Chile. Since then they have withdrawn from the country the not exactly insignificant sum of $4,500 million. It should be remembered that copper produces about 70 per cent of our foreign exchange earnings and finances a significant part of the fiscal budget. In addition, for more than half a century, Chile itself was allowed no information about either the levels of production, or the markets, or the price of copper.

For these reasons the Popular Unity Government decided to put an end to this economic dependence, and to retrieve the country's basic resources from the control of foreign capitalists. Now we own our copper, nitrate, steel, coal and petroleum resources, and these constitute the basis for our economic development.

We must produce to satisfy the needs of the Chilean masses. To achieve this, the Government planned the creation of a socially-owned property sector, a mixed sector and a private sector. We began to create the socially-owned sector by nationalizing essential resources under foreign control, by taking over a number of monopolistic industries — textiles and tyres, for example — and by bringing the private banks into state ownership.

In the mixed sector the car industry has been rationalized. The creation of firms with state participation has reduced the number of assembly plants, which was excessive in Chile. We have intensified implementation of the Agrarian Reform Law, which was passed under the previous government with our support. In 1971 we expropriated 1,300 *latifundia* and we plan to have eliminated the *latifundium* system by the end of this year by expropriating the last 2,000. As a result, more than 50% of the land will be in the reformed area and in peasant hands. Small and medium-scale properties will, however, not be affected. In the reformed area, production will be organized into co-operatives, 'Agrarian Reform Centres' — which are a Popular Unity idea — and, in some areas such as Magallanes, state farms will be established. (Magallanes had one of the largest farms in the world, covering   1.2 million hectares — larger than some European countries. It was owned by a company comprising Chilean and foreign capital.)

According to our technicians, Chile could produce sufficient food to feed more than 20 million inhabitants. Yet each year we import meat, wheat, vegetable and animal oils, and butter, spending more than $200 million in purchasing foodstuffs which Chile does not produce. 42% of the Chilean population is underfed, failing to receive the adequate biological requirements.

Only by implementing an agrarian reform as part and parcel of our economic development process, by raising the moral and intellectual level of the peasant and by treating him as a first-class citizen, by providing technical assistance, credit, seed, fertilizer and mechanization — only in this way can we become self-sufficient.

It is essential to re-structure our irrigation policy at national level. According to our technicians, there are some places where we lose or make bad use of 30% of the available water. In others the system fails altogether. The fact that 3,600,000 Chileans have no household supply of drinking water is a sufficient indication of the task before us.

The Formation of the Social Property Area

The presidential decision to nationalize copper was approved unanimously by Congress, even though this is a minority government. It involved a constitutional reform which assigned the President of the Republic certain rights and duties. Among these was the right to deduct the companies' excess profits when fixing the compensation. We reckoned 10% as a legitimate rate of profit, but in the case of copper we allowed 12%. The President was also given

powers to assess whether the investment made in the copper development plans had been efficiently used and whether it had yielded the
expected benefits and achieved what it was designed to do. Congress's
reasoning was based on the fact that the expansion and development
plans of the copper companies were financed from credit and not
from re-invested profits.

On the basis of a decision by the General Comptroller's Office
(*Contraloria*), and with regard to my own views as President on the
subject of excess profits, Chile decided that only two copper
companies, Andina and Exótica, would be compensated. The large
enterprises at Chuquicamata and El Salvador, which belong to
Anaconda (to which Exótica also belongs), will not receive any
compensation. Nor will there be any for El Teniente, which belongs
to the Braden Copper Company. The expansion plan did not produce
the results expected by those who designed it. Nevertheless we only
deducted the very small sum of $8 million for the El Teniente invest-
ments. Moreover it is usually said that if no compensation is to be
paid, then there is no further obligation on the part of the Chilean
State. Yet in fact we have had to take responsibility for credits worth
$716 million which financed the companies' expansion plans.

Economic power and capital were highly concentrated in Chile.
So too was credit. Only a few Chileans had access to credit, which
was basically concentrated in Santiago. We believe that it is vital to
establish a national banking system. Rather than presenting a bank
nationalization law to Congress, we have used a bourgeois legal disposition which permits the Development Corporation (Corfo) to buy
and sell shares. In this way we purchased bank shares through Corfo,
and 95% of total credit is now nationalized. We have now changed
the rules governing credit, reducing the interest rate which had
reached 38% per annum, and providing a greater proportion of credit
to medium-scale industrialists and farmers.

We now control not only the money supply but also export
trade through the Central Bank. The country had no foreign exchange budget, and it has suffered an endless drain on foreign
exchange due to the activities of national and foreign companies. In
view of the recognized lack of central organism for foreign trade, we
have set up a Committee for Foreign Trade as the basis for a future
Ministry of Foreign Trade.

The creation of the three economic sectors — state or social,
mixed, and private — has been heavily criticized, and has aroused
great internal opposition as well as an implacable and aggressive
campaign abroad. We never thought it would be otherwise. At the

same time we always hoped that men and nations would understand our right to live and would extend us a fraternal hand, even though their political and social orientation was different from ours, but especially when their views or situation are more akin to our own.

The Social Model

With its enormous mineral resources, and its land, forest and sea resources, Chile has great potentialities. But we are severely limited with respect to the most valuable factor, human capital, which is the only non-substitutable resource. We achieved our commercial and industrial revolution somewhat late, as we did with our scientific and technical revolution. The gap between the capitalist-industrial countries and socialist countries on the one hand, and the developing countries on the other, is now increasing.

Therefore not only must we change the structure of the social system, but we also need to integrate our nation into one whole, to give us a new profile, a new voice and fresh determination. The world cannot indefinitely remain indifferent to the plight of millions and millions of human beings. The powerful nations must understand that the dignity of man and of nations is not only measured by income per capita.

Our principle concern is with man. I am not a romantic but a Marxist, and I believe in Marxist humanism. We are struggling to allow the human couple its role as the essential basis of the family (and of the whole people which is the sum of all families together). We want work and shelter for those who have none. Bread for those who are hungry, and spiritual food for those many children who cannot even go to school. We are particularly concerned about the nation's youth — the source and strength of the future — and the aged who have been little more than beggars in this unjust society.

The masses must have real and effective participation in the exercise of power. We want to end the system in which the old and traditional oligarchy looked on its lands as a personal fief and the peasants as serfs. Tupac Amaru, the great Indian leader of Peru, once said: "We do not want the boss to eat at the expense of the Indians' hunger." We want this to become a reality, but to do this we have to take measures which wound deeply. That is why the opposition is fighting against us. Even so, we are making progress.

Our basic concern is that man should have the right to authentic liberty — something which he was always denied in a system based on the exploitation of man by man. Culture must no longer be the prerogative only of those who can afford to buy it. It is unacceptable

that thousands and thousands of people, who may have better potential than others, should be denied the chance of developing their
intelligence because, unlike those of us who went to the University,
their parents cannot pay for their education.

Nor do we want a University system which is marginal to
society's preoccupations and outside the process of change. Our
University is already committed to the transformation of Chile —
both the students and the academic and administrative staff are
aware of the hopes people have in the University, to which they have
contributed so much.

Who are we, and where are we going?
We are a nation in the southern tip of the Americas, raising a new
banner of dignity and independence, and the right to transform our
own existence, while respecting the individual and collective rights of
others. We are looking beyond our own frontiers in the hope that the
political independence of Latin America, for which Simon Bolivar,
San Martin, O'Higgins, Sucre and Morelos fought so hard, will
become a reality.

We have a hard task before us. We are well aware that only an
organized, disciplined and conscious people will achieve our historical
objective. We, the political leaders at the forefront, are only birds of
passage. But the people continue, like a thread through history —
aware of yesterday's tragedies but with the future open to their own
efforts. We have faith in Chile, and we hope to win the understanding
of others concerning the task we have set ourselves as a people. One
day we shall be proud as a people of having done what others have
not yet achieved, having done it with profound respect for man and
with the deepest affection for our country.

Chapter 2

THE CONSTITUTIONAL AND LEGAL ASPECTS
OF THE POPULAR UNITY GOVERNMENT'S POLICY

Eduardo Novoa *

In order to examine 'La Via Chilena' — the Chilean Road to Socialism- with respect to the constitution and the legal system in force in Chile, it is necessary to begin by explaining some basic intentions of the Popular Unity's programme.

In the first place it is an attempt to transfer power from one class to another; in other words, it is intended that the workers acquire real power in our society. Second, the intention is to replace the existing society and this involves breaking up its present structures, in order to achieve the final objective of liberating the classes which up to now have been exploited. The mere statement of these objectives is enough to make it clear that the Popular Unity Government has a revolutionary programme.

As an example of how revolutionary groups act when they get into power, two well known cases are worth mentioning; — one, the Russian revolution of October 1917, because it is the most important revolution of this century, and the other, the Cuban revolution, because it is the revolution nearest our time. In the Soviet Union, immediately upon gaining access to power, the revolutionaries ordered that all laws not repealed by the Revolutionary Government were to be interpreted in a manner consistent with the character and meaning of the revolution. This first stage lasted only one year, for in December 1918 it was decreed that from then on pre-revolutionary laws and legal dispositions should be neither applied nor referred to.

In Cuba the situation was different but the result was the same. When the triumphant revolution led by Fidel Castro got into power the standing legislation was not revoked but it was decreed that interpretation of this legislation should conform to revolutionary principles. To date, the pre-1959 legislation is in force but to a large extent it has been effectively annulled by subsequent legislation which the Cuban government introduced. Therefore, both in this

* President of the State Defence Council.

case and the previous one, the previous legislative bodies disappeared and all legislative powers are vested in the revolutionary group in power.

These are instances of groups who wish to develop a revolutionary programme and feel themselves in conflict with, and soon hindered by, the legislation in force. The situation with the Popular Unity Government is different in that it committed itself to uphold the principle of legality, which is not inconsistent with revolutionary determination because the principle of legality is something people have fought for and it protects them from excesses of power. Legality can be looked at as a framework which guarantees the rights and liberties of citizens and demarcates limits to the actions of those exercising power. The Popular Unity committed itself to uphold the principle of legality because the Chilean constitution and legal system is flexible. It is a system which theorists on constitutional and political law call semi-rigid in that it allows limitless modifications to its own structures by means of certain procedures which are a little more severe and demanding than those required to modify or pass new laws.

Nevertheless, the Popular Unity has criticised the content of the existing legislation which is in force. It has frequently claimed that it is a bourgeois body of legislation which is unjust, oppressing the people while protecting and supporting the most powerful groups, especially the economically powerful.

The Chilean people's profound spirit of legality and respect for institutional organisations is the basis for this promise to respect the law. Chile has now accomplished 140 years as a legally organised nation state based on respect for the law as proclaimed by the public authorities. But at the same time, the political results of recent elections have indicated that a very large majority of Chilean citizens are in favour of revolutionary changes. This is confirmed by the fact that in the 1970 elections there was a notable degree of similarity on many points in two of the presidential candidates' programmes — namely, Allende of the Popular Unity and Tomic who stood for the Christian Democrats. If one takes account of the content of the programmes and the results in terms of the percentage of total voters, it is obvious that two thirds of Chilean voters were in favour of profound revolutionary changes in the country's political, economic and social structures. This revolutionary disposition of the large majority of Chilean citizens is what gave the Popular Unity the hope that its programme could be achieved with full respect for legal procedures and the juridicial set-up.

Like all legal systems the world over, the Chilean one is simply the expression of a particular historical form of social life and organisation. These values and concepts of man and society and the economic organisation of society are reflected in a wide variety of ways in the legal system. This is not always understood by men who dedicate their lives to studying law and who so often see law as something abstract, a product of more or less absolute rationality or of a desire for justice which has achieved its peak of perfection in the legislation with which they are familiar and who for this reason regard the law as immutable and permanent. But the truth is that the legal system is neither inert nor neutral. It has its own internal dynamics and serves particular ends, — the defence of the particular historically determined society in which the system is in force. This defensive action also tends to cast as illegal all those who are against this particular form of society. Looked at in this way, a country's legal system simply becomes a mechanism created to uphold a certain social, economic and political concept and which is equipped to serve the society which created it and not to serve or be used by others.

The basic principles of the Chilean legal system upon which our legal institutionalism is built are closely related to the doctrinal concepts of the French revolution and this can be verified in both fields of public and private law. Chilean law is always concerned with the protection and development of individualistic liberal concepts within society and its purpose is to ensure that society embraces and develops these concepts. It is true, however, that by means of past ideological struggles and the pressure of the proletarian masses this legislation has to some extent been modified, but change towards a more progressive society is slow and difficult and provides no short term hope of a total transformation.

From the constitutional point of view it is also worth noting that the executive in Chile has greater powers, faculties and attributes than has the legislature, since to a large extent it can control the actions of Congress. By using the ordinary legislature, with the support of only one third plus one of either of the two branches of parliament, it can prevent a new law from emerging. If Congress does not approve the Government's proposals within the legally prescribed time limit the Government can reapply the previous year's budget. It also has the exclusive right to initiate certain laws which involve public expenditure and especially those which involve fixing the renumeration of both public servants and employees in the private sector.

It might be thought that possession of such a range of powers would make it possible, once President Allende was elected, to initiate the changes which were necessary to put Chile well on the road towards socialism. But all these powers are, in fact, suitable for a society which does not want to be changed. The President can reduce legislative activity and stop a new law going through but he cannot obtain new laws which would modify the existing system. All these powers lead to the maintenance of the status quo, but when a government which is determined to initiate revolutionary changes assumes power all these Presidential powers are worth nothing at all, because they prevent profound stuctural changes from being carried out.

In order to be able to operate, this Government has had to resort to a series of legal dispositions which lay almost forgotten. But once having used these to their maximum the moment has arrived when there is no legal mechanism by which to proceed any further.

In addition to the foregoing the very important human factor must be mentioned. It is not just a question of looking at the legal system as a set of rules which were elaborated and dictated in order to conserve a given social order, — these rules have to be applied by human beings, who when applying them inevitably insert their received concepts or those they think most valid. For this reason, in the application of its policy, the Popular Unity Government has encountered serious obstacles in the legislative field, above all in relation to the judicial powers and the Chilean Comptroller (Contra loria).

The Judiciary is a very hierarchical and closed institution as far as entry into it is concerned. In Chile, it is a professional career, starting off at the lowest level job and working up towards the position of judge; and all functions other than court activities are prohibited. In this very narrow context in which they carry out their functions and within the confines of their conservative legal training, the members of the judiciary are unfit for the needs of the day and are unable to understand that laws need to be applied in a way which makes them useful to existing society in which they live. The majority of the members of the judiciary assume extreme, traditional and individualist positions, such that, each time a difficulty arises in which the judiciary becomes involved, the interpretation they give to the law closes the way to any possibility of action on the part of extremely innovative governments such as the Popular Unity.

Something similar applies with respect to the Comptroller General of the Republic. According to the Constitution, the

Chilean legal system requires that every Presidential decree, resolution or order can be acted upon if the Comptroller General — a high level public servant with legal training — does not previously declare it to be against the Constitution or the Law. In practice the Comptroller's power is immense and if this public servant has no clear understanding of what constitutes a progressive interpretation of the law and adheres to traditional criteria in interpreting the law, then such problems as those faced by the Executive in the Popular Unity Government emerge.

All this goes to explain why during one and a half years in power, the Popular Unity has initiated so few laws with transcendental significance for national life. Excepting the copper nationalisation law, all other bills introduced by the Government involving profound institutional changes, or changes in the country's socio-economic organisation have encountered fierce opposition in Parliament. This recently ended in Congress resolving to reduce the legal Presidential powers which have existed for the last forty years. Not only was there insufficient comprehension on the part of Congress to let the new Government carry out its published election programme, but things have reached such an extreme that a few legal mechanisms which would permit no more than moderate implementation of the Popular Unity's programme are being whittled away.

After eighteen months of such resolute efforts to introduce into Chile revolutionary changes in the legally constituted system and accepting and respecting the prevailing legality, the question is posed as to whether it is still possible to think that revolutionary changes can be made lawfully.

Chapter 3

ONE VIEW OF CHILE'S PRESENT POLITICAL AND ECONOMIC SITUATION

Radomiro Tomic*

In this analysis of Chilean experience more emphasis will be put on political than economic aspects. Due to the fact that the civilization to which we belong has taken on more acute revolutionary forms in Chile than in other Latin American countries, the present revolutionary situation will be explained with reference both to Chile's past and to future developments of the process underway.

Summarizing the human and physical context, the Chilean people is a homogeneous one, despite the different origins of its people. There are no racial tensions or internal cultural antagonisms. These ten million Chileans live in an area three times bigger than England, Italy or Japan and all regions from extreme north to south and from the Andes to the sea are economically productive. Chile has many more natural resources than England, Italy or Japan, possessing a solid base of mineral, energy, maritime and agricultural resources.

In the hundred years between 1830 and the world crisis of 1930, Chile went through two different and contradictory stages. The first, the distant past in which Chile was 'constructed', lasted from 1830 to 1891. The second, more recent past, in which the values and traditional institutions of the old governing classes decayed, lasted from 1891 to 1930.

Between 1830 and 1891 Chile acquired the institutions relevant to that historical period and developed a governing class which operated these institutions efficiently. State authority was centred on the President of the Republic, but the National Congress's powers of criticism and censure were upheld. A sense of nationalism developed but without undermining the noteworthy and sincere spirit of Americanism which then existed. This governing class preached by example, and imposed on the country the same rules and standards of work and saving, and simple disciplined life as it applied to itself.

* Professor at the Institute of Political Sciences, Catholic University, Chile and Presidential Candidate for the Christian Democrat Party in 1970.

The results were notable. Chile, which had been one of the Spanish Crown's poorest colonies, became the most united, stable, modern and prosperous country in Latin America. Latin America's first National University, its first school for training primary school teachers, and its first telegraph system and railway were established in Chile. Famous Argentinians and other Latin Americans who were persecuted in their own countries by the tyrannical regimes, which were so frequent in the early days of independence, sought refuge in Chile. The 1855 Chilean Civil Code served as an example for the basic legislation in several other Latin American countries. The Chilean merchant fleet was one of the most important in the American Pacific. One hundred years ago, or half a century before the first North American dollar or engineer arrived in Chile to produce copper, Chile was the world's number one copper producer, employing Chilean entrepreneurs, work, capital and techniques. The agricultural sector produced more than the population consumed and the Chilean peso maintained parity with the North American dollar for almost half a century.

Chilean experience also demonstrates the important fact that when structures are relevant to a country's reality and collective cause then there is nothing the people cannot achieve.

The old political and social structures, which were useful at the beginning, soon ceased to correspond to new realities and new requirements. The traditional governing minority no longer served the country, and converted what it formerly regarded as patriotic duties into privileges and advantages. The semi-feudal system in the countryside and the *latifundia* became less and less efficient at feeding a growing population. National capitalism began to develop on the basis of exploitation of the working class, creating social tensions previously unknown in Chilean society. Foreign capital took over control of nitrate, then of copper and Chilean foreign trade. The enormous customs revenues from nitrate and copper provided the ruling classes with such an easy life that the old austere, pioneering and enterprising spirit of the previous generation disappeared.

The more recent past — the period of decay in institutions and of the traditional ruling class—began with the 1891 revolution, in which the Government was confronted by Congress. Both sides received military support, but Congress was victorious.

In this period, the State's authority was fragmented by parliamentarianism. Foreign capitalism took over control of Chile's external economy and capitalist exploitation provoked violent social situations in the nitrate, coal and copper industries and even in the countryside. These were cruelly repressed, sometimes with thousands of workers as victims. The first workers' organizations and federations developed and the first workers' political parties began to emerge.

In the 1920's there were two successful *coups d'état* in Chile and between 1927 and 1931 the country was under a dictatorship. In 1932 several government *Juntas* and brief dictatorships succeeded one another in the Moneda Palace. The great World Crisis had cruel repercussions on Chile, agitating the proletariat, the middle class and the youth. The old parties divided and the new mass parties were founded.

This period ended with the Popular Front victory in 1938, in which the Communist and Socialist parties participated. The Popular Front won the Presidency by a margin of only 3,000 votes and the Armed Forces respected the popular decision and did not intervene. In 1945, at the end of the Popular Front Government, Chile entered the present tormented period.

The following figures indicate how tormented this period has been. From 1830-1930 the value of the Chilean peso in relation to the dollar changed from one peso to five per dollar, but from 1930 to date it has changed from five pesos to twenty-five thousand pesos per dollar; this disaster has taken place without wars, bombed factories or economic blockades. The decline in the value of money is not, of course, an isolated phenomenon. Similar analyses could be made concerning other aspects which would equally well demonstrate the failure of the old economic and institutional structures to adapt themselves to the new requirements of the national and world revolutionary process.

Two contradictory factors characterize the present. First, there is profound national dissatisfaction with the inability of successive governments to resolve the basic problems. This has led the Chilean electorate to change the ideological orientation and political composition of its governments five times in twenty years. Second, the weight of the national democratic and legalist tradition has led Chileans to try to remedy the situation by changing their government rather than the economic system and institutions. Not one of the political forces which gained power from 1946 onwards has managed to win an immediate second term in power. This happened to the Radicals in 1952, to Ibanez (symbol of the 'strong man who would do away with politicians') in 1958, to the right-wing 'government of managers' in 1964 and to Christian Democracy in 1970. After 18 months in government the Popular Unity, in which Marxism predominates, is already suffering a much quicker loss of strength in terms of the popular vote than did the Christian Democrats, as shown by the January by-election results in O'Higgins, Colchagua and Linares. The vote obtained by the Popular Unity was 4.5% less than they obtained in the same provinces in the April 1971 municipal elections.

Before analysing the 'Chilean Road to Socialism' it is necessary to point out that in 1964 the Frei Christian Democrat Government made the first attempt to prepare the ground for participation of the people in the exercise of power. It is very interesting to analyse the Christian Democrat phenomenon in Chile. This government, which got into power on the slogan 'Revolution in Liberty', translated this into three types of achievement, which are of historical importance:

1. the Agrarian Reform Law and the expropriation of more than three million hectares, and the unionization of more than one hundred thousand peasants;

2. the tremendous efforts in education which involved a doubling of public expenditure on education and important qualitative changes, by modernizing the educational systems;

3. the development of popular grass roots organizations such as trade unions, neighbourhood, womens' and youth organizations.

But the essential aspects of the political and economic structures were left unmodified and the fundamental problems continued to have their impact, producing frustration, antagonisms, inflations, monetary devaluation and unemployment. The modest 2% rate of per capita growth achieved throughout the last thirty years was more or less maintained in this six year period, and the foreign debt repayment rose to the level of $80 million per year. In brief, it was proven once more that the traditional economic and institutional system no longer worked in Chile, despite the skill, homogeneity and dedication of its administrators.

On the other hand, the theory, which circulated in Chile at the time, that the *raison d'être* of the Christian Democrats in Chile was 'to be an alternative to and against Marxism' polarized and confirmed the antagonism between the Marxist-inspired forces and those inspired by Christianity. This also reduced the Christian Democrat capacity for action to a purely reformist bent, with neither the desire nor possibility for promoting deeper structural changes in the state, society or economy. The Christian Democrat Government vote fell from the 43% gained in the 1965 Parliamentary Elections to 36% in the 1967 Municipal Elections and to scarcely 29% in the 1969 Parliamentary Elections. This percentage was maintained in the 1970

Presidential Elections, but, isolated between the Marxist left and the Right wing, it was insufficient to win. Allende obtained 36% of the vote and the best chance of being elected President of Chile.

Allende, was not, however, elected President of Chile by the popular vote. Since he did not obtain an absolute majority, only the two Chambers of Congress could elect him President. This required the Christian Democrats to vote for him in Congress and the proposal to do so was discussed and approved by about two-thirds of the National Committee of the Christian Democrat Party. However, the Christian Democrat parliamentarians were instructed to elect Allende as President only when a Constitutional Statute of democratic guarantee had been jointly approved by the Popular Unity and the Christian Democrats. All the Christian Democrat deputies obeyed these orders, permitting the election of Allende as President. The central objective of his programme was to prepare the way for establishing a socialist society in Chile.

In order to analyse the country's political and economic situation after eighteen months of Popular Unity government, it is worth referring to the report of the Political Commission of the Chilean Communist Party's Central Committee — a notable and unobjectionable document. The section on 'Economic and Political Fronts' says "a difficult political situation exists this year which could become very serious and there is a complicated economic situation which could become extremely harsh. On the political and economic fronts, the worst possible threats to the Chilean Revolution are becoming increasingly apparent." What is under discussion is the further development of the Chilean revolution or a regression — advance towards a more democratic system or towards a tyranny based on terror. But, while there is national consensus that the economic situation during the eighteen months of government 'is difficult and may get considerably worse in the course of this year', there is of course no consensus between the Opposition and the Government on the causes.

An analysis of this situation can be centred on three questions:- is the Popular Unity Government failing to achieve its programme objectives?; if it is failing, what are the causes?; and what are the short-term prospects for Chile? The Economics Minister, Pedro Vuskovic, has said that the Government's short-term economic policy served the political objective of widening the Popular Unity Government's basis of support. He also said that electoral support was high but not sufficient. This explains the urgent need to rapidly reactivate the economy, so as to bring rapid benefit to the popular masses, and this would be impossible without rapid structural changes in the different property sectors (socially owned, mixed and private).

The idea was to widen the Government's electoral and popular support through a very rapid redistribution of income, etc., and a massive increase in the money supply. The Economics Minister's justification in terms of calculated success in the short term is the only possible justification for such a policy, because several of these measures contradict the basic requirements of socialist trans-formation in an under-developed economy such as Chile's. After one and a half years it is quite clear that the Government has not achieved its objective. Despite the measures 'to widen the electoral and popular basis of support', its electoral and popular support has diminished and not broadened.

There are other revealing signs that the Government is not achieving sufficient to bring success. For example, the profits which should have resulted from copper nationalization and which were absolutely essential for financing the social property sector have disappeared. Congress and the whole country unanimously approved of the nationalization, and it is a measure compatible with transition to a socialist economy. But, due to political and, particularly, institutional weaknesses, this Government has been unable to prevent production costs rising by about 50% and the usual $60 or 70 million annual profits earned by the North American copper companies with normal world copper prices have evaporated. There are various causes of this disaster, some attributable to the North American companies, but the most important factors were the hiring of large numbers of workers and employees with no justification from the productive point of view, the highest level of worker absenteeism in the history of the copper industry, lack of discipline in the work force, and technical inexperience.

The nationalization of the nitrate industry has meant an in-crease in annual losses from $11 million to $20 million. The drastic income redistribution outpaced the capacity to increase the supply of goods and services, and resulted in shortages. This has probably done the Government more damage with respect to its popular support than a less drastic income redistribution would have done. The massive increase in the money supply, amounting to more than 100% in one year, served to reactivate the economy in the short term but the inflationary repercussions are of such magnitude that in January and February, 1972, the cost of living increased by 10.4% according to the official price index, the second highest inflationary level for this two-month period in 15 years.

There are other negative aspects, unrelated to the economy and the Popular Unity Government's programme, which are weakening the Government more than it seems to realize. The Government is over-run by extreme leftist groups which do not belong to the Popular Unity and, not believing in the 'Chilean Road to Socialism', organize the illegal occupation of farms, smallholdings, shanty towns, rented land, commercial offices, factories, mines, schools, colleges, public buildings, roads and bridges. The Government hesitates to use public force and Opposition propaganda is therefore successful in portraying the Government as lacking in political determination and unable to enforce obedience. Illegal occupations are not only the work of the ultra-left; they are also the spontaneous action of groups of peasants, workers and miners who believe that by occupying the land or factories where they work they can draw rapid attention to their problems. Quite frequently this is seen as a means of getting the property transferred to the social sector, in the belief that there are better salaries and conditions of work there.

There is also evidence that, after 18 months in government, the somewhat difficult co-existence of the eight parties is beginning to break up. Some parties have divided and recently one authorized its congressmen to vote against the Government or to abstain on certain Government bills. Without wishing to exaggerate the structural and operational weaknesses created by the political heterogeneity of Popular Unity parties, it does seem to be a factor which makes it increasingly difficult to formulate a common policy, especially on matters not in the Presidential Programme or with respect to new situations which arise.

Nevertheless, it would be unfair to evaluate this year and a half without pointing out some of the important decisions made by this Government, which, because they are in the national interest and will help bring socialism nearer, will be respected by history. This is the case with the nationalization of copper and banking, the acceleration of the agrarian reform, to the point where the *latifundia* has been completely eliminated in Chile, and with foreign policy to date.

Why is the Popular Unity Government failing to achieve its objectives? Allende realized that it was impossible to implant Marxism in Chile by means of an armed confrontation and the dictatorship of the proletariat — the classical road in Marxist theory and experience — and that the only possible way was what has been called 'the Second Road to Socialism' or 'the Chilean Road to Socialism'. But unfortunately the Marxist parties and Allende did not see that the necessary condition for successfully proceeding along the second road to socialism is for the government to have an 'institutional majority'. Faced with the existing institutional framework the alternatives are clear; either these institutions must be destroyed by means of an armed struggle in which the subjected classes defeat the ruling classes and impose a dictatorship of the proletariat, or the institutions must be used to create a new institutional framework which facilitates a democratic and pluralist socialism – the only socialism possible in Chile. This depends upon having a parliamentary majority. Strength is necessary for the first path, a majority for the second.

Whereas in other countries this might seem unrealistic or utopian, in Chile this is not the case. A socialist framework was possible if the laws in force were used without breaking the country's principles of legality to uphold the legitimacy of Allende's government. For the 'second road to socialism' to be successful this principal contradiction had to be understood and resolved. But, with a minority in the legislature, Allende and the Popular Unity are condemned to failure in the main aspect of their task.

The Christian Democrats long since analysed this problem of the need for a parliamentary majority if capitalist political and social structure were to be replaced by socialism without dictatorship. It was very clear that, in Chile, this called for far-reaching agreement between socialists inspired by Christianity and those inspired by Marxism, that is, between the Christian Democrats and the Popular Unity, for the period following the 1970 Presidential election.

This was the policy approved by the Christian Democrat party for the Presidential campaign and maintained throughout the campaign and after. But it met with public and emphatic rejection by the Popular Unity on a number of occasions before and after the Presidential campaign. This fatal political error is the root of present political and economic problems and of the not very encouraging prospects for this Government and for socialism in Chile.

What are the prospects for the near future? The Popular Unity Government's revolutionary capacity is on the verge of exhaustion. The most important of those things which were feasible within the framework it chose – copper nationalization, state control of banks, agrarian reform – have been carried out, or only need finalizing. Will the Government accept reality or will it attempt to forge ahead by radicalizing its programme, objectives and methods? Will it accept the limitations imposed upon it by a set of institutions which it can only partially manipulate, or will it prefer to undermine them and try to circumvent them? Will the Government confine itself to 'the second road', or will it give in to pressures from those who believe that the only road to socialism is armed conflict between the 'oppressed' and the 'oppressors'?

Objectively it would be an enormous mistake to cede to this temptation. The heterogeneity of the eight Popular Unity parties, the open opposition of the large majority of Chileans to a dictatorship of any form, especially a Marxist dictatorship, and the unfavourable international context, do not give a policy of deliberate and aggressive radicalization of the Government action any chance of success.

Furthermore, not only are some of the groups which oppose the Government weaker now than they were in 1971. The Government, too, is weaker and it could be argued that the radicalization of the Government's policies to achieve socialism and greater aggressivity on its part are more a sign of weakness than strength. So what acceptable and feasible way out is there?

Important agreements between the Christian Democrats and the Popular Unity, of the sort which could have been concluded in the initial days of this Government and which were rejected by the Popular Unity, do not seem possible in the near future. But this does not mean that the country is inevitably confronted by an institutional catastrophe. The greater part of the Government's political strength and, in any case, the Christian Democrats in opposition, are against anything which would upset constitutional order, in particular extremist left and right wing efforts to provoke a meaningless armed confrontation on a national scale.

Democracy has not disappeared in this country and the basic 'institutionality' is still in order. Despite the many antagonisms, open and democratic discussions between the Government and the Opposition continues, as shown by various important matters and draft legislation in which common criteria have been found and opposing points of view reconciled. Such was the case with the Christian Democrat decision to elect Allende as President of Chile, the unanimous support by all Chilean political parties for copper nationalization, the recent agreement on modifications to the Election Laws and the legislation on Electoral Pacts, both of which will benefit the Popular Unity more than the Opposition. The same can be said for the current attempt to reach a joint drafting of the Constitutional Reform creating the three areas of the economy. It is necessary to persevere in this policy of working towards limited pacts and agreements, to prevent paralyzation of the existing institutional set-up, but it is only possible if both sides accept the rules of the game and do not abuse established facts.

The present policy of co-existence is realistic and enables preparation for the future. Within this framework of co-existence and dialogue, efforts must be made to develop the political conciousness of the people and of the political parties who affirm that without the 'unity of the people' it will be impossible to make or fulfill the only revolution which can remove Chile from its collective frustration, break down the antagonisms which prevent national solidarity, end the absurd poverty in a country with such tremendous resource potential and the heavy burden of foreign dependence. This revolution is a Socialist, Democratic and Pluralist revolution. Throughout the world, history is marching toward unity not uniformity.

It might seem that the limited roles permitted by the present Chilean situation are not heroic. But courage, the highest form of patriotism, does not always involve combat. In the words of Milton, " they also serve who only stand and wait!"

Chapter 4

THE HISTORICAL BACKGROUND TO THE PRESENT ECONOMIC SITUATION IN CHILE

Ricardo Lagos*

One of the first elements to emerge in an historical analysis of Chilean experience is the country's institutional evolution and its effect on Chilean political development.

If one main thread links and characterizes the different parts of the Chilean process, it is the slow but steady incorporation of the different social classes into political life. The very restricted oligarchic classes associated with the aristocratic landowners in the 19th century were joined by the financial and mine-owning classes. Then, in the first 20 to 30 years of this century, the middle class was incorporated, especially during the first Arturo Alessandri Government beginning in 1920. In 1938 active participation of the working class began with the Popular Front Government. Participation by the working class has been limited, acting more like a pressure group through the trade unions or through the political parties, which mainly represent workers and which have nearly always been in opposition. Increasing participation at political level is demonstrated by the distribution of seats in the National Congress, and can be measured by many other indicators such as the proportion of people entitled to vote. The rise in the number of affiliated trade unions is impressive, as is the concomitant easing of procedure for establishing trade unions. Thus, whatever the indicators used, it is evident that Chilean political and social evolution has been characterized by the increasing incorporation of different social groups. If full participation has not yet been achieved, there is at least a sizeable degree of political participation by the different social classes.

However, this political evolution has not been exactly paralleled by economic evolution. The year 1930 is crucial for understanding the process of economic evolution resulting from the crisis. Countless works deal with the types of growth before and after the crisis and they largely ignore this issue.

* Interim Secretary General, Latin American Faculty of Social Sciences (FLACSO), Santiago, Chile.

Because the Chilean economy was oriented largely towards foreign trade and was dependent on one or two basic products, the crisis severely affected the balance of payments and brought about a change in the economic system. The export dominated growth model which existed prior to 1930 became impossible after 1930, a partial change occurred in the economic structure, and different sectors of the economy experienced different rates of growth. A slow process of industrialization began, and, although some authors trace this back to 1914, the process gathered strength at this point. In broad terms, the evolution of the various productive sectors from 1930 onwards is as follows. Agriculture, which had played a relatively major role in the country's development, began to account for a declining share of the national product. Mining, dependent basically on the price of copper in the international market, maintained its share; likewise services maintained a large share of the national product (nearly 45% in the whole post 1940 period). Industry increased its share, becoming the most rapidly growing directly-productive sector. This fact to some extent explains Chilean evolution in more recent years. The higher rate of urbanization which accompanies industrial development also helps to explain the increase in political participation already mentioned.

Basically, until 1940 the pattern of growth was one in which the substitution of imports mainly takes place in items that are easily substitutable. During the 1940's industrialization concentrated on basic infrastructure sectors and this was achieved by direct state intervention, because, without new sources of energy and steel being developed, the industrialization process could not continue. The newly created Development Corporation (CORFO) was therefore a product of the ideological motivations of the Popular Front Government and of economic considerations. This stage lasted until approximately 1955. From this date, the process of industrial growth began to encounter increasingly serious difficulties; the number of easily substitutable imported items began to dwindle and, in order for the process to continue, industries requiring increasingly specialized technology and much larger sums of capital were necessary. The difficulties were compounded by the size of the Chilean market, a population of 9 to 10 million (in the late 1960's) and an unevenly distributed per capita income of around $500 p.a. are insufficient to take full advantage of certain types of modern technology. On account of the technical considerations and the capital required, the process of Chilean industrialization, which had been based mainly on Chilean capital, became very much influenced by foreign capital.

As a result, from 1930 onwards the Chilean economy has been a dependent economy; industrialization did not lessen the degree of dependence but rather modified the form it assumed. Originally dependence was of the traditional type, with a foreign enclave constituting the principal source of foreign exchange and fiscal revenue. From 1960 onwards, another type of dependence began to emerge as a result of an extraordinarily rapid increase in Chile's foreign debt. From a public and private sector foreign debt of $ 598 million in 1960, the level rose to around $ 3,000 million in 1970, making the economy vulnerable and dependent in a way which had not been the case prior to 1960.

The third form of dependence is related to industrial investment. The Chilean manufacturing sector, which was originally financed by Chilean capital, suffered a process of 'denationalization' from the mid 1950's as foreign capital began to gain importance. In 1968, the last year for which figures are available, approximately one sixth of the capital in manufacturing was foreign. If accurate information were available for 1930, the proportion would clearly be less. Thus, what would appear to be the typical development sector for national capital was gradually subjected to foreign domination, a process which is now occurring in all the most developed countries of Latin America. Thus industrialization, which was intended to bring a greater degree of autonomy and independence, brings instead a new kind of dependence.

The second characteristic of the Chilean economy is the concentration of property ownership. Until 1960 the concentration of agricultural property ownership in Chile was extraordinarily high, with the greater part of cultivated land in the hands of a few large estate owners. This concentration is affected from 1964-1965 onwards, with the passing of the Agrarian Reform Law in 1962 and its later amendment in 1966. In the industrial sector, over 80% of industrial output is produced by limited companies in which, by virtue of share holding, the concentration of industrial ownership is extraordinarily high. At the same time there is a high degree of concentration in the firms themselves — in 1965 the 52 largest firms in Chile accounted for 38% of the value added in the industrial sector.[1] The third key characteristic was that the process of development and industrialization in Chile and the influence exerted by the public sector took place within a capitalist framework.

---

[1] This increases still further if industrial conglomerates are taken into account, rather than the individual component firms.

As a result of these factors, growth has been unstable. Analysis of the statistics from 1940, the first available, up to 1960 shows a high degree of fluctuation in growth rates. During the last decade, according to ODEPLAN studies, the average rate of growth of domestic product is in the order of 4.6%, with annual rates ranging from 7% in one year to 2.2% in another. In fact the growth rate is a low one when compared with the population growth rate, and it is erratic.

Another characteristic of the Chilean economy, which has been a permanent cause of concern for various governments, is the level of unemployment. The unemployment figures from 1956 onwards, although erratic, show an average level of unemployment of between 5% or 6% and 7%.

Further, given the concentration of income, the impetus to increase production has been the consumption of the high-income groups and to some extent this has generated unused capacity in certain industrial sectors. New economic sectors, especially in the industrial field, were intended to satisfy the needs of a specific section of the population and not the population as a whole; for example, the Chilean electronics industry hardly substitutes any imports but simply imports a greater number of components and raw materials and assembles them in Chile, indicating that production is oriented towards the requirements of a minority.

Another notable feature of the Chilean economy has been the high rate of inflation.

These characteristics have undergone little change, despite efforts to use different economic policies: The Klein-Saks model in 1956 was designed to combat inflation; the model first adopted by the Alessandri Government was supposed to make growth compatible with a slow-down in inflation, trying to contain inflation in the same way as the previous model by controlling wages and salaries and achieving development through an increase in foreign indebtedness, with a rapid increase in foreign debt from 1960 onwards. The method used from 1964, which was successful until 1967, aimed at reactivating the Chilean economy as well as keeping inflation in check by increasing demand.

The political complexion of the various governments has differed, ranging from the conservative Alessandri administration to the reformist Christian Democrat administration. Nevertheless, while it has been possible to introduce some modifications into the basic economic framework, the degree of dependence, the high degree of concentration of property ownership, the degree of monopoly in industry and the 'denationalization' of this sector have undergone no substantial changes. These elements characterize the Chilean situation in 1970 and perhaps help to explain what has taken place since.

Part 2

Macro-Economic and Industrial Policy

Chapter 1

THE ECONOMIC POLICY OF THE POPULAR
UNITY GOVERNMENT

Pedro Vuskovic*

The principal task in formulating our economic policy is that of translating the basic lines of the Popular Unity's programme into concrete ways of running the economy. The programme emerged from an analysis of Chile's past experience — an increasing subordination of the Chilean economy to foreign interests; an increasing concentration in the ownership of the means of production and, accordingly, increasing concentration of control of the basic sectors of the Chilean economy by foreign interests or powerful national monopolistic interests; and an increasing concentration of national income. As a result, the rate of growth was relatively low, as was the rate of accumulation. The economy was increasingly unable to provide opportunities for productive work for the growing labour force and, hence, unemployment levels remained relatively high and strong inflationary pressures were always present.

These features, which have characterized the Chilean economy for many years, became even more acute in the period just before the Popular Unity Government came into office. The traditionally low growth rate had become, in the three years prior to the Popular Unity's assumption of power, virtual economic stagnation. Also unemployment and inflationary pressures were worse than usual.

The principal objectives of the programme, arising from this experience, can be summed up under three or four main headings. Firstly, it is necessary to restructure the Chilean economy into three spheres of ownership: a socially-owned property sector, one of joint ownership and a private property sector. The purpose of this restructuring of the economy is to transfer the strategic economic activities from private monopolistic or foreign control to the control of society as a whole. Secondly, it is necessary to achieve a rapid and substantial growth in the wage earners' share of national income. Thirdly, the restructuring of the economy and the change in income

* Minister of Economic Affairs

distribution will form the basis of a new development model, in which social and property relationships are transformed and the socialist transformation of the Chilean economy is begun.

When the main fields of concern and the economic priorities are established, certain basic political requirements emerge. In other words, economic policy is subordinate, in its content, shape and form, to the political need of increasing the Popular Unity's support. There is an imbalance between the level of electoral support with which the Government came to office and the size of the groups which will benefit from the Government's programmes. Accordingly a central objective of economic policy is to widen political support for the Government, to the extent this is compatible with other aspects of the programme.

The urgent need to achieve a rapid recovery of the economy, and to extend the benefits to the mass of the working population, cannot be undertaken in isolation from the structural changes; they are all necessarily inter-dependent. It is not possible to make deeper changes without broadening the Government's political support, and economic reactivation and income redistribution will provide an impulse to these fundamental changes.

In the absence of consolidated political power, economic policy has to be conducted within a framework of permanent political struggle; the economic situation itself, economic tendencies, and the management of economic policy become weapons in the political struggle. There is not so much room to manoeuvre when the general political struggle converges in the field of economic policy. Secondly, these objectives must be pursued respecting the obligation to implement the process within the existing legal framework, and within the structure of the existing government apparatus.

Different measures have been used to restructure the economy. One method was to apply existing legislation which had similar aims to those of the Popular Unity Government's programme. The abolition of *latifundia* in the pursuit of agrarian change is permitted by an Agrarian Reform Law, which had already begun to be applied under the previous administration. It is now being applied more rapidly.[1] Where it is politically possible to pass new legislation, recourse is made to legal and even constitutional reform, as was the case with copper nationalization. Sometimes legislation in existence for a considerable time is used to deal with cases where owners or entrepreneurs have abandoned their enterprises. There is legal

1   See Section I Part 3 on Agrarian Policy.

machinery to expropriate enterprises in such situations.

Finally, extensive use is made of direct negotiations with firms which, according to our programme, must change from private to joint ownership status, or become part of the socially-owned sector. The programme contained rather general definitions which only made reference to the type of activity which should be incorporated into the socially-owned sector. This very general reference has given rise, from the time the Popular Unity Government came to power, to uncertainty about which firms would fall within each sector. This led the Government to define policy in this field more precisely. The main criterion is the size of the enterprise. In specific activities, particularly industry and commerce, all firms whose shares or capital exceed a certain figure are liable to be transferred to the socially-owned sector.[2] Finally, a specific list of 91 enterprises was compiled.

It is essential that society as a whole and the workers should exercise control over economically strategic enterprises or activities. This is not incompatible with some degree of participation by private interests. Accordingly, the problem of deciding whether a concern should be wholly socially-owned or whether it could become a mixed enterprise is less a question of principle than a pragmatic problem, in which the merits of each case are examined individually.

The same applies to foreign capital. Here also, the individual merits of each particular case are examined, paying regard principally to the weight to be given to transfer of technological know-how and openings to foreign markets.

As a countermeasure, various forms of support are planned for that part of the economy which, according to the Popular Unity Government's programme, will continue in private hands. These range from production agreements between state organizations and sectors or branches of private activity, to important changes in the credit policy which provide these sectors with far easier access to credit, and to a statute for small-industry and artisan production.

The second objective, the reactivation of the economy, is short-term, and the starting point was one of economic stagnation. The very depressed situation became even worse between 4 September and 4 November 1970.[3] Several pump-priming programmes, par-

---

[2] All enterprises whose capital was 14 million escudos or above on 31 December 1970, were to be transferred to the socially-owned or mixed sectors. (Editor)

[3] The period between the Presidential elections and the day Allende assumed power as President. (Editor)

ticularly the acceleration of house-building and public works etc., were therefore introduced by the Popular Unity Government. The dynamic effects of these efforts were then superseded by the resulting widespread pressure of higher demand, which led to the mobilization of productive capacity in other sectors.

With regard to redistribution of income, it was decided that the wages policy should not simply restore the real purchasing power of wages in line with the rise in prices in the preceding period, but provide a more than proportionate increase. This was done after a discussion leading to the drawing up of an agreement between the Central Trade Union Confederation, as the body representing the mass of the Chilean workers, and the Government.

This wages policy was combined with a prices policy which required that wage increases were to be absorbed by the enterprises, and not passed on through price increases. This implied a decrease in the unit profit rate for some enterprises, but a substantial increase in production, and therefore, productivity would maintain the absolute level of profits.

The progress made in 1971 towards achieving the planned objective of restructuring the economy was, in general, quite significant. Nationalization of copper and other mineral resources has been completed. Substantial advance was made in agrarian reform, to the point where the complete abolition of *latifundia* — defined as productive units exceeding a certain basic irrigated hectarage — is envisaged. In the area of finance, state control now extends to almost the whole of the previously private banking sector. Considerable advance was made in bringing under social control the large wholesale distribution monopolies. In addition, progress was made in nationalizing firms or in bringing firms in important sectors of industry, such as textiles, cement, steel, coal etc., under state control.

Nevertheless, despite the progress made in 1971, there are still important decision-making centres which have not been affected. Progesss has not been sufficient to warrant less attention being paid to this objective at the beginning of 1972.

As far as economic revival is concerned, some indicators show surprising results, if account is taken of the circumstances under which the process commenced and the political conditions in which economic policy is being conducted. Output grew by 8% or 9% in 1971, a fairly exceptional rate compared with past performance. Estimates for growth in the real volume of output in manufacturing industry in 1971 vary between 12% and 14%. A considerable decrease in unemployment has been achieved — in the case of Greater

Santiago it decreased from more than 8% when the Popular Unity Government came to power to less than 4% in the most recent surveys which relate to the latter part of 1971. This represents one of the lowest unemployment rates since surveys on employment and unemployment were first begun some fifteen years ago. The rate of inflation has also decreased from approximately 35% in 1970 to little more than 20% in 1971. With regard to income redistribution, a combination of factors — the increase in real money incomes, the effects of the reduction in unemployment and other more direct ways of providing real income for the workers — has resulted in a significant increase in real incomes and also a fairly important change in the distribution of income. The National Planning Office (ODE-PLAN) estimates that the wage earner's share in national income has risen from 51% to approximately 60%.

Various different types of problem have emerged during this economic process. Some are a natural result and others have been intensified by exogenous factors. The following are some of the principal points for concern in relation to these problems.

The first was quite easily foreseeable; there has been much faster progress in income redistribution than in adjusting supply to this new structure of income distribution, resulting in more or less appreciable imbalances between supply and demand. This has given rise to shortages — the higher purchasing power of the workers is not always matched by the availability of the products they want or are in a position to buy.

Secondly, there have been major problems resulting from the accumulation of financial strains in the economic system. To a large extent, these stemmed from the need to bring about a rapid recovery of the economy. During 1971, there was quite a significant disparity between the expansion of liquidity and the rise in prices. The system of payment between firms was changed drastically, from a system which generated an enormous volume of financial credit to a system of virtual cash payment for all transactions between firms. But, in any case, another kind of problem has emerged which is reflected in this accumulation of financial stresses.

Thirdly, we have experienced a number of problems related to the control, management, and coordination of economic policy, resulting from the inherited state apparatus which is too rigid to respond to new conditions and demands. There are also, of course, the inevitable problems of learning how to carry out all these tasks.

A fourth problem arising in the course of 1971 was the decline in the rate of investment, which was mainly due to a decrease in private investment insufficiently compensated by an increase in public investment.

Finally, these problems should be seen in the context of the divergence between the subjective perception and the objective results of 1971. The very powerful ideological campaign waged by the sectors affected by the process of structural change has in some way succeeded in obscuring the objective results of the economic process during 1971. This is important, since the possibility of implementing both the programme and certain concrete aspects of the economic policy towards some sectors is lessened. The subjective perception created by the systematic campaign of the reactionary sectors renders those aspects of economic policy designed to support private sector groups, to establish new kinds of relationships and to create new possibilities of support, difficult to put into practice. It also encourages extensive alliances between groups which do not really serve their real interests. The solidarity between the large marketing monopolies and the small retailers, and between the giant industrial monopolies and the small industrialists, are examples. The chances of implementing an economic policy aimed at establishing new kinds of relationships with, and support for, small industry are weakened as long as the small entrepreneur responds to the ideological campaign of the large firms rather than pursuing his own concrete interests.

A comparison between the situations at the beginning of 1971 and 1972 reveals clear differences. At the start of 1971, the objectives of reactivation and redistribution could rely on extraordinarily ample margins of spare capacity in different sectors and the problem was how to encourage use of this. The situation today is different; in many sectors of the economy, spare capacity still exists, but in others capacity is fully utilized. There is also less flexibility in financial policy than there was at the beginning of 1971.

There are now limitations arising in the foreign sector as a consequence of a previous policy of foreign indebtedness, gradually leading to the present situation of extremely high indebtedness. The point has now been reached where, for this year and next, servicing of the accumulated debt may represent about 40% of the country's total income from exports. Such a situation is difficult to deal with in any circumstances, and much more so when some of the traditional sources of new capital inflows are dwindling or drying up completely. This is why Chile requested discussion of debts and proposed a re-scheduling scheme.

While some factors are less favourable than at the beginning of 1971, others are more so. First, there is now greater ability to manage and control the economy. The establishment of the socially-owned part of the productive and financial sectors, particularly in banking, has provided the Government with the means to act more decisively than was possible in 1971. Second, instead of having to implement programmes to get the economy moving, we now have to start from a situation where practically the whole productive system is strained. Therefore even if it were only possible to maintain in 1972 the levels of activity achieved in the second half of 1971, this would signify an industrial growth rate at least 7% or 8% higher than in 1971.

Some important advances have been made in solving some of the problems which drew a great deal of attention in 1971. This is particularly the case with the distributive and marketing system. This constituted one of the major obstacles to be faced after the first income redistribution efforts. Its whole infrastructure was designed to market goods and services to high-income groups. It was not only necessary to change the structure of supply but also to reshape the distributive and marketing channels so that products reached the mass of workers whose purchasing power had grown.

There are also other factors which are perhaps more decisive than these tangible, specific factors. The political offensive, designed to worsen some of the objective problems which arise in the process, has been intensified.

There are also other aspects which entail taking stock of some of the advances achieved and giving them a greater meaning. In fact, the creation of a socially-owned sector has three aspects. First, it signifies the beginning of a process of socialist tranformation. New production relations are being established in this sector and therefore its management will be guided by different criteria to those when capitalism predominated in these economic sectors. As a consequence, substantially greater benefits and prospects should derive from the socially-owned sector. This process has hardly begun and there is a great potential for the future to the extent that this type of management is developed in these areas. The industries forming part of the socially-owned sector are still managed along much the same lines as before, retaining many of the old methods both within the individual enterprise and in the sector as a whole.

Secondly, there is the problem concerning the role of the socially-owned sector in guiding the private sector in the same field or line of production.

The third aspect is one which, from the Government's point of view, ranks extremely high, and concerns popular participation in the implementation of economic policy. To some extent surmounting many of these problems, and the implementation of this kind of economic policy, has been a moderate administrative type of approach. The real possibility of implementing an economic policy of this kind is dependent on the extent to which it can effectively be transformed into a policy of the masses, with very active participation by the workers themselves. In this respect interesting experience is being gained with worker participation in socially-owned enterprises or in enterprises operating under state control. Participation has been organized by means of production committees for sections of the enterprise and by means of administrative councils for the productive unit as a whole. Substantial contributions have been made to what has been called 'the battle for production.' The results achieved in 1971 to a large extent came from this active presence of the workers in these sectors. The same occurs where the people participate at other levels or when dealing with other problems. When shortages first began to occur, the problem was discussed at the level of the ordinary people, and led to the formation of the *Juntas de Abastecimientos y Precios* (Prices and Supplies Committees). This is one form of active participation by the people in resolving many of the problems affecting them. Further valuable experience is being obtained and a clear picture can be obtained of future developments, leading not merely to participation by the people in resolving concrete problems but to a change in the character of the old government apparatus and in some degree in the people themselves, who will continue to become integrated and to take part in these tasks and, in so doing, are changing the very nature of the administrative machinery and of the state.

Chapter 2

SOME ASPECTS OF
THE POPULAR UNITY'S DEVELOPMENT MODEL

Jose Ibarra*

Three main aspects of the Popular Unity's development model will be explained; the strategy, the results of the Government's first year in power, and the longer-term strategy.

First, however, a brief description of the technical nature of planning in Chile is necessary. The objective has been to translate the ambitious economic, social and political aims of the Popular Unity's programme into a viable, concrete plan for action. An examination of the compatibility of these aims was therefore necessary, because it would not be possible to achieve them all simultaneously. The National Planning Office is not in a position to propose long-term goals and objectives; everything centres on a six year period since there are Presidential elections every six years which decide the future, and also one of the central features of the Popular Unity Government is its pluralism. Planning does of course require some projection into the future and the basic lines of development for the longer term have been formulated for sectors such as electricity, public works, and others where, for technical reasons, it is essential to see further ahead.

It should be made clear that the Popular Unity's plan constitutes a minimum hypothesis in that it attempts to be as realistic as possible about the results of the structural changes being undertaken. It is recognized that there is a time-lag between the achievement of economic results and the increase in awareness about this social process, and the planners do not wish to speculate on the advantages of the new organization and structure of production. It is hoped that events will show that it is possible to proceed much further and, depending on the degree of political, social and economic success, ODEPLAN will modify the annual plans, and adapt the strategy itself.

The plan is based on internally-generated resources, since much of the customary flow of international aid and co-operation has

* Deputy National Director, ODEPLAN.

either already been cut off or will be soon. Also, the foreign debt is now enormous. To increase it further would require conditions very different from the usual ones. It is not that foreign aid is unwanted. Aid is necessary, and to the extent that it is forthcoming, additional plans will be formulated, allowing faster growth. These precautions were taken not because this situation was thought desirable, but in order to secure the fundamental aim of the strategy, that of structural change.

Emphasis has been put on formulating a strategy rather than a plan, because it would be absurd to make a detailed six year plan when the very nature of what can be achieved is determined by the constant political struggle. Detailed planning is done for the annual plans. In the Popular Unity strategy the basic problems of the Chilean economy are considered to be structural ones, namely, dependence, and the existence of *latifundia* and monopolies. These structural features lead to concentration of income and property, the exclusion of large sectors of the population from the economy, and to the insufficient or inefficient use of available resources — of natural resources as well as of existing industrial capacity, but above all, human resources. The six year strategy for the 'transition to socialism' aims first at the eradication of dependence, the *latifundia* and monopolies — the worst evils of capitalism — and then at the organization of the whole population so as to meet their basic needs — a task of vast dimensions.

TABLE I

Distribution of Family Income, 1968

Income Bracket[1]	Number of Households	% of Households	% of National Income	Average Size of Family	Total (000's)	Population %	Number of Income-Earners per Household
0 – 1	518	28.3	4.8	4.5	2.345	25.1	1.13
1 – 2	591	32.3	12.4	5.1	3.009	32.2	1.41
2 – 3	330	18.0	11.8	5.4	1.798	19.3	1.74
3 – 4	139	7.6	6.9	5.7	789	8.5	1.94
4 – 5	84	4.6	5.4	5.2	439	4.7	2.02
5 – 6	55	3.0	4.3	5.6	307	3.3	1.96
6 – 8	49	2.7	4.9	5.2	256	2.7	2.04
8 – 10	28	1.5	3.6	5.9	166	1.8	1.90
10 & over	37	2.0	45.9	6.1	227	2.4	1.96
TOTAL	1.831	100.0	100.0	5.1	9.336	100.0	1.51

[1] In multiples of *sueldos vitales*, the basic subsistence wage.

To take the problem of employment. First, it is estimated that over the six years 402,000 new jobs will have to be created to absorb the natural growth of the labour force. Second, open unemployment, which was around 8% of the total labour force in December 1970 when this Government first came to power, will also have to be absorbed. The reduction of this figure to 2%, which is internationally considered sufficient to allow for job changes, will require the creation of 119,000 to 120,000 additional jobs. Third, 467,000 paid jobs are needed for women; in 1970, the percentage of the population of working age (from 15 to 64 years of age) actively employed was 87% for men, and only 26% for women. These three categories together give a total requirement of about 1 million new jobs, which, considering that total employment in 1970 was 3 million, means that an increase of 33% is needed in 6 years.

Another interesting aspect is the distribution of income. In Table 1 incomes are classified as multiples of the *sueldo vital*,[1] which represents the cost of a minimum basket of goods for a family. This year this wage is about E. 1,100. There were 518,000 families earning less than one *sueldo vital*, amounting to 28.3% of all households and receiving only 4.8% of the national income. In the income bracket from 1 to 2 *sueldos vitales*, there are 591,000 families, or 32.3% of all households, receiving 12.4% of national income. Since the average family income is about 4 *sueldos vitales*, 60% of all families had an income of only half the average, and their share of national income was only 17%. Figures showing the distribution of consumption have not yet been published, since the figures are so astounding that they are being carefully checked and analysed. They are taken from a survey of family budgets in 1968 and 1969, which covered 10,000 households from all over the country. Those in the bracket from 0 to 2 *sueldos vitales* apparently consumed very much more than their income, incurring debts amounting to 63% of income. From 2 to 4 *sueldos vitales*, families were indebted to 30% of income. These figures indicate the extent to which the extreme poverty of 60% of the population was forcing them into permanent debt in order to stay alive. Dis-saving continues up until the 8 to 10 *sueldos vitales* bracket is reached. The groups between 10 and 20 were saving 12% of their income, while in the highest ranges savings reached 40%. This would mean that some families were saving a considerable amount, but not enough to offset the debt being incurred at the lowest levels of income. It would also explain why the national income accounts show negative family saving every year.

[1] *sueldo vital* — basic subsistence wage.

The last column of Table 1 indicates the number of people employed in each income bracket. The national average for a household is 1.5 working members. However, in the 0 to 2 bracket the average was only 1.13: in those families receiving from 2 to 4 *sueldos vitales,* 1.4 members were working, and in the higher ranges the figure rises to reach two or more people per family. Here one begins to see the real magnitude of what has been called 'the excluding economy'; — in 60% of families, receiving in total only 17% of national income, on average only just over one person gets work. This economy has been incapable of generating sufficient employment opportunities for the population for all the reasons already explained. As soon as they can, men go out to work; there are few opportunities for women, and even if women want to work, they have nowhere to leave their children. The Popular Unity Government believes that employment should be provided for the poorest groups; and this is why the 467,000 jobs for women must be created.

At the same time as providing this section of the population with work, their very low income levels must be dramatically increased through the redistribution of real income. Smaller increments are envisaged for families in the remaining income brackets up to 10 *sueldos vitales* while in the higher ranges, existing levels of income will be maintained. Consumption targets are derived from these figures. It may be wondered if consumption is not being over-estimated. The Government believes that it is not. What is being proposed is simply to provide the majority of the population with proper employment opportunities, in the belief that participation must begin in the economic sphere. The most important thing is to bring income and employment to the population as a whole.

Given the existing political conditions, only income redistribution can provide the necessary impetus to mobilize and redirect the economy. This implies a complete change in the structure of demand, and a different type of investment. Investments will have a short gestation period, a relatively simple technology and will provide a large amount of employment per unit of capital, and will require only modest levels of saving. A small rise in the rate of savings should be possible, given that the basic instruments for change are the structural ones mentioned, whose significance from the strictly economic point of view is very clear.

The only way in which the logic of decision-making can change is for social criteria to be used in the most important decisions. This is why the formation of the social property sector is necessary, starting with the big monopolies, which use sophisticated technology and high levels of mechanization, and can provide surpluses and a high proportion of total savings. Other savings will not be high. Families who are only just being offered an adequate living-standard cannot be asked to save, while the Government lacks the political power to force high-income families to save more; neither can theGovernment itself save much, as the State has to provide such public services as health, education, housing, etc. These require additional state expenditure and decrease the savings-generating power of the Government. Also, the State will have to assume responsibility for the bulk of investment because last year's low rate of private investment will probably continue for some time.

The present size of the social property sector is actually quite modest — it accounted for only 10% of the national product in 1970. Even with the announced expropriations, its contribution will scarcely reach 20% to 25%, rising to 30% after six years. However, it will include the most important, and the most technically sophisticated production, from which it is possible to obtain surpluses. This is what will ensure a change in the destination of output, fulfilling the targets for the supply of popular consumption goods.

Of course, this strategy is not one that can continue indefinitely. Once the whole population is employed and organized so as to satisfy their basic needs, strategy will change. Fortunately, Chile is very rich in natural resources. Basic industries such as electricity, coal, steel, and petrol are considerably advanced, with considerable installed capacity and technical and professional capacity. The country is in a good situation from which to embark on a new stage of increasing productivity through the more complete utilization of natural resources, in order to reap the gains from international trade. Pre-investment plans which serve this strategy were drawn up under the previous Government but they are projects taking from five to eight years to mature, requiring a vast amount of investment and generating very little employment. To embark on them now would mean the renunciation of the aims of full employment, income redistribution and the meeting of basic needs. But they will have to be begun at some stage, and, precisely because of their long gestation-period, this should be as soon as possible. The Government hopes they can be undertaken with international co-operation and aid and that friendly countries will help to hasten this stage by co-operating in the completion and implementation of the studies. If this happens, the minimum target growth rate of 7% over the six years could be raised considerably.

As for the economic results of 1971, events are proving many cautious predictions to be already obsolete. Little by little, the situation is changing so as to allow the use of several new economic instruments, such as the social property sector, the nationalized banking system, etc. Preliminary calculations show that, altogether, families saved between 5% and 6% of national income, while the goal set for 1976 was only 1%.

In conclusion, savings is not the worst problem. Mobilization of resources is more important. Although it was not possible to increase total investment in 1971, public sector investment rose dramatically, especially in social programmes, while private sector investment lagged, despite all the large-scale projects it was offered. Nevertheless in 1971, as at present, there was a shortage of complete projects ready to be implemented, reflecting a failure in 'real' aspects of the economy, not monetary ones. Once projects are ready, the instruments of economic control will ensure the finance.

Chapter 3

SOME PRELIMINARY FACTS ABOUT THE MANAGEMENT AND ORGANIZATION OF THE INDUSTRIAL SECTOR

Oscar Garreton*

The management and organization of the industrial sector are very important problems and will become increasingly so as the state industrial apparatus assumes more responsibilities. The intention here is to explain what has been done so far, without entering into a theoretical discussion on alternative ways of organizing a socialist economy or on the role of the market in planning etc. However, certain introductory comments are necessary.

First, it needs to be rocognized that at present the question of power is not defined and that the struggle for it assumes very special forms. Since the Popular Unity Government has only limited power (it only controls the Executive), industrial management and control will assume changing forms, constituting a process rather than a defined situation. Second, management of the industrial sector is only one part of overall economic policy-making and some global decisions directly affect industrial policy.

The question of industrial management and control is not one of organizational charts or apparatus. It involves determining where economic power lies and what mechanisms exist to direct the economy – especially since, in Chile, to be in government is not the same as being in power. Until the Popular Unity Government it was the imperialists and the Chilean monopoly bourgeoisie who exercised control over the national economy. The State's role was basically one of support and regulation, to keep the existing system going, but never one of control or direction. This does not mean it always acted in the interests of the *gran* bourgeoisie. On the contrary, the State sometimes worked against their interests, mainly when their exaggerated demands conflicted with other social classes. As the degree of monopoly concentration in the economy heightened, regulatory

* Under-Secretary, Ministry of Economic Affairs.

action became indispensable, though it has assumed different forms under successive governments.

As Alberto Martinez and Sergio Aranda argue, the State's first task was to bolster up the capitalist system in the productive, financial and distributive fields.[1] The increasing lack of economic dynamism obliged the State to participate heavily in fixed capital investment, and in infrastructure and services investments etc. The State also regulated the relationship between the world capitalist system and the national system (especially in the copper enclave) and acted as intermediary between the two. State action in this sphere took various forms, including the statute governing foreign investment in Chile, the credit and guarantee system etc. The State also regulated relations between the Chilean capitalist system and the backward forms of capitalism in the agricultural sector. For example, by fixing agricultural prices the Government regulated the transfer of surpluses between the rural and urban sector. The State has also acted as a shock absorber, defending the system from the attacks and pressures of exploited groups and classes.

But when it is asserted that the centre of economic control is not vested in the State, this goes beyond the obvious statement that power is wielded by the dominant class rather than by the instruments which the latter use. It refers to the fact that the dominant groups, as a class, did not control industry from the state apparatus but directly from the monopolistic centres. However, they did maintain firm control over the State and over Corfo (the Development Corporation), the key apparatus in the industrial sector.

Corfo differs from other state organs in that, when it was created in 1939, it was granted greater operational flexibility, dynamism and autonomy, providing enormous possibilities for action with respect to industrial development.

Between 1940 and about 1952, Corfo grew rapidly with particular emphasis on the development of basic activities such as electricity, steel, petroleum etc., which act in support of private industry. In this period, the first efforts were made to create technologically developed industries such as engineering and chemicals, which facilitate more dynamic industrial development.

This process continued after 1952, but with a different emphasis. Industries such as sugar and fertilizers were created to help the agricultural sector; the mining sector and iron were also developed, as well as hotels and the services sector. During this period of

[1] *Chile Hoy,* Essays edited by Victor Brodersohn; Siglo Veintiuno, 1970.

conservative government under Alessandri, certain enterprises created by Corfo, like copper and rubber manufacturing, were transferred to the private sector, clearly demonstrating Corfo's role in support of this sector. This role was accentuated as Corfo also became an increasingly important source of finance for investment in the private sector.

Between 1958 and 1964 — a period of right wing government — fewer Corfo 'subsidiaries' were created while Corfo's support for private enterprise increased. The financial apparatus was further developed, and the new subsidiaries were oriented towards research and other services for private industry. Corfo also continued to absorb private enterprises which were on the verge of bankruptcy and, due to its relatively greater flexibility and efficiency compared to other organisms, it began to assume responsibilities in non-industrial sectors.

In the period 1964 to 1970 Corfo undertook certain necessary, more technological projects ('dynamic' in the neo-capitalist concept of development), which were capital intensive and which the private sector was incapable of developing. Telecommunications, electronics, computer and petrochemical industries were established and Corfo continued as mediator with foreign capital.

It would be inappropriate and unjust to take these facts as a condemnation of Corfo. On the contrary, those who created Corfo were imbued with a creative ideology and the nature of Corfo's activities show clear differences over time. The openly pro-monopoly nature of Corfo during the Alessandri period was not an explicitly intentional part of its activities in the early years. Moreover, all industrialization processes objectively require the sort of activities which Corfo developed. But the context within which this took place in Chile led to consequences not intended by its creators and early managers.

Despite the fact that Corfo is so clearly an organism of and for the private sector, its mechanisms of central control and information, even over its subsidiaries, are surprisingly weak, so much so that the latter operate with a large degree of autonomy.

In industrial planning Corfo does little more than provide projections and only a rather weak and formal financial control is exercised over its subsidiaries. The deficiency in Corfo's central apparatus is not due to technical reasons or lack of the necessary technological or communications knowledge. Important information and control systems have been created, such as the computing and simulation systems in the large modern subsidiaries like CAP (Pacific Steel Company), ENDESA (Electricity Generating Corporation) and

ENAP (the Petroleum Distribution Company), enterprises considered vital by the monopoly bourgeoisie and the imperialists. It is therefore clear that Corfo did not create these enterprises and information systems for its own purposes or to facilitate control over industry.

Analysis of the evolution and functioning of Chilean capitalism shows how the large monopoly enterprises exercised control and direction over industry from the commanding heights of the economy. However, as from 1970 the Popular Unity, in which the working classes predominate, decided to exercise industrial control through the state apparatus. This has posed various problems which must be resolved. The first, a basically political problem, is how to transform the important and dominant working class participation in the government into control over the apparatus of industrial management and, in particular, over the decisions of concrete mechanisms such as Corfo. The second problem concerns control over the monopolistic means of production, which constitute a real basis for control by the workers and their government. The third concerns the organization of the country's productive capacity. The socially-owned property sector must not be allowed to develop into a group of enterprises whose size and weight mean that they control the central directive apparatus; development of this sector must facilitate the exercise of central control over the constituent enterprises. The existence of a socially-owned property area controlled by the State and the workers is an urgent necessity but this will not automatically give them control over industry. A new form of organization with information and control systems must be brought into operation. Without this, capitalist inertia rather than the Government and the workers will continue to govern the industrial sector.

Substantial efforts have already been made to improve government control of industry. The Ministry of Economics, Corfo and Corfo's Sectoral Committees, and their related enterprises, are three mechanisms through which this operates. In establishing the new apparatus of industrial control, emphasis has been put initially on intermediate planning levels. Without these, the overall management and control apparatus would lack the organic capacity or necessary information to make it work.

The legally created Sectoral Committees in Corfo operate at the middle level in the various branches of production. The idea is to transform them into General Management bodies for each branch, which also function as the executive machinery for the social property area and as the indicative planning apparatus for the rest of the sector. Sectoral Committees have been set up for textiles, construction materials (incorporating the cement plants), electricity, electronics, leather and footwear, and agriculture-based industries.

Corfo has now been transformed into an organization with a pyramid-shaped structure consisting of the central apparatus, the sectors and their dependent enterprises. Information and control systems are being established to connect these various levels.

There has been no immediate and automatic substitution of capitalist rationality in the enterprises transferred to the social property sector by a new socialist one. The situation varies widely. Although the majority of workers, *interventors* and administrators pursue a correct industrial policy, there are occasional deviations. Sometimes workers are keen to get higher prices for their products, or dislike producing products which are not so profitable. With workers' consciousness increasing and the new planning and control system taking time to develop, enterprises often receive conflicting instructions.

The mere existence of industrial management and control indicates nothing about who controls it, and it cannot be assumed that it operates in favour of the working classes and their allies. To change effectively the nature of industrial management, the presence of the workers' political and class organizations is required at all levels of the industrial system. Workers' control is currently functioning in a more or less organized fashion (depending on the degree of organization of the groups involved), with interesting and efficient results. Although nationalization creates the conditions for workers' control over these enterprises, incorporation of the workers into management is not automatic when nationalization occurs. It is necessary to develop workers' consciousness, and the *interventor,* the State and its political apparatus, and the political parties all have a role to play in this.

Nevertheless, the fundamental question is how the working class can control the management of the economy at all levels. This problem is inherent in the current Chilean political process and is difficult to resolve. Control is being established in a variety of ways — through the dominant role of the workers' parties in the Government, through the concrete mechanisms by which trade unions participate at different levels, and through other forms of power gained by the workers as a result of their own actions and the impetus they provide to the Popular Government.

There is no question of workers' control over the management of the economy in the interests of the class as a whole in a market economy. Neither is this control necessarily to be found in a planned economy. If the working class is to control the management and planning of the system, private ownership, especially in the monopoly sector, will generally have to be abolished. Moreover, in order to guarantee that economic management is in the interests of the working class, it is necessary to incorporate the workers into control and management of the means of production at all levels of decision-making in private enterprises.

The possibilities of winning the present struggle depend on the extent to which the workers and the Popular Unity gain real power, and to which economic power is wrested from the monopoly bourgeoisie and foreign capitalists in Chile. Increasing political control will gradually permit growing control over the direction of industry, which is just beginning to develop. This process is politically the most important one in Chile at present.

Chapter 4

THE POPULAR UNITY GOVERNMENT'S EFFORTS IN PLANNING

Gonzalo Martner G.*

Reference will be made to three basic aspects of planning in Chile, — the planning system, the development model and the nature of the plans.

The Planning System. The Popular Unity programme states that a national planning system would be set up and, immediately on coming to power, the Government began to draw up an organizational scheme to establish this system. It has a pyramidal structure; at the top at Presidential level there is the National Development Council, consisting of government officials, ministers responsible for the social and economic fields, six workers' representatives and six management representatives. This is a consultative council. The National Planning Office is its technical secretariat and it is here that medium and short-term development plans are discussed.

To formulate short-term, annual and interim policy the Executive Economic Policy Committee was set up, which consists of the President of the Republic, a co-ordinating Vice-President, the Finance Minister and Economics Minister, with the Minister of Planning acting as technical adviser. This Executive Committee has, in turn, an Executive Committee, mainly consisting of the Minister of Finance, and the Minister of Economy, since the policies and concrete measures will be actually implemented through these ministries in co-ordination with the corresponding institutional sector.

ODEPLAN, the National Planning Office, also acts as an advisory Technical Secretariat for this economic co-ordination Committee.

The National Planning Office was set up in 1967 under the previous government and was based on the Development Corporation's Planning Department. In fact, Chile has a certain tradition of planning, going right back to 1939 when the Corfo Development Corporation drew up the first development plans. Subsequently, it

* Minister, Director of Planning.

successfully evolved sectoral plans such as those for steel, petroleum etc.

ODEPLAN has two basic divisions, one concerned with national planning and the other with regional planning. National planning has what might be termed an overall function, that is to say, it has divisions whose function is to liaise with the sectoral planning offices in ministries where they exist. Some of these are more developed than others, some with only a few staff, while others are relatively well staffed. For example, the Ministry of Agriculture has approximately 120 officials in ODEPA, the Agricultural Planning Office, and the Ministry of Housing also has a large Planning Office. Each Ministry has a number of decentralized enterprises and entities under it, and it is another task of the sectoral planning offices to plan these enterprises. For example, the Under-Secretary of Transport and the Transport Planning Office co-ordinate and encourage planning efforts in transport undertakings, and the Railways, Ports Authority and the National Airline each have a planning office. The system is therefore hierarchical. In the industrial sector CORFO through its industrial planning section, is responsible for controlling planning at enterprise level in its subsidiaries.

There are 18 Regional Planning Offices in the regions, each allotted an area such that the country's 12 planning regions are fully covered. The function of these offices is to prepare medium and short-term programmes and they work in conjunction with the *Intendente*[1] the principal political authority in each province. In some regions there are Regional Development Corporations.

With the creation of the Ministry for Family Welfare, planning units will be established at commune and neighbourhood level and at the level of all other popular mass organizations. But this legislation, which has already been under consideration by Parliament for a year, has not yet been approved.

This planning system is linked with the executive apparatus, Parliament, the Army, and the workers etc. The links with the Executive branch of Government are particularly strong. The planning bodies are advisers at presidential level and at the level of the Executive Economic Policy Committee; and there is also a very strong link at ministerial level. Some ministers work in close co-operation with the Planning Office and others to a lesser extent. At regional level, relationships with the *Intendentes* are on the whole fairly close. Planning Office officials are cited to Parliament to

---

[1] *Intendente*–Governor. This post is a political appointment and the Governor is Presidential representative in the Province. (Editor).

discuss draft legislation with the relevant committees. Furthermore, ODEPLAN is required to produce an annual economic report which is submitted to the President of the Republic and Parliament.

There are permanent institutional links with the Armed Forces in that the Minister of Defence is a member of the National Development Council. Secondly, there are monthly meetings between representatives of the three armed forces at the National Planning Office, where there is an exchange of information on plans to ensure that national development plans are compatible with national security plans. In addition, the Executive has given the Armed Forces a role in regional action. For example, there is a Navy representative in the Valparaiso and Aconcagua Development Corporation. In some cases, military members have been included in the quota of government representatives in the nationalized mines, especially military engineers.

Another important aspect is the relationship between planning and the national budget which constitutes a problem in all countries. In many places there is a kind of civil war between the Planning Office and the Treasury. But here in Chile there are no basic conflicts between these institutions because the functions have been split. The Planning Office proposes the overall framework and global projections for the forthcoming year to the Treasury and puts forward its idea of what the level of public expenditure and the level and composition of public investment should be. At the same time, the sectoral planning offices influence the ministerial budgets in such a way that there is already co-ordination at ministerial level when the preliminary budgetary work is being carried out. Since the process of preparing the budget in Chile is a long one, beginning in about May each year and finishing on the 31st December, there are many opportunities for discussion on criteria for determining priorities. For example, at one point, Treasury officials did not attach importance to the housing programme until ODEPLAN showed the advantage of increasing house construction.

For 1973 it is hoped to prepare an investment plan for the public sector covering the entire social area which will be the axis of government policy especially investment policy.

To sum up, a start has only recently been made on setting up a planning system and the structures are still being created, but the planning process has to be thoroughly improved and the necessary technical personnel obtained.

An important aim is that planning should cease to be a super-structure and become the basis of the system and to this end an agreement is being drawn up with the Central Trades Union Confederation (CUT) to establish a joint ODEPLAN-CUT Commission, responsible for setting up a system and procedure in each enterprise in the socially-owned sector. The first step in this new task was to create a working party which is drawing up a manual and a planning methodology for the enterprises, principally making use of the experience of socialist countries in which National Planning Office staff have studied and gained experience. The joint ODEPLAN-CUT Commission will propose operational models for planning mechanisms with full worker participation for each enterprise.

The Popular Unity Government believes that planning is a way of enhancing participation, enabling discussion on and participation in the substantive issues of development policies.

Planning Models. The new government has adopted a different view of development. Chile has already gone through the export oriented and the import substitution stages of the traditional model, and by the late 1960s these provided no further scope. Now a new development model which has certain different characteristics from previous ones is being worked out. One of the new model's basic aspects consists in transferring the impetus for development from a wealthy minority, which generated an important proportion of the total demand in the economy, to the demand generated by the bulk of the population, by redistributing income. This is not merely a problem of social justice but also one of effecting a change in the structure of production. Increasing the purchasing power of the wage earning class creates a new type of demand which should be accompanied by a change in the structure of supply and production. The allegation that the new model is only concerned with consumption is therefore wrong. The intention is to bring about a change in the structure of demand so as to transform the production structure to satisfy the needs of the vast majority of the country's population, with popular demand providing the stimulus for development.

The old model of export oriented growth is being replaced, and with it the slogan of 'export or die'. The link between the peripheral Chilean system and central capitalism will no longer be the source of development as in previous models based on the need to increase copper exports. That is to say, it involved exporting more in order to obtain dollars and to import technology, machinery, equipment etc. This does not deny the convenience of maintaining links with the rest of the world, but the emphasis must be on internal dynamic forces. The previous development model in which labour saving technology was imported, resulted in modernization in some activities and some cities, but also led to concentration in property ownership and income and to the exclusion of a large part of the Chilean population from the system and a high level of unemployment. This government proposes a development model which will end this concentration and increase participation; and to make this viable, it is drawing up a flexible planning system. It is intended that the State should assume control of the economy's most important means of production, but they should not be administered by a bureaucratic apparatus remote from the interests of the workers. Being socially owned it will possible to involve workers increasingly in the management and administration of these enterprises, but always within the framework of the national economic plan.

A flexible and dynamic system cannot be imposed by decree but must emanate from the workers' own awareness and from the ways in which participation develops. An overall strategy together with detailed planning in certain strategic sectors is preferable to a closed system and this is the type of planning being introduced in the large scale copper mines. In agriculture, a basic strategic sector, it is hoped to establish a planning system in which there is peasant participation. Sufficient progress was achieved in industry in the last 4 or 5 months for the sectoral committees in conjunction with the related enterprises to outline an industrial investment programme; and there is already a detailed industrial programme which shows that accelerated industrial growth is feasible in the coming years.

In the social sectors a more indicative and global type of planning is envisaged. Planning for housing is at present somewhat global, but will become more detailed and it is intended to reach the point where construction operations and allocation of materials are planned. A basic change has to be made in public works planning where the concentrating effect of the previous model resulted in the concentration of public works in the central area of Chile, creating an infrastructure favouring the bourgeoisie.

The change in strategy brings out a lack of cohesion between the projects on which the plans are based; at times they do not correspond very closely to the new orientation of development policy. For example, there is a surfeit of infrastructure projects, very good electrification, petroleum, highways and irrigation projects, because Chile has a civil engineering tradition. Of 7,000 engineers, the vast majority are civil engineers and it is only recently that industrial engineering has established itself. This itself limits the ability to elaborate industrial projects. The present Government's strategy is to achieve an increase in the production of consumer goods for the masses which is compatible with the development of machinery, tools, equipment, spares and other investment goods which will stimulate heavy industry. The production of consumer goods in Chile involves many medium and small projects with simple or intermediate labour intensive technology, which means they must be simpler. In addition, Chile is a developing country with an unbalanced industrial structure, lacking productive capacity in capital goods. The new development strategy places great importance on full employment and therefore an ambitious employment target has been set.

The Nature of the Plans. Efforts have been made to produce a medium-term plan for the 1971-76 presidential period, and this plan fills 16 volumes,containing a global economic plan at national level and a plan for each of the country's 12 regions. The plan consists of a diagnosis, some projections within the national strategy, and groups of projects at varying stages of progress. Some projects are only at the ideas stage, some worked out in detail, while others are actually underway. The same applies to the regional plans, which contain fully developed projects where regional development strategy is clearer and others where the situation is more difficult and the engineering capacity to elaborate the projects is not so great.

The six year plan is implemented by means of annual plans which essentially contain what might be called the government's economic policy framework and the basic investment projects which are to be carried out. A plan for 1971 has been drawn up and the 1972 plan is on the verge of completion. Some special plans have also been drawn up, such as the Reconstruction Plan, to deal with the consequences of the 1971 earthquake which entails rebuilding 35,000 homes, 10 to 15 hospitals, a large number of schools and public buildings, and there are plans to re-build from scratch various villages and small peasant settlements. This is obviously an enormous drain on resources which competes with normal construction programmes. For example, approximately 60,000 emergency dwellings were erected in the disaster area last year and cement was used to repair a large number of highways and public works.

Finally, the relationship between these plans and the foreign trade budget: a foreign exchange budget has been drawn up for 1972 — the first time this has been done in Chile — based on projections of export and import requirements. This required an estimate of the internal deficits, especially in agriculture. This mechanism has enabled control to be exercised over foreign trade and a Foreign Trade

Secretariat, the embryo of a future Ministry of Foreign Trade, has been set up. At this moment, there are some eight bodies with a role in foreign trade and it is difficult to co-ordinate both export and import policies.

Chapter 5

DISCUSSION ON THE POPULAR UNITY'S ECONOMIC POLICY

Short Term Tactics and Long Term Strategy

From speeches on economic policy it was clear that two main factors conditioned the Popular Unity's economic policy in the transition period. The first was the fact that the Popular Unity was an alliance of different social classes and groups, though with the working classes predominating; this determined the second factor which was that the transition towards socialism would be a gradual one. The class alliance under the Popular Unity was a reaction to the many conflicts created by capitalism in an underdeveloped economy. It focussed on defeating imperialism and national monopoly and *latifundia* interests, but the very heterogeneity of the conflicts made it difficult to form a unified, solid political bloc.

These two factors and the constraint of being a minority government meant that economic strategy and policy had to serve the double purpose both of helping achieve full control of power and of beginning the construction of a socialist economy. The struggle for power had to be kept in mind when discussing all aspects of economic policy. In addition the economic strategy had to be suitable for an underdeveloped economy like the Chilean one as well as permitting the transformation of the power structure.

The new strategy centred on an expansion of the private and social consumption of the popular classes through the complementary policies of income redistribution and more employment opportunities. Emphasis on the production of popular consumer goods was expected to raise the demand for labour since it was said to be more labour intensive than the production of luxury goods at existing levels of technology in Chile. Higher employment would increase the demand for popular consumption goods. This policy would also favour the development of small and medium scale enterprises, which had traditionally produced popular consumption goods. This was considered to have political advantages in terms of furthering the alliance with some middle class groups.

Concentration on popular consumer goods would also reduce the range of goods available in the limited Chilean market, facilitating rationalization and the benefits of economies of scale. Increased demand for these goods would permit the utilization of the excess capacity which existed in many industries.

Another disadvantage claimed for a strategy based on popular consumption was that it would allow a net saving of foreign exchange. While it had been recognized that income distribution in favour of the popular classes would increase the demand for imported foodstuffs, the high direct and indirect import content of luxury goods would be avoided. Foreign exchange savings on consumption items would permit higher imports of capital goods — allegedly the principal bottleneck in investment.

The transition to socialism in Chile required the control and transformation of the State by the working classes through the expansion of the socially-owned property sector and a change in the production relations, and an agrarian reform which would permit non-capitalist development in the countryside. This was a necessary part of the economic strategy because it was the only way to ensure the re-orientation of the production structure and adequate reinvestment from the monopolistic enterprises.

The central theme of discussion concerned the political aspects of economic policy. The view of one East European was that the Popular Unity seemed trapped in what Lenin had called the 'vicious circle of revolution': it needed to gain fuller control of power in order to re-orient the economy, yet it lacked the economic organization and means to do this. In this participant's view the solution did not lie in devising a set of economic policies or instruments to regulate and run a system of state capitalism, or manipulate consumption. Intensification of the political struggle was the only way to breaking this vicious circle. This depended on increasing the political activity of the masses and the working class parties of the Popular Unity, whose task was increasingly to take over the organization of production. Considerable efforts to radicalize consciousness — a kind of investment — were needed during the transformation period, in order to increase commitment to socialist transition.[1]

In the opinion of a North American social scientist this mass support could only be gained through popular mobilization and participation in the political struggle in the rural and urban sectors. It did, of course, involve the risk of alienating the middle classes but, in

[1] See Section 1 Part 5 for the discussion on participation and social consciousness.

his view, if priority were given to winning the support of the middle classes it raised doubts about the kind of socialist transformation being pursued.

Other participants did not agree that concern with economic policies was irrelevant. They felt that although the political aspects were exceedingly important, and every effort was needed to strengthen the revolutionary forces in Chile, it was necessary to pay some attention to the more technocratic and organizational aspects of how to move towards socialism. This was partly because the Popular Unity had to implement policies of some kind or other, and partly because they felt that successful pursuit of certain economic policies could help further the transition to socialism.

Certain policies with political objectives had economic implications which necessarily lead to technocratic preoccupations; for example, higher working class incomes and consumption had balance of payments implications. On the other hand, some participants felt that, while it was necessary to formulate economic policies consistent with the principal objectives, there were inbuilt dangers. Excessive concern and caution over the more technical aspects could result in the need for structural and political — even revolutionary — change being subordinated to technocratic considerations.

The timing of Presidential and Congressional elections in Chile seem to create almost insuperable problems for the Popular Unity. It was important for the Popular Unity to win a working majority in the March 1973 Congressional elections, and to this end it was attempting to use economic policy to win electoral advantages. One British economist with experience in Government felt that it was difficult to contrive policies which began the task of building a socialist economy without cutting off political support, but he also thought it was a mistake to try to use economic measures to gain electoral advantages. They could not be gained sufficiently quickly and any attempt to achieve them would rebound by spoiling the Government's image as a long term policy maker. An alternative was to build up a socialist image and educate people by setting an example, explaining to them the nature of policies which would benefit them in the long run.

According to an American political scientist's interpretation of events, the very success of the Popular Unity's economic policy involved a paradox. It had created political conditions which made the continuation and deepening of the overall transitional process even more difficult, with the opposition more active in early 1972 than it had been in the early months of the Popular Unity Government. But this situation did not seem at all paradoxical to members of the Popular Unity Government. To them it was evidence that the capitalist groups which the government intended to displace now felt their position considerably weakened. Realizing that if the present process continued the changes would be irreversible, they were now fighting back to regain political control to defend their economic interests.

The Socially-owned Sector

State control of the economy and increasing worker participation in economic decision-making was regarded by the Popular Unity as essential if the power of the old dominant groups, who controlled the State and the economy and opposed change, was to be broken and the economy run in the interests of the mass of the population.

Some participants felt that the growing state intervention over the past 40 years provided a good institutional base from which to begin the task of economic management and control. Others felt that too much emphasis on the age and size of the existing public sector obscured the real magnitude of the task confronting the Government in reorienting state intervention and expanding the socially-owned sector. The State was never neutral or independent but served the interests of the dominant class. As explained by Oscar Garreton, state intervention and the existence of a state sector in Chile had never weakened the national and foreign monopolistic interests. Little central control had been exercised by the state sector over the private sector; on the contrary, it had underwritten the initiative and autonomy of private capital. In the early years the State had developed the not very profitable basic industries which served the rest of the industrial sector and these enterprises operated with a large degree of autonomy. In the 1960's the State had begun to finance private investment. Between 1961 and 1969 direct public investment grew at a cumulative annual rate of 6.3% whereas indirect public investment (capital transfers for private sector investment) grew by 20% a year. In 1969, 65% of direct investment went to electricity, water, gas, transport, communications, housing and urban services, while 62.6% of indirect public investment went to agriculture, mining and industry, rising to 70% in 1972. In view of these figures and the fact that the State was responsible for about 75% of total Chilean investment, it was clear that most investment in the private sector was state aided.

The creation of mixed copper enterprises was another example of how the State has assisted foreign enterprises. Even with state ownership of 51% of the capital, the foreign companies owning the balance were able to take out even more profits from Chile than when they had held 100% of the shares.

Another indication of CORFO's previous harmonious relationship with the private monopolistic sector was the presence of private sector representatives on it's management Council, which had never given rise to conflicts of interest under previous governments.

Chilean participants felt that, in view of these facts, the state sector in the past could hardly be described as an embryo of socialism; this would only begin under the Popular Unity Government. The socially-owned property sector would be expanded and production relations transformed. This was seen as the only way in which it would be possible to change the power structure and begin the process of a socialist transformation. Using legislation from the early 1930's, the Government had been able to take control of industries where production was interrupted or where the 'national interest' demanded it.[2] The Christian Democrats were now attempting to block these efforts to restructure the economy. They were sponsoring a Constitutional Reform Bill which would require a separate piece of legislation for each act of nationalization. The Bill would be retroactive to October 1971, and affect what the Government had already achieved.

One European participant felt that, in view of the Popular Unity's limited political base and limited leverage on central state institutions, policy for the socially-owned sector should put as much emphasis on political as on economic performance. Rather than concentrate wholly on structural change and the expansion of the socially-owned sector, high priority should be given, in the short run, to using this sector to deliver material benefits to the Government's political base — a policy which would not be necessary for a government with complete political control and the possibility of concentrating on longer term growth targets.

Even this policy, however, was recognized to have its limits, bearing in mind both the implications for the balance of payments of the increased pressure of demand, and the degree of external dependance. Moreover the transitional nature of the current political and

---

[2] An *interventor* (Manager) is appointed by the Government when a firm is requisitioned as a result of labour conflicts, non-compliance with the law or in cases where production is interrupted due to economic problems. Until the enterprise is transferred to the socially — owned sector or, in some cases, returned to its owners, the government-appointed manager has full responsibility for running the enterprise, even though legally it still belongs to the private owners. (Editor)

economic context meant that the role of the public sector could not be discussed in terms of a stable mixed economy. The situation was complicated from both the economic and political point of view. A large number of private capitalists had been warned that there was little future for them, yet, they had still been left in control, at this stage, of a sizable proportion of production and income. Naturally they were reluctant to invest, as were smaller enterprises, who, despite government assurances, felt unsure about their future. Any tendency of the Government's prices and income distribution policies to squeeze profits would provide even less encouragement to invest.

Many Popular Unity officials therefore felt that for economic reasons alone it was necessary to transfer enterprises from the private to the socially-owned sector. If this were not done, surpluses would not be reinvested and increased popular demand would neither give rise to a new dynamism nor lead to a reorientation of production and growth.

When discussing the role of the state and the private sector, it was thought relevant to look at Soviet experience in the early years of the Revolution. In the Soviet Union, as in Chile, the first task had been to strengthen the social basis of power, by using economic measures to consolidate the union between the working classes and the peasants — the social forces on which the Revolution was based. Incentives were given to raise agricultural and peasant production and the Government implemented policies to improve exchange between the rural and urban sector on the basis of the market mechanism. Since the state sector was not sufficiently developed to provide the necessary volume of consumer goods and to maintain a high level of economic activity, capitalist production was allowed in this sphere of activity. Capitalist production was functioning in the interests of strengthening the revolutionary social forces and the transition to socialism. To prevent capitalist production becoming a dominant self-reproducing system, key sectors of the economy such as heavy industry, transport, power and banking had been brought under state control.

Several participants raised questions about the mechanisms the Government was using to cream off investable surpluses. It had been explained that price policy, rather than global tax measures or similar instruments, was to be the principal mechanism for generating surpluses, which would accumulate at enterprise level, particularly in the socially-owned enterprises; this could lead to conflicts between wages and investment at enterprise level depending on the nature of the enterprise in the socially-owned sector and the range of their decision-making powers. If wages and investment decisions were made at enterprise level, with some degree of worker participation, the conflicts would have serious social and economic implication.

Popular Unity economists explained that such contradictions did not arise in the socially-owned sector. First, the enterprises were subject to social control in so far as they were integrated into a sectoral and national planning and decision-making framework. They did not belong to the individual groups who worked in them, although this was one of the intentions of the Christian Democrat Constitutional Reform Bill on the structure of the economy. Although the enterprise was the level at which surpluses would be accumulated, decisions concerning investment would be made at sectoral and national level, though with the participation of the enterprise through the planning mechanisms.

One important aspect of the socially-owned enterprises which concerned participants was the seeming lack of any clear criteria for guiding the decisions of the *interventor*, managers and workers' councils who ran the enterprises. Although there was a feeling that these enterprises should begin to conform to different principles, they had not received clear or new guidance from the Government about how they should operate in a mixed economy in which capitalist principles still predominated.

For example, the Government's price policy of maintaining low prices for working class goods and allowing increases in others had evidently lead in some cases to socially-owned enterprises reducing production of these less profitable though socially more necessary goods in favour of the higher-priced, more luxurious items.

On the other hand, the industrial visits made by participants[3] gave the impression that, despite the profound changes taking place in some enterprises and sectors, the minimum amount of disorder was apparent — contrary to the impression conveyed by a large section of the press.

Popular Unity economists agreed that there were problems involved in trying to run a socially-owned sector in a mixed economy

---

[3] The industrial group visited three factories. Two were private joint stock companies producing electrical household appliances and steel castings respectively, though a subsidiary of the latter firm had been expropriated and another subsidiary would have to be disposed of under a law prohibiting holding companies owning enterprises in another economic sector. The third enterprise, a very large one, processed Chilean copper and aluminium, making both intermediate producer goods and final consumer goods, and had been 'intervened' in September 1971. Participants also visited the Federation of Metal Working Unions, and the Association of Small and Medium Manufacturers.

in a way which furthered the Popular Unity's social, economic, and political objectives. Progress was, however, being made in the various CORFO sectoral committees, by drawing up price and production policies for a whole sector. They also thought that the problems would diminish as the workers' social consciousness heightened.

Income Redistribution and Wages Policy

In his speech, Ricardo Lagos had referred to the process in Chile of an increasing concentration of income, and Jose Ibarra had provided recent figures for income distribution. In response to questions from participants about recent trends in income distribution, it was pointed out that during the 1960s the share of wage and salary earners had remained constant. In the latter part of the period their position seemed to improve but this only compensated for the previous decline, caused by the Klein Saks economic policy under Alessandri. However, any gains or constancy in the share of labour as a whole reflected an improvement in the situation of employees and white collar workers. Between 1960 and 1969, the share of labour increased from 52.9% to 53.1% employers increased their share from 30.2% to 32.4%, but the position of manual workers declined from 22.7% to 20.7%. In the same period property incomes rose from 17.7% to 24.5% of the national income.

Many participants acknowledged that the Popular Unity's income redistribution policy was economically, socially and politically useful. Higher incomes for the lower wage brackets could provide the necessary impetus to revitalise the economy, and from the point of view of social equity an improvement of the income level of the working classes was justified. Moreover, several European and Chilean participants agreed that a short term policy of material benefits to build up the basis of support for future change was necessary and simpler than the immediate pursuit of irreversible structural change. However, several participants felt it was necessary to analyse the mechanics of the income redistribution. Had it been carried out at the expense of the high income groups or of profits, and what had been the effects of higher consumption?

Government economists explained that the rapid growth of national income in 1971 had been passed on to the working classes mainly through high wage awards. The incomes of the higher income brackets had not been reduced through new taxation or wages legislation. The latter fact meant that in future, when it was no longer possible to achieve income distribution through such rapid growth, it would still be possible to effect an internal redistribution. The

Government's policy was to reduce the enormous income inequalities which existed within the wage and salary earning population. A start had been made in 1971 by awarding higher cost of living adjustments to the lowest paid income groups and, in a few limited cases, an attempt had been made to introduce maximum earnings.

Overall, the average level of wages had risen by 50% in 1971 with respect to 1970, and in 1972 an increase of 40% was expected. Several participants expressed concern about the danger of wage inflation; the Government had awarded sizeable wage increases in the socially-owned sector — where workers were often better organized — besides substantially improving welfare and social facilities in the factories. This set an example to the private sector, over which the Government had little control.

The Government expected the pressure for wage increases to continue, since more than 60% of the working population still earned less than two *sueldos vitales*. There was also a widespread conviction that under a government with socialist objectives it ought to be possible to achieve greater equality between workers within the same enterprise, the same industry and in different branches of production. It was also true that the better paid workers were more organised and tended to demand larger increases.

One Chilean economist explained that, when confronted by highly organized groups of workers demanding a wage increase exceeding the rise in the cost of living, the Government had tried to restrict the basic money wage increase to the increase in the cost of living. Any additional increase beyond that was to be related to productivity increases. This policy would simultaneously act on production as well as wage levels, thereby helping to avoid demand problems generated by wage rises. So far, the policy has not been widely successful, since some highly organized workers would not accept a cost of living related basic increase. However, in this speaker's opinion, the Government should persist since this was the only sensible policy.

The aspect of wages policy which most concerned the participants was that related to the level of wages and its effect on reinvestable surpluses. This was particularly relevant to the socially-owned sector for two reasons. First, the workers in many of the socially-owned enterprises were often among the better organized and were in a position to exert pressure directly on the State — in what were key enterprises. Second, to the extent that decisions on wages were made at enterprise level and that worker's participation allowed workers a say in the determination of their wages, serious problems could arise if investment decisions were also determined at enterprise level.

With respect to this problem the Government's policy was said to be quite clear; both wage and investment policy of socially-owned enterprises had to be determined at sectoral or global level in line with the overall plan and not according to the interests of individual groups of workers.

A substantial number of participants suggested that there might be other ways of achieving income distribution other than awarding high wage increases to the working classes. A different approach might even be the only way to achieve a real increase in working class incomes. With the possibilities of using idle capacity and unemployed resources now exhausted, it would be increasingly difficult to obtain substantial increases in output to match the level of demand. Moreover, in future, an expansion in output would require investment, yet continuation of the Government's 1971 policy of allowing high wage increases and of controlling consumer prices would reduce the surplus available for reinvestment.

Various alternative policies were suggested, many of which were complementary. Some related to ways of reducing middle and upper class income and consumption — increased direct taxation, higher indirect taxes on luxuries, discriminatory price policies, and the curtailing of luxury consumption, including foreign travel. Other measures advocated were ones which would act on aggregate supply and demand, to the benefit of the lower income groups and the detriment of the well-off. These suggestions included the control of supply, rationing, and forced savings.

(a) *Taxation Policy*

Given the need to redistribute income, to finance Government expenditure and to reduce the level of liquidity in the economy, increased taxation of upper income groups seemed to many non-Chilean participants an obvious solution. Moreover, one political scientist saw definite political advantages in levying taxes on specific forms of luxury consumption (such as private summer houses, cars, private schools, etc.) and applying the proceeds to build the popular equivalent — popular housing, state schools, public transport, etc. Changes in taxation policy, however, required Congress' approval and the Government's path was blocked in this respect. Congress had opposed the Popular Unity proposals to tax transfers of possessions valued at more than twenty-five annual *sueldos vitales*, which would have affected only a small proportion of all property. Proposals for a tax on excess profits had been rejected, and a proposed 30% tax on enterprises with a capital of five hundred thousand *escudos* or more had been reduced to 15% and only applied to firms with a capital of six hundred thousand *escudos* and above. A scaled charge on *bienes raices* (land and property) was rejected in favour of a general tax at the lowest rate of the proposed scale; the proposal for a graduated tax on wine and cigarettes, according to their value, was dealt with in the same way.

The Government had failed to secure approval for a law to punish tax offenders, modifying the existing over-lenient legislation. Fiscal revenue lost due to evasion of the sales tax amounted to twenty thousand million *escudos* in 1971 — higher than the total budget deficit of fifteen thousand millions in the same year. Evasion of income tax and other taxes was equally prevalent, and the total sum involved was so high that effective efforts to prevent evasion would certainly yield high returns. However, a Government economist explained that the administrative capacity to improve control of tax evasion was lacking and that the Government's 'tax consciousness' was still not sufficiently developed.

(b) *Discriminatory Price Policies and Reformulation of the Cost-of-Living Index*

A price policy which would keep down the price of necessities while raising the price of luxuries, or leaving them free from price control, had two things to recommend it. A high price for luxury goods would help reduce the level of demand for these items, and it would also absorb some of the excess liquidity of the high income groups in much the same way as an indirect tax would.

Nevertheless, such a policy would only work in the direction of the Government's overall strategy if complementary policies were applied. High prices would yield high profits and these would mainly accrue in the private sector, since the government sector did not include many luxury products, and the normal functioning of the price mechanism would then allocate resources away from Government priorities. Additional taxes would therefore have to be levied on the profits, but the difficulty of obtaining congressional approval for this rendered the idea less useful at the present stage.

However, some items in the range produced by socially-owned enterprises could be regarded as falling within the non-essential category, for example certain types of textiles, and it would therefore be possible to raise these prices substantially, and the profits would accrue directly to the state sector.

Another serious difficulty was that annual statutory wage awards *(reajustes)* were made to compensate for increases in the cost of living index. But whereas the index had at one time been based on a narrow basket of working class goods, it had been transformed in the 1960's into a national consumer price index covering three hundred and twenty or more articles, with a considerable weight for middle class type goods.

Steep price increases in these items would add to inflationary pressure by automatically being reflected in the *reajuste*.

One possible solution suggested by various economists was the reformulation of the index, removing all the middle class or more luxury type of items. Moreover, the weighting of the index indicated the necessity of doing this since the total weight assigned to products such as petrol, oil and tyres, etc., which affected the car-owner, was greater than the weight assigned to each of the one hundred and twenty-four food items except bread. Thirteen food items taken together were weighted lower than car oil. Similarly, items like televisions and telephones, which did not enter in the consumption patterns of the mass of the population, had a relatively high weighting.

In fact, the Government was reported to be seeking ways of changing the composition and weighting of the index, and of establishing a new price index to reflect the needs of the social classes it was trying to benefit. But changes in the official index required legislation, and it was therefore necessary to find a way of achieving the same objective in a way that did not depend on the approval of Congress.

(c) *Restrictions on Middle and Upper Class Consumption and Restructuring Supply*

Several Chilean and European participants argued that, in view of the fact that idle resources had been fully absorbed, further increases in real incomes and consumption of the working classes demanded a reduction in the consumption of other social classes.

Measures such as forced savings which only aimed at halting the expansion of middle and upper class consumption were not enough, since they would continue with their established consumption patterns which were influenced by foreign standards and tastes, partly through the mechanisms of capitalist dependency. It was necessary to redefine middle class consumption patterns and there were certain areas such as housing where control was vital. (The standard of housing defined as 'economic' in the law promoting house-building, known as DFL2, which provided substantial fiscal and legal benefits to house-owners, allowed a maximum of one hundred and forty square metres — a luxury by European standards. Only the upper middle class and the rich could afford to build these so-called economical houses and flats). The Government's measures only to authorise production of small cars was regarded as a step in the right direction.

According to one Government official, something in the nature of a cultural revolution was needed to change consumption habits and attitudes, but no efforts to do this had been made so far.

Various participants suggested that, in the Chilean situation, the most realistic and effective way of influencing middle and upper class consumption was to define an appropriate structure of supply in accordance with social, political and economic objectives and to manipulate aggregate supply accordingly. This involved having a clear resource allocation policy favouring those products which the government considered part of the working class basket of goods, and defining an appropriate structure of prices. Such policies would also work in favour of income redistribution.

Government officials explained that they were trying to define a basket of essential goods and services which would orient these short term price and investment policies in the manner suggested. However, the existing restricted size of the socially-owned sector limited the degree of control the Government had to operate such a policy, and the decisive element in determining the structure of supply was still the market. In the short term, therefore, the Government intended to put strong emphasis on administrative measures to absorb as much excess liquidity as possible from the middle and upper classes. New measures were being devised, but it was inappropriate to reveal details.

(d) *Rationing*

If the government's income distribution policy via wage increases were to continue and result in a real increase in consumption for the working classes some participants, particularly British, felt that some form of rationing might be necessary. This view was not shared by the Popular Unity which considered that most of the problems were caused by distributional problems rather than by real shortages, and improvement of distribution channnels would make rationing measures unnecessary. One method was for wholesale networks newly brought under government control to ensure direct supplies to retailers in poor areas, as was being done with meat. The Government believed in discussing these problems with the working classes and involving them in their solution.

In fact, the Price and Supply Committees (*Juntas de Abastecimientos y Precios*) had emerged spontaneously as the popular response to supply problems. These were neighbourhood groups in which the housewife played a dominant role. They incorporated the representatives of the various mass organizations and the local retailers and their task was to ensure fair distribution of consumer goods. Within six months of the first committee being established, there were already 450 in Santiago, covering 100,000 families or about 600,000 people. Their efforts in bringing about an improved distribution of meat to the poorer areas of the population were already showing signs of success — 20% of the country's beef consumption was now supplied through these committees. Efforts to encourage fish consumption instead of meat, which was largely imported, were also beginning to show success. Plans existed to establish wholesale and retail outlets in each neighbourhood under the direction and control of the Price and Supply Committee.

Inflationary Pressures, Price Policy and Methods of Price Control

The Popular Unity Government's price control policy had been very successful during the Popular Unity's first year in power and had played an important part in its income redistribution policy. However, many participants noted the existence of various disequilibria which would put strong pressures on prices, perhaps wiping out the gains achieved in 1971.

According to one Chilean critic, the inflationary situation in 1972 promised to be extremely serious, and could only be avoided at the cost of serious unemployment and increased foreign indebtedness. During 1971 the supply of money had increased 120% and in 1972 it would increase at least by 60% and more probably by 100%. With an increase in the money supply of such a magnitude it was exceedingly difficult to manage the situation, whatever the monetary theory backing up the Government's economic policy. In his opinion prices would have to increase in 1972 in order to change the price structure and to help create surpluses in the public sector. Moreover, during the rest of 1972 there would be a strong pressures to make up for the price increases of the previous twelve months with new wage adjustments.

If prices did not rise significantly, shortages were likely to arise and there would be strong pressure on the balance of payments.

A Government Official explained that in 1971 it had been considered necessary to keep all prices down, but in 1972 the policy had been to allow differential increases in order to modify the distorted price structure which had been inherited, so that the economy could be allowed to operate according to the market mechanism. In particular, in 1972 the Government had allowed agricultural prices to rise more than others, partly in order to improve the terms of trade between the rural and urban sector. The price of bread, oil, sugar and public transport, which weighed heavily in the budget of the mass of the population, had been increased.

However, increases in consumer prices were now to be manipulated in such a way that the income of the poorer classes would not be eroded. The new policy compensating for any increase in the price of essentials had been introduced along with the February price increases. On the basis of surveys of family consumption, and estimates of the incidence of the increased prices on the average family, the Government was awarding a fixed increase in income, unrelated to wage and salary levels.

Government economists claimed that there were various basic factors causing inflationary pressures. First, there was the increase in urban and rural wages in 1971 and early 1972. Under the Popular Unity the power of the workers to press their wage claims had increased enormously. The tendency for workers to identify socialism with greater economic equality meant there were strong pressures from the lowest paid groups to catch up with other workers, both within the same industry and in other sectors. Second, the price of imported goods had risen by 14% in 1972, and the escudo devaluation in late 1971 had increased the price of imported final goods and inputs. The third pressure came from the law governing the budget and wage increases tied to the cost of living. The Government had tried to finance these with taxes to be borne by the high income groups, but Congress had substituted taxes on mass consumption goods instead.

A fourth factor considered important by various Chilean economists were the speculative tendencies which had developed, partly as a result of the high degree of financial liquidity and the shortage of certain luxury goods, and partly because certain groups wished to use the sensitive political and economic situation to create problems for the Government. A form of 'black market' had developed for consumption goods like beef and chicken, and durables like cars and televisions.

Government efforts to expand the socially-owned sector and accelerate the agrarian reform, involving substantial payments for these assets, had also added to the high level of liquidity and inflationary pressure in the economy.

The Government estimated that overall consumer prices had risen by about 10% in January and February 1972. This was not considered alarming since in previous years prices had increased by 15% to 18% in the first quarter, after which the pace slackened. A linear projection could not be made for the whole year on the basis of the first months, since so much depended on what happened in the rest of the economy. The Government was not expecting a sustained rise in prices. However, serious disequilibria did exist which could give rise to inflationary pressures. Control of these tendencies was high among the Government's priorities. Besides the traditional instruments available for this task, the structural changes (agrarian reform, the socially-owned property sector, control of foreign trade and distribution etc.) put at its disposal new tools to fight inflation.

One new and politically important instrument involved popular mobilization, which had great advantages over policies based on bureaucratic price control mechanisms. In fact Chileans regarded wide social involvement in vigilance against unlawful price increases, hoarding of scarce goods, and speculation, as the best way of ensuring effective control. Popular organs of control were beginning to be organized at all levels. Price and Supply Committees established in working class neighbourhoods had organized themselves to carry out these responsibilities. *'Vigilante'* committees had been set up in private enterprises and the Government was beginning to discuss price policy with them for the respective industries.

In reply to questions concerning possible changes in the Popular Unity financial and credit policies, it was explained that the Government had not developed what could be called a revolutionary financial policy. With high liquidity in the banking system it was possible to use financial instruments to control its level, but the Government had not yet used these measures sufficiently.

The Government intended applying old and new policy instruments to absorb liquidity. Administrative measures planned by the Government would absorb 15,000 million escudos in 1971, an amount equal to the total budget deficit, reducing the pressure of demand of certain goods and helping to prevent speculation. For example, the Government was introducing control over the distribution of particular products (*estancos de distribucion*). In the case of cars, marketing was done through the normal channels, but the Government fixed the sales prices, the producer's income, the use of the profits, and many aspects of production. Prospective car buyers had to deposit the total price of the car when placing their order, which was one to six months before delivery date, according to the make. The car scheme would absorb 1,500 million escudos a year and the profits would help finance public expenditure.

A Government participant felt that too much emphasis had been put on the consumption and inflationary effects of the Popular Unity's income distribution policy. He pointed out that 1971 figures showed a considerable increase in personal savings. Moreover 6,000 million to 8,000 million escudos had been saved by working class groups through savings and loan mechanisms — a large proportion of which went into housing schemes which had provided 60,000 houses in 1971 for the popular classes.

Nevertheless, a North American participant thought that, as the incomes of the working classes increased, more consideration should be given to the working class savings. He recommended a scheme of financial assets, which guaranteed monetary readjustments and a positive rate of interest, in order to attract working class saving in particular. But a Chilean economist stressed that, if people in higher income brackets were allowed to subscribe for such assets, the savings scheme would work against the Popular Unity's income redistribution objective.

The Level of Investment
The decline in the level of investment from 16% to 14% of the national product was viewed by several European participants as indicative of future trends. Profits had been squeezed in 1971, and if it was correct that increased consumption had affected stocks more than fixed investment then it seemed that in 1972 fixed investment was likely to decline further. Further increases in wages and continued control of consumer prices would not encourage private investment. It would also make it difficult to fulfil the plan objective of relying heavily on surpluses generated in the state sector for financing capital investment. In the State sector, in particular, high wage increases had been awarded. Many new social benefits had also been provided for the workers, which were financed out of profits. Participants wondered how the Government was going to increase savings in order to guarantee an adequate level of investment, if it was not going to allow a very substantial increase in prices.

The relatively low price of copper was seen as a further complicating factor in relation to investment. Currently it was about 49 cents a pound, but any fall below the price of 46 cents used by the Government in calculating its internal budget and longer term investment projections would cut into the projected investable surplus and tend to limit capital goods imports.

Government officials claimed that the savings and investment situation did not give grounds for such pessimism. There was a tendency to overestimate the extent to which profits would be affected by the wage and price policy. Although unit profit margins might be lower, the use of excess capacity to supply the higher demand worked in the direction of maintaining the absolute volume of profits. Naturally, however, the Government had applied its restrictive policy more rigorously in the socially-owned sector where it was easier to gain compliance with the policy. Therefore, large surpluses had not been generated in this sector.

The decline in investment in 1971 was with respect to 1969 and 1970, years in which the level of investment was inflated by the copper expansion plans (involving credits of $735 million). In absolute terms the level achieved in 1971 was higher than in 1967 and 1968 and was mainly financed with domestic resources. Looked at from this angle, 1971 showed no decline in the capacity of the Chilean economy to generate investment. Moreover, although unit profit margins may have been affected, the absolute level of profits had been more or less maintained because of the large increase in demand and output, utilizing excess productive capacity.

One factor which Government economists claimed had affected the level of investment during the Popular Unity's period in government was the lack of suitable projects ready for implementation. It would not be easy to increase these rapidly since the Government's policy was to rely increasingly upon national engineering capacity for project preparation, in contrast to past dependence on foreign engineering groups. To the extent that this policy was pursued, project preparation could only proceed at a pace determined by the development of local engineering capabilities.

In 1972, the Government's policy was to make discriminate price increases which, while conforming to its policy of maintaining the purchasing power of lower incomes, helped to generate investable surpluses. In enterprises or branches of production which were now under state control the policy would be to ensure that the price of popular consumption goods remained low, while the price of other less essential products was raised to provide surpluses. Government officials recognized that their capacity to achieve full implementation of such a policy was limited by lack of full control over the socially-owned enterprises, but they claimed that progress was being made.

A Latin American economist felt that there was room for optimism concerning private investment in the future. With or without an income redistribution policy, private investment was bound to have declined in the political climate existing in the early stages of the Popular Unity Government. However, the redistribution of income and the consequent change in the structure of demand would not only cause a reorientation of private production but would also lead to a renewal in private investment activity. Private entrepreneurs could not remit profits abroad, nor would they be able to spend them on luxury consumption since such goods would not be available. Their only alternative would be to reinvest them in the areas indicated directly or indirectly by Government policy.

Chapter 6

DISCUSSION ON THE
POPULAR UNITY'S PLANNING EFFORTS

Five main topics constituted the basis of the debate on planning in Chile, namely, the role of ODEPLAN (the National Planning Office) in the planning process, the type of plan that had been prepared and its methodology, the plan objectives, the mechanisms for encouraging or ensuring plan implementation, and the implications concerning the foreign sector and employment.

Participants had been presented with summaries of the 1971-76 Six Year Plan and the 1971 and 1972 Annual Plans prepared by ODEPLAN. Apparently this was the first time that complete development plans had been published in Chile. However, in order to be able to evaluate the status of the plan and the likelihood of its implementation, participants considered it necessary to know more about the status of ODEPLAN within the government apparatus and its role and responsibilities.

In the experience of one foreign participant ODEPLAN in the past had not, in practice, been a key part of the planning process. From his observations, its activities had really been limited to making rather hypothetical calculations about the future of the economy. Under the Frei Government, at least, there was substantial ministerial autonomy and each regarded it as a prerogative to fix plans and policies without having some other agency revise and tailor them to achieve some degree of mutual consistency. For example, one of ODEPLAN's strategic objectives during the Frei Government was that, by 1970, Chile would be free from the need to import foodstuffs, thereby relieving the country from the need to create extra port handling and storage capacity. But, at the same time, the Ministry of Agriculture planned to build extra food storage capacity at the ports and claimed that food supplies were not the business of ODEPLAN. Had the Popular Unity Government been able to make progress in this direction in the last eighteen months, such that ODEPLAN's plans did have some real meaning? Those from Eastern Europe said that experience in socialist countries showed how important it was to have a clear and unambiguous central plan which determined the main priorities and allocation of the nation's resources, the demands on which were almost unlimited from all sectors.

This preoccupation was recognized by those involved in planning in Chile to be very important, but difficult to answer. The Government's feeling was that the situation had changed substantially. In the first place, increased importance was now given to planning. The Director of ODEPLAN now had ministerial status and participated in Cabinet meetings, in the National Development Council and in all work concerned with determining short-term economic policy in these two groups. The Director of Planning, along with the Minister of Economics and Agriculture, also participated in high level political discussions between the Popular Unity parties, such as the Arrayan Meeting in early 1972, in which the political leadership of the Popular Unit worked out the political and economic tactics for 1972 as set out in the Arrayan Declaration.

Perhaps the most important, according to one planner, was the change in the Government itself. Whereas in the previous government many ideologies existed side by side, despite the fact that it was a one party government, there was now greater political unity even though there were more parties forming the government. The Frei Government had combined pro-capitalist ministers and bureaucrats and, on the other hand, some in favour of substantial reform. In the Popular Unity all Government members were said to be socialists of one form or another working in the same direction. It was much easier for ODEPLAN to gain access to the various ministries and collaborate with them. This was also made easier by the fact that the present Government's economic team was not an improvised one but one which, over a long period of time, had been developing with considerable contact and friendship between the members, which now facilitated co-ordination.

The 1971-1976 Six Year Plan was the fruit of such co-ordinated efforts. The agricultural part had been prepared by ODEPA, the Agricultural Planning Office of the Ministry of Agriculture; the first draft of the parts concerned with mining were prepared by the Ministry of Mines' Planning Office and so on. But all these sectoral plans were drawn up within a framework of global targets, although in such a way that the final plan did not diverge from the views or plans of the various ministries. If there was any really serious problem, it was the lack of sufficient and capable personnel to work in the National Planning Office and provide assistance in response to the many requests from the different ministries.

Nevertheless, not all participants were convinced that the 1971-1976 Six Year Plan constituted an operational and integrated plan. It was agreed that the aims had been clearly set out, but there was some doubt about whether the plan was integrated so that all the sectoral targets were mutually consistent, and how well the aims were adapted to the available resources.

Essentially, the strategy of the 1971-1976 Plan was to downgrade the external sector as the source of growth and substitute consumption of the low income groups by means of redistributing income, to increase their effective purchasing power and restructure production to correspond to the new pattern of demand. On the whole, there was widespread agreement among participants that this was a highly acceptable and logical approach and some felt that there were not many models open for the Chilean economy, in view of the resource limitations. Some emphasis on consumption oriented expansion for the short and medium-term was in any case justified because such a large proportion of the Chilean population hardly participated in the economic system.

However, one view was that the plans put too much emphasis on consumption, but others thought that this preoccupation might be less justified if care was taken to distinguish between social or collective forms of consumption such as education, health and houses, and private consumption determined through market forces.

Another factor in favour of this approach was that it might avoid the difficulties of investment cycles of the sort experienced in the Eastern European countries as a result of the early attempts at forced investment in highly capital intensive heavy industry. Nevertheless, it seemed to some participants that, in changing the priorities or strategy, the planners had also tried to wish away certain important and long-standing problems or, alternatively, had not fully worked out the overall resource implications. This was said to be most clear in the case of the external sector implications and foreign exchange requirements resulting from the planned objectives.[1]

Opinions differed on how to achieve integrated, consistent plans in Chile. One view was that, for this to be done properly, it required planning and implementation both on a physical and financial basis, and that the problem could only be solved with the aid of mathematical economic models such as the Balance Method of Planning as developed in the Soviet Union, based on the use of input-output tables prepared on both an ex-post and ex-ante basis. Currently in

---

[1] See Section I Part 4 for a more detailed discussion of these problems.

the Soviet Union 15 different types of input-output tables were prepared for the country as a whole and for various constituent republics, and progress was being made in advancing from near-static models to dynamic ones, all compiled on both a physical and financial basis. It was suggested that this sort of planning, which was based on the so-called 'resource principle' and which put the main emphasis on production targets for individual goods and services, was probably sufficient for the early stages of development. It gave great weight to short-term plans and the structure of decisions was claimed to be such that they could be very quickly evaluated and implemented.

However, where the economy was quite complex and large structural changes had to take place, economic planning had to be approached in a more integral way and to be seen as an integral part of overall longer-term socio-economic planning. In this case the starting point for medium-term or perspective planning was the drawing up of a list of the general aims and purposes of economic development and of the means of their achievement. The second aspect was the scientific and technical forecasting of the available resources and their value to society. The third phase involved working out projects and programmes. These three phases were, however, only preparatory stages to the drawing up of the plan itself.[2]

A North American economist with some experience in Chile agreed that mathematical planning techniques were useful for developing countries like Chile. But other participants thought that reliance on such highly mathematical techniques and subtle instruments as used in the Soviet Union might do considerable harm at too early a stage in the planning process in Chile. To be fully effective these methods depended on a mass of reliable information and on a statistical computation apparatus which probably were not yet developed in Chile, and this might lead to decisions being taken to do no planning at all until all the information was available and all

---

[2] One such model involved the construction of a mathematical 'tree of aims', which arranged aims in a mathematical graph displaying their logical links. Its construction enabled the logical nexus between all the aims to be clarified. Similarly, a mathematical 'tree of resources' had to be constructed. The two 'trees' had to be made to interlock by means of an iterative process, which indicated the best possible way of adapting means to resources without simply cutting out some aims, and of finding the best aims to be adapted and the best resources to be increased.

The most important result was the derivation from the structure of the plan itself of certain parameters such as proper shadow prices for resources and products and shadow rates of discount etc. It was claimed this process also helped in plan implementation and decentralization of decision making, because, if prices etc. were derivates of the central plan and the Government fixed prices at these levels, firms which maximized profits in terms of these prices would be automatically working towards fulfilment of the central plan.

conditions were perfect. Therefore, some felt that at the early stage of development planning, as was the case in Chile, it was preferable to employ a less sophisticated and more practical method and rely on hunches in deciding what was important.

Moreover, it was the impression of one participant that in the Soviet Union, as in Eastern Europe, the complicated planning methods and apparatus which had just been described had grown up parallel to much simpler forms of planning and were only made operational after a long process of perfection, by which time they were obviously preferable to informed guesses or less complex methods. It was also pointed out that even sophisticated linear and non-linear programming depended a lot on the objective function which was initially devised. Very often it had been found that the results came out widely different according to small changes in the objective function. Also, sometimes the result stemming from a particular objective function gave unacceptable or even unthought of indicators, and made the planning process very complicated.

Chilean planners pointed out that the Soviet type planning process, which had been outlined, was a socialist one assuming public control of the means of production. It was therefore not possible to apply it in Chile, because Chile was only trying to plan the transitional stage to socialism. The Chilean Government's present problem was principally one of trying to make the assumptions involved in the structural transformations coherent with the changes in production and other basic macro-economic variables. The planners claimed that the mathematical model they employed, although not sophisticated, was proving useful in this task, and valuable work had been done in quantifying the effects of new economic policy instruments. Such techniques as the mathematical tree were seen as a future ideal. For the moment, however, Chile was not aiming at the sort of harmonic development which could be achieved in a socialist country, or even balanced development in the traditional sense. The intention was to proceed by jumps, making progress in one or two sectors at a time, and creating imbalances which would stimulate other sectors of the economy. For the moment, therefore, planning in Chile was to be seen as an attempt to quantify the main variables and carry out detailed planning in the sectors considered strategic.

ODEPLAN, it was explained, was currently using an input-output framework for achieving compatibility between targets and which mainly gave very broad indications of sectoral balances. In view of the fact that the available statistical information was very out of date, it had had to be brought up to date by econometric methods. Although imperfect, it was claimed that this system permitted a certain degree of intersectoral compatibility, and the intention in the future was to try to develop material balances for a limited number of goods. In the opinion of the planners, the main limitation, in this respect, was not Chile's computational or mathematical capacity but the restricted size of the public sector which limited the supply of information.

An equally important, if not more important, preoccupation for most participants was the problem of plan implementation. Even in a socialist system, coordination between action and planning at enterprise level and other levels of the economy and the central plan itself was recognized as being difficult to achieve. It was widely agreed that success in planning in Chile, especially in the present transitional phase, would very much depend on the mechanisms available for ensuring compliance with the plan objectives and making the plan operational right down to the level of those who had to put it into practice.

Physical controls ostensibly took place at several levels. Traditionally, the Budget Office and Comptroller General's Office operated tight fiscal and financial control through a fairly up-to-date accounting system which provided financial information concerning the state of progress of the investment programme. And through the Central Bank up-to-date information was available on the monetary and credit aspects of the overall programme. At the level of project control, the situation was not so uniform. Some institutions like Corfo had very detailed project control systems, and entities like Endesa (National Electricity Generating Company) used operational programming and critical path techniques of analysis, whereas in areas such as house construction and agricultural production control mechanisms were still not developed.

As far as the control of overall economic policy and the functioning of the macro-economic model was concerned, ODEPLAN kept a check on progress and results through a system of up-to-date quarterly reports on the trends in the main variables, such that the Planning Office was aware if any programmes were lagging behind. In this respect, the Chileans considered that Chile had a well developed and accurate economic reporting system.

Several participants said they had the impression that not only were there no penalties for not complying with the plan but that few mechanisms existed to encourage compliance, and the fact that the incentive structure had not been overhauled constituted a major problem. Detailed examples were provided of how, in agriculture, the existing material incentives induced people to use land extensively, which conflicted with the plan objectives. Most of the policy instruments that could be used in this sector to make planning effective, such as price policy, tax policy, marketing, credit, and technical assistance, needed revising or restructuring. Participants recognized that this was a slow process and in price and tax policy there were substantial political obstacles to changing them. Nevertheless, it was felt that the Government should perhaps pay more attention to these aspects, since, without improvements such as these, no amount of global planning would bring about the required changes.

A further important observation, based on the practical experience of one observer, was that, in the absence of clear and detailed political directives on many points of the plan, the different parties and ideological tendencies naturally gave their own interpretation to the planning messages. As a result, they were distorted as they filtered down to the different levels, creating considerable confusion at the operative level. It was alleged that there was a tendency for the Government to underestimate this problem of political differences or to shut its eyes to it. An additional problem was constituted by the fact that the lower level institutional mechansims, which were necessary for adequate planning, were insufficiently developed. For example, again in the case of agriculture, so far very few of the District Peasant Councils, which were supposed to participate in planning at grass-roots level, existed and those Councils which had established themselves were not working effectively — partly, again, because of lack of political definition at higher levels. It was also suggested that there was still need for considerable improvement in both the structure and the organization of the upper levels of the administrative set-up if the formulation and the implementation of plans was to be successful.

Two particular aspects drew the attention of the meeting, concerning the concrete details of the 1971-76 Plan. The first related to the implications for the foreign sector of the plan strategy and, as mentioned before, the impression was that the balance of payments problem had been underestimated; indeed it almost seemed as if the foreign exchange question was not part of the overall problem of resource allocation.[1] According to one participant's interpretation, the plan seemed to suggest that, with income redistribution and a new structure of consumption, the external sector would no longer

---

1   See Section I Part 4 for further discussion on trade and balance of payments problems.

be so important in the future. In other words, by changing the objectives the trade bottleneck problem would disappear. But it seemed that even with the new strategy, Chile's growth possibilities were equally likely to be limited by foreign exchange shortages as in the past. The import content of what was required to satisfy the demands of the lower income groups was considered by this participant to be far from negligible, and, in his view, not enough attention was being paid to the earning and saving of foreign exchange. The present exchange rates overvalued the escudo to the detriment of exports. In all Latin American economies, whatever the economic system, the usual indicator of successful policy had been the ability to cope with the balance of payments. Furthermore, Eastern European experience in this matter was worth noting. Participants with experience in these countries described how, when some of the small Eastern European socialist economies shifted their development strategy away from emphasis on high investment in heavy industry towards a somewhat more consumption oriented pattern, the trade dependence of these economies did not diminish, but rather increased. Yugoslavia was cited as an example of success because, within a short period of time, it had learned to give a high priority to the balance of payments problem.

In the discussion on the plan implications for the foreign sector, the planners explained that the model implicit in the 1971-76 Plan was not a closed model. Although the export sector would no longer constitute the motive force of the economy, as in the previous government's model, a substantial increase in exports of $ 1.2 million to 1.8 million was to be achieved over the 6 year period. But it was to be noted that the resulting increase in import capacity would be used to fulfil the increased popular consumption and to build up domestic productive capacity. Furthermore, it was emphasized that the proposed changes in the structure of production would, in the Government's estimation, result in a change in the old import structure, making room for an increase in imports of popular consumption goods. The planners' assumption was that these goods, towards which consumption was to be reoriented, were simpler and required fewer highly processed imported inputs, and that the technology involved was also simpler and less capital intensive, so that the import of capital goods could also be reduced for a period.

From the economic planners' and policy makers' point of view, Chile was considered to be in a state of war and, if all efforts were devoted to such orthodox traditional policies as balancing the budget and achieving a positive balance of payments situation, this would lead to a failure in the transition to socialism, because the latter required an expanding economy.

Doubt was also expressed about the compatibility of the plan's employment and investment targets. The statistics showed that 56% of the labour force between the ages of 15 and 64 was currently employed, with an investment rate of 16.6%, and the plan intended to raise the rate of investment by 1.6% to 18.2% while the 56% was supposed to increase to 64%. Nevertheless, the planners claimed that these figures were not so extraordinary or unreal if account was taken of the fact that the investment coefficient was based on a national product which would be 50% higher than the present one, so that the absolute volume of investments over the six year period would be very high — something of the order of $ 10,000 million. Investment per person, though high, would not be quite as high as the past average, but this was not deemed necessary because the planned changes in the structure of consumption and production meant that a lower rate was feasible. Productivity was expected to increase on average by about 2.3% p.a. during the six year period, which was twice the rate achieved in the past decade. Higher rates were expected in some sectors like agriculture, where mechanization and improved techniques provided substantial possibilities for raising productivity. Likewise in services, where there was high under-employment.

Part 3

Agrarian Policy

Chapter 1

THE AGRARIAN POLICY OF THE POPULAR GOVERNMENT

Jacques Chonchol*

The problems and difficulties faced by the Popular Government in the agrarian reform process can be classed in three main groups:- (i) accelerating the expropriation of large estates, in order to respond to the strong pressure from the peasants[1] and to pre-empt the spread of uncertainty, (ii) the organisation of what has been reformed and its relationships with the remainder of the agricultural sector, (iii) increasing production, which is of direct importance not only for agriculture but also for the overall development of the national economy.

With respect to expropriations, the government decided, for two reasons, to use the Agrarian Reform Law, which was approved during the Frei administration even though, in many aspects, it does not coincide with the Popular Government's agrarian policy. We are using this law because, as a Government, we are obliged to act within the legal framework, and secondly, because any changes in such a complex and controversial law as the Agrarian Reform Law would certainly have required many months of discussion, which would paralyse the agrarian reform process resulting in great frustration among the peasantry who are pressing for the acceleration of the process. Also it was felt that, given the political willingness to use the existing law much more thoroughly, it would be possible to accelerate the agrarian reform process.

This law permits the expropriation of all estates which have an area greater than 80 basic hectares of irrigated land. This is a symbolic measure used to value land of different qualities in common units, because Chile has a wide variety of different land qualities within each province. The Agrarian Reform Law established such equivalents for each region and, for example, the standard of 80 hectares of good quality irrigated land close to Santiago is equal to 500 hectares of dry arable land in the South, and in some parts 700

---

* Minister of Agriculture.

[1] The words peasant and peasantry should be taken to include small proprietors, agricultural wage labourers, share croppers, migrant and temporary rural labourers, smallholders who rent their land and other types of agricultural workers (Ed).

to 800 hectares. In the case of hill pastures it may be several thousand hectares. All properties exceeding the 80 hectares equivalent can be expropriated and this can apply to the sum total of properties owned by an individual and his spouse, so that the landowner's entire hectarage will be assessed even though he registers these estates as separate properties. This does not apply to the various properties owned by the same family and, naturally, this has created complications because, faced with the impending agrarian reform process, many large estates were redistributed between different members of a family and, in spite of continuing to function as large estates, from the legal point of view they are separate properties belonging to different persons.

There is also a very important clause which permits the expropriation of all farms and estates, including small and medium sized properties, below the 80 hectare equivalent, which according to previously completed studies are considered to be badly run, badly worked or abandoned. This clause can only be applied to individual farms, not to whole areas, which undoubtedly causes serious difficulties from the point of view of planning the whole process. In accordance with this criterion, in the past year the government decided to expropriate 1,000 of the farms where peasant pressure was strongest especially since they were also symbols of gross exploitation in the area. However, the pressure was so great that not 1,000 but around 1,400 had to be expropriated.

This year the government will terminate the *latifundia*[1] in Chile, expropriating all the remaining 2,000 properties over the basic 80 hectare equivalent, of which over 600 have been expropriated to date this year.

This process entails difficulties. First the acceleration of the process generates new expectations in the peasantry that their problems will be resolved rapidly. This is typical in a traditional system where the peasantry waits indefinitely without hope, but when there is an acceleration in the process of change, pressures and expectations are awakened everywhere.

The second problem, which is quite difficult to handle, is that the physical size of the properties does not coincide with the social characteristics and problems and very frequently the social struggles are absolutely independent of the size and other characteristics of the estate. Exploitation of the peasantry is normal in the Chilean countryside but frequently it is greater in the medium and small scale

[1] *latifundia* – agricultural system based on large estates.

farms than in the large estates. Although the medium and small scale farms function in the same way as the large estates, the economic conditions are more difficult and the enterprise is therefore frequently financed by exploiting the peasantry to a greater extent. Consequently, there is a contradiction between the need to accelerate the reform process by expropriating the large estates, which enables a large number of peasants to be absorbed, and the need to respond to peasant pressures to expropriate small properties where, at times, the social struggles have been more acute.

This gives rise to another conflict. As this process does not take place in a vacuum but within the context of a process of political struggle, each time the government expropriates one of the medium or small properties, to put an end to social conflict, the opposition uses the event in a very intelligent way through propaganda and the press to induce people to believe that, as a matter of policy, the agrarian reform is tackling not only the large owners but the smaller farmers as well. This is part of an attempt to establish an alliance between small and medium scale farmers, who fear that the agrarian reform process will also affect them, in common cause with the large landowning groups. Also many of the large estates, when threatened by the prospects of an agrarian reform, were divided between different members of the same family to escape expropriation and today they appear as artificial medium and small sized properties. However, to the peasants they still constitute the same large estates on which they lived before they were divided up and with which they continue to be confronted.

Another problem relates to the land area covered by the reform sector. In 1971, 30% of agricultural land was within the reformed sector, and this year, with the land that is now expropriated, the figure is 50%. According to the present agrarian reform law, these expropriated lands were to be organised in a transitory system called an *asentamiento* for a period of three to five years. The *asentamiento* is a joint production enterprise between the state which owns the expropriated lands, and the peasants who live there. The state provides the land, credit and technical aid, and the peasants their labour power. The same physical area as the expropriated estate is maintained and an attempt is made to run it collectively in the most efficient way possible. This principle, establishing a provisional system previous to the final decision on how the land is to be distributed, is correct because, although it may be easy to change the distribution of land, it is much more difficult to change the social relations, the attitudes and above all the mentality of the peasantry.

The simple fact of changing the distribution of the land will not automatically change social relations in the countryside. Therefore, this transitory period was established as a period of preparation for the peasantry, in which, in close contact with the state, the peasants assume a much more dynamic role in the planning and management of the production process in the new agricultural enterprises.

However,the experience of the *asentamientos* has revealed many defects, though there is no doubt that the *asentamiento* peasants were socially and economically much better off than they had been on the former *latifundia*. Normally these *asentamientos* were set up on each expropriated property. Sometimes they covered an area smaller than the old estate because the Agrarian Reform Law allowed a farmer, who ran his land well, to retain a reserve of property for himself. In general the peasants dispute this, which gives rise to important social conflicts. Also,the size of the units constituted by the *asentamientos* was too small to plan a more specialised and integrated agriculture.

A much more serious problem is that, in general, the *asentamiento* system tends to perpetuate the image of the traditional farm in the peasant's mind. An agrarian reform process is not just a question of redistributing the land, but should involve an entirely new conception of the economic and social organisation of agricultural enterprises. But, if the reformed sector enterprises are organised on the same physical dimensions as the former farms, it is very difficult for the peasant to adopt different and wider economic and social perspectives, which would facilitate other types of organisation.

Furthermore, on the traditional estates, apart from the people who lived on the farm, there were many other non-resident workers. Some were small farmers who worked partly for themselves and partly for the farm. Others belonged to the floating rural population known in Chile as *afuerinos,* and who, having no fixed abode, move from farm to farm. When the *asentamientos* were established, those who did not live on the estate but occasionally worked there, or those who worked permanently on the estate but lived elsewhere, were frequently excluded. This tended to generate conflicts, because for many peasants the progress of the agrarian reform entailed loss instead of benefit, since it provided them with less work and security than in the former *latifundium* system. As a result some peasant groups are now opposed to the agrarian reform.

Moreover, as the mentality of the peasants has not changed, many of the peasants in the reformed sector, who know that after a period of five years they can become land owners, have become very egoistic. They do not wish to incorporate into the asentamiento more people than those originally working on the farm, because they argue that when the time comes for the distribution of the land they will each get less. So, when extra labour is taken on, it is only as wage-earners and not as full asentados.[2] This results in curious family conflicts with the sons of the asentados who, when they reach working age, are employed by peasants of the reformed sector as wage-earners. In many places this new form of conflict between young peasants and asentados, has produced typical worker-employer conflicts in which lengthy petitions have been lodged within the asentamiento.

The paternalism of the state bureaucracy is also creating problems. There is a tendency for state functionaries, who are responsible for supervising and aiding the asentamientos, to do every-thing themselves, on seeing the initial incapacity of the peasantry which is just emerging from a state of dependence on the patron.[3] Thus, the production plans of the new reformed units were not made by the peasants but by the technical personnel. In fact, frequently they were drawn up without any peasant participation whatsoever. and even without discussion.

The finance of the reformed units came from the state, and in particular from CORA, the Agrarian Reform Corporation, but in a rather paternalistic way in as much as the peasants did not think they had to repay the money they received. This helped to foster the dependent mentality, and it also created a grave financial problem, which is becoming accentuated as the agrarian reform process accelerates.

Finally, there exists a phenomenen which is not only charac-teristic of the peasants, but of many farmers, and this is the resistance to accounting systems, which would keep track of their costs. Thus, at the end of a period they do not really know the economic results of running the farm. In many of these asent-amientos, where physical output was greater than in the former estate, the financial costs rose even more and there was little concern about their profitability or productivity, since they were basically bolstered up by the state, which supposedly provided finance gratuitously.

---

[2] *asentados* — members of the asentamiento.

[3] *patron*—landlord or boss but the term also connotes a paternalistic master-servant relationship which existed on the estates.

Due to all these factors, a new organisational set-up of the reformed sector was sought. The result is the Agrarian Reform Centre. These centres are organised by combining various neighbouring farms to form larger units, thereby facilitating a certain degree of specialisation. Financing these units is done directly through a bank account which can be drawn on, in accordance with the production plan prepared by the members of each Agrarian Reform Centre. The responsibility for running these centres is much more under peasant control than in the *asentamiento*. Their control operates through a general assembly of peasants, which elects the directive bodies and in which women are also given a greater degree of participation. This new form of transitory organisation, which is just beginning to be applied, has met resistance. At times, it is the peasants themselves who dislike the system which requires them to open up and expand and absorb more people into their enterprise. Political resistance exists too, following attempts to deform the image of these centres in the eyes of the peasants, by presenting them as a kind of state property in which they are never going to be given ownership of the land.

It is essential to continue searching for new forms of organisation in the reformed sector, in order to absorb a greater number of workers and at the same time facilitate more efficient work, because only 7% of the agricultural population works on the 30% of total area in Chile which has been expropriated. When the 50% figure for expropriation is achieved in the near future, if the *asentamiento* system continues, it would benefit only 15% of the rural working population and there would be large groups of peasants for whom agrarian reform would provide neither new work possibilities, nor new social opportunities. This would create an even more serious conflict, for the agrarian reform would have created a small new privileged group alongside a peasant mass unincorporated into the process and not really benefiting from it as a group.

Another important aspect is the problem of agricultural production. Even if Chilean agriculture represents only 8% of national income, it has very great strategic importance at present, from the point of view of foreign trade. Up to the 1930's Chile exported around U.S. $30,000,000 of agricultural products and imported only U.S. $15,000,000 worth. However, because of the traditionally slow rate of growth of agriculture over these last thirty years, every government had gradually to increase food imports, such that food imports have risen from the U.S. $15,000,000 of the 1920's to U.S. $200,000,000. On the other hand, exports have remained practically stagnant; the country continues to export the same U.S. $30,000,000 worth which it exported thirty years ago. The agricultural situation therefore weighs heavily on the balance of payments. Added to this, the current major income redistribution in favour of the poorest sections of the population has resulted in extraordinarily large pressure on the demand for foodstuffs, which in turn has strong repercussions on the balance of payments.

This situation makes it essential for us to implement the process of land redistribution and the reorganisation of the reformed sector without permitting a fall in agricultural production and, in the agricultural year 1971-1972, production rose in spite of the rural social conflicts, the political campaigns and the speeding up of the agrarian reform.

A very substantial increase in investment in agriculture is involved. One of the most serious problems is finance, because traditionally, in Chilean agriculture the ratio between capital represented by land and the investments on the land was very bad. In order to produce more and increase specialisation and diversification, in accordance with the quality of land, we need to make heavy investments which cannot be generated within the agricultural sector itself, since it represents scarcely 8% of the national income. In this respect, Chile presents a situation which contrasts curiously with the experience of the socialist countries. Whereas, to a certain extent, they financed their development in industry and other sectors with surpluses extracted from the agricultural sector, Chilean agriculture will have to be developed in the first stage with resources drawn from other sectors of the economy.

There is also the problem of changing the structure of production. In the traditional Chilean system, owing to very erratic cost situations, there was normally a tendency towards considerable diversification in order to assure some income, losing on some products and making up the loss on others. As a consequence, there has been a tendency to use good productive land for less profitable products. Because of the peculiar characteristics of the country, of a total land area of 75,000,000 hectares the arable area is scarcely 5,000,000 hectares, that is to say, less than 10%, and an irrigated area of 1,300,000 hectares. If we desire an agricultural sector with a high level of employment and a high rate of return, specialisation basically oriented to the export market must increase. We cannot consider establishing balance-of-payments equilibrium mainly on the basis of import substitution for agricultural products, as was traditionally the idea in Chile and many other Latin American countries. Instead of substituting imports of maize and cereals of other types, it is much more advantageous to Chile to produce more wine, fruit and vegetable products which have a high value, since these supply not only the internal market, but also all the great consumer markets in the Northern Hemisphere, with the advantage that their winter coincides with the Chilean summer. This also implies an important industrialisation effort oriented towards export, a much higher level of investment, new forms of organisation. It will also mean converting the country into an agricultural exporter; up till now agrarian policy has been seen as a function of the necessities of the internal market and not of an export policy. This also makes enormous demands on the ability of the peasantry to adapt. Though, on the whole, the reformed sector produces more, it produces more of the same traditional products because the production structure has not changed and the land is not used in the most profitable way.

Finally, it is worth indicating some of the problems involved in peasant participation. The Government has ensured that the peasantry participates to the greatest possible extent and, in order to bring this about, it has created the Peasant Councils. But various difficulties are being experienced. One is that, in order for the peasants to participate properly in these Peasant Councils, the latter need finance and also a much greater degree of recognition by the whole state apparatus, which has very paternalistic tendencies. The state functionary has normally been a person who, whatever his political leanings, feels superior to the peasant for whom he has to work. This happens, in part, because of the relationship the functionaries themselves have to the traditional oligarchy but also partly because they constitute a bureaucratic caste which feels itself to be an important part of society, definitely superior to the workers. There is therefore a permanent conflict between giving the peasants participation within the state apparatus and the resistance which they meet in practice within this state bureaucracy.

Chapter 2

THE STRUCTURE AND PROBLEMS OF
THE CHILEAN AGRARIAN SECTOR

By Solon Barraclough *

The main emphasis of this exposition will be to review some of the recent studies and information on the agrarian structure and to explain what has gone on during the last decade.

Agrarian Conflict

The first point to be mentioned is that there could be no greater error than to think that the agrarian problem is simply an economic problem. It is necessary to analyse why the agrarian problem is acute in Latin America. There are a great many conflicts of interest among rural groups and classes and this is what produces a political problem.

Agrarian conflict in Chile was not something that began in the 1960's. There were many conflicts going on throughout the twentieth century and especially after 1920. Most of these were sharply suppressed and have been almost forgotten (except for the Ranquil massacre). There has been constant pressure on the traditional agrarian structure during the last thirty or forty years. The population has increased, marketing channels have changed and rural employment problems have intensified with the invasion into rural areas of cheap urban manufactured products that displaced locally made goods. These disequilibrating factors have become much more serious during the last few years.

There has been a tendency to view the agrarian problem not only as a conflict between *campesinos*[1] and large landowners but also as a conflict between rural and urban interests. The *latifundistas*,[2] however, are not at all an homogeneous group. They can be divided into several groups, each of whom has been making

---

* International Director (FAO) of the Institute for Training and Research in Agrarian Reform (ICIRA) Santiago.
[1] *campesinos* — peasants.
[2] *latifundistas* — large landowners.

separate alliances with different urban groups. Sergio Gomez has identified a highly commercial capitalist *latifundista* group that in every sense is modern.[3] These large landowners have not used the traditional forced labour obligations in order to cut down wage costs but, on the contrary, have sought to create a free labour market. This group has tended to make alliances with the most dynamic industrial and commercial urban groups. Secondly, there is a more traditional large landowning group which is also capitalist in the sense that it is trying to maximize its profits. It does not have as good access to markets, technology and credits as the first group of large commercial farmers, however. It uses a system of labour obligation in return for the use of a small parcel of land in order to assure a supply of cheap labour. This group has tended to make alliances in the urban sectors with the more traditional urban elite groups. And, finally, there are the most traditional large landowner groups, the stereotype of the *latifundista* class, who are not so interested in maximizing profits as in the prestige and in the rental income derived from their lands.

The interlocking of rural land ownership and of the urban interests among all these groups is much greater than many people suspected. The owners of agricultural lands and of other wealth in Chile are very much the same people. To speak of a sharp division of interests between the *latifundistas* and urban property owners is really distorting the picture very considerably. This is especially true when speaking of the highly commercial large farmers.

Among the other agrarian conflicts are the many conflicts among different *campesino* groups. To think of the *campesinos* as a single interest group or class is misleading. Under the traditional *latifundia* system, most *campesinos* had a common interest in combating the *latifundio*. But when this system began to break up, complex social differentiation became evident among the *campesinos*. Part of the problem which the last government had and the present government is facing in the agrarian field derives from the fact that the *campesinado* [4] is anything but an homogeneous group with homogeneous interests. The same is true of the large landowners as mentioned earlier. Progressive capitalist agricultural entrepreneurs have very different interests from traditional rentiers.

There are also conflicts between the *campesinos* and the state bureaucracy. Of course, under the old system, the state bureaucracy was very much at the service of the *latinfundistas*. As the old system

---

[3] Sergio Gomez "Los Empresarios Agricolas" ICIRA Santiago 1970.
[4] *campesinado* — peasant classes, peasantry.

disintegrated, the bureaucracy has not changed with the same rapidity. A conflict of interest soon became apparent between the bureaucracy and various groups of *campesinos*. This conflict is made more complex by shifting alliances among groups within the bureaucracy and different groups of *campesinos*. This is another facet of the agrarian problem which should always be kept in mind.

Agrarian Structure

In 1930, about 37% of Chile's work force was in agriculture. By 1970 this proportion had dropped to about 22%, but in absolute terms the number of agricultural workers had increased from about 560,000 to about 760,000 and there is little prospect that the absolute number of farm workers will decrease during the next ten years. The relationship of agriculture to the general economy shows a similar tendency. Only about 8% of the gross national product is accounted for by agriculture and this is a parameter which has to be taken account of in all calculations about the effects of the agrarian reform and about what is possible.

Some recent studies on the agrarian structure bring up to date the data of the 1966 ICAD report.[5] Not only do these new studies explore some aspects of rural class structure more fully than did earlier ones but they also indicate some of the changes that have been taking place during the last twelve years in land tenure and the labour force.

Subdivision of the large estates has been taking place gradually during most of the last hundred years and this process has accelerated very much during the last decade. An Agrarian Reform Law had been passed during the Alessandri administration but it was never really implemented until later. During the Frei administration the government expropriated 1,408 *latifundios* consisting of some 290,000 hectares of irrigated land and over 3,000,000 hectares of dry land. At the same time there was an increase in the number of private subdivisions in spite of the fact that the new agrarian reform attempted to impede this.

To give an illustration of how important private subdivision was in this period, in 1965 ICIRA (Institute for Training and Research in Agrarian Reform) made a "base-line" study of a sample of 98, or about ten per cent, of the largest *latifundia* in the central valley. At that time there were about a thousand estates in the central valley

5 Interamerican Committee for Agricultural Development, Chile: Tenencia de la Tierra y Desarrollo Socio-Economico del Sector Agrícola. Talleres Graficos Hispano Suiza Ltda. Santiago 1966.

near Santiago, which had a basic hectarage equivalent of over 150 hectares of first class irrigated land. This year, a new study of this same sample is being carried out.[6] Thirty seven estates in the sample had been expropriated during the last administration. Most of the remainder had been subdivided during this period. Some of these are now being expropriated because the subdivisions were still over 80 basic hectares or the owners had abandoned their lands, so they can be taken over under the agrarian reform legislation. But only about 40% of the sample had been expropriated during the previous period.

Now, during the first year of the present government, expropriation has accelerated very markedly with the same agrarian reform legislation. The change in velocity of expropriation has been so great that one can speak of a qualitative change. During the period from November 1970 until March 1972 there have been 2,300 expropriations comprising about 210,000 hectares of irrigated land and nearly 3,000,000 of dry land.

What has happened to production and productivity? During the period from the Second World War until 1962 production was increasing at only about 1.8% a year. During the first 4 years of the Frei administration production jumped quite markedly to about 4% per year; then, with the severe drought of 1968, there was a drop in output giving an average growth rate during the six year period of about 2.8% per year. Last year, according to the Agriculture Planning Office's estimates, agricultural production went up by over 6% but livestock output did not increase, so the overall average was about 4.6%.

Land use changes have not yet been very great, however. In fact, land use patterns today are not too different from those when the ICAD studies were made before the agrarian reform began. Of course, there are a great many exceptions both among agrarian reform units and private holdings. A study of several private subdivisions in the Santiago area two years ago indicated that there has been an intensification of land use and this, in part, accounts for the fairly good production response which was obtained during the Frei administration. There was a tendency to capitalize and to intensify land use in areas with good markets. But on the whole the land use pattern in Chile did not change very much during these years.

Roberto Echeverria made a study in Chile on the impact on income distribution in agriculture of changes in price relationships

---

[6] The study is being made by ICIRA and the Land Tenure Centre group from the University of Wisconsin.

between 1959 and 1968.* In order to try to find out about how price changes affected the major groups in agriculture the rural sector was divided into four subsectors: 1) The *latifundista* or large farm sector, 2) the small farm producers, 3) the farm labourers who have no access to land, and 4) the sharecroppers and tenant labourers who often have usufruct rights to a small plot for which they have to pay with labour obligations and therefore have an interest both as wage labourers and also as small producers. Three non-farm groups were also included in the analysis: 1) the high income urban population, 2) low income non-farm people and 3) the foreign trade sector. The methodology adopted made it possible to gain more sophisticated insights into the impact of price changes on intersectoral income flows than can be gained by simply treating agriculture as a single sector. The most interesting discovery was that during the periods when popular wisdom indicated that changes in price relationships between industrial and agricultural products should have been highly favourable to one or the other, the differential impact on these four agricultural groups was very significant. Some farm groups would benefit while others would be prejudiced by the same price changes.

During the Alessandri period, in spite of an ideology of modernization, farm producers did not modernize very rapidly. At the same time, however, they did improve their relative income position significantly while the tenant labourers and landless workers did not improve their relative position very much at all. During the Frei period, while the prices of agricultural products in relation to those of industrial products improved, the large farm producers' relative income position deteriorated slightly on the average, largely because of higher wages. At the same time the tenants and the permanent labourers on the *latifundia* improved their income position significantly. But there was a large group of farm labourers who were becoming increasingly marginalized because of greater unemployment.

A rough breakdown of what the agrarian structure is today in terms of social classes gives the following results. About 1% of the farm workforce are *latifundistas,* (about 6,000 owners). About 4% of the rural workforce are medium size producers with 20 to 80 basic hectares each. Some 9%, or 72,000 of the workforce, are small producers roughly corresponding, under the present technology, to family sized farms who neither sell much of their labour to others

---

* Roberto Echeverría, El Efecto de las Politicas de Precios Agrícolas en las Transferencias Intersectorales de Ingreso. Memoria de la Universidad de Chile, Instituto de Economia y Planificación, Santiago 1968.

nor employ many permanent outside labourers. About 35% are *mini-fundistas* who have less than 5 basic hectares and, in general, have to sell some of their labour in order even to maintain themselves. About 7% of the agricultural workforce (some 56,000 workers) is now in the reformed area. This 7% of the workforce has nearly 30% of the country's farm land — in other words the man/land relationship on the agrarian reform units is very similar to the previous pattern on the expropriated large estates. It is estimated that the permanent workers, mostly on commercial farms, constitute about 18% while about 22%, or 169,000 others, ary temporary workers. These latter constitute a sub-proletariat with every unstable conditions of work and they are often unemployed most of the year. From an economic and social standpoint they are the group which is worst off, except for a small proportion of *minifundistas* who are also very poor. About 2% of the workforce are *empleados*.[7]

Unemployment continues to be an increasingly serious problem in rural areas. When the ICAD study was made it was estimated that about 30% of the agricultural workforce was redundant. Of course, seasonal underemployment is very great but, even taking this into account, unemployment was estimated to be 30%, most of which was accounted for by disguised unemployment and under-employment. Interestingly enough, during the last six years, although agricultural production has been increasing rapidly, unemployment and underemployment in the rural areas have not decreased and probably have increased. There has been more use of labour saving technologies and a considerable increase in the productivity of part of the farm labour force. Consequently, there is now more open unemployment among the farm labourers excluded from these gains.

With respect to other aspects of the agrarian structure, credit was very much concentrated to the benefit of the large landowners when the agrarian reform movement began twelve years ago. The ICAD study estimated that over 90% of the credit was going to the *latifundistas*. This proportion was reduced somewhat during the Frei administration. Now with the nationalization of the banks and the new credit policies one should expect that the distribution of credit will change very rapidly in favour of the *campesinos*.

Marketing was also pretty much controlled by the large landowners and by middlemen to the disadvantage of the *campesinos*. A major objective of the present Government is to change the marketing structures rapidly and drastically. As long as traditional marketing institutions remain, the effect of changes in land tenure is

---

7 *empleados* - employees, white collar workers, administrative personnel.

going to be minimal, since the relationships of the *campesinos* in the reformed areas to the rest of the economy are, to a large extent, a function of the marketing system.

The primary goals of the Popular Unity Government's agricultural policy are: 1) to increase production and productivity, 2) to improve income distribution – this implies eliminating both the *latifundia* and rural unemployment and 3) to achieve widespread *campesino* participation in political and economic decision making. The review of rural class structure just described shows something of the dimensions of the Government's problem. One of the most pressing problems facing the Popular Unity Government is to build a new agrarian structure that will incorporate the entire *campesino* population into the Government's programme and the benefits of reform, instead of only those residing on the expropriated estates. Very soon over 40% of the most productive agricultural land will have been expropriated. If present tendencies continue, however, this land will provide employment for only 12 to 15% of the rural workforce. Obviously it is going to be necessary to set up some sort of system incorporating many more of the *minifundistas*, farm labourers and other *campesino* groups, or political pressures by the *campesinos* will continue to increase.

Another very pressing problem is how to make the Government agricultural bureaucracy more functional. There are over two dozen public agencies working in the agrarian sector with overlapping functions and, in many cases, with different policy guidelines. Without administrative reorganization it will be very difficult to consolidate agrarian reform and increase production, once the expropriations are completed.

Another problem is that of prices and marketing. It is difficult to see how agrarian reform can be effective unless the distribution system is completely restructured and brought under state and *campesino* control. Also prices must be used as a planning instrument to provide incentives for the *campesinos* and other farmers to produce and invest in accordance with rational goals. Price policy can play an important role in guiding resource allocation in a socialist economy as well as in a capitalist one.

Another problem the Government has to face is how to obtain effective *campesino* participation. This will, of course, depend in part on how the agrarian reform units and the agricultural planning system are organized. The Government is proposing cooperative farms and communal *campesino* councils.[8] It also depends on

[8] Consejos Campesinos Comunales

adequate training and technical assistance. Paternalism has been very strong in the bureaucracy in Chile over a long period of time and it has not by any means been eliminated by recent changes.

The implementation of a realistic technological policy is still another problem. It is hard to see how farm wages can be as high as industrial wages in the short-run, unless massive subsidies are paid or rural unemployment is allowed to increase. A great deal could be done to reduce rural unemployment, however, by adopting a technological policy that encourages greater use of labour. Also there could be more decentralizing of small industries and especially of new agro-industries.

Another problem that was very serious during the Frei administration and continues to be so today is the financing of the agrarian reform. There are a great many studies on the financial implications of present policies and the present law imposes grave limitations. It will have to be re-examined and changed in order to permit adequate financing of massive agrarian reform. During the six years of the Frei administration about half of the cash outlay for the reform was for short-term credits but, because of inflation and a series of other factors, about 40% of the short term credits were never recovered. Obviously, now that the reform is much bigger and more complex, such losses would soon become almost prohibitively expensive.

In conclusion, the Government has made considerable progress with agrarian reform in the year and a half since it took office. There are, however, many problems to be solved. A planning system with real *campesino* participation, an efficient and progressive agricultural bureaucracy and a structure of prices, taxes, markets, credit and land tenure that provide incentives to produce and invest in accordance with the plan are urgently required.

Chapter 3

DISCUSSION ON THE AGRARIAN REFORM AND AGRARIAN POLICY

The Scope of the Agrarian Reform, New Agrarian Structures and Forms of Ownership.

Chile has gone further in land reform than most 'developing' countries, yet questions were raised about how far she really had gone and what were the future economic and political implications of this. For many participants the key figures were those which lay behind the number of expropriations. By the end of 1972, when all the large farms would have been expropriated, between only 14 and 16% of the rural population would have 50% of the land. What about the remainder, the great majority of the rural population? Solon Barraclough and Jacques Chonchol had described rural underemployment and the low levels of the population occupying *minifundia* and small agricultural holdings. A socialist agricultural policy could not abandon this 85%. Was it possible to absorb them in the towns, or was there some solution for them within agriculture?

In clarification, it was pointed out that the figure of 14-16% was based on the pessimistic assumption that, as in the *asentamiento* system, only those who lived permanently on the farm and were heads of families would be covered by the reform. It was the Government's intention that the new system of agricultural organization — the Agrarian Reform Centres[1] would in fact absorb other categories of rural labour.

The Government was also said to be optimistic about the possibilities of absorbing substantial numbers of the so-called excess rural population into other sectors of the economy. Figures for 1971 showed that the urban economy was capable of providing a considerable number of jobs even in the regions such as Puerto Montt, in the southern province of Llanquihue, far from the main industrial centres.

Furthermore, participants were reminded that the Government's agrarian reform was not limited to expropriating and redist-

1 *Centros de Reforma Agraria.*

ributing large *latifundia,* but included a variety of other policies which would improve the situation of smallholders and subsistence level producers on *minifundia.* It was intended — *inter alia* — to encourage small proprietors and *minifundistas* to form cooperatives and this and other aspects of the agricultural strategy would raise the number of agriculture-based jobs and rural incomes.

One opinion, shared by several European participants, was that perhaps from a long term political point of view there was no need to be so discouraged about the real scope of the land reform. Since the present reform left a large element of potential political tension in the countryside, it provided a basis for a further radicalization of politics and demands for more radical changes in rural organization. It was also suggested that, in this context, the forms of ownership and organizational structures which were to be adopted from the outset in the Agrarian Reform process were vital factors because they influenced the future success of agricultural policy both from the general social and political point of view. Account had to be taken of the potentially conservative nature of certain forms of ownership and organization, such as peasant small holdings or collective ownership by groups of peasants, since, once having benefited from the agrarian reform, they would not easily cede to a later reorganization of their land or be persuaded to make changes in the form of ownership. Perhaps, therefore, the Government should start out from the very beginning with state ownership of the land, which should be worked collectively in large single units.

The experience of some socialist countries was worth considering in relation to this problem. In both Poland and Yugoslavia private farming constituted the basic property form in their agricultural sector and this had not been the result of recent ideological changes in their approaches toward property structures in agriculture. The decision taken in Yugoslavia, in 1950 and 1951, not to continue pressing farmers into collectives was said to be the only alternative to an enormous decline in agricultural production, which would have prejudiced further development of the overall economy. The reasons for retaining private farming in Poland were the same as in Yugoslavia, though the development of their agrarian sector had subsequently been somewhat different, and in both cases the pre-World War II small-holding structure in the agrarian sector explained the subsequent pattern of development. Bulgaria with many small farmers, although very similar to Serbia, the largest part of Yugoslavia, had had great success with collectivization, so much so that large quantities of high quality Bulgarian agricultural products were now to be found in many West as well as East European markets. Something more than a large farm, therefore, was obviously necessary for successful cooperative agriculture and the attitudes of peasant cultivators and farm labourers towards landed property was considered of vital importance. Even the farm-workers on *latifundia* in Chile might be attached to the idea of private as opposed to collective farming, and it would be interesting to know whether they regarded themselves more as salaried workers or farmers and similarly with the other groups of people who worked the land in Chile.

On this point, recent field work among different groups of *campesinos* in Chile, concerning attitudes towards individual plots of land as against some sort of collective unit, showed very interesting results. On the older *asentamientos,* which were established between 1964 and 1970, about 60% of those interviewed were in favour of private individual holdings, and 40% in favour of some sort of collective unit. On the agrarian reform centres, the situation had reversed and only 25% were in favour of private plots whereas 75% were in favour of some sort of collective operation. But, more interestingly, on the reserve of land retained by the owner upon expropriation in the earlier period and on the farms which had been subdivided in the earlier period, in the hope of avoiding expropriation, 80% of the workers were strongly in favour of collective units. Among the *minifundia* groups or small producers, those who had good market relationships were strongly in favour of private plots and resisted the idea of collectivization, whereas the poorest *minifundia* owners and the temporary workers tended to be receptive to the idea of collective operation of the units.

Of course, the kind of reformed agricultural system which could be effectively implemented also depended, to a large extent, on the capacity of the state to administer large-scale reform and structural changes. It might be rational to implement a partly individualist land reform, abandoning the peasantry in a kind of Chayanov [2] situation, where they were left to exploit their own and their family labour, on the assumption that high yields would be obtained from intensive family exploitation of small pieces of land, because, if one was instituting collective units like the agrarian reform centres, then the capacity of the state machine to administer them was of crucial importance.

The impression among some foreign participants was that in Chile the traditional Chilean State continued to function unchanged

2 Chayanov A The Theory of Peasant Economy. Ed. Daniel Thorner *et. al.* American Economics Association, Translation Series. Homewood. Irwin 1966.

along with the system of patronage which operated in the bureaucracy, and that inter-party political conflicts within the state
administrative machinery made it very difficult to coordinate and
carry out, in practice, any decision which was made at the centre, if
any decisions at all were made. Therefore, if, because of the political
obstacles involved, it was impossible to transform the nature of the
State, then more consideration should perhaps be given to greater
flexibility and variety in agrarian ownership and organization. More
room should be given to smallholder .production both in small
holding areas and on the newly reformed areas, since this form of
ownership and production was less 'administration intensive'. Those
Eastern European countries which began their transition to socialism
after World War II with an initial individualist reform, followed later
by collectivist reforms, were cited as a useful example to study,
though the difficulties of making this latter transition should not be
underestimated, owing to the conservative tendencies inherent in the
initial system, which had already been described.

Government officials involved in the agrarian sector agreed that
the administration of the agrarian reform constituted a real problem
for the Government. The existing state machinery was quite anarch-
ical because, as the state apparatus grew, in order to escape central
control many new autonomous institutions had been created, each
keen to preserve its own independent action. The Government was
aware of the urgent need to reorganize and rationalize these state
organisms. But, unlike in certain revolutionary situations, such as the
Cuban one, given the existing internal balance of power in Chile it
was impossible to make a complete break with the traditional state
apparatus and start from the beginning with a completely new
institutional framework. The traditional state bureaucracy, with all
this involved in terms of attitudes and resistance, would have to be
transformed from within − an effort which would obviously create
many problems for the Government. Nevertheless, it would be a
mistake to determine the scope and velocity of agrarian reform
according to the existing administrative capacity. Rather, the
Government's obligation was the reverse. The agrarian reform should
be accelerated, thereby forcing the State to solve the administrative
problems this created, such as the need for more and better trained
technical personnel, etc.

The Government's intended policy was, in fact, to organize the
agrarian sector on the basis of land areas which incorporated
different forms of ownership and size of landholding. Where possible,
production units would be large but, whether these large agricultural

enterprises belonged to the peasant cooperative or whether they belonged to the socially-owned property sector, they would in all cases be managed by the agricultural workers themselves. This would take place within the context of national planning, which was to be decentralized to a certain extent to permit substantial autonomy at local level.

It was also intended that these new organizational units would incorporate agriculture-based industries such as fruit and vegetable processing plants and technical and other services necessary for the proper functioning of these various activities.

Another point to be taken into account was that it was not the Government's intention to limit new forms of organization to expropriated *latifundia* areas. It was hoped that the situation of the small peasant cultivator could also be improved by new cooperative forms of organization. But it was admitted that, although great efforts were being made, progress was difficult in view of the traditionally individualistic attitudes of small-scale peasants, however poor they were.

The question of agricultural property ownership in Chile still seemed to be open. One solution proposed was to nationalize the land, redistributing the rental income through the planning process and other government mechanisms. Another alternative, considered feasible according to a non-Chilean economist with considerable experience in the Chilean agrarian sector, was to use fully the tax and price mechanism, using a land tax to the value of practically the full rental income of the land to provide funds for reinvestment in line with the national plan. This scheme would depend on the consolidation of the planning and administrative mechanisms at local level and considerable strengthening of the District Peasant Councils to improve their participation in production and, to some extent, reinvestment decisions. Of course, such a redistributive scheme would have to ensure that some of the income from agriculture flowed to a broader base of the rural population than just the reform beneficiaries and there would, by definition, be an exemption for subsistence level farmers, since they didn't have sufficient cash income to pay rental taxes. One opinion was that it was much more important to act rapidly and get some pattern into effect in the countryside rather than procrastinate in search of some ideal solution.

There was, therefore, considerable interest to learn how far the Government had gone in promoting new forms of organization and participation in the agricultural sector, in improving social communication, and in increasing the level of awareness among the peasantry. How many agrarian reform centres had been established, and how successful had they been in integrating the rural areas in which they have been set up and in incorporating the rural population excluded from the *asentamiento* scheme? How far had the question of self-management and participation versus central or national control been resolved, in view of the ideological differences on these points within the Popular Unity Government?

Those who worked in one capacity or another in the agricultural sector in Chile agreed that the *asentamiento* system had too many defects and great efforts were needed to replace it with a better system. But experience with new forms of organization in the countryside was still somewhat limited and by early 1972 only 30 to 40 agrarian reform centres were beginning to function.[3] Everything depended on the interest and willingness of the peasants to set up such a system since the Government was trying to implement the system by means of a continual dialogue with the peasants rather than by administrative decree. The first obstacle to be overcome was the confusion and resistance of the peasants resulting from the campaigns waged by opposition groups in an attempt to distort the

3 A group of participants spent a one-day field trip in the agricultural sector, and visited different types of agrarian structures. Judging by the particular examples of *asentamiento* and agrarian reform centre they visited. the group thought the latter had definite advantages over the former in terms of providing greater employment. Whereas the *asentamiento* occupied 30 heads of families in full-time employment as *asentados* on 1,000 acres, the adjacent reform centre employed 112 peasant workers on about 800 acres, and the proportion of irrigated to non-irrigated land was about the same. According to workers from one production committee to whom the group spoke, had their agrarian reform centre become an *asentamiento*, under the old rules, only 60 or 70 of the 112 would have received full-time employment. Yet this centre was also able to employ another 30 or 40 seasonal labourers and provide part-time employment for a few women. Moreover, they were aware of the fact that with better organization of the land there were opportunities for incorporating some of the additional seasonal labourers as full-time members. For example, they envisaged further investment works, re-forestation, and better re-organization of their work loads.

Another crucial aspect noted by the group, when comparing the *asentamiento*, agrarian reform centre and a state farm, was that of wage levels and investable surpluses. There were considerable differences in the daily wage and in the remuneration mechanisms in each system, which could be important in determining the long run economic viability of the respective systems. Enquiries on the spot revealed that the agrarian reform centre wages, which the workers fixed themselves, were 30 escudos a day —that is, 3 times greater than in the *asentamiento*, and 10 escudos less than those on the state farm. These wages had risen to 30 escudos from 8 escudos in the course of two years, which, even taking account of re-adjustments for inflation, involved a doubling of the wage level. One of the ostensible merits of the agrarian reform is the possiblility of capturing surpluses previously wasted on landlord consumption and of converting these into productive investment in the agricultural sector. However, under the agrarian reform centre scheme and the *asentamientos* there seemed to be some risk of these investable surpluses being diminished, by peasants granting themselves excessive wage and consumption levels. On the state farm, a very productive one, this did not appear to be such a problem. Wage increases apparently involved a bargaining process between the workers and the state management, so there was some degree of government control over wage and consumption levels.

concept of the agrarian reform centres. Progress was therefore slow because it depended on an educational process as much as on an administrative decision.

Likewise, the Government saw no easy solution to the problem of participation versus central control. It was natural that the actions and responses of the peasantry should continue to be determined by local and individual circumstances rather than the whole complex of national requirements. A long process of learning by experience, education and dialogue between the Government and the different groups of rural workers would therefore be necessary before an acceptable system evolved which gave due weight to local and national interests and considerations. Nobody doubted, however, that a rigid system of agricultural planning was bound to fail, both because of the great complexity of the Chilean agricultural sector and the existing political demand for a large degree of autonomy at grass roots level.

The Illegal Occupation of Land

The recent *tomas*[4], or illegal occupation of farms in Chile, gave rise to an exchange of opinions which helped put the problem into perspective. The impression had been given by Radomiro Tomic earlier in the meeting that the frequency, role and significance of illegal occupations were such as to cause great concern. But, as several people indicated, certain sectors of the national and international press, politicians and other interested groups had exaggerated the number of *tomas* in order to create uncertainty and alarm, and arouse anti-government feeling. It was claimed that most of the *tomas* were the result of outstanding labour conflicts, such as the frequent cases where workers had seized the land on which they worked as a means of forcing the employer to pay the family benefits to which they were due, or the obligatory social security contributions. Moreover, the occupation was usually of brief duration, often lasting only the few days it took for the labour inspector or other authorities to solve the conflict in question. Also, most of the occupied farms were small and medium-sized, which tended to corroborate the fact that most occupations were the result of labour conflicts, since it was precisely these groups of employers who were less strict in adhering to the labour regulations, etc., and exploited their workers most. This also explained the fact that the land affected by these illegal occupations was not more than 1% of the total which, in turn, accounted for the fact

---

4 *'Tomas'* — Chilean word for illegal occupation of agricultural land, urban sites and buildings, literally meaning take-overs.

that the *tomas* had not caused agricultural production to fall in 1971.

There were cases where the peasants, whose family land could be subdivided no further and could not provide enough work for further generations of sons, had occupied the lands of large farmers as a solution to their problems. Nevertheless, to give a concrete example of the exaggerations involved, Time Magazine reported something like 378 *tomas* in Cautín in early 1971 whereas there had been 54. Twenty-six of these were Indian re-occupations of stolen Indian lands to which they had titles proving their ownership, and in other cases there had been labour disputes such as the one where, in retaliation for the formation of a union, the owner had temporarily stopped the wages of his workers.

The Government thought that these problems in the country-side were to be expected when a government tried to carry out a thorough, even revolutionary, agrarian reform. Many of the conflicts and *tomas* were spontaneous but, since there would always be some groups with a different perspective and strategy from the Govern-ment, it was not surprising that political groups on the ultra-left had sometimes been involved. But, whatever the motive force in the final act of illegal occupation, the objective fact of peasant exploitation in the countryside could not be overlooked and the Popular Govern-ment would not resort to solving the problem by using repressive measures against the peasantry. The Government's method was to enter into a dialogue with the peasants and solve the problem slowly through discussion and persuasion, in the hope of maintaining an orderly process of change in the agrarian sector. It was difficult to say whether this constituted restraining the class struggle in the countryside, as some had intimated, since there was so much class differentiation in the agricultural sector that it was probably not possible to speak of one rural class.

The Model and Role of the Agricultural Sector

A large number of points came up for discussion on the model and role proposed for Chilean agriculture in the short and in the long term, and the relationships between the agricultural and industrial sectors of the economy. What image of the Chilean agricultural sector had the Government in mind for the long term? Did they intend to follow the Danish or New Zealand pattern, with a very efficient export-based agriculture; or was the idea to concentrate on being an industrial country with a very diminished agricultural sector, with food imports financed by industrial exports?

Whatever the intended long-term model and role was for the agricultural sector, participants felt there was no questioning its short-term importance even though it contributed only 7% of the G.N.P. The agricultural sector had a vital role to play in the transition towards socialism, in so far as the country's capacity to resist external pressures depended on its agricultural production capacity. If this could be increased and the growing dependence on food imports decreased, external financial problems and pressures would have less impact. Also, the relationship between the short and the long term, and the strategy for restructuring agriculture and industry, could not be discussed except within the context of the particular conditions and characteristics of the Chilean economy.

As had already been pointed out, Chile now had an import structure which only permitted a reduction in imports at the cost of serious socio-economic dislocations. Whereas twenty years ago it would have been possible to stop importing luxury consumption goods like radios, cars, etc., there was now little scope for cutting down imports since it would involve cutting off supplies of inputs to certain industries, causing them to shut down or cut back production, creating outright unemployment and under-employment. Already 20% of total imports were agricultural imports. It was estimated that these would more than likely rise to 25% or 30% within the next couple of years if the restructuring of the agricultural sector affected production, and the success of the internal income redistribution policy accentuated the need to import such agricultural goods as meat and wheat. The balance of payments situation was likely to worsen because, due to price trends and technological, administrative and other problems, export earnings from copper might well decline, and capital receipts might not be so easily obtainable in the future.

Several non-Chilean economists felt that this stucture of the Chilean economy could not be radically altered in the short term and therefore had to be taken as an important global factor which conditioned the Government's strategy and severely limited the possibility of achieving many significant changes simultaneously. The Government would have to decide on an overall strategy and ordering of priorities among sectors which would determine the short and long-term role for the agricultural sector.

The intention of the Government's long-term policy was to work towards a specialized, intensive agriculture, with emphasis on export products in which Chile had a comparative advantage and which provided high yields and high employment per hectare. This assumed a high degree of integration between agricultural and industrial strategy, because great emphasis was to be given to the processing of agricultural goods. Moreover, the Popular Unity Government's intention was to promote rural development by decentralizing agriculture-based industries, establishing small and medium-scale processing plants in areas where the products originated. In the short and medium term the Government considered that substantial emphasis still had to be put on increasing the production of basic goods like wheat and maize, which Chile currently imported in large quantities.

It was within this context that the apparent contradiction between the Government's two objectives of agricultural mechanization, for which the 10,000 tractors mentioned by President Allende were being imported, and rural full employment could be resolved. An important objective of the Popular Unity Government's agricultural policy was said to be the employment of the maximum possible number of people on the land, and to solve the problem of rural under-employment and unemployment as rapidly as possible. One opinion was that, with only 22% of its population in agriculture in Chile, a relatively small increase in non-agricultural growth should make it possible for agriculture to absorb the sector's unemployed and under-employed and all the natural increase in the rural population.

But, the problem of rural unemployment and under-employment was more complicated than it appeared at first sight, because the geographical distribution of the rural population did not coincide with the growth points in agriculture which tended to provide more employment. It was therefore partly a question of increasing mobility. Also, the definition of rural redundancy or unemployment was arbitrary since very few peasants in a traditional society were completely idle, though there were signs that unemployment in the rural work force had increased during recent years with the advance of agrarian reform and mechanization on the commercial farms.

Nevertheless there were large reserves of labour in the country-side which could be mobilized, especially during the seasons when they were more redundant. Studies done by ICIRA showed that in some parts of Chile, especially the south, the ratio of labour demand in the winter months to the main agricultural season varied from 3, 4 and even 5 to 1, depending on the crops. A change in cropping patterns would spread out the demand for labour more evenly over the seasons, and, as certain crops were more labour intensive, a change in crop patterns would also help absorb more labour than did the present production structure.

There was general agreement that in the past there had been indiscriminate mechanization. The desire to get rid of a troublesome work force and the existing price relationships constituted incentives to mechanize. The availablility of cheap and easy credit at a time when the price of labour was rising (mainly as a result of the social security obligations imposed on employers on behalf of the workers) provided a hidden subsidy to mechanization. To the individual employer it made economic sense to mechanize, but from the overall social and economic point of view it resulted in indiscriminate and irrational mechanization. In the future, agricultural planning also required a technological strategy and an accompanying incentive structure to encourage rational mechanization, if both total output and the total demand for labour were to be increased. The tractors which were being imported would, in fact, mainly be provided to peasants who had received land without equipment under the agrarian reform and would be used to cultivate 200,000 new hectares in 1972. [5] More land under cultivation meant more opportunities for work, and the peasants on the land reform units were said to be very aware that an additional tractor which enabled them to convert fields from pasture into grains or sugar beet also created additional labour requirements during the rest of the year.

Participants pointed out that a rural development strategy which mobilized redundant labour in the off-season could also contribute to the rural investment strategy. It was thought that Chile should look carefully at the successful Algerian example of rural work forces which were organized to carry out rural investment programmes in irrigation and were rewarded with food provided through PL 480. The Indian effort of 'Shramdan' had not been successful, however, because it was organized on a volunteer basis and did not concentrate on immediately productive investment works. The Andes range perhaps provided scope for the building of small hydro works by rural work forces, as an alternative to the existing emphasis on high technology, skill and capital intensive large-scale dams and irrigation works.

It was agreed by those familiar with the Chilean situation that there were many possibilities for using seasonally redundant labour in rural public works. The Government was in favour of policies

---

5 Of the total of 18,000 tractors and harvestors in Chile only 2,000 belong to the reformed sector.

along these lines, although little advance had been made in implementing any plans or projects of this nature. Many aspects of the irrigation system did need improving, and the mobilization of the excess labour or low productivity farm labour from the *minifundia* and the underemployed casual labourers could greatly improve the efficiency of the irrigation system. Other rural investments in which the seasonal labour surplus could be used were the construction of feeder roads, storage facilities and, in particular, re-forestation, which complemented well with other agricultural activities.

Agricultural Policies

(a) Investment
Analysis of the present state of the agricultural sector in Chile indicated that its development depended on a large investment effort, which would involve the transfer of substantial resources to this sector from the rest of the economy, while the latter still remained essentially capitalist. This was the reverse of the process in the Soviet Union, but in Eastern European countries, particularly the German Democratic Republic, industry financed the collectivization of agriculture, reducing in the short term otherwise feasible rates of increase in industrial workers' consumption. Peasants there had been given good prices and enormous resources were put into the industrialization of agriculture and into education and training, in order to provide incentives for collectivization.

In the case of Chile, the Government was already making efforts to change the terms of trade between agriculture and the rest of the economy. In 1971 agricultural prices increased by about 25%, and industrial prices by about 15%, and the price adjustments of January and February 1972 maintained this tendency. The relatively unfavourable situation of the agricultural sector in the past was described as partly due to the high degree of monopoly power existing in different industries supplying goods to the rural economy. These industries accumulated surpluses for private consumption and savings, instead of reducing prices. Now that these enterprises had been transferred to the social property sector, it would be possible to change their price policy and in this way help increase real agriculture incomes.

One possibility already mentioned of capitalizing the rural sector at less cost to other sectors of the economy was the acceleration of government rural public works programmes, utilizing seasonally redundant labour, but this depended on the right type of project and technology being chosen.

Two particular aspects of rural investment policy were discussed, one concerning irrigation and the other concerning education. In reply to questions concerning the importance attached to irrigation, the Minister of Agriculture has pointed out that the Government considered the question of irrigation relevant to both the short-term and the long-term strategy. At the beginning of 1972, 1,300,000 hectares were irrigated and it had been estimated by the Ministry of Public Works, which was responsible for irrigation, that parts of this system could be substantially improved by building more dams to ensure continuous supplies of water and that a further 600,000 hectares could be provided with irrigation from the existing principal irrigation works. But the Government regarded the inefficient use made of existing irrigated land as perhaps the most serious aspect of the problem. It was partly an investment problem caused by the traditional division in Chile between, on the one hand, what were regarded as irrigation works proper, under the responsibility of the Ministry of Public Works which dealt with the large-scale engineering side of the matter, and, on the other, actually putting land under irrigation ('puesta en riego') which was currently the responsibility of the Ministry of Agriculture. Lack of coordination in the past had resulted in an over-proportionate effort in large irrigation works, and the present Government intended to rectify this problem by setting up one single national irrigation authority. In addition, the system was not working to full capacity because of poor ditch construction and poor irrigation techniques. Irrigated land was also inefficiently used, in so far as the traditional crop pattern which concentrated on cereals still occupied large irrigated areas which would be more profitably applied to other products. The Government was aware that a lot could be done to improve irrigation which did not necessarily imply very heavy investments.

In relation to rural education, the Popular Unity Government's policy was to expand rapidly training of government officials, and especially, peasant leaders and agricultural workers. According to one person involved, these programmes were still insufficiently well organized to provide the type of training in book-keeping and farm management plans, etc. required by cadres or peasants. Progress was partly hampered by the number and diversity of institutions in the agrarian sector, even though the Government had ordered the different agencies to co-ordinate their efforts. Mass communication methods had not been used so far but, on the basis of a project involving UN help, by early 1973 they expected to begin using closed circuit television, films and slides to expand and improve these training activities.

(b) Crop Diversification

Various speeches and interventions had made it apparent that the Government expected the proposed changes in crop patterns to fulfil many objectives. In other words, this policy would be employment and high income yielding, export oriented, and presumably involve low risk. However, it was doubted whether all these objectives could be achieved simultaneously. From the technical point of view a change in crop patterns could probably be implemented successfully, since there were ample detailed soil and resource surveys showing this to be feasible. This still left the problem of price policy, since, of course, the main method of encouraging changes in cropping patterns was through price differentials and price stabilization for certain products.

In relation to price stabilization, one view was that within a few years, when there was less pressure on the balance of payments, it should be possible to build up buffer stocks for some food grains by importing. This would then permit the Government to control the free market price through buffer stock operations, and obtain the surplus grains from the collectives, co-operatives and individual farmers without compulsion.

Many shared the opinion that one of the most pressing problems for the Government was the need to reform the whole incentive structure so as to induce the desired pattern of production and labour absorption. The present structure seemed to be more or less inherited from the *latifundia* system and encouraged peasants to continue producing relatively extensive crops. Calculations from one *assentamiento* with good irrigated land were quoted, showing that under the existing system of accounting and incentives, where only direct costs were taken into account, wheat was still cultivated since it yielded a peasant 120 escudos per day worked, whereas sugar beet would have given him 37 or 40 escudos. If, on the other hand, indirect costs such as rent for the land, depreciation on capital and interest had to be included in the costs, then it would have been far more advantageous to have cultivated sugar beet. It was also pointed out that under the *asentamiento* system, days not worked were not counted as costs, since the members were paid whether or not or however hard they worked and the incentive structure had not been adjusted to mobilize this labour for investment purposes.

(c) Marketing and Credit

Adequate and relevant marketing structures were generally seen to be crucial to the success of the agrarian reform and rural development policy. One view was that if proper socialist relationships were to be developed government control over the circulation of goods from the industrial sector within the agricultural sector was necessary, in order to ensure an improvement in the terms of trade for agriculture. According to details provided, the Government had already begun to improve marketing mechanisms and to increase state purchases by setting up State Purchasing Agencies for wheat, maize, pork and other products, and the Government was marketing a large part of the smaller peasants' and agrarian reform areas' cattle production.

The new policy was to link state purchases to production contracts and credit and technical assistance. However, Chile was said to be experiencing problems similar to those of socialist countries who had tried to impose a single purchasing agency. When the black market price was higher than the fixed guaranteed price, many producers naturally sold their output through private outlets.

The latter situation also perpetuated the problems of credit recuperation, described earlier. The management of credit in Chile needed further consideration and other countries' experience might be helpful. In Ceylon, the Government's method of ensuring credit repayment was to mortgage one of the peasant's assets as a security against repayment of credit. This asset was the rice ration book which entitled each person to two free pounds of rice per week, provided through the co-operative store which also provided the agricultural inputs. This system was said to ensure that loans were repaid on time.

In view of the Popular Unity Government's policy to nationalize banks and distribute credit through these banks to agricultural enterprises and peasants, it was suggested that some mechanism was also needed to help spread the risk. In India, the State had set up an Agricultural Credit Corporation, which really constituted an accounting device by which the State Corporation took over about 80% of the risks of non-recovery of credit from the regional and local nationalized banks. This encouraged the banks to pursue a more open lending policy towards small farmers from whom it was normally difficult to recover credit.

The Worker — Peasant Alliance

On the basis of the theory that a sucessful revolutionary process required the solidarity of the urban and rural working classes, a

North American political scientist asked what was being done in Chile to foster and strengthen the peasant worker alliance. The importance of taking such action was said to be underlined by recent events in Bolivia which demonstrated how, once the initial alliance had broken down, a new conservative government could use the peasants against the workers and weaken the impetus for social and economic change.

Due to the complex class differentiation in the rural population and the variety of sectoral interests among these groups, discussants doubted whether this problem could be stated in these very simple terms for Chile. Declarations of solidarity by different organized groups were in any case not enough; the alliance could only result from concrete actions in a very slow process, due to the complexity of the rural sector with its many conflicting interests. Great efforts were currently being made, not only by leftist splinter groups but also by the opposition parties, to capitalize on differences among the *campesinos* for political purposes. The strategy of the National Agricultural Society,[6] in defence of its own interests, was to sow confusion and deliberately try to align the small producers and the earlier beneficiaries of the agrarian reform against the remainder of the *campesinos;* for example, early in 1972 it met with the Agricultural Workers Central Trade Union Organization to discuss agricultural problems, forming a rather strange alliance of interests.

6 *Sociedad Nacional de Agricultura* — an association of large-scale landowners.

Part 4

Chilean Foreign Policy and External Sector Problems

Chapter 1

THE POPULAR UNITY GOVERNMENT'S FOREIGN POLICY

Anibal Palma*

The full development of the Popular Unity Government's domestic policies requires an international policy based on the principles of non-intervention and self-determination for all peoples and un-conditional respect for treaties and international agreements which were freely entered into, as long as this does not limit national sovereignty. Adherence to these principles facilitates the peaceful co-existence of all states, irrespective of their socio-economic system. In its international relations, Chile has practised idealogical plural-ism, despite sterile efforts by others to create ideological frontiers in Latin America and to separate its peoples who, in their different ways, are seeking to live in dignity.

Chile shares a common destiny with other Latin American peoples, and the Popular Unity Government has paid particular attention to its relations with other Latin American Republics. No effort has been spared to remove the obstacles which hinder this central aim of Chilean foreign policy. Chile has upheld its commit-ment to the Latin American Free Trade Association and given full support to the development of the Andean Region, which is pushing ahead with policies for economic complementarity and integration between the member countries. For Chile, the re-establishment of diplomatic relations with Cuba represented an act of reparation for an international injustice. Even though the international situation in 1972 is not the same as in the 1960's, there has been no significant change in the attitude of certain reactionary international groups towards progressive governments, although their tactics may have changed, and this is now beginning to show itself with respect to Chile.

The common Latin American interest in ending under-development and dependence places us alongside other peoples in Asia and Africa who face a similar challenge. Without denying the particular situation of Latin America, the main feature of current

* Under-Secretary for Foreign Affairs.

history is the strengthening of the efforts of developing countries to work together to achieve their objectives. Participation as a full member of the Group of Non Aligned Nations, which Chile joined in September 1971, corresponds to the Popular Government's overall foreign policy objective of extending links with all countries which, like Chile, find themselves in a dependent situation which restricts sovereignty and hinders full economic development and the achievement of social justice.

With this same objective in mind, Chile continues to participate actively in the Latin American group in international organizations, seeking to strengthen the unity of the whole developing world, despite the temporary or more lasting differences which separate countries. By seeking out and emphasizing the factors which unite rather than divide us we shall make Latin America a developed and progressive entity, capable of confronting the challenge and aggression of the world's more industrialized countries.

Chile has extended its network of international and diplomatic relations, especially among socialist countries and various young African countries. With respect to the socialist countries, Chile has given more rapid proof than other more powerful countries of a pragmatic and realistic approach to present world reality. The decision to establish closer relations with African countries was motivated by the common interests we share with all the under-developed countries, and the need for unity in our search for solutions which are satisfactory to all.

Our policy of closer relationships with Western Europe, Canada and Japan has been furthered by attempting to diversify our trade and strengthening our cultural and technical assistance relationships, and we believe that our efforts to forge links with all European countries are being reciprocated.

The Government has defined its own position in relation to the Organization of American States (O.A.S.) and the United Nations and this was set out in the statement to the General Assembly of the O.A.S. in San Jose, Costa Rica, on the 15th April 1971, and in the 26th Session of the United Nations. Chile wants the O.A.S. placed firmly within the United Nations system as a complementary regional grouping which would facilitate the dialogue between the United States and Latin America. We believe that the future of the O.A.S. depends on its capacity to overcome the two fundamental myths on which it is at present based — two more or less implicit assumptions which hide and falsify reality. The first is that the O.A.S. is composed of twenty-three equal states and the second is that the interests, objectives and ideals of the constituent states largely coincide. In fact, the difference in power between the United States and each individual Latin American country is so great that it is impossible to achieve efficient and constructive work on the false basis of believing them to be equal. The divergence of North American and South American interests, in various economic and political aspects, is so obvious that it is impossible to build up anything solid and lasting if such an important factor is ignored.

With respect to the United Nations Organization, Chile feels that the Charter principles are still valid and correspond to the aspirations of the world's peoples, but they must be translated into positive action to alleviate the problems of mankind amid the revolutionary transformations which are currently affecting society. The Charter must become the mechanism for solving problems relating to world peace; it must fully guarantee national sovereignty, respect for free self-determination of peoples and the social and economic progress of developing countries.

Also related to the question of United Nations' principles, agreements and recommendations is the question of the exercise of a country's sovereign right to retrieve its basic natural resources. In exercise of this sovereign right, and backed by the whole nation, the Government nationalized the country's main basic resource, copper. This did not constitute an act of hostility towards any country. Yet Chile, like other countries which struggle for independence or for economic emancipation in order to consolidate their independence, has been subjected to imperialist pressures.

The nationalization of our basic resources was not only based on the executive mandate provided by the unanimously approved Constitutional Reform, but also on numerous international agreements which uphold the right of nations to freely dispose of their natural resources, such as the resolution on Strengthening Peace and National Security, approved by the Political and Security Commission of the last United Nations General Assembly. The latter qualified as a possible 'menace to international peace and security' any action or measure which tended to put pressure on a state which decides, according to due internal procedures, to nationalize its basic resources. This resolution, which was approved by an overwhelming majority in the Plenary Session of the General Assembly, clearly sets out the inalienable right of nations to their natural resources. The agreements adopted by the last meeting of CECLA[1] in Lima, previous

---

[1] CECLA — The Latin American Coordination Committee.

United Nations' resolutions, and some articles of the O.A.S. Charter, follow the same lines.

The important problem of rights to territorial waters also concerns the exercise of sovereignty. For developing countries such as Chile, the full use of natural resources in the ocean adjacent to the coastline is principally a question of economic necessity in order to improve the welfare of the population. In general, this is what has prompted an increasing number of countries to claim sovereignty and jurisdiction over 200 nautical miles of coastal waters in order to regulate the conservation and exploitation of these natural resources. However, Chile is convinced that the aims which are being pursued would be prejudiced if, throughout the area over which jurisdiction is exercised, the freedom of shipping or air movements were restricted.

The gap between the advanced capitalist countries and the developing countries of Asia, Africa and Latin America, is clearly increasing. In spite of speeches, declarations and international agreements, it is quite clear to most of the world's peoples that the traditional development models are unsuccessful and that the more prosperous countries continually fail to fulfill their commitments to help eliminate underdevelopment. The systematic refusal of many industrialized countries to adopt measures which would correct international trade disequilibria is an example. This has meant that the participation of dependent countries in international exchange is increasingly unequal; that, due to the particular orientation of financial assistance, the Third World nations have become net debtors; that technology transfer has been minimal and on very onerous terms; and that our natural resources have been subjected to uncontrolled exploitation.

Comrade Almeyda's* words summarize the Popular Unity Government's position:-

"only by projecting our desire for justice, liberty and democracy into our actions at international level can we help to ensure that our internal efforts will not be in vain and that some day they will be matched by the actions and efforts of all peoples. By respecting the principle of non-intervention in the internal affairs of other countries and not claiming or seeking leadership, but acting discreetly as we are accustomed to, we shall ensure that our conduct in bilateral relations with all countries and our actions in international organizations will be a positive contribution to universal peace and a stimulus to all men and all peoples, who, like ourselves, wish to see justice reign throughout the world."

---

* Minister for Foreign Affairs.

Chapter 2

THE NATIONALIZATION OF COPPER

Jorge Arrate*

Copper accounts for 70% of Chile's exports and accordingly for a very large proportion of its foreign purchasing power. Copper finances a high percentage of the fiscal budget and, at the same time, accounts for a large volume of internal purchasing power. If effectively rationalized, the purchases of the large-scale copper mines could be used as an instrument of industrial and regional development.

What follows constitutes a brief outline of some of the basic problems which have arisen during the process of nationalization of copper which began in December 1970, when a constitutional reform bill was sent to Congress. It is not intended to give a chronological account of the process of nationalization, but to pose three or four of the basic problems and to explain, in each case, what in fact actually happened, rather than provide a complete theoretical or in-depth analysis.

A first central problem was to determine the compensation due to the expropriated companies. The Constitutional Reform, which was finally passed unanimously by the Chilean Congress, set out a strictly formal juridical procedure to determine the amount of compensation, involving several stages, which is still not yet concluded. Of the many ideas and procedures contained in the Constitutional Reform, perhaps the most interesting one, from a political point of view, and the one which is most important to analyse, is the clause which confers on the President of the Republic the power to deduct from compensation — that is, the book value assessed by the Comptroller General — an amount corresponding to the excess profits obtained by the nationalized undertakings from 1955 onwards. The year 1955 was taken as a base line in the Constitutional Reform, because it was in that year that the Copper Department (which is now the Copper Corporation) was set up and, as a consequence, from that date the State exercised a minimum control over the activities of the foreign companies exploiting Chilean copper.

* Vice President of the Chilean Copper Corporation.

The principle establishing the presidential power to discount excess profits, a power which the President of the Republic made use of in promulgating the corresponding decree, constitutes a new concept, both from the legal point of view and from the point of view of the procedures traditionally used in determining compensation or expropriation. The aforesaid legislation establishes that the President may fix a normal rate of profit for the large-scale copper mining companies and may deduct from the compensation all profits in excess of that level. When promulgating the corresponding decree, the Constitution and the President himself considered different criteria for determining what might be considered 'normal' or 'acceptable' profitability, although the Constitution does not use these specific expressions.

Some of the criteria which were mentioned and which were actually used in the President's decree are, for example:-
1. a 14% limit established in the Cartagena Agreement of the Andean Pact (relating not to the overall rate of profit earned by foreign enterprises but the return on their foreign investments);
2. certain precedents in Chilean legislation such as the Telephone Agreement, entered into some years previously with a foreign company, in which a maximum profit rate was agreed. But, basically, the criteria which influenced the final decision stemmed from a study of the profitability of the foreign copper companies in their international operations. Since these international firms have investments in many countries throughout the world, it was thought necessary to compare the rate of profit on all their operations with the rate obtained on their Chilean operations. This produced some fairly surprising results. The rates yielded in Chile in some years reached approximately 40 or 50% of book value, whereas, in their overall international operations, neither Anaconda Co. nor Kennecot Co. obtained more than 10 to 12% profit. To express the same problem in another way, while only 18% of Anaconda's investments were in Chile, approximately 80% of its total profits were obtained here.

Another similar criterion was to study investments in the mining sector throughout the world, both investments by the expropriated companies and those of other international companies. Here it was noted that the rate of profit on foreign investment made by this type of company in Europe or Canada varied between 9 and 12%, according to United Nations statistics. However, a similar calculation for investments in dependent countries revealed far higher rates of profit. Thus, both the comparison between the overall international profit rate and the rate of profit in Chile for these companies, and the comparison between the average rate on foreign mining investment in industrialized countries and the dependent countries, showed a marked imbalance. This is a result of the dependent relationship, a relationship which involves exploitation. The legislation establishing the presidential power to deduct excessive profits was intended to correct this.

A second problem is that, once the bill nationalizing copper had been passed, the basic task of organizing the five production units had to begin. These five mines: El Teniente, Chuquicamata, Exótica, El Salvador and Andina are extraordinarily large. Two of them are the largest of their kind in the world — Chuquicamata in open-cast mining and El Teniente in underground mining. It was necessary to transform these five units, which were almost completely separate, into a group. In fact, it involved dealing with five concerns which were really outside the country's economy, whose policies were not defined in terms of Chile's economic development needs but corresponded to the world-wide operational level of a group of foreign companies. This involved an enormous and difficult task of reorganization, for which the experience of the personnel involved was not especially relevant. Each company had different administrative procedures and each was organized differently. El Teniente, for example, had a duty manual setting out the internal adminstrative system and organization, whereas in others, such as Chuquicamata, this did not exist. Some companies, like El Teniente, had an engineering project team with about 200 engineers developing projects for the company, but Chuquicamata had no such engineering group. Wage and salary levels in the different firms varied. Personnel carrying out the same job in Exótica and Andina received different salaries and had different benefits and insurance schemes.

The basic task in future, as far as organization is concerned, will be to establish uniform central criteria for the five different units, to incorporate them as a unit into the Chilean economy, and to plan them as one entity in the context of Chile's overall economic planning.

A third problem is that of management and participation in the copper industry. Copper workers occupy a relatively privileged position in Chile. The term 'relatively' is used because no one familiar with the hardships of work and life in the mine encampments could assert that the wage level of copper miners is extremely high. But, compared with the wages of other workers in Chile, such as coal miners, who have equally hard jobs, the copper workers' wage levels and social benefit entitlements are favourable. For many years copper workers were accustomed to use trade union power to defend themselves against the foreign company. This resulted in tough discussions and long strikes, whenever there was a dispute in the large copper mines.

This is of great importance to an understanding of what has been happening in the copper mines since the Popular Unity Government assumed power, and government representatives assumed control of the various mines in July 1971, once the nationalization legislation was passed. In the first place, the relationship which existed between the former company and the workers was transformed into a different relationship or, at least, into a strong desire for a different relationship on the part of the new executives, who are not only copper mining technicians but also politicians, and frequently rely for support on their party and on the workers who are Government supporters. In these circumstances, the former trade union is seemingly left without an enemy to fight. This poses a problem which can only be resolved by a policy of worker participation in the copper industry; this is compatible with the tradition of trade union strength in the mines. Some mistakes have been made, by transplanting without modification, criteria used in other productive sectors into the copper mines. An example of this is the complete separation of trade union activity from participation. On account of this, the trade union in the large mines has been confronted with a new power group constituted by the workers' representatives on the Administrative Council and, on the other hand, enterprise executives who have a political rather than technocratic orientation.

The results obtained to date have been very positive, despite the complexities. Since the Popular Unity Government has been in power it has been faced with seven disputes in the copper sector. The one at El Teniente will have to be settled by the 31st March. Of the other six, four have been settled without a work stoppage and the two at El Salvadore and Exótica were settled after strikes of about seven or eight days, when the strikers returned to work under the conditions originally proposed by the enterprises and the Copper Corporation. Thus, comparing the industrial relations during the months the Popular Unity Government has been in power and what occurred prior to nationalization, a notable improvement has occurred in relations with the workers and in the workers' efforts to increase productivity. And losses suffered by the Chilean economy through strikes or stoppages in the large-scale mining sector have been reduced.

The final problem concerns the so-called 'Day of National

Independence', referring to the day on which both Chambers of Congress unanimously passed the Nationalization Law. The achievement of national independence is a process, the first step of which was Chilean acquisition of all foreign owned mining property. But the transfer of ownership does not constitute complete independence because every day Chile comes up against different dependency relationships which have to be broken, re-orienting policy to achieve true independence as quickly and at as little cost as possible.

There is, for example, the serious problem of the international copper market and Chile's present balance of payments situation, which has necessitated a re-negotiation of the foreign debt. This situation stems basically from the marked fall in copper prices in 1969, 1970 and 1971. In 1970 the price of copper occasionally rose to between 70 cents or 80 cents a pound, with an average for the year of more than 60 cents. In 1971 the average price was 48 cents, and the average for the first two months of 1972 has been 50½ cents a pound. In addition, the devaluation of the dollar has to be taken into account. For some time now Chile has been trying to reach agreement with other copper-producing countries to protect the price of copper and for this purpose participates in CIPEC (International Committee of Copper Producers and Exporters) together with Zambia, Zaïre and Peru. Various real possibilities of influencing the international copper market have been studied (since the producing countries are in no position to control it). But so far the studies have not borne fruit.

The problems of the price of copper and of opening up new markets and breaking the dependence on certain consumer countries have to be constantly borne in mind. Since nationalization, marketing has been in Chilean hands for the first time in Chilean history and those responsible have already experienced the problems peculiar to the international copper market. While the opening up of China may not be of great importance as a copper market, it is of major significance in terms of breaking Chile's dependence on traditional markets. China is a market with extraordinary expansion possibilities, since China's present *per capita* consumption of copper is perhaps only one twentieth of that in industrialized countries.

A similar problem occurs in the case of supplies; 95% of the capital goods, equipment and spare parts for the copper industry were purchased from the United States, involving a new kind of dependence on the former owners of the copper enterprises. In order to break this link, a policy of resorting to new suppliers is being developed, not because of a political prejudice but because purchases should be made from the cheapest source. The North American copper firms did not pursue such a policy; they simply purchased in the United States because the dollars they spent had never even entered Chile, owing to the special conditions they enjoyed which permitted only partial return of their dollar earnings to Chile. This is very different from present procedure, under which 100% of the copper industry's foreign exchange earnings must be remitted to the Central Bank.

The problem of technological progress should also be mentioned. There are countries such as Japan and Canada which have developed a fairly advanced technology in the copper industry, including small producers such as Finland with extraordinarily advanced technology in copper processing, smelting and refining.

New ties of dependency are discovered with every problem that arises in mining, ties that were not known of before or whose real magnitude was not appreciated. Thus, the process of nationalization is not yet complete and has not even reached a definitive stage; it is a process which has only just begun. The policies which are formulated with respect to each of these matters, and the way in which the remaining ties of dependence are confronted, are vital factors for achieving real national independence. Copper nationalization was only the beginning of the process.

Chapter 3

DISCUSSION ON THE
POPULAR UNITY'S COPPER POLICY

Copper nationalization and compensation

A central theme in the discussion on copper problems was the question of compensation for nationalization. From the speech made by Anibal Palma on Foreign Policy, the impression had been conveyed that the Government seemed to think that United Nations Resolution 1803, concerning the sovereign right of nations to nationalize their basic natural resources, put the Chilean copper nationalization beyond criticism and that there could be no objection to its actions on this point. However, an economist pointed out to the meeting that some countries still tried to challenge nationalizations which were apparently compatible with the UN Resolution. A recent example was the British attempt to challenge in certain European courts the nationalization of oil resources in Libya. Nevertheless, more to the case in point, the United States courts accepted as traditional international law the right of every country to nationalize its own national resources, as had been demonstrated in the Sabatino case.

The real problem was therefore the question of compensation. As Eduardo Novoa had pointed out, there were wide divergencies in interpretation among lawyers concerning what was the due compensation referred to in UN Resolution 1803. In the General Assembly and in the Economic and Social Council there had been a lengthy debate on this Resolution, in which the United States had wished to insert the wording 'full, effective and prompt compensation'.

However, this suggestion had to be withdrawn for the more flexible term 'due compensation'. The Soviet Union, Afghanistan, and one or two other countries, wished to eliminate all mention of compensation, in order to avoid the idea that there was something automatic about payment of compensation on nationalization. On the final vote on the compromise wording, the phrase 'due compensation' was adopted by something like 32 votes against 22 for the Soviet recommendation, with about 20 abstentions, indicating how divided opinion was on this matter.

At the present time it was impossible to speak of an agreed international law on compensation. The pre-World War II position of almost general agreement on the payment of due compensation was said no longer to exist and there was no firm and uniform principle which had legal force internationally.

In the case of copper, the United States still maintained its traditional view that compensation should be 'full, effective and prompt' based on some kind of market value concept, whereas the Chilean Government was calculating compensation based on adjustments for excessive profits in the past, as had been explained by Jorge Arrate. One participant suggested that two other well-known cases of nationalization, the Anglo-Iranian Oil Company and the Suez Canal Company, were instructive cases for Chile to study. Both of the multinational companies concerned had submitted their first claims on the basis of profitability and then subsequently on the basis of book values.

It was pointed out that economists generally assumed that if compensation for assets was determined according to a reasonable percentage of the book value, the company being nationalized would get something less than it deserved because book values were supposedly low historical values, not adjusted for inflation. However, it was argued that this view was mistaken because, as experience on the above two cases showed, although the claimants were awarded only a proportion of what they had demanded, on the determination of this compensation the share values of these entities rose well above the pre-nationalization stock market values. In other words, the shareholders of Anglo-Iranian and of the Suez Canal Company got substantial capital appreciation ranging from 150% to 300% after receiving only about 60% of the book value claimed for the assets.

In the case where British enterprises, such as electricity, gas and steel, were nationalized in the early post-war period, the courts held that shareholders' rights were completely covered if they were awarded share values, that is, no more than they would have got by simply selling their shares. In the British coal industry, where asset values were awarded, the shareholders benefited from capital appreciation. The Zambians apparently paid a sum for their copper mines which was not excessive in so far as there was no resulting appreciation of the Roan Selection Trust shares after the decision to pay 51% of the share values had been announced.

Thus, if moral or equity considerations were involved in calculating compensation, and if it was decided to ensure that shareholders did not lose money they had invested, then partial asset values seemed more than sufficient.

The Contribution of the Copper Industry to the Chilean Economy

Several people thought that it was important to clear up the confusion which seemed to exist in evaluating, from the overall national economic point of view, the costs, profits and financing in the copper industry in terms of local currency, and the related issue of the surplus generated by copper for the rest of the economy.

In the first place it was thought necessary to clarify the point concerning the escudo income from copper production, which was often used by critics to confuse the situation. All the copper industry's foreign exchange earnings had to be sold to the Central Bank at the required rate for this type of transaction, which currently was 15.8 escudos per dollar. If the Government suddenly were to devalue the escudo in relation to the dollar, the Copper Corporation would then receive more escudos for each dollar earned and much less if the escudo were revalued. Changes in the exchange rate therefore automatically changed the escudo income of the copper industry quite substantially. It was argued, therefore, that the escudo income could not be taken as an indicator of the performance or profitability of the large-scale mining sector, since it was heavily influenced by a monetary variable, and on the latter basis the copper industry could switch from being highly profitable to unprofitable or 'inefficient' from one day to the next. The indicators which, according to the Government, ought to be used to assess efficiency and performance were indices of physical output, productivity and the foreign exchange earned for the country.

The index used by the Copper Corporation to measure output in the various mines was that for fine copper production, be it electrolytic, blister, refined or concentrated. On this basis total copper production in 1970 was said to be 540,000 metric tons and 571,000 in 1971, which was less than the programmed increase. In Chuquicamata there had been a small decrease in output according to this index.

However, it was argued that to gain a more precise idea of the productive effort in each mine it was necessary to take into account the total tonnage removed, including both the mineral rock and the rubble (since there were parts of the mines where it was necessary to move large quantities of the latter before extracting the mineral-bearing rocks). Taken together, the total of mineral and ballast removed from Chuquicamata showed an enormous increase in 1971 over 1970, but a lot of this effort went into removing the ballast left in place by the former mining company which had attempted to extract as much mineral as possible before finally being taken over, and had worked on the faces where the mineral content was high and easily extractable.

On the basis of these and other indicators, it·was recognized that during the last two years there had been an increase in the cost of production, though not so great as certain sections of the opposition press made out. These cost increases were due partly to a rise in wages, partly to the higher price of some domestic inputs whose prices had been readjusted by a greater percentage than the price of copper, and partly to the initial problems involved in taking over such a large industry.

There was wide agreement that the benefits to Chile of the copper industry were to be mainly assessed in terms of the net flow of foreign exchange earnings which the industry generated. The large-scale mines were said to be earning the equivalent of $600 million in foreign exchange a year, of which they themselves spent approximately $70 million, providing a net flow of $530 million to the economy as a whole. As a result of nationalization the former out-flow of remittances had stopped and the surpluses available to Chile were accordingly higher.

The statistics presented showed that foreign exchange earned by the copper industry financed something like 60% of Chilean imports. It was suggested by one participant that, to the extent that imports were capital goods, the Chilean copper industry could be regarded as Chile's capital goods industry. But there existed the danger that, unlike nationally-produced capital goods which could go straight into productive processes, the foreign exchange earned could very easily be used to finance imported consumer goods. There was now an even greater danger of this than in the past, with the increased pressure of demand resulting from the Government's income redistribution policy. It was therefore suggested that the Government needed some sort of institutional mechanism to ensure that these copper surpluses were devoted to capital accumulation rather than to immediate consumption purposes.

One foreign economist who had studied the Chilean copper sector thought it unfortunate that successive Chilean governments had apparently never formulated a specific policy or accounting principles, which, in recognition of the fact that the country's mineral resources were not renewable and the revenue flows not perpetual, could have fixed a depletion allowance or earmarked the economic rent component of government revenue from wasting resources, in order to allocate them to industrial expansion. The laws passed during the Aguirre Cerda administration, which earmarked certain copper taxes for particular investment, were a very partial approach, and it was suggested that the Venezuelan concept of 'sembrando el petróleo' (sowing petrol) should be studied to see whether some such idea could be incorporated into Chilean development plans.

Another exceedingly important aspect relating to copper foreign exchange earnings was. the impact on the balance of payments and the debt-servicing problem. The foreign exchange requirements for servicing the Chilean debt had risen so high that it now required more than 35% of Chile's total export capacity to finance it, in other words, approximately $400 million.

A Chilean economist who had worked in the previous administration claimed that the Popular Unity Government had estimated a substantial balance of payments surplus for 1971, but in practice, a large fall in foreign exchange earnings had probably converted the expected surplus on current account into a deficit. This short-fall in expected income was mainly due to the failure of copper earnings to live up to expectations, and according to one opinion this must have resulted from the non-fulfilment of copper production plans since the price of 46 cents a pound used in the Government's balance-of-payments projections had been maintained: in fact, the price during the year was 48½ cents a pound.

Production, Price and Marketing Problems.
It was agreed by those working in the copper industry that output problems were to some extent to blame; the new administration had experienced difficulties in reaching production targets. However, it was claimed that this failure could not be attributed to the Popular Unity administration. In the first place, those reponsible for making the projections had relied on the previous government's claim that by the end of 1970 the copper industry expansion plan would be completed, thereby permitting an increase in annual production of 60%. It was only later, in July 1971, when the Popular Unity Government took over the mines, that the real state of affairs had become clear. As had already been explained, the pre-nationalization exploitation policy in Chuquicamata subsequently involved the new administration in a tremendous effort to remove large quantities of rubble before extracting ore. Output in Chuquicamata was therefore

lower than anticipated in the projections for 1971.

Other mines had inherited technological problems which interfered with production plans. According to Japanese, French and Russian experts, the foundry at Caletones below 'El Teniente' had a serious flaw in its engineering design. The long-standing problem of water shortage at 'El Teniente' had been given insufficient recognition in the projections such that that problem also accounted for the failure to teach targets.

Those explaining the Government's position considered that the price factor could not be ignored because, although it was true that the projected price and the effective price had in fact diverged very little, and to Chile's advantage, what really mattered from the balance of payments point of view was not the projected balance of payments figure but the real situation, and it was recalled that between 1970 and 1971 the price had fallen by 12 cents a pound, from 60 to 48 cents. With each cent fall in price representing a loss for Chile of $18 million a year, there had been a consequent reduction in the copper foreign exchange inflow of approximately $216 million, which contributed to the actual deficit on current account in 1971.

Several commentators remarked on the importance of improving marketing arrangements, in order to gain increasing influence on the price of copper. Currently 200,000 tons of copper were sold on the London Metal Exchange, constituting a very small proportion of the total of 3 million tons of copper marketed throughout the world each year, and yet it was through this metal exchange that the world copper price was determined. In view of the importance of prices for the main exporters, it was suggested by various participants that more effort should be made to establish joint marketing arrangements in order to exert greater influence on the price, though it was also recognized that it would be extremely difficult to get other major exporters to join forces with Chile, Peru, Zambia and Zaire.

Another suggestion was that the copper-exporting countries should press UNCTAD III for a scheme of compensation for export short-falls. Unfortunately this scheme also depended on international action, but there were many other countries which were interested in such a scheme for their own primary products, as for example Ceylon with respect to tea, and agreement on a scheme such as this might be easier to achieve than getting all major exporters to combine.

The Chilean Government considered the question of influencing copper prices, instead of leaving the price to be fixed by the London market, as one of prime importance. They saw several possible ways of influencing the price but each was fraught with difficulties. The first step forward had been taken by Chile, Zambia, Peru and Zaire in agreeing to a producers' price for the copper sold on contract, but it was recognized that this had had little real significance as yet, because the producers' price was currently the same as the London Metal Exchange price.

From the copper producers' point of view, the liberty to sell copper to whomever it wished was regarded as an equally important aspect of marketing policy. Chile was said to have made considerable advance in this respect, having gained access to several new markets in a short space of time. Since the Popular Unity came into power they had begun to sell copper to the Soviet Union, North Korea, China and other socialist countries. Annual sales to China would be 65,000 tons for the immediate years ahead, but there was every expectation of selling much more as Chinese copper consumption expanded with increasing industrialization, although the possibility of China discovering and exploiting her own copper resources was not to be ignored.

Expansion and Diversification of the Copper Industry.
Various foreign economists suggested that now that the copper industry had been nationalized it could begin to play a new and more extended role in the Chilean economy. The experience of other countries like Sweden and certain, mainly agricultural, countries was quoted to point out the possibilities of industrializing on the basis of processing raw materials. There was wide agreement that there seemed to be considerable scope in Chile for forward linkages since the present stage of development of the Chilean copper industry was fairly limited. Some thought there was scope for integrating the copper industry into the national economy through backward linkages, producing nationally some of the currently imported inputs. Apparently such ideas had been discussed in the past, and many projects had been examined without anything concrete materializing until the 1967/1968 'Chileanization' agreement, which provided for some advance in the refining and manufacturing of copper. Participants wondered whether the Popular Unity Government had concrete plans for diversifying the copper industry in addition to expanding existing activities.

It was recognized that there were important reasons why copper manufacturing industries tended to be located near the main consumers, and the varying sources of copper supplies over time – as mines became depleted – had to be taken into account. An international or regional approach to the establishment and location of vertically integrated industries in the copper sector, say between Chile and Peru, might help obviate or forestall some of the problems resulting from future resource depletion, and at the same time provide for the growing regional demand for copper products.

The Popular Unity's concrete plans for the copper industry included a total investment of $90 million in 1972 in the large-scale mining sector to correct the technical problems, inherited from the previous government's expansion programme, which were limiting the expansion of copper production. In addition, in order to continue diversification in the industry, the Government had recently approved a project to produce annually 100,000 tons of copper-wire using a continuous process, though only about half that quantity would be produced in the initial period. This industry was considered one of the fundamental bases of the copper processing and manufacturing industry. Other projects had also been elaborated jointly by the Copper Corporation (Codelco) and the Development Corporation (Corfo), and the Government had just approved six investment projects for producing copper products for export. Likewise, efforts were being made to produce nationally some of the inputs required in the copper mining sector, and it was reckoned that the existing capacity in smelting and in engineering shops in Chile was sufficient to permit domestic production of some of the spare parts and repairs which were currently being imported. In 1971 a small start had been made by substituting domestic products for $500,000 worth of imports. In addition, a large import substitution project to be located in Antofagasta had been approved. The estimated cost was in the order of $5 million and it was expected to save the country $7 million annually for simple spare parts which were not difficult to make.

In examining the industry's external dependency and the problems that would have to be faced in running and developing it, it was generally agreed that one of the crucial tasks facing Codelco was the formulation of a technological policy. Chile as a large producer would have to develop its own technological advances, but it was recognized that the effort to formulate such a policy and to incorporate local science and technology into the copper industry would be starting from a very low base. Chile still had very few copper technologists or economists and in the past there had been little or no research into copper ores, or mining and processing techniques, or the industry's problems.

With United Nations' help a first and important step had been taken under the Popular Unity Government in setting up a Mining and Metallurgy Research Centre which, with international technical assistance, would begin to develop mining and, in particular, copper technology. Also, the University of the North and a group of Rumanian engineers were collaborating to improve copper production processes, and apparently there were already signs of success on one research project concerned with a new effusion process for copper processing which required large quantities of nitrate and coal — two nationally-produced inputs. Emphasis was also being put on improving the training of technical personnel and skilled workers, and a foreign scholarship programme had been worked out for this purpose with the Chilean National Science and Technology Commission.

Labour Policy in the Copper Industry

Labour and wage policy problems in the nationalized copper industry were problems which preoccupied several participants, some of whom felt that these had been very much underestimated. One participant felt that the experience of Zambia supported the Chilean view that, once the copper industry had been nationalized, labour problems occurred less frequently because the workers felt a greater sense of participation, identification and responsibility. Optimism was expressed on the Chilean side concerning the possibility of abolishing restrictive work practices and similar labour problems in the copper industry now there was more discussion with the workers. But others doubted that traditional workers' demands, taken up through trade unions, would abate, or that there was necessarily any real identity between the interests of the workers in the nationalized industry and the national interest. One European economist agreed that the continuation of normal trade union activities in a country and industry which had been liberated from foreign ownership could be regarded as anti-national. Trade union pressure for high wages in foreign-owned industries was to some extent in the national interest if and when no national profits tax was imposed on the foreign enterprise, since in this case it might help syphon off potential profits and reduce remittances abroad. But, as in the Chilean case, these wage earners then became a privileged group and it was politically impossible to reduce their wages once the industry was nationalized. Nevertheless, an inflationary situation provided the opportunity of implementing a differential wage-adjustment policy in which it might be possible to discriminate against the highest paid workers.

On the whole, however, wages should be kept as low as possible, instead of being allowed to harmonize at the exaggerated levels permitted by the high productivity industries, which had the highest absolute advantage from the foreign trade point of view. This would supposedly permit a faster rate of industrialization because there would be higher investable surpluses and the attraction of cheap labour, which might prevent excessively capital-intensive technologies being employed.

Chapter 4

DISCUSSION ON TRADE
AND BALANCE OF PAYMENTS POLICY

Introduction

Introducing the session on Chile's external sector, Dudley Seers raised several important questions relating to the foreign trade and payments situation and the Popular Unity's objectives and strategy.

The first concerned the planning of foreign exchange allocations. An annual foreign exchange budget is usually regarded as one of the principal tools of short-term planning but, as President Allende pointed out in his inaugural address, no such budget existed in Chile before the Popular Unity took power. This seemed to require urgent attention, for the structure of the economy, as inherited by the Popular Unity Government, was particularly dependent on imports of equipment, materials and foodstuffs. Although Gonzalo Martner had said that the Government's policy was to move away from the export-oriented models of the past, one could also describe the inherited model as largely import-dominated and it was not very easy to switch away from this.

Dudley Seers echoed the view of many participants that the summarized documents made available to the round-table did not provide sufficient information to permit discussion of the balance of payments over the plan period. More details were needed concerning the projections for exports and imports which underlaid the plan's national income and savings projections. Also some indication was needed of the sort of trade-offs in exports and imports the Government had postulated to achieve its foreign trade and payments objectives. No doubt the Government had more than one set of projections, since the capacity to import depended on the volume and price of copper exports, which were subject to considerable fluctuation. Although he could understand the need for confidentiality, more information would allow a more fruitful discussion.

Another important set of questions concerned the exchange rate. First, a notable gap had developed between the legal rates of exchange and the black market rate. This encouraged Chilean manufacturers to under-invoice when exporting and importers to over-invoice. Dudley Seers felt that the level of exchange rates merited discussion since with higher exchange rates it might be easier to develop the export of manufactures, particularly those products for which home demand was, or would be, insufficient to absorb existing productive capacity, if the income redistribution policy were successful. But a more basic problem which needed to be discussed, particularly in relation to the foreign exchange problem, concerned the emphasis to be put on price policy and the market mechanism, as against the use of controls to steer the economy, granted that Chile would be a mixed economy at least for some years.

The Popular Unity's Trade Model

With regard to the alleged difficulty of switching away from an import-dominated model, Gonzalo Martner said that Chile was discovering enormous new import-substitution possibilities. The copper, nitrate and coal-mining industries were important examples for which sound possibilities existed of producing, nationally, a large quantity of spare parts, machinery and, in the future, heavy transport vehicles. Plans were already underway for an engineering industry in Antofagasta to produce anything from mineral crushers to conveyor belts and small tools required in copper production, substituting $7 million of imports annually. Similarly, substantial import-subsutution possibilities existed for agricultural implements and machinery. A loan to finance a plant in Concepción was under negotiation.

The Government regarded agrarian reform as one of the principal instruments for achieving import-substitution of foodstuffs, and this demonstrated the links between different aspects of the Government's objectives and strategy. Of the total of $1,200 million of imports, $320 million were capital goods. The balance consisted of intermediate goods and final consumer goods, the majority of the latter being food products. However, the $300 million food import figure included a large amount of primary products for processing in the Chilean food industry, leaving $180 million as the real figure for imports of food ready for consumption. There was therefore considerable scope for import-substitution, to produce and process in Chile agricultural products for the majority of the population, ending food imports of a type which only went to the privileged upper-income groups.

The Government was confident that in the short term, through agrarian reform and import-substitution, $300 million of foreign exchange could be liberated for other uses, even taking into account the social problems in the countryside.

Some Latin American economists expressed doubts about an analysis which distinguished between an 'easy' and a 'difficult' import-substitution phase in Chile and other Latin American countries. The early so-called easy import-substitution industries had, in their time, required skilled personnel, advanced technology and large quantities of capital, which were supposedly the very factors which made later import-substitution efforts more difficult. The substitution of imports had become increasingly difficult in a different sense, in so far as the process had to be sustained by imports of capital goods and intermediate imports, thereby limiting the quantity of foreign exchange available for consumer imports. The resulting change in the structure of imports constituted a sort of 'structural trap' which, because of foreign exchange shortages, presented the Government with difficult and costly socio-economic choices when imports had to be restricted.

However, with regard to import-substitution in the traditional sense of establishing domestic sources of production to substitute for imports, it was claimed that new medium and long-run opportunities now presented themselves in Chile in the mining and industrial sectors. It was natural that the foreign subsidiaries which had been responsible for a large proportion of industrial and raw materials production had preferred to purchase their supplies from their own international contacts rather than purchase or develop local substitutes. The nationalization of many of these foreign enterprises had now removed one of the factors limiting the import-substitution process.

There was concern among non-Latin participants over the emphasis on import-substitution. They wondered what kind of concrete and quantitative considerations supported these import-substitution plans and warned against an indiscriminate and ultimately costly import-substitution policy. A vitally important aspect which should not be overlooked was the question of technological innovation. It was most important that the import-substitution industries should not lag too far behind technologically. But there were also substantial foreign exchange costs involved in keeping up with a wide range of technology, even if technological exchange and aid were resorted to as a partial solution to the problem. No country alone, however technologically developed, could keep up with technological innovation and, in the case of copper-mining machinery, innovation was continuous. Even Britain and the Soviet Union exchanged and purchased information from one another.

In particular, the wisdom of producing the copper industry's input needs in Chile was questioned, because it was thought that perhaps this was technologically too sophisticated and costly on industry for Chile, at this stage. But in reply it was pointed out that the products to be produced in Chile for the copper mines were relatively simple ones such as rails, pipes and tubes, tanks, drills and transport equipment, which were more or less standardized and not subject to rapid technological change. They involved a fairly simple and inexpensive production technology, of a sort which already existed in Chile. The capital cost of the project, which would substitute $7 million to $8 million worth of imports a year, amounted to only $5 million. Obviously because of profits and exchange considerations, the North American companies which had owned the mines were not particularly interested in Chile as a source of many inputs, preferring to purchase them in the United States. Now the mines were nationalized, Chilean production of these inputs was perfectly rational and feasible.

According to another Chilean economist, two other factors justified this decision. First, Chile's natural resource advantage was in minerals and Chile already had a large diversified mining industry which in future would be further diversified and expanded. An industry producing inputs for the copper industry would also serve other types of mining enterprise, since many of the inputs were similar. Second, Chile was a member of the Andean Pact, which included two other important mining countries — Bolivia and Peru. Longer-term considerations made it feasible to think that Chile could also develop a comparative advantage in this sector, with access to an important regional and maybe world market. Moreover it might prove possible to set up an Andean multinational enterprise for the production of mining equipment.

In relation to the question of the model implicit in Chile's balance-of-payments projections, Gonzalo Martner explained that, in so far as exports were concerned, the Government planned important qualitative changes. Efforts were to be made to open up new markets with new products especially in the European socialist countries and China, and eventually Africa and Asia. Exports of manufactures, in particular to China, were under discussion and certain agricultural exports would be increased: the commercial agreement with Cuba constituted the first concrete step in this direction. The Government intended that the production released as a result of government policies towards the upper class, would be devoted to the export markets.

Scandinavian countries were cited by one speaker as the sort of model which Chile should follow as far as exporting was concerned. They were said to concentrate on a few export lines which could be produced in very large quantities to supply a large number of countries. This did not require them to be in the forefront of a number of complicated fields of advanced technology. This would be more sensible for Chile than embarking on car and refrigerator production for export.

Some participants felt that, judging by the information in the background documents and in the interventions made by government personnel, there seemed to be some lack of clarity concerning bottlenecks, priorities and timing in relation to foreign trade and payments. To be able to make proper judgements more information was required. Likewise, participants wondered whether specific, well-defined quantitative and qualitative considerations had led to such decisions as the one to import 10,000 tractors, which could affect employment adversely, or to produce machinery for the copper industry domestically. Were the trade and payments figures sufficiently integrated and coherent, such that the policies outlined were more than aspirations? Had the Government studied the full implications for the price system, and the terms of trade between town and country, of importing $300 million worth of food in the agricultural year beginning May 1972? Furthermore, in order to decide what products Chile was going to import and export, and in order to put into effect radical changes in the structure of foreign trade, a coherent, explicit strategy was surely required. But, from the information provided, some people felt that no sufficiently clear indication of the Government's long-term policy on this point had been given.

From the questions and observations of participants on this topic, Jose Ibarra* concluded that there had been some misunderstanding concerning the trade model, arising from the statement that it was not an export model. It was really a question of emphasis and, in contrast with the previous government's efforts to increase copper exports to provide the impetus for development, export and import policies were now to be a direct function of the Government's principal objective of increasing the standard of living of the mass of the population, by organizing the population to produce the goods

* Deputy Director of ODEPLAN, responsible for National Planning.

necessary for raising these living standards, and providing employ-ment etc. The import requirements necessary to fulfil this objective were calculated first and the level of exports necessary to facilitate these imports were derived from this figure. The Government regarded this as a complete change from the previous model, though it was recognized that it still required a tremendous export effort.

The Short-Term Current Account Problem

At this juncture it was suggested that the emphasis in the discussion so far had been mainly on the Government's medium and long-term plans in relation to trade and payments, whereas Chile's real problem appeared to be a short-term one of how to get through the next two or three years. Some felt that the Government was taking too optimistic a view of the situation and of its future possibilities of manoeuvre.

According to ODEPLAN estimates, exports of $1,176 million and imports of $1,174 million were expected in 1972, resulting in a small positive balance on current account. However, a foreign econo-mist claimed that the surplus was over-estimated in view of the fact that copper exports would only reach an estimated $800 million to $850 million. Furthermore, the increase in food imports, which government officials had referred to as reaching an annual figure of $280 million or $300 million, had also to be taken into account. There was therefore little probability of a small current account surplus materializing. According to his rough estimates there would be a net services outflow of about $50 million on the invisibles account. Government figures for debt-servicing in 1972 were of the order of $400 million, and, provided that normal inflows of com-mitted aid were not interrupted to bring pressure on the Govern-ment, the capital inflow would be between $250 million and $300 million. The estimated total deficit in 1972 on current and capital account would therefore be in the order of $150 million to $250 million, depending on the food import bill.

This prospective balance of payments situation had to be viewed against that of the basic reserves which must give cause for some concern, since it appeared that they had been almost totally used up during 1971. Precise figures of the reserve position had not been given to the meeting. This was understandable in view of the political sensitivity of such an issue, especially at a time when the debt re-negotiation was underway. However, faced with such a critical shortage of reserves, and with the prospect of a further $200 million outflow, the Government's optimism was thought to be misplaced.

Chile was more than likely to face increasingly strong pressure by those foreign banks and financial interests which had provided the short-term credits which normally financed Chile's imports and exports, especially as the Government had declared itself committed to very radical changes to effect the transition to socialism.

However, a Latin American economist with experience in government claimed that the Popular Unity's trade plans would not put abnormal pressure on the balance-of-payments current account. In his opinion, it was not the state of the current account which gave special cause for concern or provoked political pressures by foreign creditors. He took the view that detailed analyses of the balance of payments situation could be misleading. The estimates and analyses just presented had led to the incorrect conclusion that pressures on the short-term financial situation would be felt once the reserves were run down. However, Latin American countries had always worked with low reserve margins and, irrespective of their adequacy for short-term debt servicing, once governments took certain political decisions, foreign banks which normally financed current imports with short-term credits would exert pressure. Certainly their refusal to continue to renew the credit lines created serious short-term financial problems and rigidities for the governments concerned. But it was essentially a political problem.

The earlier speaker still insisted that the creditors would nevertheless look hard at the current balance. The Chilean planners had absorbed into the foreign exchange budget, to pay for current imports, the $170 million or so which, before nationalization, had been remitted abroad as profit by the copper companies. Foreign creditors would naturally argue that this sum should be set aside to repay their debt, and they would apply pressure for this to be done.

Jose Ibarra did not believe the Government was being optimistic regarding the trade and payments situation and he explained the projections and assumptions underlying them. The trade projections for 1976 (see Table 1) showed a total import requirement for 1976 of $1,836 million. The projections, based on what was now shown to be a false assumption concerning copper exports, had been drawn up on the basis of an out-of-date fifteen sector input-output model, brought up-to-date by econometric methods and first-hand information concerning the changes in the intervening period. Tests on the revised model in 1969 and 1970 had given a sufficiently good estimate of the actual import requirements to justify the planners' confidence in the projections for inputs and intermediate imports.

From existing information on consumption levels according to income strata, and from the projected income distribution, the new composition had been calculated for 1976. With the aid of the input-output model, intermediate imports had been calculated on the assumption that there were no substantial changes in the historical technical coefficients for imports. This hypothesis was a very pessimistic one since it did not take account of the effect of the import-substitution efforts the Government was pursuing.

The export projections of $1,798 million were based on the assumption that in 1976 copper exports would be 60% higher than in 1970, and assumed an average price of 50 cents a pound. Apart from copper, the traditional export projections were conservative estimates of the prospects for expansion, as envisaged during the final months of the Christian Democrat Government.

Thus, on the basis of a 1976 imports requirement of $1,836 million, composed of 50% intermediate products, 23% capital goods and 27% consumption goods, and without any new deliberate export policy nor even import-substitution, the trade account would be almost balanced in 1976.

However, the short-term situation was difficult, not only because the copper price was low but also because of the attitude adopted by certain North American enterprises. For example, North American banks have practically cut off the more or less automatic short-term credit lines, such that from a monthly credit flow of almost $220 million immediately before the 1970 Popular Unity election triumph, the flow diminished to about $20 million by the beginning of 1972. Likewise, the distraint ordered by the New York courts on the assets of the Copper Corporation (Codelco), the Development Corporation (Corfo) and many other Chilean State enterprises, had enormously prejudiced the possibility of carrying out further commercial operations in the United States. (This harmed not only the Copper Corporation but all Chilean industries which depended on North American spare parts, machinery and equipment.) Moreover, the fact that international credit agencies like the World Bank and the Inter-American Development Bank had not granted the Popular Unity Government any long-term credit was aggravating the short-term balance of payments situation.

Various possible solutions to this short-term problem were suggested. It was generally thought that little could be done in the short term to improve the level of *exports*, and attention was therefore focused on the *imports* side. One view, shared by several participants, was that an analysis of the import bill indicated that consumption goods were the most obvious item to act upon. The import bill was composed of $345 million for crude oil, chemicals, basic metals, spares and components for use in Chilean production; $175 million for consumer goods and $300 million for capital goods. The import of capital goods could not be cut back without affecting growth and it would be hard to reduce imports of intermediate goods without affecting production and employment. Some changes in production patterns might be possible, allowing a saving in this item; but any more autarchic solution in the short term would involve such enormous changes in the system of production that it was out of the question. One therefore came back once again to the possibility of imposing some degree of restraint on certain kinds of current consumption, which seemed the only rational solution to the problem of an enormous demand for the import of food and other consumer goods.

However, the Chilean official view was that it was essential to maintain the level of popular consumption, and that import restrictions should only apply to the more luxurious goods and the inputs for industries producing non-essential products. A serious centrally directed and coordinated national effort was recommended, which would involve the mass mobilization of public opinion and the incorporation of grass-roots organizations and workers organizations such as the production committees, vigilance committees, neighbourhood price and supply control committee, etc. The idea would be to involve everyone in identifying wastages of foreign exchange, postponable imports and alternatives which were less costly in terms of foreign exchange. This method was preferable to facing a crisis in which mass opinion would not be mobilized behind the Government. It was perhaps the only way of ensuring success in the task of substituting and controlling imports.

A closer examination of state enterprise import policies was also recommended since, in the past, due to reasons of internal financial control and undervalued exchange rates, these enterprises had tended to go against the general policy of import-substitution and imported many of their inputs.

Another suggestion was that an effort should be made to rationalize the variety of machinery imports to ensure against the import of too many different models or makes of essentially similar machines. This would help reduce repair and maintenance problems in Chile and would enable further rationalization of the imported spare parts, or facilitate their domestic manufacture.

In considering these comments and suggestions concerning the short-term current account problem, a Government participant thought that the problem lay not so much with capital goods as with consumption and intermediate goods. In both traditional and new markets now open to Chile, it was current practice to receive an 80% immediate and automatic credit for capital goods purchases, whereas imports of intermediate and final consumer goods had to be settled in cash immediately. In so far as credits were available for the import of capital goods, this automatically reduced the immediate foreign exchange requirements.

Commenting on import rationalization schemes, it was pointed out that the Government had set up a Foreign Trade Secretariat to reorganize the import system, and intended to cut the existing time lag of eight months between the initial decision to import and the actual receipt of the goods. It was hoped that this would cut back the level of stocks required and in particular, curb speculative stocking, since in 1971 the level of industrial raw materials imports had increased in far greater proportion than the 14% increase in industrial output.

Rationing and import restriction, as a solution to the short-term problem, was regarded as too economistic a way of looking at the matter and was rejected by Government participants, who stressed that the starting-point for any realistic discussion of the matter was the recognition of the objective internal political situation. Sufficient details had been given about this political background for participants to see that the Government had to take account of the fact that the Popular Unity was an alliance of groups whose interests were not completely identical. The Government therefore had to steer a difficult course between internal and external pressures.

A brief discussion arose on Chile's reserves. According to one Chilean critic, the Popular Unity Government had inherited $500 million in international reserves on assuming power. It was alleged that through economic mismanagement almost the whole sum had been dissipated in the brief space of just over a year. However, government personnel said that the position needed clarifying. The sum involved was of considerable importance — equalling the sum of two recent average years of capital goods imports (excluding investment for the large copper mines). Nevertheless, it had been the result of high international copper prices and an accumulation of autonomous private foreign capital inflows for direct investment and a certain amount of new loans not related to specific investment activities. In other words, these reserves had resulted from a combination of coincidences.

Nor, it was argued, could it be claimed that they had been dissipated in foreign trade in 1971. It was admitted that there had been pressure — in particular in late 1971 — on imports as the economy recovered, especially for machinery, spare parts, food and certain other inputs. But the Government asserted that during 1971 no significant changes had taken place in the relative magnitudes of imports and exports, imports having increased only 5.6% over the previous year. The fact was that a large part of these reserves had had to be used to repay the inherited short-term debts which had partly been contracted to finance the copper industry's expansion plans.

In his final comments on the Government's balance of payments model and the foreign trade projections, Jose Ibarra thought that the various policy measures, such as the encouragement of exports, the substitution of imports, including capital goods, and efforts to rationalize even small import categories, were far from contradictory. They all pointed to the need for organization and planning. He felt that the problems faced by the Government because it had changed the traditional rules of the game had had their beneficial aspects. They had been presented with concrete problems of how to organize Chilean society, and these were a challenge to the masses to organize themselves for their gradual solution. For this reason it was impossible to give complete and ready answers to many of the questions and preoccupations which had been voiced. Answers would emerge as time went by, and the Government felt very optimistic about the future. On the other hand, certain other answers could not be given because of the extremely serious foreign policy implications.

The Balance of Payments: A Capital Account Problem

Several participants, especially Chileans, were anxious to stress that Chile's basic balance of payments problem was not a trade problem of the sort frequently experienced by mono-export developing countries, but was a capital account problem, mainly related to the unprecedented level of accumulated foreign indebtedness. Scheduled debt repayments due in 1972 totalled approximately $400 million, equal to about 40% of the year's export earnings.

The fact that, of a total gross capital inflow of $729 million in 1969, the net inflow after debt-servicing was only $246 million was sufficient evidence, in the view of one European participant, to support the view that Chile's balance of payments problem was a capital account problem. Since 1967 it appeared that Chile had virtually been borrowing to finance the outflows for existing debt.

This situation was not untypical of 'developing' countries. Discussing different solutions to the balance of trade problem was consequently missing the nub of the issue.

Various possible solutions to the balance of payments problem were put forward, with most emphasis on the question of debt. The first suggestion was that debt repudiation should be considered. It was argued that there was little point in negotiating with the powerful political and financial system whose precise intention was to limit the debtor country's freedom of manoeuvre, both in financial and other areas, and to maintain its influence in the debtor country.

A participant from a developing country, with a debt problem at least as acute as the Chilean one, pointed out that implicit in the debt repudiation strategy was the idea that the debtor country could turn to a highly autarchic solution, since reneging the debt would lead to retaliation and escalating trade disruption. The long-term costs and benefits of this solution should therefore be considered rather more carefully, especially when, as in the Chilean case, there was a democratic framework involving periodic elections.

The suggestion that debt repudiation was an answer to Chile's problems was rejected by another economist from a developing country. Refusal to repay would mean that all further transactions between Chile and the lenders would stop. In his opinion, Chile could not possibly face such consequences since the foreign exchange components of even the unambitious 1972 investment programme were considerable and absolutely vital. It was not possible to think of bringing to a halt the copper expansion programme, or the plans for the iron ore complex, the Concepción oil refinery and lubricating oil plants, steel production, the Santiago underground railway system etc. Interrupting such projects would have a drastic effect on employment as well as having many other grave economic implications.

Nevertheless, it was pointed out by another participant that if several countries, such as Chile, Ceylon, Ghana and Pakistan, could agree to repudiate their debts simultaneously or impose their own conditions for debt repayment, then, of course, the risks and costs consequent upon one country doing this could be reduced. The forthcoming UNCTAD III to be held in Santiago might provide a timely forum for such ideas as this.

It was suggested that the figure of $400 million for credits due in 1972, which would absorb about 40% of the year's export earnings, was so high that it hardly fitted within a conventional economic analytical framework. Political factors were certainly involved and it was necessary to know the composition of these credits in terms of national origin and types of credit outstanding, in order to analyse the situation properly.

Another participant agreed that it was important to have detailed figures available because there was a mistaken tendency to assume that the whole debt was government to government and could easily be rolled-over by existing diplomatic and other pressures. The total outstanding debt in 1969 was $2,300 million, of which as much as $800 million constituted suppliers' credits and bank loans. Loans from the World Bank, I.D.A., and the Inter-American Development Bank were $250 million and government loans were $1,250 million. From the figures, and from his own experience, he concluded that a large part of the pressure on the Chilean Government would be coming from those who extended suppliers' credits and bank loans, and the finance for copper expansion and the 'Chileanization'[1] between 1967 and 1969 — which was probably extended on quite onerous terms. Normally, it was not possible to approach these creditors in the same way as governments to negotiate debt re-scheduling. In re-negotiating the debt, Chile should concentrate on obtaining a postponement of instalments on the World Bank and foreign government loans, or on obtaining new 'soft' loans. It was also suggested that the Chilean Government should consider the idea of linking changes in the source of imports with debt re-scheduling efforts, providing new export possibilities to some countries as an incentive to roll-over or extend the outstanding debt.

Two alternative ways of dealing with the capital account were suggested. The first involved exploring the possibility of obtaining commodity or free foreign exchange assistance from socialist countries. A $25 million interest-free loan from the Chinese People's Republic, repayable over 15 years, had enabled Ceylon to get through a very difficult year. Another suggestion was that countries should work together at international level to establish some form of multilateral assistance, as a substitute for bilateral lending. One example of this was the proposal for linking development finance with the I.M.F.'s special drawing rights to provide a substantial pool of aid to finance trade.

According to Gonzalo Martner, there was a good chance of obtaining new credit and of success in the debt re-negotiation. In early 1972, there were $600 million of unused credits still out-

---

[1] 'Chileanization' refers to the process by which the Chilean Government became joint owner with the North American companies of some of the large copper mines in Chile, during the Christian Democrat Government.

standing in Chile's favour, some a legacy from the previous Government and some new. An extension of these credits, especially from socialist countries, Western Europe and Japan, was under discussion.

The new credits were to be used in new projects. For example, loans were being requested from socialist countries to establish small and medium-scale light industries, in both the manufacturing sector and in agriculture-based industries, in contrast to the emphasis of previous governments on large-scale enterprises. However, some large projects were also envisaged, as, for example, the expansion of the Huachipato steel mill to raise production to one million metric tons. For this, $150 million of the total cost of $300 million, including the costs in domestic currency, had already been negotiated.

Another success claimed was financing the import of 10,000 tractors, which would provide a strong impulse to the agricultural sector. The doubts expressed by several participants about the wisdom of importing so many tractors into Chile, in view of the employment problem and the Government's declared objectives, were said to be misplaced. The Government did not believe that the tractors would reduce employment since they would be used to extend the cultivated area and thereby increase labour requirements.

The Government also felt that the payments problem was undoubtedly on the capital account. Under the previous Government, debt repayment had been facilitated both by capital inflows for direct investments and by new loans. The Popular Unity Government was asking not to be forced to renounce its basic social, economic and political objectives in order to repay the inherited obligations, but to be allowed to pursue its development objectives and to receive a sufficient inflow of capital to allow it to keep up with the debt repayment. A large increase in debt was not necessary since the commercial deficit would be approximately $36 million by 1976 and debt interest would be about $100 million. An estimated total inflow of $600 million was therefore required for the whole period 1971-76. If the required aid was not forthcoming from either old or new sources, in particular from the socialist countries, then very great efforts would have to be made to increase exports other than copper, and to substitute imports. Also a certain amount of sacrifice in consumption might have to be considered, as for example, substituting fish for beef.

Exchange Rate Policy.
Gonzalo Martner claimed that the question of exchange rates was primarily a problem of capitalist economies. He thought that in

neither Hungary, Bulgaria, Yugoslavia nor the Soviet Union, was there any concern over the rate of exchange. As foreign trade came under state control, the problem of exchange rates would be increasingly less relevant, and would cease to be a dominant aspect of economic policy. The Government did not attribute particular importance to the existence of a black market since the total volume of transactions there was considered to be relatively small.

Linking the foreign exchange problem to price policy, the Government thought that, with tight state control and the capacity to mobilize exports and imports more easily, it would be able to subsidize the internal domestic price of those products whose import price seemed too high. Similarly, if prices were uncompetitive, it would be possible to provide subsidies and other stimuli to production which the Government wished to see exported. As in all countries, the price system in Chile, which still had a market economy, had to serve various objectives, including the stimulation of certain sorts of investment and the use of certain natural resources and human resources. But since structural transformation and popular control of the means of production had been given a higher priority in the Government's programme, the question of an adequate price structure was only now receiving the proper attention of policy-makers.

European and North American participants with considerable experience of Eastern Europe agreed that in the command-type economy still in existence in the Soviet Union, Poland and some other Eastern European countries, in which domestic prices were fixed and trade was conducted through foreign trade enterprises, it was not necessary to worry about the exchange rate. Foreign trade enterprises purchased domestic production at fixed prices and sold it abroad at whatever prices they could obtain and imported goods were sold at the fixed domestic prices, the difference being covered by subsidies or withdrawals into the central budget. This system was based on fixed domestic prices and physical allocation of resources, but this did not appear to be the sort of model the Government was aiming for in Chile. Moreover, in Hungary and Yugoslavia, which were socialist market economies, the level of foreign exchange rates was very important. Hungary had a very complex system of export subsidies and import tariffs to ensure an adequate exchange rate balance, and no country could afford to leave such questions aside.

In so far as state control of foreign trade was concerned, it was pointed out that the Government was not yet in a position to manage or control a complete monopoly of foreign trade. However, by the end of 1972 about 90% of the total value of exports would be in the control of state enterprises, and 60% of imports. Copper accounted for a large percentage of exports and, on the nationalization of the foreign companies, the Government automatically gained control of exports. Iron production and export was also in the hands of the State. Even during the previous Government special state enterprises existed to export agricultural output, especially from the *asentamientos*. These were now being expanded. State import enterprises had also existed for many years in Chile and they would assume greater importance, especially in relation to the main foodstuffs — cereals, vegetable oils, butter, sugar, etc. Certain textile inputs were already being imported in this way.

State control of foreign trade would in addition facilitate tasks of rationalization and the effective control of payments. In the past, a foreign exchange budget and official control mechanisms had existed, but these were more formal than real. The Popular Unity Government would be far more rigorous in the future in its import policy and would exclude items not essential for the smooth functioning of the economy or for the popular masses.

Greater control would enable the Government to stamp out the illegal drain on foreign exchange resulting from the frequent practice of over-invoicing of imports.

State control of *all* external flows was, in the opinion of an economist from a socialist country, an essential feature of any attempt to achieve a transition from capitalism to socialism. The experience of his country had shown how important it was to create a barrier, by controlling trade and capital movements, behind which the Government could do what it deemed necessary to transform the structure of the economy.

Another view was that the nationalization of foreign trade or a state monopoly of foreign trade, though important, was not in itself a solution. If one wished to retain any role at all for the price mechanism in determining what should be imported and exported, one had to face the question of what exchange rate system the country needed and what complementary export subsidies and tariff policies were required to bring about the specialization which was among the primary objectives of Chilean foreign trade policy. Decisions about what Chile ought to specialize in, however, could not be made outside the context of a coherent national strategy concerning the desired changes in the structure of production and of foreign trade.

Rounding   up   the   discussion,   Government   participants recognized the importance of looking at the exchange rate problem within the context of the overall price policy. In this matter, as in others, the Government was only just getting around to developing and implementing new policy instruments. The exchange rate had been purposely kept low for a long time in order to contain inflationary pressures and to keep down the price level. This done, the Government was now attempting to implement a differential price policy and was carefully studying a new exchange rate policy, which in fact took account of many of the criticisms which had been voiced.

Chile and The United States

A political scientist from the United States felt that the discussion on the foreign trade strategy, foreign exchange and debt etc., had taken place within a vacuum and had not considered in sufficient detail the position of the United States, the conditions it had imposed from the moment Allende took power, and the constraints under which Chile was acting. Furthermore, quite irrelevant analogies were being used when discussing Chile's situation. It was not possible to extrapolate from the past experience of, say, Yugoslavia or Mexico, in relation to some foreign trade or payments problem. Each case had to be seen within its own international context. At the same time as President Nixon and Premier Chou En-lai were engaging in friendly discussions after a long period of enmity, the United States Government had frozen the accounts of Chile because it now had a democratically-elected socialist government. One participant posed the question: Was it possible to draw on non-Latin experience since the United States still believed in the Monroe Doctrine and regarded the Latin American hemisphere as its own special sphere of influence?

The United States had not tolerated certain political and social changes in Latin America, and was not going to. Socialism was not a negotiable matter for the United States, which would extract a heavy price from any country seriously attempting to establish such a system. Only when this kind of consideration was made explicit was it possible to discuss the kinds of strategy open to the Popular Unity Government.

A contrary view was that, in view of the past record of the United States, a somewhat surprising degree of elasticity was beginning to manifest itself in its relationships with Chile. Perhaps the United States was intentionally refraining from a hardline position in order to avoid driving Chile even further to the left.

Government participants agreed that the Government could not ignore the international background. Moreover, taking into account different possible contingencies the Government had drawn up more than one balance of payments solution.

Part 5

Participation and Socialist Consciousness

Chapter 1

THE POPULAR UNITY GOVERNMENT'S WORKERS' PARTICIPATION MODEL: SOME CONDITIONING FACTORS

Joán E. Garcés*

This analysis will concentrate on the political aspects of worker participation in the management of enterprises, trying to identify the presence and interaction of a series of social, economic and political factors which influence the current process of general transformation in Chile. It is necessary to examine how the Government's policy operates in this field and contrast it with the two principal alternatives — namely the schemes advocated by the extreme left and by the Christian Democrats. Almost forty years ago Lukacs emphasized the importance of organizational problems as the point of convergence between theoretical and practical problems. He pointed out that the differences which arise in concrete discussions of the development and implementation of organization originate in different theoretical premises. In fact, the question of participatory mechanisms in the management of factories and farms etc. is essentially an organizational problem, in so far as their definition also determines the mechanisms for decision-making, for managing enterprises and for incorporating these into the overall productive process.

Theoretically, it is not difficult to distinguish the fundamental difference between capitalist and socialist schemes of participation. They differ in content because the capitalist system starts out with concepts of workers and capital and their respective roles in decision-making, and of the inevitable division between wage earners and management, whose main links are with the owners of capital. All these are absent from socialist forms of enterprise organization. The real difference, however, lies in the meaning given to participation in the socialist and capitalist forms of participation. Capitalist participation is a response to the need to absorb or neutralize social tensions and the pressures on traditional forms of enterprise organization. The representatives of the owners of capital are the

* Presidential Adviser

effective decision-makers, because only minority representation of workers exists at any level, and is often consultative. Also, since capitalist enterprises and their participation schemes function within an overall capitalist economic framework, the existing capitalist social relations are never really questioned. On the other hand, in a socialist enterprise the division between wage earners and management and the social relations are modified. These differences are very significant and they bear strongly on the main options which are being discussed in enterprises, trade unions, political parties, the Government and in Parliament.

The way this problem is now being confronted in Chile involves an apparent paradox. A few months ago the Popular Unity Government, in agreement with the Central Trade Union Confederation, transformed the meaning and content of participation and instituted socialist forms of participation in all enterprises in the socially-owned sector. These were hitherto unknown in Chile. The only previous experiments with participation — in 1969 and 1970, under the Christian Democrat Government — were relatively timid ones, i.e. the Consultative Councils established in enterprises like the National Air Line and the Social Security Fund, with no participation in decision-making organs. Workers' representatives were appointed to the Management Councils of the Central Bank, National Television, Chilectra (Electricity Generating Corporation) and Inacap (Training and Productivity Institute), but they were minority representations.

The new socialist forms of participation still operate within a capitalist context; cultural values, beliefs and sentiments derived from the capitalist mode of production predominate. All types of workers' organizations and representatives of all political opinions enjoy absolute freedom to manifest anti-socialist, pro-capitalist ideas. Also, the mechanisms ·for selecting and appointing workers' representatives to the Administrative Councils, and for appointing political representatives to important state positions obey liberal democratic criteria. They are based on universal suffrage, and a Rousseaunian type of legitimacy which allows organized forces which are fighting for the survival of capitalist society access to the state decision-making mechanisms. At the moment the pro-capitalist forces have a majority in Parliament and there are no formal obstacles to their winning control of the Executive if they can count on sufficient popular electoral support to defeat the parties with a socialist orientation.

This complex situation gives rise to several far-reaching needs, which can be summed up in two points. First, the socialist forces must consolidate and develop new participatory mechanisms by convincing and persuading the workers, without being able or wanting to resort to more effective means of persuasion in so far as they are to some extent limited by the existing pluralism which the Popular Government programme explicitly recognizes. In trying to convince the workers, the socialist oriented parties and trade unions are faced with a systematic, intelligent and well organized opposition campaign, which is also aimed directly at the workers, exploiting the defects or irregular features of the first attempts at participation. They face endless propaganda which advocates solving wage problems according to the extreme capitalist criteria of stimulating desire for private gain among workers.

The second and most important need is to bear in mind that, for interacting practical and strategic reasons, the political and economic model demands efficiency in all aspects. Within the capitalist economic system, a series of social and economic innovations in institutions and organizations are being introduced, which will tend to alter the economic base of capitalism and form the embryo of future socialist forms of organization. It is also necessary to keep the overall productive process fully integrated, in order to gear the economy to uninterrupted growth and to maintain state authority over each decision-making unit, in order to regulate the market which continues to function according to capitalist rules. Within this role of a 'benefactor' of 'intervening' state, the workers' representatives in decision-making mechanisms may still be opponents of socialism.

Socialist groups, whose tactical criteria differ completely from those of the Popular Unity Government, are also active. They help to establish participatory mechanisms which belong to a transformation process in which the existing legal and institutional limits on decision-making are circumvented. This philosophy favours complete liberty of action and decision and eventually arbitrariness, in order to surmount the barriers and controls encountered by a revolutionary movement in a non-revolutionary situation.

It is worthwhile analysing this alternative whose impact, though small to date, is having clear repercussions. It advocates spontaneous decision-making at factory level which, if it became widespread, would, because of its own internal logic, result in complete disorganization of the productive process. This is totally incompatible with the Popular Unity Government's tactical objectives. It would cause a decline in the level of production, posing inevitable social and economic problems for the middle classes who are so important in

Chile and who play a decisive role in the present political process pursued at present in Chile. An economic crisis would not only pose problems for the Government, the organized working classes and the middle classes. It would have repercussions on the popular base — the Government's main support in so far as the least politically conscious groups are more susceptible to pressures by anti-socialist forces, who continually sow disillusion among the public about the benefits of a socialist alternative to the existing system.

A confrontation between middle class and popular groups, in a country in which the procedures for designating the political authorities or electing representatives are open at all levels, from students to school teachers and in enterprise participation mechanisms, would result in the Popular Unity Government losing its majority backing. However, to ensure the proper functioning of the state and of all representative institutions, a majority backing is indispensable. The revolutionary process has reached a relatively advanced stage, producing exceedingly acute social tensions, and in such a situation any confrontation between groups of socialist workers and the anti socialists and openly pro-capitalist ones would probably be violent.

This revolutionary perspective has its own internal theoretical logic and, even though it seems paradoxical, this is shown in the methods used by certain imperialist institutions. The Secret Documents, relating to the intervention by the ITT and certain North American Government Agencies in the internal affairs of Chile between September and October 1970, show clearly that the basis of the plan to divert the normal electoral process on September 4, 1970 was to create an economic crisis and political disorder by employing ultra-leftist tactics. These documents talk explicitly of using the extreme left to provoke public disorder and disturbances in the productive sector, which would lead to military intervention and interruption of the electoral process.

Attempts such as these have been made throughout the Popular Unity's sixteen months in government. The pro-capitalist groups' need to create economic disorganization and political crisis coincides to a surprising degree with the internal logic of certain ultra-left participation models, and both result in the need for an armed dénouement of the social struggle.

However, the economic and political path being followed in Chile requires economic order and continuous economic growth. Substantial economic dislocation would upset the political programme and, in so far as social conflicts are posed and solved in political terms, this would block the path. If Chile's present problems and dilemmas are to be resolved without resorting to open physical violence, the Government's participatory mechanisms must correspond to the perspectives within which it operates.

The Popular Unity Government's programme considers the social property sector as the basis of any progress towards socialism. Parliament, however, has just approved the first stage of a bill in which this sector is to be organized in a way similar to workers' capitalism, in which profits are distributed among the workers and even among private institutions which, by means of special participatory mechanisms, would be authorized to run state and socially-owned enterprises. This Christian Democrat bill makes no clear distinction between the socially-owned sector and the private sector. It establishes a two-way flow between them, such that there is no guarantee that the social property sector will be irreversibly consolidated. Furthermore, the bill upholds capitalist production relations.

Decision-making at production unit level is important for determining the nature of the rest of the economic system. If, at the moment, it is tactically irrational to adopt the extreme-left's solution, the Christian Democrat alternative is not only irrational but also misleading and basically non-viable. The Christian Democrat scheme proposes extending to the industrial sector the neo-capitalist *asentamiento*-type organization which they developed a few years ago in the agricultural sector. This implies entrusting 80% of the country's foreign exchange earnings (produced by the 150 enterprises which are intended to belong to the social property area), 100% of its financial apparatus, and 40 to 50% of industrial production (equal to 25-30% of Gross National Product) to between 100 and 120 thousand workers, or about 4% of Chile's active population who work in the 150 enterprises which are intended to belong to the social property area. It would upset the whole economic growth process. Moreover, the organization on these lines of the dominant economic sector, which is still capitalist, would mean that the principal capitalist characteristics of profit motive, competition, continuous capital accumulation etc., would develop within the working class itself.

It is unrealistic to apply at worker level the essential mechanisms for the concentration of private property. The internal dynamic of capital accumulation would soon assert itself. It would seriously disintegrate social organization, in fact the whole of Chilean society, because the profit expectations of workers in the dominant sector would conflict with the needs of the rest of Chilean workers.

The social conflict between the minority which own the means of production, and the mass of the workers would be replaced by the upsurge and development of antagonisms among the workers themselves.

Chapter 2

PARTICIPATION UNDER THE POPULAR UNITY GOVERNMENT

Luis Figueroa*

The Government inherited an economy which, while it was not actually stagnant, was growing far too slowly. Like other Latin American countries, Chile depended economically on foreign monopolies. The economy contributed far more to these foreign corporations than it ever received from them.

The economy also functioned within a highly restrictive framework. In agriculture, for example, production was limited and prices were high. The large landowners made huge incomes. In industry and trade, the story was the same. To restrict production and keep prices up — so as to get large surpluses — installed capacity was not used to the full.

As a result the workers suffered a gradual but definite decline in real wages. At workers' congresses demands were raised for a geniune anti-inflationary policy, and not a mere paper one, and consequently the Popular Unity Government proposed a wholly new approach. In the fight against inflation, previous governments never faced up to the need to modify the entire economic structure. They were content merely to tinker with the superstructure. The workers' view was that if inflation was really going to be tackled seriously, a number of basic changes had to be made.

The first was to reintegrate into the economy the production of the basic materials essential to Chile's development — copper, iron, nitrates, iodine, etc. which all have a decisive influence on the availability of foreign exchange. In its first year, therefore, the Government took steps to nationalize these basic industries or to transfer them to the socially-owned sector of the economy. The state sector is intended to be the main lever of development, containing the basic sources of wealth and the monopoly industries with the highest concentration of capital and the strongest influence on each branch of the economy. A sector of this nature is in a position to

* President of the Central Trade Union Confederation (CUT)

generate surpluses to further industrial development, thereby making possible the uninterrupted development of the economy as a whole along social lines.

The workers began to participate in a structure which they themselves had helped to create, not only through the electoral battle, but also through the struggle they had kept up for many decades to get this type of measure adopted.

By 'workers' participation' we mean participation in the production and marketing mechanisms. But participation should not be limited to the economic sphere. It must extend to the whole of economic and social life, ranging from the production committee in a section of an enterprise to the administration of the whole company, right up to the level of regional and national economic planning. On this basis, different forms of participation are being developed. In the socially-owned and mixed sectors of industry, production committees are being established at grass-roots level. The election of representatives has also begun to the administrative councils of enterprises.

This is democratic not autocratic participation. It has been agreed with the Government that its representatives will be appointed by the central government whereas those of the workers will be elected by direct secret ballot, with individual and proportional representation. Workers participate in accordance with their different occupational grades in their place of work: shop-floor workers, administrative workers and technical management workers. The administrative councils are made up of eleven members – five of them to be elected by the workers and five to be appointed by the Government, with the administrator or director of the firm appointed directly by the President of the Republic. Of the five workers' representatives, three are elected from the shop-floor section (i.e. by the workers and staff directly involved in production); one from the administrative workers, and one from the technicians, engineers and professional graduate staff. This form of participation does not divide them according to political, religious or other ideologies; on the contrary, it enables them to participate by virtue of their role in the productive process.

As for participation in other fields, it has been agreed, and a bill has been passed by Congress, that the workers should take over complete control of all social security organizations. As far as the management and administration of social security is concerned, it will not be the Government or the employers, but the workers – the direct beneficiaries – who will manage, control and administer all aspects of social security in this country. This is extremely important since Chile has no comprehensive social security law and there is no co-ordinated overall system of social security. We need, first of all, to reform the existing legislation in this field and then to change the highly bureaucratic structure of the organizations.

We also have arrangements for participation in health. Agreement has been reached on setting up local health councils, in which the community participate through neighbourhood committees and union organizations. We are looking into a way of reforming the system, so that participation will extend to its general management; this is a move in the direction of a single national health scheme, which will enable fuller use to be made of the various facilities and installations.

The luxury of squandering resources cannot be allowed to continue; we need to rationalize health policy so that it reaches the broadest sectors of the population at the lowest possible cost. This also applies to other activities, such as sport and leisure. A programme of building popular resorts is underway; half of them are administered by the workers themselves and the other half by a government body. However, in future, all communal leisure will be organized directly by the workers through their union organizations, as will the development of physical culture and sport, through the construction of playing fields, with contributions from socially-owned enterprises, voluntary labour inputs from the workers, and financial help from the unions themselves.

Participation must now also be extended to distribution and marketing. While it is true that this new approach to economic development is benefiting more and more sectors of the population, it is also coming up against those sectors whose interests are affected by the new set-up. Foreign industrial corporations, whose Chilean companies have been nationalized, and those powerful enterprises which dominated the various sectors of the economy, are unwilling to lose the control of the economic and political life of the country which they were able to exercise by virtue of their financial and industrial power. Naturally they are putting up a fight.

The whole process, which must not only be strictly democratic, but calm and peaceful as well, is confronted with obstacles and difficulties because of this clash of interests. The workers, as a matter of principle, are in favour of the process developing peacefully, though this does not mean that they are incapable of defending it in other ways. This briefly is the situation we are faced with.

Putting this new programme into effect has brought a real increase in workers' incomes. In 1971, the first year of the Popular Government, a system was introduced for granting wage readjustments without these being reflected in price increases. The capitalists extracted enormous surplus value by means of inflationary mechanisms, policies of capital accumulation and the whole previous general policy. They should have been able to absorb these new wage adjustments during the first year without adding them on to prices, simply by making full use of their installed capacity. For under the old order the majority of companies were only working at 60% or 70% or 80%, at most, of their installed capacity, i.e. one or two shifts. Very few firms had uninterrupted work for three shifts. This meant that there was a longer and slower period of recovery of invested capital.

In 1971, there was no re-investment in the private sector. By using the same amount of installed capacity in the manufacturing sector there was in fact a quite spectacular increase in production. This facilitated the implementation of a prices policy in 1971 which was designed to bring about a minimum readjustment in prices, taking into account the increase in the cost of imported raw materials that are not subject to national control. The workers' share of the national income increased from 51%. to 59.7%. This fact is most important and one for which the workers, as a class, are grateful to the Popular Government, since it obviously means a real improvement for them.

Wages policy could also be reorganized. An example shows clearly the anarchy prevailing in the public administration wage-structure; no less than 176 different pay-scales still exist, so that a lift-attendant or a driver in one ministry does not earn the same as his counterpart in another, although both have worked for the same number of years. First of all, upward readjustments must be made, to put right any injustice, by bringing about substantial improvements in the wages of the hardest-hit sectors. Also a new wage classification must be drawn up, based on the function each person carries out.

In the private sector the situation is much more complicated and serious. The union structure here differs from that of other countries. There are workshop unions, company unions, unions for manual workers and unions for white-collar workers (both these last groups are wage-earners, but the ruling class devised these rules of the game in order to keep them divided and to attack them more easily). Now the whole situation is changing, and the CUT has drawn attention to the need to set up integrated unions based on direct ballot by all the workers in each company. These unions will combine manual workers, white-collar workers, technicians, engineers and university graduates.

In the private sector there were some 3,500 claims for the renewal of annual collective agreements, and, in 1971, between 1,500 and 2,000 collective disputes had to be dealt with. This involved a labour inspector, and at least three people from the employers, meeting at least three times in the conciliation board, and as many times again in face-to-face meetings — all of which means quite a considerable waste. Now the workers have called for a new set-up. In the public sector, it will involve a move towards a single wage-scale and, in the private sector, the establishment of tripartite legal commissions with government, workers' and employers' representatives, to draw up collective agreements in each branch of the economy at a national level. This new way of fixing a wages policy will undoubtedly mean a big saving for the country in general, and new benefits for the workers.

Finally, the workers consider that, under present conditions, the socially-owned sector of the economy constitutes the basis for further development of the country. It was generally agreed before the victory of this Government that the economic system operating in Chile, with its agricultural, industrial and mining structures could not solve the problems either of the country or of the workers, and that basic changes were necessary. There were widely divergent points of view on the different forms new structures might take, but the basis for the whole discussion is the victory in the elections of the Popular Unity Government on a platform known to the entire Chilean people. Now this programme is being carried out and we workers believe that the socially-owned sector of the economy should be the sector to be expanded, constituting the first step towards the eventual establishment of a socialist economy. In fact, the foundations for this are only now beginning to be laid; at this juncture it cannot be said that the socially-owned sector is significant. But certainly the character of the state enterprises which existed previously is now undergoing a fundamental change with the workers being brought into the administration.

For the workers, a state enterprise ceases to be a state enterprise when they begin to take part in its control, administration and planning. It then becomes a socially-owned enterprise serving the whole of the community.

Chapter 3

DISCUSSION ON THE QUESTION OF PARTICIPATION

Introduction: The Meaning of Participation
In order to give some structure to the discussion on participation, and to focus part of the discussion on concrete aspects of participation, David Lehmann presented a few preliminary ideas on the content and meaning of participation.

Participation was a term which gave rise to considerable mystification and confusion on both the left and right of the political spectrum and tended to mean all things to all men. Participation had no meaning as an abstract term and it was necessary to distinguish between different types. First there were what could be called con-flictive and administrative participation — the former depicting a situation in which politically and socially powerful forces bargained with each other in a conflict situation and the latter describing the co-option of workers onto administrative committees, for example. Each form had different consequences and these would vary in different contexts.

A second distinction could be made between participation in the application of national policies and participation in the elaboration of these policies. This was very important in the context of the question of workers' control and the use of surpluses generated by enterprises. Again, the consequences of one type or another were very different, and contradictions might result from attempting to implement both forms simultaneously. There was a difference between participation in the consumption and distribution of goods, as with the Popular Supply & Price Boards *(Juntas de Abastecimiento y Precios)*, and participation in decisions about production and planning. It was also necessary to differentiate between participation which involved an economic interest in enterprise profits, and participation in the taking of decisions, with profits under the control of the central planner.

However, whatever the kind of participation under consideration, David Lehmann felt it was essential that it be an organized activity if it was to produce meaningful results, because spontaneous participation usually resulted in power being monopolized by a few people who then manipulated the rest.

Some aspects of participation were closely linked to the question of incentives which could become an important issue of debate in Chile as in Cuba. Moral and material incentives could not be understood, discussed or resolved in the abstract with a kind of unitary model of human motivation. The production and technological situation was one determinant of workers' attitudes to production and the amount of remuneration they expected to receive. Where technologies were not very advanced, or where assembly-line technology or piece-work was easily applied, it was difficult to use moral incentives because some groups of workers would have higher bargaining power and it would be wrong to hope that these workers would be prepared to make extra efforts for the collective good or to compel them to do so. Yet the extra effort is often required from precisely these sectors with high bargaining power.

David Lehmann also thought that the analysis of other countries' experience in participation provided some insights into the problem, and some socialist countries had wide experience of different types of participation. While the German Democratic Republic had little conventional workers' control involving participation in profits at enterprise level, with collective farms as an exception, there existed a multiplicity of representative organizations throughout society. An estimated quarter of a million people were involved in representative organizations, committees, municipal, provincial and national councils, and production councils, and were therefore participating in some way or another in decision-making on all levels. Furthermore, the Party, with some 2,000,000 workers out of a population of 17,000,000, stretched into every production unit and allowed participation by a large number of people, though not on a democratically elected basis. This type of participation was not immediately related to decisions on material rewards.

In Yugoslavia, participation was mainly at enterprise level and was linked to material rewards, such as the distribution of profits etc. This gave rise to such problems as the emergence of monopoly positions and the development of regional and social inequalities, which had all been reinforced by the participation of West European capital in joint enterprises with Yugoslav capital. This raised problems of the relationship between participation and planning, which in a socialist system should go hand in hand.

The Chinese case was, according to David Lehmann, a further

example to note, even though it was very specific to Chinese culture and history. During the early period of the Chinese Revolution and the land reform, one method used to develop an independent consciousness of the peasantry was the confrontation between village and landlord in the trial and punishment of the latter. Another important aspect, which was very specific to China and the ideology of Mao Tsetung, was the relationship between the Party and the masses, especially during the early revolutionary period and during the Cultural Revolution, when certain Party leaders attempted to create a confrontation between the masses and the Party so that the Party should not become too isolated from popular control. Yet on the other hand, there did seem to be a problem for the Chinese Government of a lack of central control, combined with a lack of information about what was really happening at local level.

In Cuba, the question of participation was still unresolved. Established institutionalized channels for participation still did not exist but the issue continued to be the subject of lively debate there.

There was widespread agreement with David Lehmann that one cannot speak of participation in the abstract. The meaning of participation depended on many factors such as which class held power in society, the particular stage that society had reached, and the society's democratic and political traditions. Countries with different histories and traditions would develop different forms of political and economic participation.

Participation was sometimes spoken of as though it were a form of socialism, or as though it signified the organization of a socialist economy, but most agreed that this was not a correct analysis. In fact, there were two main ways of looking at the question of participation in Chile during the transition period. In the first place it was to be seen as part of the fight for power, which involved substituting the old bourgeois apparatus by a new one at all levels of social and political life and not just in the work place. The reorganization of the economy by the workers themselves was to be seen as part of this struggle for power. Moreover, the content and meaning of participation was not fixed for all time and, once the power struggle had been won by the working classes, the forms of participation would change.

·Several Chileans suggested that participation had a vital role to play in Chile in ensuring the irreversibility of the transition process. Increasing real and effective participation of the workers was seen as one of the surest guarantees that they would not allow any retreat from the road to socialism.

Participation could also be conceived of as an instrument to raise the level of consciousness. In learning how to manage both the economy and political affairs, right from top to bottom and vice versa, the workers' political and social awareness would increase. This would also widen the political bases of the Popular Unity, by incorporating increasing numbers of workers and peasants and middle class groups during the transformation process.

Also, apart from the fact that Chile was not yet a socialist state, it was claimed by an Eastern European participant that the concept of participation did not adequately describe a socialist democracy, because the latter comprised a far more complex system than the existence of certain participatory mechanisms. The word 'participation' always tended to suggest that there existed some power beyond the people in which the people should participate, whereas once the working class had gained power the people would exercise it daily in all their political, economic and cultural activities. This speaker also claimed that an essential feature of socialist democracy was democratic centralism because without central democratic leadership, democratic participation was impossible. But democratic centralism only functioned properly when every member of society contributed through their respective organizations, whether they be factories, political organizations, or even the state apparatus. Therefore in his view, it was not the form of participation which was the basic factor but the full realization of the principle of socialist democracy.

There was quite a wide degree of consensus that in any discussion of participation in Chile the central problem was one of power, control over the legislature as well as the executive. Control of power was seen by many to be necessary if a democratic socialist society was to be constructed in which the people exercised power in all senses of the word, participating in decisions at all levels of economic, political and social life. The bourgeois democratic state possessed some democratic forms but it was based on the exploitation of man by man and the structure of the system itself involved minority control of the majority, with the latter being consulted only once every six years in Chile in the Presidential elections.

It was recalled that earlier in the round-table discussions, Ricardo Lagos had referred to a gradual process of incorporation of different groups into political life. Many participants felt this growing participation was more formal than real and that formal indicators such as the percentage of population eligible to vote, trade union membership etc. were inadequate. While these facts did help explain how it was possible for a popular government to emerge, it was probable that there had also been a process of concentration in the real centres of decision which meant that there was little, if any, improvement in real access to important decision-making.

Forms of Participation in Chile

Considerable attention was focused on concrete forms of participation, with frequent emphasis on the fact that participation took different forms at different stages of a country's political and economic development.

Russian experience was said to illustrate very well how the struggle for power and the subsequent stage of socialist consolidation each required very different, if not contradictory, kinds of participation, as amply demonstrated by the history of the first eight months of war communism and the New Economic Policy in the Soviet Union. The revolution was fought as an alliance between the peasantry and the proletariat and it derived its whole motive force from the desire of these two social groups to take into their own hands the real power of decisions. Power could only be conquered by workers controlling their factories, peasants their land etc.; the motive force of the revolution thus involved dispersed decision-making. However, Lenin realized very clearly that socialism could not be consolidated or survive for long without an overall system of planning and decision-making to ensure consistency and long-run viability. This required a certain concentration of power and the restriction of participation at the local level, compared with the earlier period.

The crucial problem for any revolutionary movement and process was how and when to make the transition from one form of participation to the other. It was suggested that had it not been for Lenin's knowing exactly how and when to effect the transition and implement the New Economic Policy, the system might have disintegrated. Even during the first eight months Lenin had tried to shift the emphasis from participation at factory level to participation through the trade unions.

In explanation of the Popular Unity's approach to participation in the socially-owned sector, it was claimed that the problem had to be looked at in relation to the kind of socialism which was desired, which depended on the interpretation given to the nature and importance of the contradictions inherent in capitalism.

One way of looking at the contradictions inherent in capitalism centred on the contradictions between the owners of the means of production and their allies — the *gran* bourgeoisie — and the wage-earning masses, to which there was no solution within the context of a capitalist society. Capitalists responded to wage increases with inflation, temporarily neutralizing the rise in wages and the struggle for income distribution. With control over investment in capitalist hands, no legal measure could restrain inflation without preventing growth, and capitalists were therefore the dominant class.

The Popular Unity's interpretation was said to be a more difficult but more important way of looking at the contradictions inherent in capitalism. This emphasized the way in which the capitalist mode of production functioned (monopolization, unequal income distribution, increasing foreign control of national industry) and the consequent restraining effect on the development of an economy like the Chilean one.

The first focus was said to suggest a 'participatory' form of socialism or self-management to solve the problem of who should take the decisions at enterprise level, resolving the problem by identifying workers' income with that of the enterprise. But the other contradictions inherent in the way the capitalist system worked would not be resolved.

The second focus led to a form of socialism which could solve both contradictions simultaneously. It was characterized by effective popular participation at enterprise level and in society as a whole, but enterprises belonged to all workers and the whole of society and not just to those who worked in them.

The essential difference was that 'participatory socialism' was ostensibly based on the premise that capitalism and socialism had the same economic rationale, with the same criteria for economic resource allocation obtaining under both modes of production. Participatory socialism also assumed that both socialism and capitalism could develop underdeveloped countries, the former with participation, the latter with capitalist values dominating.

These features were said to be what basically distinguished the Christian Democrat 'workers' enterprises' from the Popular Unity's participation proposals for the socially-owned sector, and they emanated from different analyses of capitalist society and not from the desire for more or less workers participation in enterprises.

To some, the Chilean road to socialism seemed to involve a paradox if, as had been suggested by some Government participants, there really was no intention of progressing beyond parliamentarianism or 'macro-democracy' to establish workers' management or 'micro-democracy'. 'Micro-democracy' was seen by many as a necessary though not sufficient condition of socialism, or for the take-over of political power by the working class. To insist on the retention of parliamentarianism or 'macro-democracy', which had been described as the essence of the Chilean road to socialism, and oppose full 'micro-democracy' seemed inconsistent to some — and only if the latter supplemented the former, would the Chilean case deserve as its label, 'the Chilean road to socialism'.

It has been claimed by members of the Government that different forms of participation existed in Chile and that the participatory mechanisms instituted by the Government were consistent with the requirement for the overall political, social and economic well-functioning of the state apparatus, and especially the state's regulatory or directive functions. But such statements, and the claim that the Popular Unity's view of socialism entailed "effective participation both at the level of the enterprise and society as a whole", provided participants with no indication of the actual schemes of participation evolving in Chile and the problems involved. It was felt that the discussion should not concentrate too much on theoretical aspects of participation but that some thought should be given to the immediate and more concrete issues concerning participation, especially in the intervened enterprises and socially-owned property sector.

During the industrial sector visits made by one group of participants, it was learned that in 1971 the Government had issued a document which set out a kind of participation model. At the top, the old board of directors was replaced by an administrative committee consisting of five or six directly-elected workers' representatives rather than union nominees, and an equal number of government nominees and the *interventor* — a presidentially-appointed director — as chairman. However, it appeared that there were great variations in the application of this model. Many problems were apparent too. For example, the appointment of state nominees raised political problems in a Popular Front-type government and it was not surprising, therefore, that there were cases in which the state nominations had not been made. Also, the question arose as to whether these nominees should be professional or political appointees, whose main function was to activize the enterprise politically. Should they be from within the enterprise itself or from outside? Often the appointment of a technocrat as *interventor* had led to management difficulties. One union group had explained that in their industry workers' representatives preferred to co-operate with a worker as *interventor* or director rather than with a professional man, however highly qualified and politically motivated he was. However, owing to the inherent educational limitations in a worker's background, it was not easy for him to acquire the knowledge necessary for fixing sales and purchasing policies, or for giving effective production directives. One solution which suggested itself was the type of arrangement to be found in a very large intervened industrial firm in which the administrative committee, headed by an *interventor* with 24 years' experience as a worker, was really a figurehead with most of the important technical and financial decisions in effect being taken by professional advisers from Corfo — the State Development Corporation. However, it was important that the advisers should carry out this function without antagonizing the administrative committee or abrogating to themselves authority, such that the committee felt that it was not taking the final decisions itself. Perhaps a necessary ingredient for this was a degree of political commitment and idealism on the part of the professional advisers.

A further point made was that these difficulties were likely to be compounded by the fact that the technocrats from Corfo would probably be significantly younger than the workers who had been appointed to administrative positions.

Another participant who had also briefly examined the Government's scheme for the structure of worker-participation committees considered the scheme very complex and almost baroque. Fifty separate committees, often with overlapping membership, were to be set up in various shops, sections and departments of an enterprise of about 1,000 workers. Although an elaborate hierarchical structure existed on paper, it was not clear if there was to be any real hierarchical relationship between the committees. At the top there was the administrative committee and below that a co-ordinating committee, both with responsibilities for the whole enterprise; in the absence of further details about their respective roles, the scheme was not at all clear. It was generally felt that excessive complexity should be avoided. One solution would be to transfer some functions, especially of the lower level committees, to the trade unions.

There were a number of aspects which still remained unclear. What was the composition and role of the administrative councils, and the role of the non-worker members? Who appointed them, and to whom were they responsible? Were the administrative councils the principal mechanisms through which worker participation was supposed to operate? Did these councils exercise current control over the enterprise and therefore meet very frequently, or were they intended as an annual review mechanism—and who determined the role of these councils?Did these councils have any role in dealing with concrete matters such as price fixing, or in determining production plans, long-run investment plans and enterprise wage policy? Then there were questions about the management, below the general manager: who appointed them? who determined their salaries, etc? What was the relationship between the administrative council and the trade union within each enterprise?

In describing the current situation in relation to participation, Luis Figueroa stated that the administrative councils, although situated in what seemed a strictly economic context, were to be seen as a new form of controlling political power because in capitalist society those who wielded economic power also had political, legal and all other forms of real power in society. Workers' participation in the production units therefore constituted a form of political power operating through the national economy, with the administrative councils gradually assuming the former functions of capitalist company directors in relation to production, reinvestment, wages etc., but with one great difference. Whereas the board of directors of a capitalist enterprise operated mostly independently of outside institutions like banks or other enterprises, in the new situation the enterprise's powers of decision-making at production unit level had to be integrated into sectoral and overall national decision-making. For Luis Figueroa and many other Chileans a social sector firm only had real social significance if, on the one hand, there was active participation of the workers in the powers of decision-making and, on the other, this took place within a sectoral and national planning framework. From the workers' point of view, the planning of the creation and consolidation of the socially-owned area of the economy was vital, for this sector constituted the political, moral and economic embryo of the new socialist system.

It was recognized that, even with participation, the workers would still be faced with conflicts — now with enterprise executives rather than the capitalists — though the nature of the contradictions would be different. Previously, full agreement with the capitalists was rarely possible and contradictions were resolved through strikes, which constituted a direct class confrontation. In the new situation, in which the character of property had changed, these contradictions could be resolved by different means because the owners were now the whole of society. Conflicts could be studied and resolved by the gradual and partial resolution of all the problems of the workers, taking into account both the specific interests of the workers in a given enterprise, the interest of workers as a class *and* the interests of the nation as a whole.

As far as participation in enterprise planning was concerned, the situation was said to vary widely from one enterprise to another in Chile. Moreover, the public sector contained a great mix of enterprises, ranging from hotels and steel production to large-scale copper mining, and there was no uniformity in their planning methods. Under the Popular Unity Government large-scale enterprises, like ENDESA (Electricity Generating Corporation), ENAP (National Petroleum Company), and CAP (Pacific Steel Company), had begun to discuss their expansion plans with the workers' organisations, and the workers were now involved in discussing the copper industry's production plans. Various experiments along these lines were also taking place in manufacturing. However, the Development Corporation's sectoral committees had taken most initiative in formulating production and investment plans and these would be discussed in the individual enterprise's production committees before being finalized or made public.

It was explained that the involvement of workers in production and investment planning also assumed other forms in Chile. Workers were being involved in the discussion of regional plans and projects, through the Regional Planning Offices. For example, the Antofagasta Planning Office had brought together all the workers belonging to production committees in this essentially mining province, to discuss production targets for 1972. The Government hoped that this very diversity of forms of participation in planning would finally produce an improved system which ensured the effective implementation of plans. Also, the dominant view among Chileans was that it was preferable to let the various forms of participation emerge and evelop for a few more years before trying to rationalize and institutionalize them. It was felt that premature limitation of the forms of participation could lead to unnecessary rigidities, and ran the risk of formalizing schemes which prevented proper contact with all workers in favour of a more convenient system involving a few workers' representatives.

It was also claimed that for the Government to stipulate the forms of participation to be followed would be too paternalistic, it being preferable to encourage or permit the workers to work out their own forms of participation in the initial period.

It was partly for these reasons that the Popular Unity was strongly opposing the Constitutional Reform Bill presented by the Christian Democrats to Congress, which not only tried to institutionalize and limit the socially-owned property sector but also attempted to establish participatory mechanisms similar to those which in other countries had earned the name 'workers' capitalism', or 'profit-sharing', because the workers themselves ran the state, or socially-owned, enterprises.

The view that it was paternalistic to set out some pattern or model for participation was subjected to criticism on the basis that such abstract thinking was not very constructive. It was argued that, unless some ideas and models of participation and techniques to create it were developed, anarchy would ensue and result in the complete absence of any meaningful participation. Nevertheless, it was recognized that there was a danger that excessive attention to organizational charts would mislead the Government into believing that such neat and coherent constructs really reflected the way in which power was wielded and decisions made in the factory or on the farms. It would be important for a proletarian government to understand the real situation operating behind these formal constructs and it was suggested that Chilean sociologists might make a useful contribution in this field.

Participation in Yugoslavia and the Soviet Union

Picking up an earlier suggestion, various non-Chilean participants thought that other countries' experience with participation might contribute some useful ideas and the lessons drawn from this experience might help focus attention on the more important aspects.

The Yugoslavian self-management system gave workers the freedom to fix the price, wages and investment policies for their enterprise and the workers selected their own management. Enterprises were free to integrate or hive off certain activities and were subject to little control with respect to foreign trade.

The main problem was said to be the varying preferences for different types of manager. Some people in industry strongly favoured professional management while others, in particular the trade unions, favoured 'self-management', that is, workers' and workers' council decisions on almost all day-to-day decisions about production and management. This problem was not yet resolved and there was no clear idea of how it would be.

Another problem concerned income differences arising from attempts by individual groups of workers to remedy their situation.

Social and regional differences did exist in Yugoslavia but were almost negligible compared with Chile. It was also true that they were increasing in Yugoslavia but there were efforts and pressures, particularly by the Party, to reduce them. But the most serious problem was said to be the differences between individual enterprises. Workers were the private owners of the means of production and because there were large inter-enterprise differences in technology, capital per worker and monopoly power, workers' incomes varied substantially between enterprises. This created a social problem but, from the economic point of view, what was even more serious was that this structure of distribution was the basis of wage inflation. Owing to the existence of a labour market, the attempt by lower-wage enterprises and industries to catch up with the higher-paid industries constituted a wage inflation mechanism. In fact, from 1960-61 onwards a chronic wage inflation had set in as workers became increasingly independent in wage and price policy formation.

This seemed to be a problem which, according to several people, was likely to affect Chile very seriously, especially in view of the enormous disparities in labour productivity between different branches of activity, such as copper and agriculture.

In Yugoslavia, the Government's response to inflation had been a rather restrictive monetary policy, and the rate of growth of the Yugoslav economy, especially from about 1963 onwards, slowed down.

To counter the large differences in productivity between sectors which had generated wage inflation, the Government should have restructured the tax system so that taxes were proportional to the value of output, and surpluses or differential rents were syphoned off from individual enterprises, utilizing them to relate income more closely to the work actually done.

Apparently the Yugoslav Government had not so far intervened in this way because it still did not realize that since 1960 the mechanics of the Yugoslav economy had completely changed. Some economists claimed that, particularly after 1965, it had developed into a Keynesian economy in the sense that short-run economic activity was dependent on demand and not on capacity, whereas many often still thought in terms of a Sayes Law type economy in which capacity determined economic activity.

Two further reasons explained wage inflation in Yugoslavia. First, the profit-sharing system and the difficulties this entailed for wage control made it easier for wage-push types of inflation to arise. Second, a factor which was perhaps peculiar to the Yugoslav economy, was that to the extent that decision-making was governed by workers' interests which were viewed essentially in material terms, there was a greater tendency for worker-managed enterprises to respond to an increase in demand by increasing price rather than output, than would capitalist enterprises in a similar environment. The workers' management system seemed to have more of an inbuilt inflationary bias than its counterpart capitalist system.

It was also suggested that the Yugoslav economy was more like a Friedman-type economy than a Keynesian one, although its capital market was relatively underdeveloped. The monetary influences which operated on the economy worked strictly through the money supply and there was little of the flexibility of a classical Keynesian-type economy with regard to the absorption of savings.

As regards the overall performance of the Yugoslav economy under widespread workers' self-management, opinions in Yugoslavia were said to vary widely. Analysis restricted to the earlier period concluded that self-management was a very efficient way to organize the economy and those concentrating on the second period drew more pessimistic conclusions. The verdicts were based on historical analyses comparing the development of self-management and economic growth. Worker participation had begun in 1951 but from 1951 to 1960 there was no real workers' management in so far as they were not free to fix prices and wages or utilize the investment funds. During this period, because of changes in economic policies (especially in 1956 when priorities shifted from heavy industry to consumer goods industries) there was a high rate of growth, particularly from 1956-1961 when it was the fastest in the world. The subsequent poor overall performance of the economy was more the result of the Government's economic policy than the system of self-management, in the view of many Yugoslavs.

Another participant, who had studied Yugoslavia closely, explained that, as a matter of deliberate policy, 'micro-democracy' had expanded slowly in Yugoslavia in order to develop the necessary prerequisites. In 1972, factories still did not have genuine worker participation in the central decisions. For example, although worker-managed enterprises could initiate ideas concerning major investments, the final decision was not the sole responsibility of the enterprise. This interdependence in decision-making was also thought to apply to other economic decision areas. However, one unique feature of the Yugoslav system of participation, which was important to take into account when assessing the value of participation to those concerned, was the power of the workers to change their bosses.

Among the prerequisites which had to be developed to permit genuine worker participation in serious decision-making at enterprise level, was an understanding, on the part of works-managers, of the overall macro-framework within which they operated. Awareness of their interdependence with workers outside the enterprise was necessary because, without a certain degree of social consciousness, the necessary self-restraint would not be forthcoming.

Some observers felt that the simultaneous movement towards fairly centralized control, through direct instruments in the state sector, and a multi-tiered system of participation developed at enterprise, consumer and ministerial level, would cause problems in Chile. At a time when profits were being squeezed because of short-term requirements and pressures for wage adjustments, there was a danger of a slowing down in the decision-making process. The Government might lose its power of central control over the state sector. It was possible, therefore, that within a few years Chile would be in need of structural changes in order to recapture the ability to control the state sector.

The problems arising from the combination of the Yugoslav self-management system and government economic policies, were seen by some as a warning to Chile. The overall results in what was supposed to be a workers' state were not in the interests of the working class as a whole, though some groups of workers had bene-fited. In the relationship between participation at the lower levels and the central planning system in Chile, there lacked a mechanism which centralized at a high level the experiences and views of the whole working class. The parties in Chile which declared themselves workers' parties would have to give this priority over their efforts to achieve conciliation with middle-class parties and movements. Also, if government officials existed who were not under the direct control of organisms representing the whole working class, then, as in Yugoslavia, it was likely that economic policies which did not co-incide with, or further the interests of, the whole working class would be implemented.

Others agreed that the political parties, rather than the trade unions or the state machine, were the relevant mechanism for trans-mitting workers' demands from the bottom to the top. However, the possibilities of party workers helping to demonstrate the whole process through ideological education was limited by the very small numbers of cadres available. The Communist and Socialist parties were said to have very few political cadres dedicated to full-time political work. A more concentrated effort by the Popular Unity parties was needed to develop urban and rural working class con-sciousness.

Chileans in particular doubted whether workers' self-manage-ment on Yugoslav lines was a constructive or viable form of participation for Chile, or would lead rapidly in the direction of socialism. Workers in the privileged monopoly enterprises, which had been transferred to the social property sector and were then given the benefit of self-management, would fight to retain or improve their income advantages instead of struggling for the construction of a socialist society. Many Chileans thought that the Christian Democrats and the supporters of their Constitutional Reform Bill had this in mind, when proposing neo-capitalist ideas concerning workers' enterprises.

One view was that workers' management in the social property sector was regarded as neither politically nor economically viable. This sector generated 80% of the country's foreign exchange earnings, accounted for 100% of the financial sector and between 40% and 50% of industrial output — altogether 25% to 30% of G.N.P. Under a workers' management system the decisions affecting such vitally important magnitudes would rest in the hands of no more than 100,000 to 120,000 workers or 4% of the active Chilean population.

About 60 worker-managed enterprises already existed in Chile but they were all small, more or less artisan-type, enterprises with a total of about 1,500 workers between them. The workers had assumed the management functions when the firms went bankrupt or the owners abandoned the country during the previous Government. However, it was interesting to note that in March 1972 these firms sent a joint letter to Luis Figueroa, the President of the CUT (Trades Union Confederation), asking to be integrated into the social property area with all the conditions, restrictions and duties that this involved.

Discussion shifted to the experience of the Soviet economy. Decentralization and participation were being introduced there as part of the economic measures to achieve a higher standard of living, which now constituted the country's current main objective. To achieve this, labour productivity had to be raised and technical progress increased and this in turn involved three important reforms — namely (1) individual enterprises were to be granted greater independence, such that they no longer had to follow centrally dictated norms and indicators; (2) the economic and financial situation of individual firms would in future reflect their own efforts; and (3) there would be increased worker participation in management. However, these reforms were taking place in a context in which the Government continued to control most prices.

The first steps involved participation in the formulation of long-term plans for 1990 and the annual operational plans. To ensure proper plan fulfilment, moral and material incentives were being developed. One new form of incentive was the establishment of three central funds for (1) technological development; (2) individual incentives and (3) social and cultural activities including nursery schools, housing and sports facilities. These funds received what was left after paying off credits, taxes and the contribution to the State, and the decisions concerning how much of the balance should go into each fund was determined jointly between the enterprise's management and the unions. Initially 190 enterprises were subject to these decentralizing reforms, but now all production branches and sectors, including transport and commerce, were going over to the new system. Results had been very positive; workers' enthusiasm had increased and production efficiency had risen. The incentive fund depended directly on enterprise performance, and if it were increased too much, relative to the development fund, this would affect technical advance and within a few years the incentive fund itself would diminish.

Most prices were centrally determined in order to prevent inflation and were fixed for long periods at a time. However, the prices of goods which did not have widespread use throughout the economy were fixed by the enterprise in conjunction with the marketing organizations. The stability of prices facilitated enterprise planning and provided firm expectations regarding the growth of the three new enterprise funds.

The question was raised as to what kinds of mechanisms had been established to prevent growing inequalities between workers in the most advanced and the less advanced industries, resulting from the economic reforms. In reply, it was pointed out that the new philosophy concerning wages was that workers who worked most received most, and that in efficient enterprises where economies in the use of materials and power, and rationalization and good organization resulted in costs substantially lower than prices, the benefits should be passed on to the workers. However, minimum wages were fixed for a large number of branches and sectors, especially those where conditions were worst, and any wage differentials came from the incentive funds.

Looking back over post-revolution history in the Soviet Union, one speaker suggested that it was only during the first eight months of the Soviet régime that there was worker participation in operative decision-making at factory level. Workers' control of the factories and syndicalism were abolished after this difficult period, and worker-participation in productive decisions and price policy was never re-introduced. Since then one-man management and responsibility for production decisions had been predominant though there was some participation through production committees which were specially concerned with inventions and how to make production more efficient at shop floor level. But suggestions were passed up for the management to accept or reject. Also there was participation through the trade union factory committee on matters such as factory amenities, health and social justice, but not production decisions.

The Problem of Historical Analogies

Many references had been made to other socialist revolutionary situations in an attempt to compare and contrast experience on participation with the Chilean one, according to a Chilean participant, and certain seemed to infer that solutions to transformation problems from radically different historical contexts were being suggested as suitable for Chile. The question of historical specificity, a fundamental Marxist point, had in his view been almost totally neglected in the discussion with the attendant risk of drawing unscientific, erroneous conclusions.

The problem was illustrated with the example of dual power, in which new institutions like factory committees spontaneously developed parallel to the existing bourgeois ones, as in the model of the *soviets,* which one participant had postulated as the fundamental basis for developing revolutionary consciousness. This was indeed what had occurred in Russia under Kerensky but it was claimed that there was a difference between the institutional framework of Kerensky's Russia and that existing in Chile under Allende.

The *soviets* — revolutionary factory committees — evolved in response to the problems posed by the Russian revolutionary process itself. In 1917 the state apparatus and its role as main regulator of the existing production process had been destroyed and trade unionism was not yet very developed. In contrast, Chile had a long tradition of strong trade unionism and class struggle and it had not been necessary to destroy the state apparatus in order to allow the workers' movement to take power. In this speaker's view a system of dual power in Chile would cause serious disruption in the overall revolutionary process.

Important differences were also pointed out between the Yugoslav and the Chilean situation such that the systems of participation and, eventually, self-management would assume a totally different character. In Yugoslavia the working class had achieved hegemony because the whole of the state apparatus was in the hands of the working class and not just the executive, as in Chile. Nor did the Yugoslav working class have to compete in conditions of complete equality with the bourgeois class in expressing and organizing themselves, and conquering and reconquering the state apparatus. The dictatorship of the proletariat did not exist in Chile but rather an advanced form of liberal democracy, in which totally opposing social classes and tendencies co-existed, and they engaged in increasingly severe confrontations as the revolutionary process advanced. While this liberal bourgeois state remained unchanged, operating on the Rousseaunian lines of majority representation and majority will, it remained open to changes in control. To the extent that the organized workers' movements were able to control parliament as well as the executive, further institutional changes could be made as the revolutionary process advanced.

Workers' Interests and the Common Good

In the debate on participation and the socially-owned property sector, several possible causes of conflict between the interests of particular groups of workers and the interests of the working class as a whole were identified. If workers' participation was to extend to wage and price fixing at enterprise level, this raised awkward problems concerning income distribution, inflation and capital accumulation. With worker participation in wage setting, the tremendous disparity in economic power and productivity between highly concentrated industries and smaller enterprises, combined with the pressures arising from the demonstration effect, would make it even more difficult to successfully manage a co-ordinated incomes policy and keep prices in check.

In the opinion of other participants, there was not necessarily a contradiction between workers' participation in wage setting etc., and the interests of the working class as a whole. Whether or not micro-level decisions had macro-level repercussions depended on the overall economic and political decision-making system, and the way the individual decision-making unit was integrated into this system.

In their view, the real decision which determined the level of wages and salaries was, in effect, taken when the overall allocation of resources was decided on and the basket of goods and services to be produced was determined. Real wages were determined by the transformation of effective income into real consumption, and therefore, enterprise-level decisions could only influence to a limited extent the overall economic situation. For this reason, there was not necessarily any real problem in concentrating at enterprise level all those decisions most related to enterprise efficiency and to the optimum use of the enterprise resources, as well as the decisions of a social welfare nature. The technical complexity of the problem did not mean there was no solution to it.

It was also suggested that, where a socially-owned and private sector co-existed, worker participation in profit decisions in the former involved an apparent contradiction. If the workers wished to maximise their reinvestable surplus they would need to exercise a degree of self-restraint in their salary demands, but restraint on prices, in the interests of the common good, would rebound to the benefit of the private sector, whose inputs from the socially-owned sector would be relatively cheaper.

This sort of issue raised important policy problems for both the Government and workers' management committees and also raised questions concerning working class sacrifice and the attitudes and role of trade unions in the future. Was there any chance of getting the working classes to understand or accept a certain amount of sacrifice in consumption, and of introducing some form of rationing, in view of the need to preserve foreign exchange resources for vital capital goods imports and to build up stocks?

Another crucial question was how the CUT would act in this complicated class struggle. Would it function as a class organization waging the workers' economic demands through the existing class parties, supporting the Government? Or, would the CUT maintain a certain independence from the political parties and the Government *per se* and concentrate on pushing the workers' claims? There was a difficult course to steer between pressing the workers' demands to the point which caused a profound socio-economic crisis and toppled a government which provided the only real chance of the workers taking power, and, on the other hand, frequently conceding to the government's position and subordinating their specific interests to the overall policy and strategy.

Several Chileans present felt it was necessary to clarify the attitudes and behaviour of the Chilean working classes. Compared with the working classes in many other countries, the Chilean proletariat was said to be much less concerned with narrow economic interests and pressing their rightful claims. Otherwise they would have supported more firmly the paternalist reformist governments in Chile. Their ability to form an overall view of the need for profound transformation had provided a solid backbone to the left political movement for many years.

Nevertheless, it was recognized that it would be completely utopian to suppose that the Chilean proletariat, which included people in a wide range of different situations with correspondingly different attitudes, was solely motivated by political consciousness and gave no thought to the improvement of their economic circumstances. Under the capitalist system they had always been forced to sacrifice in order to finance the economic growth of the parasite class and their increasing monopoly power. Now that the workers' parties were in power, the achievement of a new economic, social and political status for the working classes was to be the basis of the new society being developed, and the Popular Unity Government felt obliged to improve the situation of the proletariat immediately. This was also dictated by the special nature of the politico-economic process underlying Chile's road towards socialism. Also, if, as was clear, the Government did not have sufficient control over prices, incomes and expenditure to prevent inflation, then it needed sufficient power to ensure that the burdens of inflation did not fall on the working classes.

One view, which the Popular Unity shared, was that there should be no attempt to limit working class wage demands in the interest of some abstract common good. The workers' struggle for improving their own immediate economic situation was correct and necessary, because it was the only objective political force which could enforce a redistribution of income and power in favour of the working classes, in the present political context. If sacrifices were to be made by any group, then it should be the higher income classes.

Chapter 4

DISCUSSION ON SOCIAL CONSCIOUSNESS AND SOCIALIST COMMITMENT

Introduction

The importance of social consciousness and socialist commitment had been frequently referred to and it was recognized that, in view of their increasing importance as the transition period progressed, it was necessary to analyse in more detail the ways that social consciousness could be heightened and also the obstacles to its development. Bertram Silverman and James Petras in turn provided some introductory ideas to stimulate the discussion, which helped to clarify the issues and evaluate the magnitude of the task ahead.

In Bertram Silverman's opinion, success in the Chilean road to socialism depended on the critical task of developing socialist consciousness. It was a factor directly related to Chile's economic strategy and economic organization. But, whereas a great deal had been heard about legal restrictions on economic policy, there were no apparent limitations on the organization of workers and peasants or on the development and mobilization of socialist consciousness and commitment. The latter were questions of political will, organization and strategy. Yet, various participants had suggested that progress in relation to economic reforms was more rapid than the organization and mobilization of the rural and urban working class in the transformation period.

It had been indicated that 85% of the rural population remained outside the agrarian reform, a large proportion of rural workers remained unorganized and 70% of the small and medium peasants had been affected by agrarian reform. It was not clear whether the agrarian reform had significantly modified the conservative traditional peasant mentality; there were indications that it had contributed to class conflicts between rural workers and peasants. Some studies showed considerable support for collectivization but against this background the commitment to organize the rural proletariat and peasantry appeared to have been very limited, with relatively few full-time party cadres working in the rural sector. A further cause for concern was the fact that 85% of Indap's[1] technical staff, working with peasants, were from opposition parties. This problem of the old bureaucracy influencing the process of socialist development had been of great concern to Lenin during the early stages of the Soviet Revolution, and would have to be dealt with by the Chileans.

Bertram Silverman thought such problems as these were critical because they were related to economic strategy. For example, the re-distribution policy resulting from the agrarian reform posed the problem of how to extract marketable surpluses to ease tensions in the cities and help resolve the balance-of-payments problem. The fostering of collective consciousness could help in confronting this problem, and could be achieved by increasing the organization of both rural and urban workers by involving the latter in the development and organization of social consumption, such as schools, health centres etc.

He felt, too, that the organization of workers in small and medium private enterprises outside the critical economic sectors was also very important, particularly when the transition process began to increase the divisions within society. The first stage of transition was relatively easier because the expropriation of the *latifundia* and the foreign monopolies united the nationalist aspiration of both the working and middle classes. Once the process began to affect the national bourgeoisie, conflicts would certainly begin to appear. A strategy aiming primarily at reducing the fears of the middle class, rather than the organization of committed social consciousness in the working classes, was likely to undermine the base of Government support once the development process called for increasing economic sacrifices. Moreover, such a strategy raised serious doubts about the meaning of socialist transformation.

Unless socialist consciousness were developed, Bertram Silverman thought the workers would question the need for sacrifices. Socialist commitment was not merely an educational process but a dialectical one resulting from participation by rural and urban groups in the struggle to achieve socialism. Attempts to implement socialism from above left the workers completely outside the process. He regarded the development of national and social consciousness as essential, as Chile entered a new phase of economic development. The structural transformation undertaken had exposed further limitations of the old economic system. As had been made clear, the re-distribution and consumption strategy had created production and invest-

---

[1] Indap — *Instituto de Desarrollo Agropecuario:* Agricultural Development Institute. This Government Agency provides assistance to small and medium-scale peasants.

ment problems, and accentuated the difficulties of reviewing the foreign debt. Moreover, the structural transformations had created unavoidable administrative problems and organizational inefficiency. At this point socialist consciousness and the need for sacrifices became critical, but how could this consciousness be developed without mass organization and mass participation in the transition, or without forging rapidly ahead with the process of building socialism?

The Popular Unity's consumption strategy and its relationship to social consciousness was considered sufficiently important by Bertram Silverman to merit special attention. The Popular Unity's short-term strategy of achieving further income re-distribution to increase the consumption of lower-income groups without seriously affecting middle-class consumption levels was understandable. But such a strategy tended to reinforce self-interest, private gain, rising expectations, and divisions within the working class. Therefore, the question was how to break down this narrow economic self-interest, and develop a broader socialist consciousness, by raising real incomes in terms of collective investment and consumption in education, health, recreation, etc. The development of social rather than individual incentives would be a useful mechanism. The active participation of workers in collective projects and Cuban experience in this field had much to offer.

Cuban experience also highlighted some of the important issues concerning the development of social commitment and socialist consciousness, even though, unlike the case of Chile, the process really began once the problem of control over state power had been resolved. Cuba had invested a great amount of energy in the initial stages in developing socialist consciousness and had risked alienating part of the middle classes, and also risked incurring serious inefficiency problems because of the lack of cadres. Also, in confronting the dependency problem, Cuba placed serious restrictions on its future economic development possibilities because of the resulting embargo and loss of United States markets. But the Cuban process of mobilization and rapid redistribution of income paid off in terms of increased social consciousness and commitment to the revolution, which not only provided the leadership with mass support but also facilitated the creation of a new economic system.

In view of the apparent lag in developing socialist consciousness at this stage of the transition period, it was hoped that more concrete details would be given of the measures contemplated by the Popular Unity to develop mass organization and a social, collective mentality among the working class. Unless more was done to mobilize the masses, the economic consolidation process faced serious risks, with poor response, or even worker-disaffection, manifesting itself when confronted by inherent contradictions such as that between incomes policy and production goals.

Why did bourgeois ideas still predominate among the workers in Chile? According to James Petras, this problem was a reflection of the relative weight of the working class in Chilean society and not of the influence of the bourgeois political parties. Chile could be characterized as an over-modernized, semi-industrialized society with a still relatively small working class, a large service sector, and a very large *empleado* class.[2] Consumption patterns tended to reflect the past and future relations between manual and non-manual labour, with the *empleado* rather than the proletarian ideal predominating. The only way the working-class movement could develop as an independent group was by an increase in its relative size though greater emphasis, in future, on industrialization away from service or unproductive activities.

Another point to which James Petras drew attention was the attempt to inculcate socialist consciousness in a class society when the Government itself assumed responsibility for maintaining it, even if ostensibly for the transition period only. Under such a system, worker response to appeals for greater productivity would be "increased production and sacrifices for whom?" According to James Petras, two strategies were open to the Government in dealing with this problem. The first was a radical one involving drastic levelling and the rapid expropriation of all the means of production as the counterpart for socialist appeals for sacrifices in production and consumption. The second strategy would be to recognize that a progressive welfare state was being developed, not revolutionary socialism, and on that basis encourage worker support for a social democracy by providing socialized health services, better housing, higher salaries etc.

The context in which change took place was also important. For example, if part of the agricultural economy continued in capitalist hands, a capitalist peasantry was likely to result. Expropriation and reform on a farm by farm, or sector by sector basis, could fragment the working class and peasantry rather than create solidarity, lead to uneven development of the different social sectors, and increase the likelihood of income differentation. Conflict was built into the Popular Unity's development strategy, based as it was on the co-

---

2 *empleado* – literally, employees; denotes white-collar workers, clerical and administrative staff etc., as opposed to *obreros* – workers, especially manual workers.

existence of a public, private and mixed sector — and their conflicting social forces. This was likely to lead to serious problems especially because, as the process of change developed and conflicts became manifest, the Government appeared to feel these should be contained while the Opposition was willing to exploit them.

James Petras felt that it was still not possible to talk of a working class consciousness in Chile because a complex situation existed in which no single group dominated. There were workers whose consciousness was limited to economic matters, others with a revolutionary socialist consciousness, and the large majority in between who were willing to express one or other according to the immediate circumstances. Worker consciousness had to be understood with reference to the wider institutional context which conditioned it. The narrow self-interest of the workers was the product of 150 years of experience of the workers' movement and had also been promoted by the working class parties. To the degree that inequality existed, socialism would be understood by the workers as more work and not the collective good. To expect the masses to give a lead to the trade union leaders in the changeover was unrealistic. It was necessary for the political leadership in the parties, and in government, to respond to the challenge and create a dual system of power alongside such opposition institutions as Congress, by promoting new mass organizations like peasant and worker councils, and housing and neighbourhood committees, in a gradual evolution towards new forms of organization and representation. The conflicts arising over concrete political issues, and those between the new organizations of the masses and the old political institutions, would create class tension and polarization and thereby change the consciousness of the masses.

General Discussion

A wide divergence of opinion existed over whether there really was a notable lag in the development of socialist consciousness in Chile. Some Government members agreed that economic change had proceeded more rapidly than had changes in attitudes, and that the development of a revolutionary socialist consciousness had just begun.. Others argued that working class consciousness had begun to develop as far back as the beginning of the century when the first Chilean workers' movements were established. In their view the working class parties, especially the Communist and Socialist parties, had a very developed revolutionary socialist consciousness and they had played a significant part in fomenting it.

Taking his own personal experience, one participant felt that progress in social consciousness was not really slow. On a visit to Chile, twelve years previously, the country appeared troubled and pessimistic, concerned more with its past than with its future. The attention of North American social scientists at that time was focused on whether even the Christian Democrat Party would be able to develop into a viable political unit. In 1970 and 1972 Chile still appeared to be a troubled country, but its attention and energies were concentrated on the future.

To Chilean participants, at least, it was not surprising that bourgeois ideas and logic still influenced the working classes and their leaders, and that revolutionary socialist consciousness seemed to develop slowly, even in the transitional period. The means of communication and of influencing public opinion still remained largely under the control of the Chilean bourgeoisie and certain national and foreign monopoly groups, with far longer experience in handling them than the groups who were trying to develop revolutionary socialist consciousness.

Another speaker suggested that there was an understandable tendency to exaggerate the power of the communications media. If they really were such an effective means of controlling the consciousness of the masses, it was difficult to understand how, in a situation such as the Chilean one where 90% of the media was controlled by the Opposition, the Popular Unity had been able to win the elections.

Socialist consciousness developed through concrete experience in the class struggle and the fight for improved socio-economic and political conditions, and more rapidly the more intense became the class struggle. But the real problem, as several participants were quick to point out, was whether consciousness changed only as a result of changes in the 'superstructure' — i.e., institutions — or through more profound changes in the basic social structure and nature of the State. To a Marxist, the fundamental aspect was the nature and influence of productive relations. It was impossible to discuss the problem of generating new political values and class consciousness among the workers without referring to the transcendental influence of production relations and the relations between work and property.

The current debate on, and struggle for, the consolidation of the social property sector was, then, exceedingly important. The process to establish the material base for social transformation would have a profound effect on social consciousness. The reactionary forces in Chilean society were said to have clearly understood this and fought hard to protect their interests. But less conservative groups had not understood this — although they questioned the old system, they often advocated a reformist policy of marginal changes. If the social property sector was not consolidated, it would be impossible to achieve a radically new socio-economic system by democratic means, because the economic and political advances gained by the workers would be undermined. Seeing that progress could not be made through the democratic proccess, they would look on force as the only alternative.

But if the Popular Unity did manage to consolidate the social property sector, the class enemy would be much less clearly defined and would react more violently — a point which the working classes did not always understand. The history of countries with the longest experience in constructing socialism was said to testify to this fact.

This pointed to the need for political education. History showed that social struggle alone did not automatically give rise to socialist consciousness; it also depended on deliberate efforts by political parties and trade unions to raise the level of political awareness. The Chilean Socialist and Communist parties, particularly, had played a significant part in fomenting the growth of socialist consciousness over a long period of years, but there still remained an enormous task ahead.

It was urged that one should not forget that the current initial stage of the Chilean Revolution took place in a capitalist socio-cultural context. The capitalist criteria of rational behaviour, based on maximum profit, continued to operate at the level not only of factories and farms but also of the national economy. The creation of the socially-owned sector would not necessarily substantially modify this all-pervading influence. Other countries which had started out with complete nationalization had still experienced serious problems in modifying attitudes and creating social consciousness. As a result, Chile was likely to experience problems of investment motivation in the private and mixed sectors; and in the socially-owned sector inefficiencies would arise — all of which would lead to production difficulties and inflation.

Inflation itself was often regarded as a strictly economic problem, but in Chile it was also part and parcel of the values and habits inherited from a capitalist socio-cultural context. Therefore, many Popular Unity measures and mechanisms would have to overcome not only the resistance of opposing political groups but also the wide-spread inbuilt resistance emanating from a capitalist context.

The Soviet Union, China and Cuba had only attempted to formulate the theoretical solution to this problem several years after the revolutionary process had begun. Thus, discussion of Stakhanovism, of the Cultural Revolution in China, and the 'new man' in Cuba, began long after the revolutionary forces were in complete control. In Chile, however, it seemed that the modification of behaviour and values was closely related to the very problem of gaining more power in the short term. Several participants felt the Popular Unity Government should pay more attention to implementing a system of social communication to combat opposing influences, and to develop a social consciousness and a socialist ethos.

In view of the importance of education in developing consciousness, some European participants were surprised that so little had been said about this aspect. Chile appeared to have ambitious plans for the quantitative expansion of education, but the plan documents seemed to make little reference to structural and qualitative changes. According to one view, it was not a question of using education as a vehicle for political propaganda, but rather of providing the sort of education and outlook relevant to the short and medium-term economic structure of the country.

The case of Ceylon was cited. The educational system and its underlying philosophy were quite unsuited to that country's real socio-economic conditions. The recent aborted uprising was partly related to the existence of a large number of well-educated unemployed, and people in government were aware of the need to end the emphasis on urban, white-collar jobs. The status and rewards of white-collar jobs would in the future be such that young people would see rural and agricultural activities as worthwhile and profitable. This would mean giving university education less emphasis, and formal education would end on completion of secondary education except for those going on to very specialized professional courses. It was intended that secondary education would also include a period of practical work experience. Alternative courses of action to implement these ideas were currently being discussed in Ceylon. A first step had been taken in this direction — government white-collar workers at all levels, including top civil servants, were now expected to do a period of manual work. This would change the attitude to manual work.

Chilean participants pointed out that official statistics did not fully reflect the real situation. The Popular Unity Government had had to limit itself to its statutory educational activities. Any efforts to democratize and modernize education in Chile require parliamentary sanction, but the reactionary parties had little substantive interest in legislation permitting workers and peasants access to the universities. The trade union movement itself was therefore developing and financing its own educational system. In 1971 it had set up trade union schools in which 2,500 trade union cadres had received training. In addition, direct agreements between the trade union movement and the universities had enabled many workers to receive a university education. Four hundred youths had entered the School of Medicine to learn medical techniques, and 2,000 workers were attending night classes in the State Technical University. An agreement had also been reached with the National Training Institute (Inacap) to include social education in its training programme for skilled manpower, so that workers could learn about social class structure, the role of the working class, trade unions, government, and the country's political institutions and democracy. The CUT had also recently drawn up a programme for continuing education which went right through from training in literacy to learning a profession or trade.

Popular Unity politicians and technocrats regarded the participation of the proletariat at all levels of society, including enterprises, as being one of the most important ways of educating workers and fostering socialist consciousness. Beside formalizing the growing power of the workers, participation in the running of factories and farms would help wean them away from past attitudes to the purpose of political and trade union struggles. Changes in consciousness resulting from participation in Popular Unity committees, in committees in 'intervened' factories and in peasant councils, was claimed to facilitate changes in the existing capitalist structure which the left political leadership would otherwise be unable to bring about. The Government was said to be planning other ways of trying to develop political awareness and revolutionary consciousness in order to permit the country to progress to further stages along the road to socialism.

Part 6

Future Prospects for the Popular Unity Government and
the Chilean Road to Socialism

Chapter 1

IS THE 'CHILEAN ROAD TO SOCIALISM' BLOCKED?

Alain Joxe*

Preconceived ideas that the present movement for reform in Chile is based on a compromise between Left and Centre, and cannot therefore lead to socialism, need to be re-examined. Whatever the final outcome, Chile at this moment is in a revolutionary situation controlled by a coalition adminstration — reformist in as much as it is a coalition (the Popular Unity), but revolutionary in as much as it includes revolutionary parties and militants acting more or less in harmony with the ultra-left and who aim at going beyond reform. But, beyond this political framework, there is another, less apparent and defined, situation which needs to be analysed, if an answer is to be found to the question, 'Is the Chilean Road to Socialism blocked?'.

Had this question been asked in 1969 with regard to Frei's 'Revolution in Liberty', the answer would certainly have been 'yes'. The Christian Democrats, the party then in power, had a majority in Congress but were no longer actively pursuing their programme, in particular the Agrarian Reform. They were increasingly and openly operating in favour of preserving the *status quo*. The party's inertia was not the result of the usual problem created within the political institutions of Chile by the interval between the Presidential and the Congressional elections. The main obstacle was the combination of the dominant socio-political forces in the national and international field. This period also marked the final days of the Alliance for Progress, of which Chile had been one of the chief beneficiaries. Rivalries within the dominant class led to support being given to two candidates of the Right — Alessandri and Tomic (the latter being selected for his leftist rhetoric). Allende owed his victory at least as much to the division of the Right as to the unity of the Left, winning with a slightly lower percentage of the vote than he obtained on his

* Centre d'Etudes de Politique Etrangère, Paris

last defeat in a Presidential election. The collapse of the 'Revolution in Liberty', which reflected the collapse of Kennedy's plan for Latin America, swung the political balance to the Left.

Can today's situation be regarded as comparable with that of the Frei years? Can it legitimately be said, as it often is, even within the slightly disillusioned parties of the Popular Unity, that the Popular Unity has worn itself out more rapidly during its period in power than the Christian Democrats did after 1964? The answer is no, in as much as the loss of momentum — if there is any such loss — is due to fundamentally different causes. The social and economic reforms and innovations introduced in Chile since Allende became President are of such importance that this 18 month period has been filled with many more possible causes for exhaustion. A government tends to spend itself in exercising power and the ingenious and exhausting efforts of the Popular Unity Government to exercise power to the utmost, within the flexible but narrow framework of the existing laws, is certainly one cause of the loss of momentum. This is often confused with failure, but it can also be seen as the price of success in innovatory political activity. Successive reforms have been carried out at a rate, and with a political purpose, different from that of the Christian Democrats. They are leading towards a real and irreversible political and social confrontation — the transition to socialism. What is referred to as 'exhaustion' is essentially a measure of the hostility of the privileged classes which are under attack.

Thus any purely empirical comparison of the behaviour of political groups on the traditional political stage, leads to errors of perspective, but these errors themselves form part of the ideological warfare conducted by the privileged groups which are on the defensive.

A different political context already exists. The blocking of the 'Revolution in Liberty' was synonymous with the slowing-down of a middle-class modernizing reformist movement. The blocking of 'the Chilean Road to Socialism' must inevitably take the form of a repression of the movement for the revolutionary transformation of society which, under various more or less confused forms, has already penetrated the masses. The first obstacle was resolved by the traditional expedient of elections. The second will be accompanied by a degree of violence and unrest. The forces now on the move are no longer electoral forces, and, though the Right will endeavour to channel these forces into the electoral process, it will only be able to do this by force.

To determine whether or not the road to socialism is blocked, the road itself must first be defined. The description which Luis Corvalan, the General Secretary of the Communist Party, provided in 1962 has not altered to any great extent. It involves two stages:-

1. *Democratic Revolution:* Agrarian Reform, expropriation of foreign investments, and of extractive industries, expansion of the state controlled sector of the economy so as to make it the dominant sector; redistributional and social welfare measures for the benefit of the lower classes. These latter measures were intended to foster or facilitate the mobilization of the masses in support of the revolution.

2. *Consolidation:* the working class becomes the controlling force, thus smoothing the way to socialism.

The overall scheme was to begin with elections and to end without armed confrontation.

The first stage is well under way though certain aspects are still only mid-way to full implementation. Since 'transition' to the second stage of transition to socialism can only be defined as the sum total of the achievement of the various aspects of the first stage, the intended strategy seems to be foundering on a number of separate fronts where tactical difficulties and Clausewitzian 'frictions' render short-term performance vitally important. The question which therefore needs to be asked is whether the Chilean process is blocked, or whether it should employ different means from those originally planned.

It is not possible here to enter into detailed theoretical discussions on transition. For present purposes a more modest and obviously empirical attempt will be made to examine a few current concrete and sectoral processes, in order to make a provisional though necessarily partial and impressionistic diagnosis.

The Popular Unity Government is at a turning point, dictated by the accumulation, over a relatively short period, of a series of internal and external constraints and pressures. Whether the Government likes it or not, the solution which will be found in the coming months to a whole series of urgent problems will tend either towards the collapse of the Chilean process and increasing compromise with anti-socialist forces or towards a revival of the revolutionary process. Arguments that in its electoral programme the Popular Unity never claimed that the transition to socialism would be effected under the present presidency, or whether this view was shared or refuted by responsible Chilean political decision-makers, of one tendency or another, are of purely superficial interest. The truth is that world interest in the Chilean process stems from the possibility of transition to socialism and the fact that large-scale mobilization of the Chilean masses is based on the prospect of eliminating capitalism, not modernizing it.

This makes it difficult, if not impossible in the present process, to distinguish clearly between the 'obstruction' to modernization and the 'obstruction' in the movement towards the transition to socialism, both with respect to the anti-capitalist and the reactionary forces. The counter-offensive of the Right, which for many months has seemed imminent, now seems not far off.

In the lobbies of Congress, a legal impasse, aimed at creating a governmental crisis as the result of the abortive confrontation of the executive and the legislature, is being prepared. The imperialist counter-offensive at present assumes the discreet form of blocking Chilean funds in the United States and the negative attitude adopted by the United States in the Paris negotiations on the refinancing of Chile's external debt. The threat to the Chilean economy, opportunely recalled to mind by the publication of the 'ITT secret documents', far from promoting an upsurge of nationalism in middle-class circles, provoked a rebound to the Right. In these circumstances, a Popular Unity victory in the 1973 Congressional elections can in no way be regarded as a certainty. Consequently the possibility of controlling the legislative power, which is needed if the revolutionary reforms are to be carried out in a legal manner, is jeopardized. This electoral victory would allow the Popular Unity to govern, to show what it can do, and to firmly establish the popularity it needs to ensure the victory of another Left candidate in the 1976 Presidential elections. Theoretically, a Congressional victory in 1973 and a Presidential victory in 1976 fulfil the same role as, generally, armed struggle does in the destruction of the bourgeois state. The prospect of an electoral defeat inevitably creates the probability of confrontation, though such a confrontation is not uniquely determined by such a formal event as the date for elections. It is therefore necessary to identify the obstructions which operate at the level of the Government's socio-economic policy in order to understand their possible effect at the more political level.

*   *   *

Action on socio-economic factors is being pursued on three main fronts: agrarian reform; the extension of the 'socially-owned sector of production'; and the foreign debt, treated as a particular case in the general framework of international conflict between under-developed and developed countries.

1. *Agrarian Reform.* The Agrarian Reform is going ahead at full speed. Nevertheless the growth of popular awareness, and the creation and organization of a class of peasant owners initiated by the Christian Democrats under the Frei government, raises fresh problems. Until a few years ago, organized demands for land by Chilean agricultural workers hardly existed. As a general rule, with certain sectoral or regional exceptions, the *inquilino* — and, indeed, the *minifundista* — would have switched over, without difficulty, to a co-operative or socialized form of agriculture, once the *latifundista* class had been eliminated. Today, Chile is experiencing a real agricultural revolution which will lead to the elimination of the *latifundia* and the *latifundista* class. Though the desire to eliminate the *latifundistas* remains a unifying factor among the various categories of agricultural workers, the Popular Unity must come to grips with the peasant problem. The fact that the Christian Democrats continue to mobilize apparently to their benefit certain 'anti-feudal' revolutionary elements among this new peasantry (still partially 'in power' in the *asentamientos*) emphasizes certain contradictions within the popular rural classes. In analysing this phenomenon, the various Popular Unity groups all too often do little except to take up a political stance, since the political views adopted by the Christian Democrats (favouring the interests of the small and medium peasant proprietor classes) have led the Popular Unity groups to adopt diametrically opposed positions. Thus, while seemingly bent on maintaining a certain degree of state domination in the Agrarian Reform Centres, the Government is compelled, by virtue of the pressure exerted by the competing forces, to make concessions, either to the Left, or to the capitalist agricultural sector. This general line, together with its exceptions, can only be defined as *strategy* or *tactics* from the traditional political point of view; it cannot be regarded as a clear definition of the strategy of the working class in relation to the peasant problem. If this political opportunism continues, it is obvious that the new peasant class, whose differences with regard to the working class need be in no way antagonistic, could, as a class, only support the latter through the medium of the Christian Democrats, as a political tendency. From the general political point of view, this implies all manner of further compro-

mises and constitutes one of the first points which act as a brake on the process.

2. *Extension of the socially-owned sector.* By nationalizing the banks and mines and, particularly, the copper mines, the Government has been able to appropriate the surplus and to control the main source of foreign exchange. But the mines are not the dominant sector of the economy, merely the main source of finance. Moreover, on a world scale, investment in raw materials exploitation is no longer the principal point of imperialist pressure, viewed as a still expanding system. The decisive stage of the development of the nationalized sector has therefore not yet been reached, neither in the strategically-important sectors from the point of view of the anti-imperialist struggle, nor in the sectors of fundamental tactical importance from the point of view of the internal political struggle. All monopolistic enterprises were originally to be embraced in the expansion of the socially-owned property sector; but the Government has announced its intention to include 91 companies, most of which are already occupied, 'intervened', or requisitioned. Though this number still represents a sufficient nucleus to ensure government control of production, it cannot be allowed to diminish further, for both economic and political reasons.

In this context the Christian Democrat opposition (obviously allied to the Right, despite denials by the 'Tomic' tendency, which is currently powerless) seems bent on depriving the Government of this basic requirement for the further development of its policy. The definition of the three sectors of production (social, mixed, private) is to be put to a constitutional reform vote, for which the Christian Democrats' votes are indispensable. The small radical party PIR (Party of the Radical Left) was given responsibility for negotiating a compromise formula. Implementation of the Popular Unity's economic programme may be slowed down by the unprecedented maze of Chilean parliamentary procedure or it may well be completely blocked by an abortive legal confrontation. If the Popular Unity fails to find a way of avoiding this hold-up or of breaking through this obstruction, it will be paralyzed and will lose control of the economy as well as of the legal-political system.

It still has four years left in office in which to govern under impossible conditions. It runs the risk of losing the 1973 elections, and of having to depend more and more on the goodwill of the Christian Democrats. Allende's government would then be described as the moment in Chilean political history when the dependent Chilean bourgeoisie astutely left to the popular parties the task of reforming the system, in order to avoid the civil war which the foreseeable blunders of the Alessandri group would probably have unleashed. (The Christian Democrats voted in favour of Allende as President in Congress.) Once the core of state monopoly capitalism has gained sufficient strength, but within limits which ensure the reversibility of the socialization process, and after having finally reinforced the state apparatus (in which the parasite middle classes are traditionally entrenched) with new, more or less opportunist classes, Allende would then have to hand over power to Frei in 1976 in disastrous ideological confusion. This at least is the picture of events preferred by the Christian Democrats. The alternative, put forward by the orthodox Right, is the rapid removal of Allende, this year, by putting him on trial in the High Court on a charge of unconstitutional action. Senator Bulnes of the National Party advocated this scheme on 9 March, during a televised broadcast; but this is an extreme position and assumes that the President has completely lost his popularity, if the impression that Parliament is nothing but a cynical elite is to be avoided. Allende is, however, still extremely popular, even if the Government is beginning to be criticized for day-to-day problems. It is therefore very improbable that the Right will suceed in carrying out its scheme, unless they combine it with some form of violent, fascist-type action.

Nevertheless, due to lack of power to carry through its economic reform programme, the Government is undoubtedly heading for political collapse, particularly if its mass mobilization campaign continues to rest on the assumption that its policy of redistribution of real incomes will increase its support. Short-term economic tactics of this nature are a mistake, as nearly everyone agrees today. The discontent created by supply difficulties cancels out the satisfaction normally associated with a real increase in the workers' purchasing power. Conversely, owing to its failure to continue and intensify the political struggle for power, the Government, defenceless in the face of sabotage, the black market, and speculation, and politically powerless to introduce exceptional measures such as the rationing of certain commodities, will certainly experience economic collapse. The struggle for 'political power', which would change the existing balance of forces such that the Government's economic plans went unhindered by parliamentary obstruction, is not a political struggle within the framework of the established institutions of the middle-class State, but a political struggle at the level of new institutions for the masses, which signify the beginnings of dual power.

3. *External Pressure.* The external debt has been an additional paralyzing factor limiting internal room for manoeuvre. In this respect the Chilean economy has several vulnerable points: plan implementation depends on an adequate supply of unsubstitutable vital goods, paid for in dollars. Delivery is threatened less by the weight of the overall debt than by the possible withdrawal of all short-term commercial credits. Should the United States decide to resort to a confrontation by closing off credit possibilities, Chile will soon find herself in an impossible financial situation, and active preparations are being made on the assumption that such a decision may be taken before the end of the year. The presence in Santiago of the UNCTAD Conference will provide Chile with a few months' respite, since one does not embark upon the economic strangulation of a small country while it is playing host to a vast assembly of expert observers, paid to find a solution to the under-development of the Third World. But good strategy obviously precludes counting upon the indefinite prolongation of the hostile inaction which up until now has characterized America's reaction. It may be that the Russians and the Chinese are already in a position to provide tactical support in the form of hard currency credits. But nobody wants a repetition of the Cuban case, neither the Chileans nor the Russians, and this means having to suffer a certain number of indignities. The most serious, perhaps, in the present phase (in which a large number of variables which determine the future of 'the Chilean Road' appear to have become distorted) is the fact that the onus of the debt will weigh heavily on the image of herself which Chile wishes to project to the outside world and may lead to a number of temporizing decisions at home. The implementation this year of the programme for redistribution of real incomes will inevitably mean a lowering, for the first time, of the real living standards of the privileged classes and, consequently, to a natural intensification of the class struggle. To meet this situation, which already exists, the Government should not slow down, but accelerate, their political process. But this tendency, for which Vuscovic, the Minister of Economics, has been responsible, is not compatible with the reasonable middle-class image necessary to reassure creditors.

These three points of obstruction are clearly reflected on the political scene by an appreciable acceleration of the polarization process and by an increase in the military's role as arbiter. To explain this development, it must be borne in mind that the Communist Party has, since assuming governmental responsibility, endeavoured to keep open more political options than any other party. To its

Right, it leaves the way open to negotiation with the Christian Democrats; to the Left, with the MIR through the intermediary of the Popular Unity — two sets of negotiations which cannot remain compatible indefinitely. Success in one implies failure in the other. The Communist Party has never abandoned the hope of reaching an understanding with the left wing of the Christian Democrat Party — the MAPU (United Popular Action Movement), then the MIC (the Christian Left Movement), have only partially and temporarily fulfilled this hope. The MAPU very quickly took a Marxist-Leninist turn when it renounced its Christian origins, barring its chances of enticing away the Left militants still adhering to the Christian Democrat Party. The MIC, which has not renounced its purely Christian ideology, has on many occasions adopted ultra-left points of view despite the 'responsible' centralist policy preached by the Minister of Agriculture, Jacques Chonchol, one of its principal leaders. It seems that the Christian Democrats cannot throw in their lot with the Popular Unity without ceasing to be Christians and without ceasing to be moderates, representing the middle class. Hence the desirability of negotiating with the Christian Democrat Party, such as it is, trying to neutralize it through its internal divisions rather than attempting to split it further. These negotiations, which the Tomic faction condemns as 'anti-capitalist and anti-putschist', have less and less chance of leading anywhere for the moment. The 'Freist' group is at present in control of the Party machine and is openly operating in alliance with the orthodox Right of the National Party, and even with the 'Patria y Libertad' (Fatherland and Freedom) fascists.

For several months now, the Communist Party, or more precisely, the Popular Unity, has been engaged in conversation with the MIR. These discussions, held in President Allende's presence, are unlikely to lead anywhere. The MIR would like a basic discussion about the whole revolutionary process and about strategy. The Communist Party opposes this, arguing that the MIR is not a member of the Popular Unity and that the only purpose of discussion is to seek tactical agreements, aimed particularly at restraining the 'opportunist and adventurist' activities perpetrated in various sectors on the basis of exploiting a certain mass spontaneity. According to the Government, Mirist activities cannot be associated with the strategy of alliance and class conflict theoretically defined by the Popular Unity (to alienate neither the medium-scale peasants, nor the middle-class industrialists). But the MIR continues to function as a police force and anti-plot organization and their advice is sought in cases of emergency. The Communists, whilst recognizing that MIR militants would be brave and useful militants in the event of the fascist Right deciding to resort to open armed conflict, have no hesitation in launching an extremely violent propaganda campaign against them through commercial advertising media, in which they are depicted as agents acting in the interests of the CIA. It seems likely that there will be no rapprochement between the Popular Unity and the Christian Democrats, and also perhaps an irreparable breach between the Communist Party and MIR.

The Armed Forces and the Political System

In general, observers of the military scene agree on the paradoxical existence of, on the one hand, increasing discontent and concern within the armed forces over government policy, and on the other, a genuine manifestation of satisfaction over their mounting prestige and recognized status, never granted by previous governments, and an increasingly clearly defined process of integration into and, as it were, commitment, on the part of the officers, to the economic and social currents precipitated by the Government's policy. These two aspects coexist in the maintenance of traditional loyalty to the President, on the one hand, and on the other, in the use of certain precise control mechanisms to prevent conspiracies materializing in a confrontation.

1. *Discontent and Concern.* On the whole, the officers' attitude to the Government reflects the same reticence as that from the entire upper-middle class to which they from now on belong; especially since the improvement in their status granted by the Popular Unity. The causes of contention stem from difficulties associated with supply shortages, apprehension at the prospect of the reorganization of society, and of an upheaval for which they see no need. The level of professional qualification (or military sub-culture) of senior officers is archaic, more so, probably, than that of the young officers, all of whom have been partially trained in the United States. They have received no systematic training to enable them to analyse the political and social factors which both underpin and undermine the Chilean revolutionary process. Awareness of the overall issues affecting society is only just beginning to awaken among the military. Collectively, they remain ensconced behind their purely professional principles, individually, they adhere closely to the standard patterns of their class of origin and to moderate options of Right or the Centre. There is, of course, a good deal of anti-communism, and the

absence of any form of global analysis prompts the majority of officers, who have no real ties with the business world, to regard with suspicion the development of a situation which seems very disorderly, and to not consider relating it to the existence of a right-wing and imperialist plot. The officer corps therefore constitutes a breeding ground for military conspiracies, which in Chile are the romantic and almost innocent speciality of retired officers. These extra-murally organized conspiracies do gain verbal support from a not insignificant number of serving officers, giving the conspirators the illusion of considerable strength. But this strength collapses on the vital day, under various pretexts, because there is a considerable difference between lending a sympathetic ear to now retired friends and taking part in unlawful activities against a legitimate government which so far has given nothing but cause for satisfaction.

Whereas this widespread feeling of unease and discontent among the armed forces is nothing more than the ideological reflection of the privileged classes, whose high standard of life is from now on threatened, the officers are in fact a privileged part of the bureaucracy. Traditionally paid in kind, their standard of living is not endangered by price manipulations, fiscal policy or differential salary adjustments. The Right, fearing that the significance of this differential treatment may become obvious to the military, endeavours to use this fact for its own ends. In its polemical newspapers it occasionally abuses the officer corps with the taunt that 'the Army has allowed itself to be bought with a car and house.'

The Armed Forces' self-attributed role of guardians of the law calls for their intervention only in the event of serious violation of the law on the part of the Government, or serious armed disturbances. The Chilean legal framework is sufficiently elastic to turn the process of defining its 'violation' into an interminable legal controversy. Until Congress, still dominated by the Christian Democrats, decides to head for an insoluble legal conflict, 'moderate' violations of the law will continue to be legally perpetrated. These occur every day; they are common to both Right and Left and incur no risk whatever of automatic intervention on the part of the Armed Forces. But should the Right and the United States decide to strike a heavy legal blow and drive the President into a position from which there is no legal way out, there is absolutely no valid reason to believe that a considerable proportion of the military would not choose, as in 1891, to defend the President by a show of anti-parliamentarianism and patriotism, as characteristically traditional of all the armies in the world as their anti-Left tendencies.

The anti-parliamentarian criticism that 'the President isn't allowed to govern' is voiced not only by certain generals but also by shanty-town dwellers. The Government is therefore anxious to get the military to participate — as far as the Armed Forces' constitutional attitude of non-involvement in political issues permits — in the actual social upheaval itself. This has been done, not by giving preference to officers holding leftist views, but by utilizing their social and technical qualifications for administrative and implementation purposes. As a result of this policy, traces of 'Peruvianism' and 'Caamanism' are gradually beginning to appear within a group which up till now was cut off from the large popular movements.

2. *Benefits and Participation.* The main economic benefits include special credits for house construction; pay readjustments more favourable than those applied to equivalent civilian salary grades; new uniform allowances; etc. There are also two important professional benefits. Firstly, there is a new armaments purchase programme which has not been published. The amounts involved are apparently fairly substantial and not budgeted for, and will, of course, directly affect the balance of payments.

Secondly, relations with the Cuban Army will provide professional benefits. Chilean sailors and airmen have always manifested a genuine desire to acquire professional expertise. The 'Unitas Manoeuvres' organized by the United States have, for example, always been justified by the Navy from the purely professional point of view. 'If the Russians were to suggest joint manoeuvres, we would immediately accept,' a naval officer declared at the end of the Frei administration. Today, the friendly relationship with the Cuban State makes it possible for Chilean pilots, up to now accustomed only to flying old subsonic Hawker Hunters, to train in Migs together with their Cuban colleagues, and for the sailor to become acquainted with the ultra-modern Soviet equipment used by the Cuban Navy. But these visits are still only isolated occurrences.

As regards participation, at inter-ministerial level, the Government has set up numerous bodies or committees through which Armed Forces' representatives are invited to present the 'national defence' point of view. An ODEPLAN-Armed Forces' joint commission meets monthly and is responsible for co-ordinating the development plan and the security plan. The Army has been entrusted with special responsibilities in certain southern frontier regions, either on account of the traditional fear of frontier action from Argentina, or in order to control the arms traffic conducted from the neighbouring country by the extreme Right or revolutionary Left. In the Nuble province, the Army is responsible for rapidly training several thousand peasants as tractor operators.

The Government has conferred new importance on the 'Military Work Service', created at the time of last year's earthquake to carry out reconstruction and public works. It encourages intellectual exchanges between Army officers and Government departments by means of frequent departmental meetings and technical talks at the Military academy. The military now shares in the administration of regional development and of the mines, with a number of military engineers detached to the mines as 'interventors'. In the province of Magallanes an outgoing *Intendente*[1] has been replaced by a general.

The Army is ready to step in to ensure the replacement of middle-class political groups where issues of modernizing political reform and the recovery of national resources are concerned. Even in this moderate capacity, the military may suddenly appear as a substitute for the middle-class parties in the Popular Unity. With the responsibilities of power, and obliged to present their views in the collective decision-making organs where they are confronted with representatives of political parties, it is probable that the Armed Forces, contrary to the intention of the Executive, will be increasingly driven towards assuming the role of a further middle-class party, presenting a radical or Tomic type position within the Popular Unity.

On the other hand, increased military participation in the responsibilities of the Popular Unity Government obviously entails a concomitant increase in authoritarianism where political procedures are concerned. Even if in the short term it provides an assurance against confrontation, in the medium term the 'entry of the military into the Popular Unity' would imply the abandoning of consolidation and a slowing-down of the revolutionary dynamic.

The answer to the question 'Is the Chilean Road to Socialism blocked?' is that the Chilean Road, defined in the programme of the Popular Unity based on an idyllic electoral process, is certainly blocked; but then, what long-term political plan has ever been realized in strict accordance with its pre-election design? A more apposite question to ask would be whether all possibility of transition to socialism *without civil war* is from now on blocked to Chile. In spite of all the tensions, and without wishing to pose as a prophet,

---

[1] *Intendente:* Provincial Governor, this is a political appointment and the *Intendente* is the President's representative in the province.

it does not seem that civil war is likely, even though the adversaries are armed (or perhaps because they are armed). Chile is the only real historically old national state on the continent. It is also the only country where a conscious and irrepressible politicized Left has been established for several generations. There will therefore be a Chilean Road to Socialism. But, without confrontation — victorious confrontation — this road will inevitably be via the slow conversion to socialism of the Armed Forces, of the Christian Democrats and of the middle classes, detaching them from the imperialist pole of attraction. And that will not be a question of a legislative agreement.

Chapter 2

DISCUSSION ON WHETHER THE CHILEAN ROAD
TO SOCIALISM IS BLOCKED

The Nature of the Chilean Road to Socialism

The question whether the Chilean Road to Socialism is blocked
addresses itself basically to two problems:

i   do the difficulties encountered constitute permanent obstacles
     to achieving socialism by the chosen strategy, and

ii   would another strategy be more relevant and successful?

Discussion centred on the nature of the Chilean Road to Socialism,
and the various stages to be passed through. It was emphasized that,
as President Allende and the Popular Unity had often declared,
neither the Government nor its programme was socialist: the Popular
Unity's intention was to set in motion a long process, which would
eventually lead to socialism, and which would involve passing
through certain not easily distinguishable stages. The Popular Unity
was leading a democratic revolution against imperialism and the
oligarchy — an essential first stage in a developing country such as
Chile — by retrieving Chile's basic natural resources from foreign
control, ending the domination of the *latifundia* in the countryside,
and putting an end to foreign and domestic monopoly power. The
fact that the class alliance was not purely anti-imperialist, but also
attacked the interests of the foreign-linked national bourgeoisie, was
seen as a guarantee against the renewed development of external
dependence.

There was nothing particularly Chilean or unique about this
gradual advance by stages towards socialism. Lenin, in his work on
'Proletarian Strategies in the Bourgeois Revolution', had already
written about it in 1905. The need for an initial programme that was
essentially anti-imperialist and democratic rather than socialist, not
only corresponded to the Chilean situation but also to the major
lines of historical development in the twentieth century. The only
aspects of the Chilean Road to Socialism which could be regarded as

authentically or particularly Chilean were the specific forms the process took, which were determined by history and national circumstances.

The essence and uniqueness of the Chilean Road to Socialism lay in the fact that the process was to take place within the bourgeois institutional framework, and would use it whenever possible to effect radical changes, gradually transforming the system into a socialist one. But was this gradual strategy the only one open to Chile, especially if no further advance was possible by this route? Were the frequently discussed radical or revolutionary routes to socialism real alternatives?

Some doubted whether the Popular Unity really had a concerted and defined strategy. Recent declarations by the Communist, Socialist and Radical Left (PIR) parties could be held to indicate a lack of determination and certainty within the Government concerning the means to be used and the speed of change. The interaction of these different internal pressures would eventually determine whether the gradual, legal road to socialism, or the more radical one, would be followed. Government acceptance as a *fait accompli* of certain illegal or marginally legal activities in the industrial and rural sectors, more akin to a radical strategy, was seen as a further indication that there was no single unanimous Government view on the path to be followed.

The more general view, however, was that the Popular Unity was united in rejecting a direct unconstitutional confrontation and in supporting a strategy using the existing legal procedures, as long as these were sufficiently elastic to advance their programme to open up the way to socialism. The only source of power considered legitimate by the Popular Unity was the support of the broad majority of the Chilean population. One of the Government's current tasks was to try to widen its support. Any differences of opinion which existed within the Popular Unity were over the tactics to be adopted rather than the strategy itself.

In fact, it was claimed that the protagonists of a violent confrontation were now the powerful national and international groups who previously had always argued in favour of pacific social evolution.

A violent confrontation very much suited the Government's political enemies which now felt threatened by the fact that the people had gained partial power by means of the bourgeois democratic rules of the game and not by armed struggle. The people had gained control of the executive, and intended to go on from this position of partial power to increase its strength and win the legislature. The world-famous I.T.T. papers [1] were concrete evidence of the conspiratorial efforts that had been made to subvert the armed forces and provoke the left to violence, in an attempt to create a climate favouring military intervention (contravening established constitutional processes) in order to prevent Salvador Allende assuming the Presidency. The willingness of the right wing to resort to illegal and violent tactics was an aspect of Chilean reality which should be borne in mind when assessing possible alternative strategies, because whether the path chosen by the Popular Unity was a fruitful one depended very much on the reactions of Chilean right wing groups and their imperialist allies.

The workers were said to be clear about their reaction to an open violent confrontation outside the democratic constitutional framework initiated by the dominant classes. In accordance with the CUT decision of 4 September 1970 they would take over factories, farms, and service industries, including those not already expropriated. If they and their government won in this violent confrontation, they would impose their own conditions and measures to ensure that no such conspiracy could develop in future to threaten the workers' government. In such a situation the whole course of the process of transition to socialism would change radically, and the old political system would cease to function. The capitalists were to take note that, if they wished to maintain power and control over their enterprises, they should take care to maintain the struggle within legal channels. Any efforts to the contrary would mean the immediate loss of the means of production which the workers would never return.

Did the Popular Unity have any real choice when formulating the programme and strategy which it would present to the electorate? Many pointed out that, even with a moderate platform, Allende had only managed to gain 36% of the national vote in the Presidential elections. Had he presented a more radical programme he could never have gained even this degree of elecoral support. Moreover, only two of the original six constituent parties of the Popular Unity have a consistently Marxist ideology and the others would never have lent their support to a radical strategy to implant socialism violently. In other words, neither the Popular Unity nor the Marxist parties had

---

[1] *Documentos Secretos de la ITT*, Santiago, Quimantú, 1972. Published in English under the title *Subversion in Chile: a case study in US corporate intrigue in the Third World*, Nottingham, Bertrand Russell Peace Foundation, 1972.

sufficient power, based on electoral support, to carry through a radical alternative.

There was a wide degree of consensus that a more radical approach was no real alternative in the Chilean case. While it had a certain romantic appeal, it was completely unrealistic if Chile's history and present reality were taken into account.

Other important factors such as the reactions of the military and the possible economic consequences had to be taken into account in assessing the feasibility of the 'radical' road to socialism. In an economy as complex as Chile's, it was feared that a radical solution might engender greater economic dislocation and disintegration than the so-called reformist one, and therefore possibly work against other political and economic objectives of the Government. In particular, it could affect its ability to maintain or increase its political support.

Nevertheless, it was claimed that to suggest there were no alternatives was to take too static a political view, since it only took account of the immediate political possibilities in 1970 and 1971. Also to take a very deterministic view of the alternatives was a mistake. New perspectives which appeared closed in the early stages might open if the political consciousness of the masses was substantially heightened by the process under way. The options open to Chile could not be fixed for all time since a transition period was characterized by fluidity. Events in 1970 showed how difficult it was to talk about clearly defined solutions. The Popular Unity and the labour movement had had to organize and mobilize in order to make it absolutely clear to certain of the opposition forces that, unless Salvador Allende, the candidate who had obtained the biggest popular vote, was allowed to take power, the consequences would be very costly. So far, the road had not been an easy, peaceful or particularly democratic one, and there was no guarantee that it would be so in the future.

While there was a wide consensus that, at the present juncture, the Chilean Road to Socialism was the Government's only realistic strategy, opinions diverged as to the nature of the problems and obstacles which confronted the Popular Unity and about the prospects for further advance in implementing its programme. Some feared that the deteriorating political and economic situation could become sufficiently serious during 1972 as to endanger the position of the Popular Unity and prevent this particular democratic form of advance towards socialism from proceeding much further.

Five main factors were mentioned as causes of the Popular

Unity's problems; the increasing lack of flexibility in the legal and constitutional framework; the actions of the opposition and right wing; the ideological heterogeneity of the Popular Unity; the failure of the Popular Unity's short-term objectives and the incompatibility of its short-term objectives with its long-term objectives; and finally the activities of the ultra-left.

The Legal Framework

Eduardo Novoa, in one of the opening speeches, had cast doubt on whether the legal means left open to the Government were sufficient to enable it to carry through the vast programme of economic, social and political transformation which remained to be effected. However, the example of widespread political agreement on constitutional reform permitting the nationalization of copper was sufficient evidence for some participants to conclude that there still remained considerable flexibility in the Chilean legal system. In their view, given the degree of openness of the Chilean system and the degree of social mobilization, Congress could not fail to reflect the collective national consciousness or popular will. Moreover, they considered it very likely that a large majority would certainly support such fundamental transformations as the elimination of private monopoly power and privilege and the establishment of a new decision-making system, as set out in the Popular Unity's electoral programme. The legal system would respond to massive manifestations of opinion and facilitate the desired changes.

Others were not so confident that it was possible to continue to rely on legal means and constitutional procedures to change the system and achieve rapid and profound social, economic and political changes. The entrenched opposition, which virtually controlled the political institutions, was using them in a determined effort to block the Popular Unity's programme of transition to socialism. The prospects for the Popular Unity and the struggle for socialism were therefore not encouraging unless the political spectrum changed and support for the Popular Unity Government increased to the point which would give it control over both branches of Congress.

Others were not so pessimistic about the Government's room for manoeuvre. A European economist thought that several legally determined economic instruments such as the *estanco* were available to the Government and would enable it to proceed with its economic policy without new legislation. A wide range of policy measures existed which a government could employ to exercise control over the economy which did not involve new forms of organization or new statutory powers. Even if there were legal obstacles to expanding the socially-owned sector, the Government could reorganize the existing state sector and use it as an instrument of economic control and orientation.

The Activities of the Opposition and the Extreme Right-Wing

In the view of Popular Unity speakers, right-wing reaction was one of the most serious sources of difficulty for the Government. In response to the attack on their basic interests, the Chilean right-wing and the foreign groups — particularly the North American imperialists who were losing their privileges in Chile — had naturally begun to react. Their opposition to the Popular Unity Government was expected to become even more entrenched in 1972. The events revealed in the I.T.T. papers were sufficient evidence of the lengths to which the right-wing would go and exposed the myth of its unfailing commitment to the democratic legal process.

Another important point in this connection was that the concepts of 'legal' and 'illegal' no longer exhausted the possibilities of discussion. A third notion, 'extra-legal', was regarded as particularly important in the current *impasse* in Chile, in which the opposition was trying to change the nature of government by stripping the Executive of its powers and instituting an embryonic parliamentary system.

In making efforts to limit the Government's power, and by preventing progress towards the implementation of the transition programme, the opposition groups were not playing according to the rules of the game. They were making improper use of their political rights in order to immobilize the Government and to force it, in turn, to take so-called 'extra-legal' steps.

If the opposition groups continued to try to force the Government into extra-legal or even illegal activities to fulfil its programme, some suggested that it might become necessary for the President to use his residual powers to protect the Presidential office and prerogative against the attacks and manoeuvres of Congress. Another suggestion was that a limited degree of Presidential dictatorship might be necessary if the Popular Unity was to survive; and, whatever the constitutionally-established powers the President had at his disposal, a vital factor was the attitude of the Chilean armed forces towards the legal and constitutional tradition in Chile and towards the Popular Unity.

The Political Heterogeneity of the Popular Unity

The political heterogeneity of the Popular Unity Government was said to be sapping the strength of the Government. Among the Government's eight components, there were three obvious main groupings. Firstly, there were the Socialist and Communist parties who wished to develop a Marxist-Leninist form of society but who took a historical perspective and determined their strategy and tactics in the light of Chilean reality. Secondly, there were militant groups who did not seem to take a historical perspective, and urged a radicalization of the Popular Unity strategy in the hopes of gaining complete power for the working classes during the life of the current Popular Unity Government. The third group was composed of social democrats who were completely opposed to Marxism-Leninism. It was therefore hard to see how such a heterogeneous political alliance could adhere to a clear, common long-term strategy to build a Marxist-Leninist socialist state, though they might combine tactically on points of common interest to defeat the right-wing opposition.

As the problems faced by the Popular Unity Government mounted, there would be increasing internal crisis in the Popular Unity, according to one opinion. Already in early 1972, there had been one occasion on which one Government party had ordered its parliamentary members to vote against a government bill.

In reply to the argument that ideological heterogeneity and internal contradictions weakened the Popular Unity's efforts, it was recalled that the previous government, a one-party Christian Democrat government, had warned of the dangers of a Popular Unity government becoming a one-party government which would do away with democratic institutions and personal liberty. But the very arguments about political heterogeneity were sufficient evidence of the fact that the Popular Unity was a truly multi-party institution which represented different social classes. It still maintained its unity after eighteen months in power, and the fact that there were differences among the eight parties was not a cause for apologies or regrets. It reflected the intention that the new Chilean politics should be characterized by permanent discussion, which was the essence of democracy.

Short-Term Policy Achievements
and Compatibility of the Short-Term and Long-Term Objectives

The long-run objective of establishing a socialist society implied certain unavoidable short-run decisions on policy. The Popular

Unity's short-term policy was alleged by one critic to be primarily one of widening the popular base of the Government by increasing the masses' purchasing power through a massive redistribution of income and increase in the money supply. The Popular Unity's policy ostensibly attached no importance to capital accumulation, unlike that of other countries which had attempted to establish socialism. One Christian Democrat view was that sacrifices were needed from all sectors if there was to be a transition towards socialism. This implied discipline, hard work and saving, rather than higher consumption for the rural and urban working classes. The Popular Unity's short-term objectives were therefore incompatible with the long-run objective of achieving socialism. However, the necessary but unpopular measures could not be taken unless the Government had a clear majority in both Chambers of Congress.

In this respect its short-term policies had been a failure in their own terms, because they had not produced the expected results. Support for the Popular Unity was said to have fallen by 4%. Moreover, if this policy had not brought success in the very short term, it was most unlikely that support would increase later in 1972 because by then the economic situation would be even more difficult.

This description of the objectives of the Government's short-term economic policy was criticized from various angles. Although it was true that emphasis had been put on income redistribution, with the result that the share of wages in the national income had risen from 51% to 60%, it was claimed that the purpose was not simply to gain electoral advantage. Income redistribution was a moral obligation to the people. Without some increase and a narrowing of the most glaring inequalities no revolutionary process was possible.

The question arose as to whether loss of popular support, if there had been any such loss, could be taken as condemnation of a socialist, or would-be socialist, government. In many circumstances substantial changes had had to be made which were bound to lose a government some support. The burden of many of the measures which were intended to improve the overall economic situation would fall on government as well as opposition supporters. The enormous inequality in income distribution in Chile meant that for a long time Chile had virtually been divided into two nations. It was naive to think that it was possible to reorganize the economic system and to develop a one-nation state without harming the interests of certain groups or without losing some popularity. It was possible that the more successful the Government was in effecting the transition to socialism, the greater the proportion of the inherited productive capacity it would have to abandon. If the Government was at all successful in its tasks, certain luxury items, for example, would not continue to be produced since there would no longer be people to afford them. A loss of capacity which could not be converted to better uses should not be regarded as a failure, for, if the per capita income of the mass of the population was to be increased, then the overall average per capita income might have to fall.

It was also important to remember that even though the lower income classes had benefited from the income redistribution policy, there would be a lag in the recognition, by the urban and rural working classes, of the popular, revolutionary nature of the structural changes and policy measures undertaken by the Popular Unity Government in its sixteen months in power. The error was to regard this lag as permanent, as Radomiro Tomic had, and as one which would worsen with time. On the contrary, the popular lack of recognition of the merits of these measures was temporary. The awareness of the Chilean people would deepen as the process continued, and in time the popular classes would provide increased and more decided support for the Popular Unity Government. The impression was that the Government was only losing the support of the floating voter of the middle classes and of groups with a low level of political consciousness.

The observations of Radomiro Tomic concerning the evolution of Government support and the election results were the subject of considerable debate. Comparing electoral support during the early period in government, it was observed that the Christian Democrat vote in September 1964 was 56% and in March 1965 was 43%. In other words, it suffered a decline of 13% and not 7% as had been stated. On the other hand, the Popular Unity vote had increased from 36% in the Presidential elections in 1970 to 50% in the April 1971 municipal elections — an increase of 14%. Furthermore, in the senatorial by-election in 1971, to replace Salvador Allende in Magallanes, the Popular Unity candidate obtained more than 50% of the vote. According to calculations based on the recent senatorial election in the three provinces of Linares, Colchagua and O'Higgins in January 1972, the overall national decline in the Government vote was approximately 2%. This suggested that the Popular Unity was still supported by 48% of the electorate in early 1972, comparing the figures with the 50% obtained in the Magallanes senatorial by-election. It was also pointed out that Linares, Colchagua and O'Higgins, where the Popular Unity lost to the opposition candidate, were mainly agricultural areas traditionally unfavourable to the left.

Even so, the Popular Unity had maintained its percentage of the vote. Had elections been held in Concepción or Antofagasta the results would probably have been more favourable to the Government.

It was suggested, however, that if meaningful comparisons were to be made concerning the growth or decline in political support during the first year of the Frei and Allende administrations, it was necessary to use similar units as the basis for comparison. In analysing the early Frei period, Tomic had compared national Congressional election results with those of the Presidential elections. In contrasting the results over a similar period during the Allende administration, it would have been more scientific to use national election results rather than by-election results. The only national elections which had taken place since the Popular Unity took power were municipal elections, but it was claimed that these had taken place too soon after the Presidential elections for useful comparisons to be made.

In reply to these latter points concerning the respective electoral performances of the Frei and Allende administrations, it was pointed out that the calculation that the Popular Unity was losing support of some 2% was based on a comparison of the percentage of votes obtained in the January 1972 Congressional by-election with April 1971 municipal election results in the same three provinces, and not with the results of the earlier Presidential election of September 1970.

Ultra-Left Activities

The activities of ultra-left groups and the Government's relations with these groups was considered by some as another factor which made the Popular Unity's position more difficult. These groups, which did not belong to the Popular Unity, did not believe in the Chilean Road to Socialism. They advocated and practised direct action in order to provoke a confrontation with the opponents of socialism. There was ambivalence within the Popular Unity towards the ultra-left. Some Popular Unity groups argued that the ultra-left's activities furthered the aims of the right-wing and the imperialists, while others allegedly regarded them as a useful element of support. The fact that the Government did not adopt a hard line with the ultra-left to restrict its activities, and was prepared to enter into discussions with the MIR, supposedly caused many non-Marxist Chileans to doubt the Government's declared adherence to its legal, constitutional strategy. This was alleged to encourage the extreme right-wing to engage in equally reprehensible forms of action which added to the Government's difficulties.

In clarification, a Popular Unity politician pointed out that the Popular Unity discussions with the MIR constituted an attempt to unify the revolutionary forces on the basis of the Government's principles and programme and to defend and maintain the stability of the Popular Government.

The Future of the Popular Unity;
Political Alliances and the Role of the Christian Democrat Party

While the relevance or importance attributed to these five complicating factors varied largely according to the political persuasion of the discussants, there was a large measure of agreement that the fundamental question which had to be answered was whether the organized working classes really could move beyond their situation of partial power to take over the legislature, thereby opening up new possibilities for institutional change.

If the existing bourgeois liberal system prevailed and the class struggle continued, with a gradual heightening of the political consciousness of the proletariat, there seemed to be no obstacles in the internal logic of the Chilean bourgeois state to prevent the workers winning sufficient strength to gain control of the legislature as well as the Executive.

However, during this pre-socialist stage of the revolution, this depended to quite a large extent on the ability of the proletariat to ally itself with other popular classes and, in the opinion of some participants as well as some Popular Unity parties, it was also necessary for the Popular Unity to form an alliance with those sections of the middle class, antagonistic to monopoly interests, which still had an economic role to play at this stage of the revolutionary process. In view of the dangers of such a process, it was claimed that an alliance led by the working classes guaranteed that this gradual pluralist process would lead in the direction of socialism.

A central question in this respect was the nature and role of the Christian Democrat party. Radomiro Tomic had claimed that the Popular Unity had committed an error in refusing, both during and after the Presidential elections, to ally itself with the Christian Democrats. They had rejected what was a unique historical opportunity to form a 'united people'. However, this argument seemed to contradict his other claim that the existence of so many heterogeneous parties in the Popular Unity Government militated against the effectiveness of the Government.

Obviously not all would agree that the composition of the Popular Unity was one of the principal causes of its difficulties. Nevertheless, many did believe that the continued existence of the Popular Unity Government over the next five years depended mainly on the position adopted by the Christian Democrat party.

In the opinion of some participants, the attitude of the Christian Democrat party to the formation of a political alliance, which would guarantee a majority for the forces in favour of change and the construction of socialism, needed further clarification and analysis.

The impression had been given by Radomiro Tomic that the Christian Democrat party had worked unanimously for this idea, but had met opposition from the Popular Unity. Yet the 1969 Christian Democrat Congress decision, and the party's current attitude towards the Popular Unity, seemed to indicate that the Christian Democrat party, or at least a majority of it, had not wanted to contribute to the formation of a united left, but had impeded it. In 1969, the Christian Democrat Congress discussed at length whether to present a joint candidate with the left wing parties in the 1970 Presidential elections, or whether to go forward alone as a 'centrist' alternative to the Popular Unity on the left and Alessandri on the right. The first idea was rejected in favour of the second and the decision received the support of the then President, Eduardo Frei. As a result, a section of the Christian Democrat party resigned. Along with other small leftist groups, it formed the M.A.P.U. (United Popular Action Movement) which later joined the Popular Unity.

It was, however, true that in October 1970 two-thirds of the Christian Democrat party's National Committee had voted in favour of instructing their Deputies and Senators to vote for Allende when, in the absence of an absolute majority for any one Presidential candidate, Congress had to choose between the two candidates with the largest number of popular votes. The Christian Democrat's decision on this vote contrasted with that of other parties on similar past occasions when both Chambers of Congress had had to choose between Presidential candidates. Previously the candidate with the most popular votes had in fact been selected by Congress, but in each case the party whose candidate had come second in the direct popular elections voted in Congress for their own candidate. In 1946 the Conservatives voted for Cruz Coke, in 1952 the Radicals voted for Pedro Enrique Alfonso, and in 1958 the FRAP (Popular Action Front) voted for Allende.

However, the subsequent attitude adopted by the Christian

Democrat party during the Popular Unity administration cast doubt on its seriousness in working towards a majority government. The activities and political behaviour of certain prominent Christian Democrats had allegedly encouraged panic, lack of confidence and economic dislocation during the early months of the Allende administration, and seemed to be inconsistent with the thesis that the party was seeking to help the transition to socialism.

More recently, the Christian Democrat party had presented a Constitutional Reform Bill defining the three areas of property ownership — social, mixed and private — which the Popular Unity saw as an instrument for slowing down the creation of the socially-owned sector of the economy and preventing its consolidation, thereby striking at the roots of one of the vital aspects of the Popular Unity's strategy. Furthermore, in the Colchagua, Linares and O'Higgins by-election in January 1972, the Christian Democrat party had joined forces with the right and presented a common candidate. This hardly seemed to indicate any great enthusiasm for a transition to socialism. It was suggested that perhaps there was more than a grain of truth in the phrase, 'He who wins with the right is won over by the right'.

It was acknowledged that the Christian Democrat party was not a monolithic, politically homogeneous block, even after the recent break-away of small groups such as MAPU and the Christian Left. The future leanings of the Christian Democrat party were therefore not completely pre-determined. It was a multi-class party which embraced a belief in social reform, in transition to socialism and in a certain form of capitalism. In practice these could hardly be conciliated. In the recent past it had seemed to identify more closely with the dominant classes in Chile than with the popular classes. If the three main groupings continued, it was not absolutely clear which way it would lean in the future.

Others were more convinced that the future would see a Popular Unity and Christian Democrat rapprochement. They saw various points of consensus in Chilean politics; there was agreement between different ideological groups that the Chilean economic system was not viable, that a deep-rooted social and economic reconstruction was necessary and that a new socialist type of society should be aimed for. However, at present these groups were divided into two main opposing forces — one socialist and revolutionary and the other reformist. Nevertheless, according to the depth of their respective analyses concerning Chilean reality, it was thought that there were processes at work, resulting from the structural disequilibrium of Chilean society, which would unite these two groups into one party in the future, permitting progress towards a socialist society.

What was the likelihood of an electoral pact in the near future between the Christian Democrat party and the Popular Unity? One prominant Christian Democrat view was that the Popular Unity alone would benefit from such a pact, because the Christian Democrats would in effect stand alongside rather than within the Popular Unity alliance; therefore it was unlikely that in future elections the Christian Democrat party would suggest joining the Popular Unity and then suffer rejection as in the past. On the other hand, it was not logical to expect the party to commit political suicide and withdraw from the scene of political struggle. That would be tantamount to flying in the face of normal political action in which options and tactics, rather than principles and moral imperatives, are the basis for action.

The view of one Popular Unity politician was that its past refusal to accept the Christian Democrat proposals for a united people's platform was based on the lessons of the Popular Front experience of 1938 in which the bourgeois reformist parties constituted the backbone. The political spectrum had changed since then and it was now the working classes who would play the fundamental role, although other groups might join forces with them. The Popular Unity for its part hoped there would be constructive points of contact and agreement in the future between themselves and the Christian Democrats, so that the Chilean revolutionary road to socialism would be widened to include the Christian Democrats.

Serious differences between the Popular Unity and the Christian Democrats did exist, however, and one of the major points of conflict in which neither side appeared willing to compromise, concerned the three property areas. The Christian Democrat party's Constitutional Reform Bill was aimed at controlling the growth of the social property sector by permitting only those additions to this sector which were decreed by new legislation, such that, in future, government administrative or executive decisions to transfer an enterprise to the social property sector would not be sufficient. The Christian Democrat Bill also included proposals for new forms of property ownership and industrial organization because they did not favour the idea of a large state-capitalist sector. The Popular Unity objected to these proposals because they were clearly designed to slow down the development of the socially-owned property sector, the very basis of their overall strategy for achieving socialism. The proposals for worker-participation were equally objectionable since, as had been explained earlier, they would put tremendous power into the hands of a small percentage of the work-force and would encourage capitalist ideas.

SECTION TWO

Official Chilean Documents
and
Background Papers

THE POPULAR UNITY'S PROGRAMME

Programme presented to the Chilean people during the Presidential Election campaign in 1970

INTRODUCTION

The parties and movements of which the Popular Unity's Co-ordinating Committee is composed, without prejudice to our individual philosophy and political delineations, fully agree on the following description of the national situation and on the programme proposals which are to constitute the basis of our common effort and which we now present for consideration by the whole nation.

Chile is going through a grave crisis, manifested by social and economic stagnation, widespread poverty and deprivation of all sorts suffered by workers, peasants*, and other exploited classes as well as in the growing difficulties which confront white collar workers, professional people, small and medium businessmen, and in the very limited opportunities open to women and young people.

These problems can be resolved in Chile. Our country possesses great wealth such as copper and other minerals, a large hydro-electric potential, vast forests, a long coast rich in marine life, and more than sufficient land, etc. Chile also has a population with a will to work and progress and people with technical and professional skills.

Why have we failed?

What has failed in Chile is the system — a system which does not correspond to present day requirements. Chile is a capitalist country, dependent on the imperialist nations and dominated by bourgeois groups who are structurally related to foreign capital and who cannot resolve the country's fundamental problems — problems which are clearly the result of class privilege which will never be given up voluntarily.

---

* The word peasants and peasantry should be taken to include small proprietors, agricultural wage labourers, sharecroppers, migrant and temporary rural labourers, smallholders who rent their land and other types of agricultural workers. (Editor)

Moreover, as a direct consequence of the development of world capitalism, the submission of the national monopolistic bourgeoisie to imperialism daily furthers its role as junior partner to foreign capital, increasingly accentuating its dependent nature.

For a few people it is good business to sell off a piece of Chile each day. And every day this select few make decisions on behalf of all the rest of us. On the other hand, for the great majority of Chileans there is little to be gained from selling their labour and brain power and, in general, they are still deprived of the right to determine their own future.

The 'reformist' and 'developmentalist' solutions, which the Alliance for Progress promoted and which the Frei Government adopted, have not changed anything of importance in Chile. Basically, the Christian Democrat Government was nothing but a new government of the bourgeoisie, in the service of national and foreign capitalism, whose weak efforts to promote social change came to a sad end in economic stagnation, a rising cost of living, and violent repression of the people. This experience demonstrated once more that reformism cannot resolve the people's problems.

The development of monopoly capitalism prevents the extension of democracy and exacerbates violence against the people. As 'reformism' fails and the people's capacity to struggle increases, the most reactionary sectors of the dominant classes who, in the last analysis, have no recourse but to use force, become firmer in their position. The brutal forms of violence perpetrated by the Frei Government, such as the activities of the Riot Police Unit, the beating up of peasants and students, and the killing of shanty town dwellers and miners, are inseparable from other and no less brutal forms of violence which affect all Chileans. People living in luxurious houses while a large part of the population lives in unhealthy dwellings or has no shelter at all also constitutes violence; people who throw away food while others lack the means to feed themselves also commit violence.

Imperialist exploitation of backward economies takes place in a variety of ways: through investments in mining (copper, iron, etc), industrial, banking and commercial activities; through the control of technology which obliges us to pay exaggerated sums for equipment, licences and patents; through American loans with crippling conditions which require us to purchase from the U.S.A. and with the additional obligation to transport these purchases in North American ships. Just one example of imperialist exploitation is the fact that from 1952 to date, the U.S.A. invested US$ 7,473 million in Latin

America and received back US$ 16,000 million.

Imperialism has taken resources from Chile equivalent to double the value of the capital accumulated in our country throughout its history. American monopolies, with the complicity of bourgeois goverments, have succeeded in taking over nearly all of our copper, iron and nitrate resources. They control foreign trade and dictate economic policy through the International Monetary Fund and other organisations. They dominate important branches of industry and services, they enjoy statutory privileges while imposing monetary devaluation, the reduction of salaries and wages and the distortion of agricultural activities through their agricultural surpluses policy.

They also intervene in education, culture and in the communications media and they try to penetrate the Armed Forces, making use of military and political agreements.

The dominant classes, acting as accomplices in the process and unable to defend their own interests, have increased Chile's foreign indebtedness over the last ten years. It was argued that the loans and arrangements with international bankers would increase economic development. But the only result is that today Chile holds the record of being one of the world's most indebted countries in proportion to its population.

In Chile government and legislation is for the benefit of the few — that is they only serve the large capitalists and their hangers-on, the companies which dominate our economy, and the large land-holders whose power still remains almost intact.

The owners of capital are only interested in making more money and not in satisfying the needs of the Chilean people. For example, if it appears to be a good business proposition to produce and import expensive cars they use our economy's scarce resources for this purpose, ignoring the fact that only a minute percentage of Chileans have the means to purchase them and that there are far more urgent needs to be satisfied. The improvement of public transport and provision of machinery for agriculture are obvious examples of such urgent needs.

The groups of businessmen who control the economy, the press and other communications media, the existing political system, and the threats to the State, when it hints at intervention or refuses to favour all these interests, are an expensive burden on the Chilean people. For these groups to deign to continue 'working' — since only they can afford the luxury of working or not — the following conditions are necessary. They have to be provided with all kinds of assistance. Important businessmen pressure the State under the threat that, unless the help and guarantees they request are authorized, there will be no private investment.

They have to be allowed to produce the products they want with money belonging to the whole Chilean people, instead of producing the goods needed by the great majority; and to transfer the profits obtained to their foreign bank accounts. They wish to be allowed to dismiss workers if they ask for better wages; and to be permitted to manipulate food distribution and stockpile food products in order to create artificial shortages and thereby raise prices in order to continue enriching themselves at the expense of the Chilean people.

Meanwhile, a large proportion of those people who actually produce face a difficult situation. Half a million families lack housing and as many or more live in appalling conditions lacking sewage, drinking water, light, and healthy conditions. The population's education and health requirements are insufficiently provided for. More than a half of Chile's workers receive wages which are insufficient to cover their minimum vital needs. Every family suffers from unemployment and unstable employment. The chances of employment are impossible or uncertain for countless young people.

Imperialist capital and a privileged group not exceeding 10% of the population receive half of the National Income. This means that out of every hundred escudos produced by Chileans, 50 end up in the pockets of 10 of the oligarchy and the other 50 have to be shared among 90 Chileans from the poor and middle classes.

The rising cost of living creates havoc in people's homes, especially for the housewife. According to official statistics, the cost of living has risen almost 1,000% in the last 10 years.

This means that every day Chileans who live from the proceeds of their work are robbed of part of their salaries or wages. The same happens to retired people, craftsmen, independent workers and small scale producers, whose meagre incomes are daily eroded by inflation.

Alessandri and Frei gave assurances that they would put an end to inflation. The results are there for all to see. The facts prove that inflation in Chile is the outcome of deeper causes which are related to the capitalist structure of our society and not to increases in incomes, as successive governments have tried to make us believe in order to justify the system and restrain workers' incomes.

On the other hand, the large capitalist can defend himself from inflation and what is more he profits from it. His property and his capital become more valuable, his construction contracts with the State are revalued, and the prices of his products always rise ahead of wage increases.

A large number of Chileans are underfed.. According to official statistics, 50% of children under 15 years of age are undernourished. This affects their growth and limits their learning capacity. This shows that the economy in general and the agricultural system in particular are incapable of feeding Chile's population in spite of the fact that Chile could support a population of 30 million people right now–that is, three times the present population.

Yet, on the contrary, each year we must import hundreds of thousands of dollars worth of food products.

Most of the blame for the food supply and nutritional problems of the Chilean people can be attributed to the existence of *latifundia* which are responsible for the backwardness and misery which characterize the Chilean countryside. Indices of infant and adult mortality, illiteracy, lack of housing and ill health in the rural areas are markedly higher than for the cities. The Christian Democrat Government's restricted Agrarian Reform Programme has not resolved these problems. Only the peasants' struggle, backed by the whole nation, will resolve them.The present struggle for land and the abolition of the latifundio is opening up new perspectives for the advance of the Chilean people.

The growth rate of our economy is minimal. In recent five year periods the average rate of growth has been scarcely 2% p.a. per capita; and since 1967 there has been no growth at all. On the contrary, we have moved backwards according to the Government Planning Office's figures. This means that in 1966 each Chilean had more goods than he has today, which explains why the majority are discontent and are looking for an alternative for our country.

The only alternative, which is a truly popular one, and one which therefore constitutes the Popular Government's main task, is to bring to an end the rule of the imperialists, the monopolists, and the landed oligarchy and to initiate the construction of socialism in Chile.

THE ORGANIZED PEOPLE IN UNITY AND ACTION

The growth in size and organization of the labour force and the growing struggle and consciousness of its own power reinforce and propagate criticism of the established order, the desire for profound change and conflicts with the established power structure. There are more than three million workers in our country whose productive efforts and enormous constructive capacity cannot be put to good use within the present system, which only exploits and subjects them.

These organized forces, in a common effort with the people to mobilize those who are not sold out to national and foreign reactionary interests, could destroy the present system and, by means of this united struggle on the part of the large majority of Chileans, progress could be made in the task of liberating themselves. The Popular Unity alliance has been formed precisely for this purpose.

The imperialists and the country's dominant classes will struggle against a united people and will try to deceive them once again. They will say that freedom is in danger, that violence is taking hold of the country, etc. But each day the popular masses are less and less taken in by these lies. Social mobilization is growing daily, and is now reinforced and encouraged by the unity of the left wing groups.

In order to encourage and guide the mobilization of the Chilean people toward the conquest of power, we will set up Popular Unity Committees in every factory, farm, poor neighbourhood*, office or school, to be run by the militants of the left wing movements and parties and to be composed of the thousands of Chileans who are in favour of fundamental change. These Popular Unity Committees will not only constitute electoral organizations. They will interpret and fight for the immediate claims of the masses and above all they will learn to exercise power.

This new form of power structure which Chile needs must begin to develop itself right now, wherever people need to be organized to fight over specific problems and wherever the need to exercise this power becomes apparent. This system involving a common effort will be a permanent dynamic method for developing our Programme, constituting a practical school for the masses and a concrete way of deepening the political content of the Popular Unity at all levels.

At a given point in the campaign the essential contents of this Programme, enriched by discussion with and the support of the people, and together with a series of immediate government measures will be set out in a People's Act *(Acta del Pueblo)* which the new Popular Government and the Front which sustains it will regard as an unrenounceable mandate.

Support for the Popular Unity's candidate does not, therefore, only involve voting for a man, but also involves declaring oneself in

* The word used in the original Spanish text is *'población'* and refers to various types of low income housing areas in towns and villages. These include slums, illegally occupied squatter settlements, temporary shanty towns and permanent but poor housing developments promoted by the government and housing associations or constructed by means of self-help programmes in which technical and material assistance is provided by the government. In the rest of this document references to low income housing districts or low income neighbourhoods should be taken as referring to all these different low income housing areas. (Editor)

favour of the urgent replacement of our present society, the basis of which is the power and control exercised by large national and foreign capitalists.

THE PROGRAMME

Popular Power

The revolutionary changes required by Chile can only be carried out if the people of Chile take power into their own hands and exercise it in a true and effective manner.

In the process of a long struggle, the Chilean people have achieved certain democratic liberties and guarantees which will require vigilance and constant battle if they are not to be lost.

The revolutionary and popular forces have not united to simply fight for the substitution of one President of the Rupublic by another, nor to replace one party by others in Government but, rather, to carry out the profound changes which are required by national circumstances, based on the transfer of power from the old dominant groups to the urban workers, rural population and progressive sectors of the urban and rural middle-classes.This popular triumph will therefore open up the way for the most democratic political government in the country's history.

As regards the political structure, the Popular Government has the double task of preserving and making more effective and real the democratic rights and achievements of the working classes, and transforming present institutions in order to install a new system of power in which the working classes and the people are the ones who really exercise power.

The strengthening of democracy and working class progress

The Popular Government will guarantee the exercise of democratic rights and will respect the social and individual liberties of all sectors of the population. The freedom of worship, speech, press and of assembly, the inviolability of the home, and the right to unionize will be made effective, removing the present obstacles put up by the dominant classes to limit them.

In order to put this into practice, the unions and social organizations formed by manual workers, white collar workers, peasants and rural workers, shanty town dwellers and inhabitants of low income neighbourhoods*, housewives, students, professional people, intellectuals, craftsmen, small and medium businessmen, and other groups of workers, will be called upon to participate in government decision making at the relevant level. For example, in the social security institutions we will establish a system of management by the contributors themselves, ensuring that the governing bodies are elected democratically and by secret ballot. As for firms in the public sector, their governing committees and production committees must include direct representation of manual and white collar workers.

The Neighbourhood Committees *(Juntas de Vecinos)* and other organized groups of inhabitants of poor neighbourhoods will have ways and means of controlling the activities of the pertinent national housing organizations and of participating in many aspects of their activities. It is not just a question of these particular examples, but of a new philosophy in which ordinary people achieve real and effective participation in the different organisms of the State.

Likewise, the Popular Government guarantees the right of workers to employment and to strike, and the right for all people to obtain a proper education and culture, fully respecting all ideas and religious beliefs and guaranteeing the freedom to practise them.

All democratic rights and guarantees will be extended, by granting to social organizations real means of exercising their rights and creating the mechanisms which will allow them to participate in the different levels of the State's administrative apparatus. The power and authority of the Popular Government will essentially be based on the support extended to it by the organized population. This is our notion of strong government — the very opposite of that held by the oligarchy and imperialists who identify authority with the use of coercion against the people.

The Popular Government will be a multiparty one, composed of all the revolutionary parties, movements and groups. The executive will therefore be truly democratic, representative and cohesive. The Popular Government will respect the rights of the opposition as long as they are exercised within the legal framework.

The Popular Government will immediately proceed to effectively decentralize the administration which, in conjunction with

* The original Spanish text refers to *'pobladores'* which generally means 'settlers'. But in this context reference is being made to both inhabitants of shanty towns and squatter settlements and to the inhabitants of new low income housing estates constructed for or with the aid of working class people who are often immigrants from the countryside. In the rest of the text the word *'pobladores'* will usually be translated simply as inhabitants of poor neighbourhoods and should be read as including the various categories just listed. (Editor)

democratic and efficient planning, will eliminate the centralization of the bureaucracy, replacing it with real coordination between all parts of the administration.

The structure of the municipalities will be modernized according to the plans for coordinating the whole state administration, while granting them the authority due to them. They will become local organs of the new political organization, possessing sufficient finance and powers to enable them to deal with the problems of the local districts and their inhabitants, in conjunction and coordination with the Neighbourhood Committees. The Provincial Assemblies must begin to operate with the same purpose in mind.

The police must be reorganized so that they can never again be used as a repressive force against ordinary people but, instead, ensure that the population is protected from anti-social behaviour.Police procedures will be made more humane, effectively guaranteeing full respect for human dignity and physical integrity. The prison system and prison conditions at present constitute one of the worst aspects of the present judicial system and must be radically transformed with a view to reforming the lawbreaker.

A NEW INSTITUTIONAL ORGANIZATION: THE POPULAR STATE

Political Organization

The new power structure will be built up from grass roots by extending democracy at all levels and by organizing the mobilization of the masses.

A new political constitution will validate the massive incorporation of the people into governmental power.We shall create a unicameral form of government with national, regional and local levels, and in which the Popular Assembly will constitute the supreme power. This people's Assembly will be the only parliament, expressing the sovereignty of the people at national level and in which all the various currents of opinion will be expressed.

This system will enable us to root out the evils suffered in Chile under dictatorial presidencies and corrupt parliamentary rule. The powers and responsibilities of the President of the Republic, the ministers, Popular Assembly, regional and local government organizations and political parties will be precisely redefined and coordinated in order to ensure the functioning of the legislature, efficiency in government and above all respect for the will of the majority.

All elections will take place simultaneously in an orderly process so as to establish the necessary harmony between the different expressions of the popular will and to ensure that these are expressed coherently.

Organizations representing the people may only be created by means of secret and direct universal suffrage of men and women of over 18 years of age, including civilians and military personnel, and literate and illiterate people. The members of the Popular Assembly and other organizations representing the people will be subject to control by the electors through consultation procedures, which would also allow for their mandate to be withdrawn. A rigorous code of conduct will be established requiring deputies or high level civil servants to lose their mandate or post if guilty of acting on behalf of private interests.

The economic policy instruments to be used by the Government will constitute a national system of planning, and they will be executive instruments to be used to direct, coordinate and rationalize government activities. The operational plan must be approved in the Popular Assembly, and workers' organizations will play a fundamental role in the planning system.

The regional and local organs of government in the new People's State will exercise authority in the relevant geographical areas and they will have economic, political and social powers. In addition they will be able to make proposals to and criticize the higher levels. However, in exercising their powers these regional and local bodies must work within the limits set by national laws and by the overall social and economic development plans. Social organizations with specific attributes will be integrated into each of the different levels of the Popular State. It will be their duty to share responsibilities and develop initiatives in their respective spheres of influence as well as analyse and solve the problems within their competence. These attributes will not in any way limit the complete independence and autonomy of these organizations.

From the very day the Popular Government assumes power it will provide ways of ensuring that the influence of the workers and people is brought to bear on the administrative decisions adopted and on the control over the operation of the state administrative machinery. These constitute decisive steps in the elimination of an overcentralized bureaucracy which characterizes the present administrative system.

The Organisation of Justice

The organization and administration of justice must be based on the guaranteed principle of autonomy and on real economic independence.

We visualize the existence of a Supreme Court whose members are appointed by the People's Assembly, the only limitation being the natural suitability of the members. This Court will be free to determine the internal, personal or corporate powers of the judicial system.

It is our intention that the new administration and organization of justice will come to the aid of the popular classes; it will operate more rapidly and in a less burdensome fashion.

Under the Popular Government a whole new concept of the judicial process will replace the existing individualistic and bourgeois one.

National Defence

The Popular State will pay special attention to the preservation of national sovereignty, which it also views as being the duty of every citizen.

The Popular State will remain alert before those threats to our territorial integrity and the country's independence, which are encouraged by the imperialists and by those groups of the oligarchy in power in neighbouring countries who encourage expansionist and retaliatory pretensions as well as repressing their own people.

The People's State will establish a modern, popular and patriotic concept of the nation's sovereignty based on the following principles:

(a) The guarantee of the national integrity of all branches of the Armed Forces. In this sense we reject the use of these forces to repress the people or their participation in activities of interest to foreign powers;

(b) The provision of technical training with contributions from any modern military science, as deemed convenient to Chile and in the interests of national independence and of peace and friendship among peoples;

(c) The integration of the Armed Forces into different aspects of national life and the increase of their contribution to social life. The Popular State will find ways of making it possible for the Armed Forces to contribute to the country's economic development without prejudice to its primary task of national defence.

Following these lines, it will be necessary to provide the Armed Forces with the necessary material and technical means and to establish a just and democratic system of remuneration, promotion and retirement, which guarantees economic security to personnel in all ranks while serving in the forces and on retirement, and which provides real possibilities for promotion through the ranks on the basis of individual merit.

THE CONSTRUCTION OF THE NEW ECONOMY

The central policy objective of the united popular forces will be the search for a replacement for the present economic structure, doing away with the power of foreign and national monopoly capital and of the *latifundio* in order to initiate the construction of socialism.

Planning will play a very important role in the new economy. The main planning organs will be at the highest administrative level, and the decisions, which will be democratically determined, will be executive in character.

The Socially Owned Sector

The process of transformation in our economy will begin with the application of a policy intended to create a dominant state sector, comprising those firms already owned by the state and the businesses which are to be expropriated. As a first step, we shall nationalize those basic resources like large scale copper, iron and nitrate mines, and others which are controlled by foreign capital and national monopolies. These nationalized sectors will thus be comprised of the following:

1. Large scale copper, nitrate, iodine, iron and coal mines.
2. The country's financial system, especially private banks and insurance companies.
3. Foreign trade.
4. Large distribution firms and monopolies.
5. Strategic industrial monopolies.
6. As a rule, all those activities which have a strong influence on the nation's social and economic development, such as the production and distribution of electric power, rail, air and sea transport, communications, the production, refining and distribution of petroleum and its by-products, including liquid gas, the iron and steel industry, cement, petrochemicals and heavy chemicals, cellulose and paper.

In carrying out these expropriations, the interests of small shareholders will be fully safeguarded.

The Privately Owned Sector
This area includes those sections of industry, mining, agriculture and services where private ownership of the means of production will remain in force.

In terms of numbers these enterprises will constitute the majority. Thus, for example, in 1967 out of 30,500 firms (including artisan establishments) just 150 firms monopolistically controlled the entire market, received most of the assistance from the State, and most of the bank credit, and exploited the rest of the country's businessmen by selling them raw materials at high prices while buying their output at low prices.

The firms which compose this sector will benefit from the overall planning of the national economy. The State will provide the necessary technical and financial assistance for the firms in this sector, enabling them to fulfill the important role which they play in the national economy, when the number of people they employ and the volume of output they generate is taken into account.

In addition, the patenting system, the customs tariffs, and the social security and taxation systems will be simplified for these firms and they will be assured of adequate and just marketing of their products.

These firms must guarantee the rights of workers and employees to fair wages and working conditions. Both the State and the workers in the respective firms will make sure that these rights are respected.

The Mixed Sector
This sector will be termed mixed because it will be composed of enterprises combining both State and private capital.

The loans or credits granted to the firms in this sector by development agencies may take the form of contributions, thereby making the State a partner rather than a creditor. The same holds in those cases in which the firm obtains credits with the backing or guarantee of the State or one of its agencies.

Intensification and Extension of the Agrarian Reform
In our view the Agrarian Reform process should be complementary to, and simultaneous with, the overall transformation which we wish to promote in the country's social, political and economic structure, such that its implementation is inseparable from the rest of our

overall policy. Existing experience in this matter has shown up gaps and inconsistencies which suggest a reformulation of the policy for the distribution and organization of land ownership on the basis of the following guidelines:

1. Accelaration of the Agrarian Reform process, expropriating the holdings which exceed the established maximum size according to the characteristics of the different regions, including orchards, vineyards and forests, without giving the landowner the priority right to select the area to be retained by him. The expropriation may include the whole or part of the expropriated farm's assets (machinery, tools, animals, etc.).

2. The immediate cultivation of abandoned and badly exploited state lands.

3. Expropriated land will be organized preferably on the basis of cooperative forms of ownership. The peasants will be given titles which confirm individual ownership of the house and garden allocated to them, and the corresponding rights over the indivisible land of the cooperative as long as they continue to be members. When the circumstances warrant it, land may be allocated to individual peasants, with the organization of work and marketing being promoted on the basis of mutual cooperation. In addition, lands will be allocated to create state agricultural enterprises using modern technology.

4. In certain qualified cases land will be allocated to small farmers, tenants, sharecroppers and trained agricultural workers

5. Minifundia properties will be reorganized by means of progressively cooperative forms of agricultural work.

6. Small and medium peasants will be given access to the advantages and services provided by the cooperatives operating in their geographical area.

7. The defence of the indigenous Indian communities which are threatened with usurpation of their land will be ensured, as will be the democratic conduct of these communities, the provision of sufficient land and appropriate technical assistance and credit to the Mapuche people and other indigenous groups.

Policy for Economic Development
The Government's economic policy will be carried out by means of a national system of economic planning and through control

mechanisms, guidelines, production credit, technical assistance, tax and foreign trade policies, as well as through the management of the state sector of the economy.

The policy objectives will be:

1. To resolve the immediate problems of the working classes. In order to achieve this we shall divert that part of the nation's productive capacity at present used to produce expensive and unnecessary products for high income groups to the production of cheap, high quality mass consumption goods.

2. To guarantee work and adequate wages to all Chileans of working age. This will involve devising a policy which generates a lot of employment while making adequate use of national resources and adapting technology to national development requirements.

3. To free Chile from subordination to foreign capital. On the one hand, this means expropriating imperialist capital and implementing a policy for increasing our capacity to self-finance our activities and, on the other, it means that we must determine the conditions under which non-expropriated foreign capital may operate, and achieve a greater degree of technological independence and greater independence in international transport, etc.

4. To secure rapid and decentralized economic growth, which will develop the country's productive forces to a maximum, achieving the optimum use of the available human, natural, financial and technical resources in order to increase labour productivity and satisfy the need for greater independence in the development of the economy, as well as those needs and aspirations of the working population which are compatible with a dignified human life.

5. To implement a foreign trade policy which will tend to develop and diversify our exports, open up new markets, achieve growing financial and technological independence and put an end to the successive scandalous devaluations of our currency.

6. To take all necessary measures to achieve monetary stability. The fight against inflation is already implicit in the announced structural changes. But it must also include measures which adjust the money in circulation to the real needs of the market and include the control and redistribution of credit and efforts to keep interest rates low. Measures must also be taken to rationalize marketing and commerce, to stabilize prices and to prevent price increases which emanate from the demand structure and reflect expenditure patterns of the high income groups.

The achievement of these objectives is guaranteed by the fact that it will be the organized masses who will exercise economic and political power, a situation which is represented by the existence of the public sector and of the overall planning of the economy. Government by the people will ensure the fulfillment of the indicated targets.

SOCIAL TASKS

The Chilean people's social aspirations are both legitimate and possible to satisfy. For example, Chilean citizens want decent housing without crippling rent increases, schools and universities for their children, adequate wages, a once and for all end to increases in the cost of living, stable employment, appropriate medical attention, street lighting, sewers, drinking water, surfaced roads and pavements, a just and efficient social security system, which is not based on privilege and which does not provide starvation level pensions, telephones, police, nursery schools, sport fields, holidays, tourism and popular beach resorts.

The satisfaction of these rightful aspirations, which in fact constitute rights which society must recognize, will be the principle concern of the Popular Government.

The basic aspects of Government action will be:

(a) The definition of an incomes policy, with the immediate creation of committees, which, with the participation of workers, will determine what constitutes a subsistence wage and minimum wages in different regions of the country.

As long as inflation continues, wage readjustments related to the cost of living will be decreed by law. These adjustments will be made every six months or whenever the cost of living rises by more than 5%.

High level salaries in all Government departments, and above all the salaries of those appointed directly by the President, will be limited to levels which are compatible with national circumstances. Within a certain technically determined period, we shall begin to set up a system of equal minimum wages and salaries for equal work, wherever the work is done. This policy will first be introduced in the public sector, gradually being extended to the rest of the economy respecting, however, the differences made possible by varying levels of productivity in different firms. In the same way we intend to eliminate wage and salary discrimination between men and women or for reasons of age.

(b) To unify, improve, and extend the social security system, maintaining all the legitimate advances made so far, eliminating the abuse of privilege, inefficiency and bureaucracy, improving and speeding up treatment and attention, extending social security to groups of workers not yet included, and making the contributors responsible for the administration of their Social Security Schemes, which should function within the overall planning framework.

(c) To provide all Chileans with preventive and curative dental and medical care financed by the State, by employers and by social security institutions. The whole population will join in the task of protecting public health. Medicines, etc. will be provided in sufficient quantities and at low cost, on the basis of a strict control of laboratory costs and the rationalization of production.

(d) Sufficient funds will be provided for a large housing programme. The industrialization of construction will be developed, controlling prices and limiting the amount of profits made by the private or mixed enterprises operating in this field. In emergency situations, plots of land will be allocated to those families requiring them, also providing them with technical and material assistance to build their own houses.

One aim of the Popular Government's housing policy is for every family to become a house owner. The system of readjustable rents will be eliminated. The monthly mortgage or loan repayment and rents, to be paid by house purchasers and tenants respectively, will not exceed 10% of family income as a general rule. We shall undertake the remodelling of cities and suburbs to prevent poor people being forced to the outskirts, respecting the interests of such inhabitants of redeveloped areas as small businessmen, by assuring them of a future in the same area.

(e) Full civil status of married women will be established, as will equal legal status for all children whether born in or out of wedlock, as well as adequate divorce legislation which dissolves legal ties and safeguards the woman's and children's rights.

(f) The legal distinction between workers and white collar employees will be ended, both being classed as workers in future and the right to unionize will be extended to all those who do not have this right at present.

CULTURE AND EDUCATION

A new culture for society

The social process, which will begin when the working class wins power, will develop a new culture which considers human labour with the highest regard, which emphasises the desire for national assertion and independence and which develops a critical understanding of present reality.

The profound changes which have to be undertaken require a socially conscious and united people, educated to exercise and defend their political power, and scientifically and technically prepared to develop the transitional economy towards socialism, and a people wide open to creativity and the enjoyment of a wide variety of artistic and intellectual activities.

If, today, the majority of intellectuals and artists fight against the cultural distortions of capitalist society and attempt to convey their creative efforts to the workers and link themselves to the same historical destiny then, in the new society, they will continue this effort but from a vanguard position. A new culture cannot be decreed. It will spring from the struggle for fraternity as opposed to individualism, for the appreciation rather than disdain of human labour, for national values rather than cultural colonization, and from the struggle of the popular masses for access to art, literature, and the communications media and the end of their commercialization.

This new State will involve the whole population in intellectual and artistic activities not only by means of a radically transformed educational system but also through the development of a national system to promote popular culture. A large network of Local Centres for Popular Culture will encourage ordinary people to organize themselves and exercise their rights to participate in and promote culture. This system of Popular Culture will stimulate literary and artistic creativity and it will multiply the links between writers and artists and a very much larger public than their existing one.

A Democratic, Integrated and Planned Educational System

Action by the new Government in this field will concentrate on providing the best and most extensive educational facilities possible.

Both the general improvement in the working classes' living conditions and the recognition of the responsibilities borne by teachers at different levels will influence the extent to which these proposals are fulfilled. Also, a National Scholarship Programme will be established which will be sufficiently broad as to ensure the inclusion and continued education of all Chilean children, especially the children from working class and peasant backgrounds.

Furthermore, the new Government will implement an emergency plan for the construction of schools, relying on contributions of national and local resources mobilized by grass roots organizations. Luxury buildings which are needed as premises for new schools and boarding schools will be expropriated. In this way, it is hoped to create at least one integrated school (both basic and middle levels*) in each rural district, and in each urban residential district and low income neighbourhood.

In order to provide the special requirements needed for the proper development of pre-school age children, and to facilitate the incorporation of women into productive work, we shall rapidly expand our nurseries and nursery schools systems, granting priority to the most needy groups in our society, As a result of this policy, the children of urban and rural workers and peasants will be better prepared to start school and continue to benefit right through the normal school system.

To make the new teaching system a reality, new methods are required which put emphasis on the active and critical participation of students in their teaching, instead of perpetuating the passive attitudes they are expected to adopt at present.

In order to rapidly repair the widespread lack of culture and education resulting from the present system, we shall set in motion an extensive popular mobilization campaign aimed at the rapid elimination of illiteracy and the raising of the educational level of the adult population. Adult education will be mainly organized around work centres, until it is possible to have a permanent system of general, technical and social education for workers.

The transformation of the educational system will not only be the task of technically qualified people. It is also a task requiring study, discussion, decision and implementation by teachers', workers', students' and parents' organizations within the general framework of national planning. Internally, the planning of the schools system will pay particular attention to the need for integration, continuity and diversification in teaching.

In the executive management of the educational system there must be real representation of the aforementioned social organi-

---

* The basic level of education lasts 8 years commencing at 6 years of age, and the middle level lasts 4 years, following completion of the basic level. (Editor)

zations, which will be integrated into the Local, Regional and National Education Committees.

In order to achieve effective educational planning and turn the idea of a unified national and democratic school system into a practical reality, the new Government will take over responsibility for private educational establishments, starting with those educational institutions which select their pupils according to criteria of social class, national origin, or religion. This will be done by integrating the staff and other resources of the private education sector into the state system.

Physical Education

The Popular Government will be constantly concerned to ensure that physical education and participation in all kinds of sports is possible right from the earliest years at school and in all youth and adult social organizations.

University Democracy and Autonomy and the
Role of the Universities

The Popular Unity Government will give strong backing to the Universitary Reform process and it will resolutely push forward this reform. The democratic outcome of this reform process will constitute an important contribution by universities to the revolutionary development of Chile. On the other hand, the reorientation of academic teaching, research, and extension functions towards national problems will be encouraged by the Popular Government's own initiatives.

The State will allocate sufficient resources to the universities to ensure the fulfilment of their functions and to ensure that they become fully democratic public institutions. In line with this, the members and employees of the universities will be responsible for running their respective institutions.

As class privilege is eliminated from the whole of the educational system, it will be possible for children of working class background to enter university and for adults to gain access to higher education either by means of special scholarships or through a system which simultaneously combines study and work.

The Mass Media

The mass media (radio, publishing, television, the press and cinema) are fundamental in helping to develop a new culture and a new type of man. For this reason it is necessary to redefine their purpose, putting emphasis on their educative role and ending their commercialization, and to adopt measures which allow social organizations the use of these communications media, eliminating the harmful effects of the monopolies. The national system of popular culture will be particularly concerned with the development of the film industry and the preparation of social programmes for the mass media.

THE POPULAR GOVERNMENT'S FOREIGN POLICY

Aims

The main lines of emphasis of the Popular Government's Foreign Policy are:-

The assertion of full political and economic autonomy for Chile.

The establishment of diplomatic relations with all countries, irrespective of their ideological and political position, on the basis of respect for self-determination and in the interests of the Chilean people.

Ties of friendship and solidarity will unite Chile with dependent or colonized countries, especially those who are fighting for their liberation and independence.

The promotion of strong interamerican and anti-imperialist sentiments based on foreign policies which are the expression of entire nations rather than on policies formulated solely by foreign ministries.

Efforts by nations to achieve or maintain self-determination will be given decided support by the new Government as a basic condition for the existence of international peace and understanding. As a consequence, our policy will be one of alertness and action in defence of the principle of non-intervention and we shall resist any attempt by the imperialist nations to discriminate, pressure, invade or blockade. We shall reinforce our relationships, trade and cultural exchanges and friendship with socialist countries.

Greater National Independence

The active defence of Chilean independence means that we must denounce the present Organization of American States as an agent and tool of American imperialism, and fight against all forms of Panamericanism which are implicit in this organization. The Popular Government will attempt to create an organization which is really representative of Latin American countries.

It is considered absolutely necessary to review, denounce or renounce, as befits each case, those treaties or agreements which involve commitments limiting our sovereignty, and, in particular, treaties of reciprocal assistance, pacts of mutual aid or other pacts which Chile signed with the U.S.A.

The Government will reject and denounce foreign aid and loans which are extended for political reasons, or involve conditions requiring the investments derived from those loans to be made in ways which prejudice our sovereignty and are against the people's interests. Likewise, we shall repudiate all types of foreign charges imposed on Latin American raw materials such as copper and the obstacles put in the way of free trade which, over time, have made it impossible to establish collective trade relations with all countries of the world.

International Solidarity

The Popular Government will demonstrate effective and militant solidarity with those struggles in which people are fighting for freedom and for the construction of a socialist society.

All forms of colonialism and neo-colonialism will be condemned and we will recognize the right of those peoples subjected to these systems to rebel. Likewise, we shall condemn all forms of economic, political and military aggression provoked by imperialist powers. Chile's foreign policy must be one of condemnation of North American aggression in Vietnam, and one of recognition of and active solidarity with the heroic struggle of the Vietnamese people.

In the same way, the Chilean people will demonstrate meaningful solidarity with the Cuban Revolution, which is the vanguard of revolution and construction of socialism in Latin America.

The Middle Eastern Nations who are struggling against imperialism can count on the solidarity of the Popular Government, which supports the search for a peaceful solution based on the interests of both the Arab and Jewish peoples. We shall condemn all reactionary governments which promote or practise racial segregation and anti-semitism.

Policy for Latin America

With regard to Latin America, the Popular Government will advocate an international policy which asserts the identity of Latin America in the world.

It is our view that Latin-American integration must be built on the basis of economies which have liberated themselves from imperialist forms of dependency and exploitation. Nevertheless, we shall maintain an active policy of bilateral agreements in those matters of interest for the development of Chile.

The Popular Government will take action to resolve frontier problems which are still outstanding on the basis of negotiations which exclude imperialist and reactionary intrigues, and which take into account both the interests of Chile and the interests of the peoples in neighbouring countries.

Chilean foreign policy and its diplomatic expression must break away from its bureaucratic habits and lack of initiative. Moreover, our foreign policy must derive from the peoples of many nations with the double purpose of, on the one hand, taking up the lessons learned from their struggles for application in the construction of our socialist society and, on the other, of offering them our experience, in such a manner that it is in the very practice of the idea that we shall build up the international solidarity for which we are fighting.

THE POPULAR GOVERNMENT'S FIRST FORTY MEASURES

1. **An end to enormous salaries!** We shall put a limit on the high salaries earned by those appointed directly by the President. We shall not allow people to hold simultaneously various paid posts such as advisory posts, directorships, representatives.

We shall do away with administrative promoters and political mongerers who use their official positions to promote their own ends and the interests of their friends and business and political acquaintances.

2. **More advisors? No!** All civil servants will belong to the normal staff grades and none will be exempted from the Administrative Statute's conditions. We will not have any more advisors in Chile.

3. **Honest administration.** We shall put an end to favouritism and grade jumping in the Public Administration. It will not be possible to remove civil servants from their posts without due cause. Nobody will be persecuted for their political or religious beliefs. We shall ensure the efficiency and honesty of government officials and the civil treatment of the public.

4. **No more unnecessary foreign trips.** Foreign journeys by government officials will not be allowed except for those which are really necessary in Chile's interests.

5. **No more use of government cars for pleasure.** Under no circumstances will the government's cars be used for private purposes. Those vehicles which are available will be used in the service of the public, — for transporting school children, for transporting people requiring medical attention from low income housing districts, or for police duties.

6. **The Civil Service will not enrich its employees.** We shall establish strict control over the incomes and property of high level public officials. The Government will no longer allow public officials to use their position to enrich themselves.

7. **Fair Pensions.** We must put a stop to millionaire level pensions whether they be for parliamentarians or any other public or private group, using the resources to improve pensions at the lower end of the scale.

8. **Fair and timely retirement.** We will give retirement rights to all people over 60 years of age who have been unable to retire because their contributions have not been paid.

9. **Social Security for Everyone.** We shall incorporate into the Social Security system all people in small and medium scale commerce, industry and farming, and independent workers, artisans, fishermen, small scale miners and housewives.

10. **Immediate and full payment of pensions and benefits.** We shall finally pay the increases in pensions due to retired members of the Armed Forces and we shall arrange for the proper and due payment of retirement pensions and widow's pensions under the Social Security System.

11. **Protection of the family.** We shall set up a Ministry for the protection of the family.

12. **Equal family allowances.** All family allowances will in future be fixed at the same level.

13. **Children are born to be happy!** We shall . provide free education, books, materials, exercise books etc. for all children throughout the basic level.

14. **Better meals for children.** We will provide breakfast for all children in the basic level and lunch for those children whose parents cannot provide it.

15. **Milk for all Chilean children.** We guarantee a daily ration of ½ litre of milk to all Chilean children.

16. **Family welfare clinics in all poor areas.** We shall set up family welfare clinics in all working class neighbourhoods, slums and squatter settlements.

17. **Real holidays for all Chilean students.** The best pupils selected from the basic educational level throughout the country will be invited to the Presidential Palace at Viña del Mar.

18. **Control of alcoholism.** We shall overcome alcoholism, by providing possibilities for a better life and not by repressive means. We shall stop abuse of the drinking laws and licensing regulations.

19. **Housing, lighting and drinking water for all Chileans.** We shall undertake an emergency plan for the rapid building of houses. Also, we shall ensure the provision of drinking water and electric lighting in every block.

20. **No more readjustable 'CORVI' payments.** CORVI, the Housing Corporations dividends and the loan repayments it receives will no longer be readjusted in line with rising prices.

21. **Fixed price rents.** We shall fix rents at an amount corresponding to 10% of family income as a maximum. Key rights will be abolished immediately.

22. **Vacant sites, No! Housing, Yes!** We shall build on all disused public, semi-public and municipal sites.

23. **Property taxes on mansions only.** We shall free from the payment of property taxes the owners of dwellings with a surface below 80 square metres as long as the owner lives there permanently and the house is neither a luxury house nor a beach villa.

24. **A real Agrarian Reform.** We shall intensify Agrarian Reform, which will also benefit medium and small scale farmers, *minifundia* holders, sharecroppers, employees and temporary rural labourers.

25. **Medical attention without bureaucracy.** We shall eliminate all the bureaucratic and administrative obstacles which hinder or make difficult the provision of medical attention to contributors and unemployed people.

26. **Free medical attention in hospitals.** We shall abolish payment for medicines and examinations in hospitals.

27. **No more artificially high prices for medicines.** We shall drastically reduce the price of medicines by lowering the import duties and taxes on the raw materials.

28. **Scholarships for students.** We shall establish the right of all

good students to obtain a scholarship for the basic and middle school levels and university education, taking into account performance and the family's economic resources.

29. **Physical education and popular tourism and holidays.** We shall promote physical education and we shall establish sports fields in schools and all neighbourhoods. Every school and low income urban or rural housing district will have a sports field. We shall organize and promote low income tourism and holidays.

30. **A new economy to put an end to inflation.** We shall increase the production of items of popular consumption. We shall control prices and prevent inflation by immediately setting up the new economic structure.

31. **No more links with the International Monetary Fund.** We shall renege the commitments with the International Monetary Fund. We shall put an end to the continual shameful devaluation of the escudo.

32. **No more taxes on food.** We shall stop increases in taxes which affect basic food necessities.

33. **Abolition of the sales tax.** We shall abolish the sales tax and replace it by another more just and expedite tax system.

34. **No more speculation.** We shall severely penalize economic crimes.

35. **No more unemployment.** We shall ensure the right of all Chileans to work and we shall prevent unjustified dismissals.

36. **Work for all Chileans.** We shall immediately create new sources of employment by implementing plans for public works and house building, by setting up new industries, and by carrying out development projects.

37. **The Riot Police Unit will be disbanded.** We shall ensure law and order in lower and middle class residential areas and the protection of the individual. The police and detectives will be restricted to crime prevention duties. We shall disband the Riot Police Unit incorporating its members into the normal duties of police vigilance against delinquency.

38. **An end to class justice.** We shall set up a rapid and free legal procedure, in which the Neighbourhood Committees will cooperate, to examine and resolve special cases such as quarrels, ruffianism, abandonment of the home and acts which disturb the community.

39. **Legal advice bodies in all neighbourhoods.** We shall set up Legal

Advice Bodies in all low income neighbourhoods and districts.

40. **The Creation of a National Institute of Art and Culture.** We shall create a National Institute of Art and Culture and schools for training in the arts in all districts.

THE TWENTY BASIC POINTS OF
THE POPULAR UNITY GOVERNMENT'S AGRARIAN REFORM

ONE. Agrarian Reform and agricultural development will not be isolated factors, but will form an integral part of the overall plan for transforming the economy into one which serves the whole people. This implies that Agrarian Reform will not only involve the expropriation of all *latifundia*, the distribution of land to peasant producers and rural labourers and the provision of the technical assistance and credits which are necessary to enable them to produce what Chile requires, but also includes the transformation of commercial and industrial relationships for the sale and purchase of products required by peasants for consumption and for production. The marketing and processing of agricultural output must be in the hands of the State or peasant or consumer cooperatives.

TWO. The benefits of Agrarian Reform will be extended to the groups of medium and small farmers, smallholders, employees, sharecroppers and temporary labourers who have so far been excluded from these benefits.

THREE. The peasantry, represented by unions, cooperatives and small scale farmers' organizations will replace the representatives of the large estates in all Government departments and agencies. The Popular Unity Government will only deal with these representatives of the rural population because it is they who are the true representatives of the 98% of the population which lives from agricultural activities or depends on an income from agriculture.

At the level of the Ministry of Agriculture and Agrarian Reform, as it will then be called, under whose direct responsibility will be placed all branches of the State which deal with the agricultural sector, a National Peasant Council will be set up to advise the Minister and top civil servants and officials of the various government agencies. This Council will be democratically elected by the grass roots peasant organizations.

At the same time Regional Peasant Councils will be formed in each of the country's agricultural zones in which the officials responsible for the zone and the elected peasant representatives will participate on an equal footing. All the measures necessary for implementing Agrarian Reform and agricultural development will be adopted in these National and Regional Peasant Councils—i.e. expropriations, land distribution, credits, marketing of products and inputs, etc.

FOUR. Agrarian Reform will no longer be implemented on a farm by farm basis but by areas and, in each of these areas, productive work will be guaranteed for all peasants and rural labourers in the area either in direct work on the land, or in the processing and distribution of the products, or in the provision of the general services required in production.

FIVE. We shall employ new legal concepts to help us to achieve integration and cooperation by the united action of the various rural organizations of wage earners, employees, sharecroppers, temporary labourers and small and medium scale farmers. This will involve an increase in the number of tasks to be carried out by the unions, agrarian reform settlements *(asentamientos)* * , rural cooperatives, indigenous Indian communities and other types and forms of small farmers' organizations, such as the small farmers' committees.

Furthermore, the Popular Government will end the present mockery of the law whereby agricultural employers refrain from paying the 2% employer's contribution required by the law governing peasant unions inducing the bankruptcy of the rural workers' trade unions.

SIX. Areas under forest will also be included in the Agrarian Reform.

SEVEN. Only small and medium scale farmers will be excluded from expropriation, and only those larger scale farmers whose social and economic contributions to agricultural production and rural community development are recognized by the peasants will have the right to retain some land. And in any case, the right to retain some land will not be accompanied by the preferential right to select this piece of land, since it may be necessary to offer other land so as facilitate the restructuring of peasant holdings.

---

* *Asentamiento*. This was a transitional system adopted during the Christian Democrat Government and during the first year of the Popular Unity Government to manage the expropriated estates for a three to five year period. The *asentamiento* coincides with the boundaries of the old estate and is run as a unit on a cooperative basis by the agrarian reform corporation and *asentamiento* members. During this transitional period the peasants are trained to take over full management responsibilities and Government agencies provide technical assistance and credit. According to the law the peasants may decide whether the land will be divided into individual holdings or be organized and operated on a cooperative basis on the expiry of the *asentamiento* period, though the Government may impose cooperative ownership operation if there are overriding technical reasons for doing so. (Editor)

EIGHT. Working capital will be included in expropriations so that, right from the very beginning, expropriated holdings have the capital necessary for farming operations.

NINE. Technical assistance to peasants will be provided without charge and special credit, technical assistance and training programmes will be drawn up for the most backward groups especially the indigenous Indian committees.

TEN. Each peasant will have family rights to his house and garden. Production will be organized preferably under the cooperative system, though in special cases individual cultivation and ownership of land may be considered.

ELEVEN. By means of credit, technical assistance, regional and national planning, we shall orient production towards high priced products both for export and for the home market. Credits for certain types of labour intensive products, such as pigs and poultry, will be reserved for small farmers and other peasants to help increase their income and improve their social and economic situation.

TWELVE. At an early stage of the Popular Government the Agrarian Reform Law will be fully enforced, making use of all powers that the present Government does not wish to use or has not been able to use, such as allocating land to cooperatives, defending the interests of sharecroppers and tenants, reorganizing irrigation areas and systems, etc. The necessary amendments to the present Agrarian Reform Law will be discussed and approved by the National and Regional Peasant Councils before being sent to Parliament.

THIRTEEN. The State will guarantee the purchase of that part of the peasants' output which is not marketed at official prices through the normal channels, and gradually the State will make anticipatory contracts for all livestock and agricultural output which is planned according to the country's needs.

Advance credits for production will be granted to small peasants in cash only, and not in the form of credit notes as happens in most cases at present and which involves the further exploitation of those peasants who can only get their credit notes discounted at burdensome rates and on unfavourable terms.

FOURTEEN. Agriculture-based industries will preferably be located in the agricultural regions which at present suffer most severely from agricultural unemployment or underemployment.

FIFTEEN. The State will nationalize all monopolies controlling the marketing, preparation and processing of livestock and agricultural products or the necessary inputs for agricultural production. These enterprises will be either directly managed by the State, with advice from the Peasant Councils, or they will be handed over to rural cooperatives.

SIXTEEN. A national social security system for all rural workers will be set up, especially including those small farmers who are at present excluded from social security. In the same way, we shall ensure that social security arrangements for farmers and agrarian reform settlements will be continued.

SEVENTEEN. Special programmes will be undertaken to improve and to construct rural housing because, until now, peasants and rural workers have been excluded from all previous housing improvement programmes.

EIGHTEEN. We shall set up rural hostels in the principal towns in agricultural areas,so that passing migrants and temporary labourers or peasants on business in town have somewhere to lodge which also provides them with support and guidance in carrying out their tasks, especially in relation to public services, education, health, etc.

NINETEEN. A general policy for education will be developed through adult literacy programmes, publications of books, news-papers and radio programmes for the rural population, and through courses on agricultural technology in line with the region's production plans. At the same time, theatre, art and other cultural activities will be promoted, which will help develop the character of rural communities.

TWENTY. A special effort will be made to push ahead with plans for the protection of natural resources, forestation plans, etc., and with plans for making better use of irrigated areas.

SUMMARY OF THE SIX YEAR PLAN
1971 – 1976[1]

National Planning Office, Republic of Chile

[1] This summary of the 1971-76 Development Plan, prepared from 16 large volumes of national and regional plans, and was not intended for professional economic use. Unfortunately it does not do justice to the plan; it omits details of the employment targets and foreign trade and payments objectives and does not adequately reflect the degree of detail and integration achieved in the plan. However, despite its inadequacies the summary is included here in order to provide some minimum indication of the Popular Unity's Planning efforts. For further details consult the following Plan documents: Republic of Chile, Estrategia Global del Plan de la Economia Nacional 1971-1976, ODEPLAN 1971, Santiago; and Plan de la Economia Nacional 1971-1976 ODEPLAN Serie I, Planes Sexenales Vols. 1-16, 1971.
(Editor)

INDEX

The New Development Strategy for 1971-1976

The development of Chilean society, based on a high degree of foreign dependence, has resulted in a series of acute social and economic imbalances. Property and income have been concentrated in relatively few hands; the economy was structured to satisfy the requirements of the highest income groups, while a large part of the population has been economically and socially 'marginalized'. Through their control of property and income the minority groups have traditionally wielded political power.

In 1971 the country began a new historical phase, in which the working classes came to power on the basis of a demand for radical change in people's living patterns, in the country's institutional structure, in production relations and the control of the means of production, so as to lay the foundations for a new society.

In defining an operational strategy for the development of this new society during the transitional period, the Government's first concern is the existence of sizeable social groups who are not incorporated in the main processes and advances in Chilean society. Even when employed, these people endure miserable living conditions, which prevent them from exercizing fully their civil rights or from making decisions, as free citizens, concerning their own future.

The Government has also taken into account the substantial numbers of small and medium-scale businessmen and tradesmen, and self-employed white collar and manual workers. Both the quantitative importance of these groups, and the fact that their income level puts them in a similar position to the majority of the working class, make it only appropriate that they should participate fully in the definition of the transitional process.

Another important factor defining the strategy is the existence of under-utilized or idle capacity in nearly all economic sectors.

Furthermore, as far as land tenure is concerned, legal measures already exist to abolish the *latifundia*. There is sufficient organizational experience to carry out changes and improvements in the agricultural sector to ensure that land reform results in increased production, thereby raising the peasants' standard of living.

The strategy chosen by the Government involves the incorporation of the entire population into the process of change. The problem of inequality in the living conditions of the majority of the population must be solved. immediately. This involves two simultaneous processes: a large increase in employment and a substantial increase in real terms in the salaries and wages of the lowest income groups.

It will be necessary to build up an economically predominant socially-owned sector to ensure substantial changes in the composition of supply so that it corresponds more closely to social requirements. Consumption is to be based on the satisfaction of the basic needs of the majority, which means that these people must first be organized to defend their own interests and attend to their own needs. Also, maximum advantage must be taken of natural resources and relatively simple production techniques with high labour intensity. To achieve this, it is necessary for a substantial proportion of total production to be planned according to social criteria.

For economic expansion, we are counting on the surpluses generated by the foreign and monopolistic enterprises which will become part of the socially-owned sector, and on savings made in the Government's day-to-day activities.

Until full employment is reached — including within this concept a substantial decline in underemployment (part-time jobs or jobs in low productivity activities such as agriculture and services) — emphasis will not generally be put on productivity increases obtained by mechanization but rather on careful choice of efficient labour-intensive techniques, especially for middle and small-scale projects. However, the average cumulative increase in productivity which has been considered in the plan is 2.3% per annum –higher than the 1.5% a year achieved in the period 1960-1969.

In the longer term, once the employment objectives have been achieved, some important high productivity projects will be undertaken, which will permit Chile to compete with new types of products on a large scale in international markets.

Economic Aspects of the 1971 – 1976 Strategy

The employment target fixed for this six-year period involves creating 988,000 new jobs. This figure is obtained by first estimating the normal increase in the labour force: 402,000 people; second, reducing open unemployment (which in 1970 was about 6%) to a frictional rate of about 2%, which requires the creation of 119,000 new jobs. Finally, in order to raise the family income of the lowest-paid groups, the necessary conditions will be created to allow a far larger proportion of women from these families to work. This means an increase of 467,000 new jobs. (In order to assure the greater participation of women in the labour force a big effort will be made to equip nurseries and day-care centres. In addition, working hours for women will be made more convenient and half-time jobs will be provided.)

The increase in employment, combined with higher productivity, will yield an overall growth of about 50% in the gross domestic product for the period 1970-1976. This implies an annual average cumulative rate of growth of 7%, much higher than in any comparable historical period.

An increase in consumption of the majority of the population is regarded as the main dynamic element of the transitional economy, therefore a substantial rise in the rate of saving cannot be considered. The proposed target is slightly above the average historical rate of domestic savings (15.8% in 1970). Thus aggregate consumption would grow at the same rate as output — that is, at about a cumulative average of 7% a year, or 5% *per capita*.

In the new context, the enterprises in the socially-owned sector must generate savings equivalent to about 10% of output, if the savings targets are to be achieved. This is an extraordinary responsibility for the workers and executives in the socially-owned sector.

As regards the sectoral composition of production, the proposed strategy departs fundamentally from past patterns. The sectors which grew most rapidly in the past were basic metals, chemical products, and durable goods in general, since demand from the highest-income groups was concentrated on these products. This was also the case for all types of services, especially commerce and personal services. If previous trends were to continue, sectoral growth would become increasingly unbalanced. But on the basis of the new structure of demand, the production increases calculated for 1970-1976 show a relatively even increase in output of the different sectors, except in construction. The extraordinary growth proposed for this sector is a consequence of the great importance attached to housing, schools, hospitals and other construction for public services, in order to satisfy social needs, such as recreation, holidays and tourism, sports, and other activities.

A general analysis of the shares in the national product projected for 1976 as compared with 1970 shows that the Government will increase its share from 9.39% to 11.56%. Output generated by enterprises will increase slightly from 77.86% to 78.19%. However, the ratio between private and socially-owned enterprises will undergo substantial modification. Private enterprises, which in 1970 produced 68% of the total national product, will account for only 48%, and the socially-owned sector will increase its share from 10% to 30%.

Salaries and wages will increase their share in national product from 35% in 1970 to 46% in 1976. The gross profit of enterprises will be affected by the redistribution of income, falling from 35.5% of the product to 23.5%. For private enterprises the decrease will be from 30.6% to 13.4%. However, the gross profits of enterprises in the social property sector will increase from nearly 5% to just over 10%. This is due to the fact that the socially-owned sector will include expropriated monopolies, which had a higher profit margin.

With respect to the distribution of the available income among the factors of production, there will be quite a strong internal redistribution in favour of wage-earners and the self-employed, whose share will increase from 51% to nearly 61% of total product, while that of owners of capital and entrepreneurs will decrease from 18.6% to 8.3%.

The share of available income going abroad will decline from 3% to 1.2% since the nationalization of basic resources and other foreign controlled activities means that the profits of such companies will now remain within Chile.

To reach these targets, a total level of investment of about 125,000 million escudos (at 1970 prices) or $10,700 million is needed over the six-year period (at an average exchange rate of 11.7 escudos per dollar).[1] This investment will cover replacement needs as well as the requirements for increasing productive capacity. With respect to the composition of investment, 25% will be assigned to social investments, 17% to basic infrastructure and transport equipment, 5% to electric power and the remaining 52% to directly productive activities.

In the new strategy, the capacity to import is no longer a basic element but constitutes an adjustable factor in the structural transformation and reorientation of the economy towards the needs of the majority of the population. Therefore, although the programmes for export promotion, import substitution and economic complementarity play an important role in the plan, none is decisive for the overall success of the strategy.

---

[1] United States' dollars.

Total exports will reach $1,798 million with a faster growth rate during the early years as a result of copper exports.

Total imports will reach $1,836 million in 1976, comprising 28% capital goods, 22% consumption goods and 50% intermediate goods. The proportion of imports to gross product will decline from 15.4% in 1970 to 14% in 1976. This small decrease in the import coefficient is due to the change in composition of demand, to special efforts to substitute imports of capital goods, and to strict control over luxury imports. The plan envisages a deficit on trading account, which will reach $38 million in 1976. To this should be added the servicing of the foreign debt and other capital payments, thereby requiring further resources to be obtained from abroad.

Objectives of the 1971 — 1976 Plan
The objectives to be achieved by 1976 are:

1. greater economic independence by taking over from foreign control basic resources such as copper, iron, nitrate, and also the financial, industrial and marketing activities;

2. the transition from an 'exclusive' economy to an economy with full popular participation; the target is to increase the proportion of the active population from the 30.7% in 1970 to 36% in 1976;

3. an improved distribution of national income, offering a more just and more dignified life to the Chilean people and increasing the purchasing power of wage-earners, which will provide a growing market for domestic industry;

4. a restructuring of the productive apparatus so as to improve the standard of living. This implies producing goods of popular design in each branch and line of production;

5. an increase in the rate of accumulation and a change in the pattern of investment. To achieve the investment rate necessary for increased production, the surpluses which previously left the country or were spent on luxury consumption will be mobilized for Chile's own benefit;

6. an expanded socially-owned sector, transforming it into the motive force of development and creating operational sectors which will facilitate an increase in efficiency and improved planning in the socially-owned sector;

7. a higher national output, moving from the existent stagnant economic situation to one of sustained development. These production targets will be achieved by means of Annual Plans, which

will be implemented in accordance with the guidelines set out in this Six-Year Plan.

Plans for the Productive Sectors
1. *Agriculture*
A fundamental aspect of the transformation strategy is the implementation of a far-reaching land reform. Basically, it is intended that this reform will promote rapid and substantial change in the land tenure system and in the existing agricultural production relations. The following are the Popular Unity Programme's basic points relating to land reform:

- acceleration of the land reform process, by expropriating land in excess of the maximum established allowance;

- immediate incorporation into the cultivated area of abandoned and poorly exploited state lands;

- expropriated lands will be organized preferably on co-operative ownership lines. Peasants will have titles which accredit their ownership of the house and plot of land assigned to them and of their corresponding rights in the indivisible co-operative lands;

- in certain cases, land will be assigned to small farmers, tenants, share-croppers and to trained agricultural workers;

- reorganization of *minifundia* property through the gradual formation of agricultural co-operatives;

- the inclusion of small and medium-scale proprietors in the advantages and services of co-operatives operating within their geographic area;

- support and enlargement of indigenous Indian communities.

In order to organize the reformed area, a new form of organization — Agrarian Reform Centre — has been created which is compatible with the present Agrarian Reform Law. This is a transitory socio-economic organization, which is to be introduced in the areas expropriated by the Popular Unity Government. The internal structure of these centres will include a General Assembly and Workers Assembly; Control, Production and Welfare Committees; and Production Teams.

The peasants will be integrated into the decision-making process through the National Peasant Council, to participate in the agricultural development plans and policies.

As a longer-term objective a reorientation of the productive process is planned, synthesized in the following three policies: technical change in agricultural activities — changing from extensive to a more intensive agriculture; changes in the regionalization of production; and industrialization of rural areas.

Production plans
Agriculture and cattle production are to grow by 46% between 1971 and 1976. The production of cereals will increase by 31%, and root crops by 42%. By 1976 it is aimed to have doubled the 1970 production of dry pulses. In relation to oil and sugar crops, it is planned to double the 1970 production level of sunflowers and to increase sugar beet production by 60% and raps by 50%.

An increase of 43.7% in cattle production is planned, which means that in 1976 22,000 more tons[2] of beef, 10,000 more tons of lamb and 8,000 more tons of pork, 38,000 more tons of chicken, 556 million more litres of milk and 685 million more eggs will be produced than in 1970. For vegetables, fruits and vineyards a 50% increase is projected for the six-year period.

The main programmes are:

1. Agricultural development and technical assistance programme; aimed at rationalizing productive processes by means of technical and financial assistance at farm level. This involves improving out-of-date cultivation, irrigation and soil-use techniques, the improvement of mechanization, and greater use of selected seeds, pesticides, fertilizers and other inputs. This will cost 1,560 million escudos and will benefit an area of about 312,000 hectares.

2. The improvement of irrigation techniques and the new irrigation programme will allow 114,000 extra hectares to be put under irrigation, requiring a total investment of 1,171 million escudos — (47% for investment in irrigation, 48% for improvement of irrigation techniques and 5% for the purchase of materials and equipment).

3. A programme to improve soil use and management techniques, consisting of technical assistance to develop the efficient use of agricultural soils, to increase yields and for the defence of natural resources.

4. Re-forestation programme. This includes four initial projects involving an investment of 1,340 million escudos over thirty years. An investment expenditure of about 666 million escudos is pro-

---

[2] Throughout this document 'tons' should be taken as meaning 'metric tons'.

grammed for the six-year period. These projects are:

(a) A national re-forestation programme costing 83 million escudos in the provinces from Valparaiso to Osorno, with plantations of pine (*pinus radiata* and Douglas fir), eucalyptus and also indigenous species.

(b) An integrated re-forestation programme costing 63 million escudos, covering 75,000 hectares over the six-year period, mainly in 'agrarian reform settlements', peasant cooperatives and on the lands of small proprietors.

(c) A re-forestation programme costing 93 million escudos in the northern provinces of Tarapacá and Antofagasta, planting an area of 80,000 hectares with Tamarugo (*prosopis tamarugo* species). This will make it possible to begin a sheep-rearing programme.

(d) A pine (*pinus radiata*) re-forestation programme, at a cost of 425 million escudos, covering 300,600 hectares in the provinces from Talca to Malleco. The aim is to ensure normal supplies for the cellulose and paper industry as well as for the many lumber yards in this area.

5. An infrastructure programme including about 23 projects which will allow nearly 400 extra hectares to be cultivated and the improved cultivation of approximately a further one million hectares. Seventeen projects will be completed during the period, including the Chungará project in Tarapacá; Calama irrigation in Antofagasta; irrigation of Paloma, Choapa-Illapel, Elqui and Hoya de Limarí in Coquimbo; Puntilla del Viento, irrigation of Rengo, El Manzano, Maule Norte, Pencahue, from Aconcagua to Talca; Digua and Maule Sur in Linares; Laja-Diguillín in Ñuble; completion of the South Bío-Bío and Cautín projects in Malleco and Cautín.

6. Other infrastructure investments for marketing and agricultural industries. This programme has a total cost of 1,280 million escudos for the 1970-1976 period.

7. A programme of agriculture-based industries, including wheat and pulse, canning and preserving of fruit and other products, potato processing, industries based on livestock, beer industries, milk-dehydrating plants, basic oil extraction plants, beet sugar mills, forage dehydrating plants, etc., with a total investment of 2,400 million escudos.

8. Industrial projects to support agriculture, establishing factories to produce agricultural machinery and implements such as ploughs,

motor-saws, levellers, water carts, etc. There are also projects for new plants to produce super-phosphates and ammonium phosphate.

2. *Fishing*

The fishing sector will become an alternative important source of protein products, and will play an important part in the process of export diversification. Also, in accordance with the policy of making the most of natural resources in activities with rapid maturity and low capital intensity, special impetus will be given during the period to fishing activities, both for the domestic and the export market.

It is hoped to increase domestic annual per capita consumption from 20 kilos per inhabitant to 34 kilos by 1976, signifying an increase in production from 193,000 tons a year to some 375,000 by 1976. The expected increase in exports is shown in the following Table.

Increase in Exports

(Thousands of Dollars)

	Average 1966-1967	Goal 1976
Frozen	6,120	12,000
Dry salted	80	500
Canned	300	14,000
Flour/oil	17,050	25,000
Dry seaweed	1,000	6,000
TOTAL:	24,550	57,500

As a result of recent fishing research, it has been possible to determine the enormous production potential of certain exportable high value species, such as oysters, large and small mussels in the Southern region, and also for protein concentrates for human consumption.

Fisheries production programme

In order to achieve the fisheries sector's production targets the following programmes have been drawn up:

1. Renewal of the fishing fleet with an approximate investment of $3.2 million.

2. Renewal of the industrialized fishing fleet at an estimated cost of about $17 million, with a high percentage of national components.

3. Artificial cultivation especially of oysters, with an investment of $1.5 million, and of mussels with a total cost of $25 million, producing some $14 million during the first year of production.

4. Industrialization of sea products, including canning and freezing industries, and industries for producing protein concentrates and dry salted fish.

Fisheries infrastructure programme

It is intended to create specialized fishing ports, with an industrial district and shipyards for boat repair and maintenance. The establishment of a fishing-port in the Bío-Bío area with an investment of about $5 million is the first priority. It is also proposed to install a fishing base in Valparaiso region at an estimated cost of $3 million. An investment estimated at $500,000 has been allocated for the improvement of fishing port facilities in the port of San Antonio.

It is planned to mechanize the ports of Iquique and Arica, investing $1 million and $800,000 respectively.

In the short term, the installation of a central terminal in Valparaiso is planned at a cost of $1 million. There is also a plan to set up terminals in Santiago, Concepción, Constitución, Tomé, Temuco, Puerto Montt, Chacabuco and Punta Arenas.

3. *Mining*

The development of a dominant socially-owned area in the mining sector, which is responsible for exploiting resources according to social criteria, will permit the abundant surpluses generated in mining to contribute fully to the country's overall development. This implies a gradual move away from capitalist towards socialist relations of production, in which it is vital that the workers become conscious of the fact that the great contribution they make to the economy, in terms of productivity and generation of foreign exchange, cannot be for their own exclusive benefit.

In concrete terms it is planned to achieve an increase in production with the expanded installed capacity in the large nationalized companies, and to reorganize medium-sized mines, eventually doing away with the smallest mining operations.

It is of great importance to implement measures for the nationalization of foreign trade in this sector, since this will allow the country to take full advantage of the possibilities opened up by this new type of foreign relations.

All these short and medium-term measures will be in accordance with the general policy of making more rational use of the subsoil resources and integrating them into large industrial complexes, which will be set up to develop heavy industry, specialized machinery and exports, which add most value to existing natural resources within the country. This implies studying in depth the resource potential and undertaking applied scientific research in order to determine how to make the best use of these resources.

The production and expansion programmes for mining activities envisage a 60% increase in copper production with respect to 1970, which means an output of 1,130,000 metric tons of fine copper and an investment of about 945 million escudos, not including the investments necessary to solve technical problems resulting from the expansion programmes.

The production of fine copper will increase from 94,600 to 246,500 metric tons, which will be achieved when ENAMI's (National Mining Corporation) mixed plants come into operation as in Baquedano, El Salado, Paipote, Combarbalá, Vallenar, etc., and the independent medium-scale mining plants (Lagasca and Michilla) begin operations. The Ventanas Refinery will be expanded in order to reach an annual output of 200,000 tons of electrolytic copper by 1975.

ENAMI's expansion programme includes several projects which will facilitate an increase in its activities. These include

1. three expansion projects, the first of which is the expansion of the Rio Salado concentration plant and the other two are part of the expansion of the Ventanas complex; these projects will result in an increase from 48,000 to 120,000 tons a year of smelted copper, an increase from 100,000 to 200,000 tons a year of refined products, thereby increasing the proportion of copper which is processed domestically;

2. mineral treatment plants will be set up in Baquedano, El Salado, Paipote, Combarbalá, Vallenar and Calama, which involve a total investment of 329.8 million escudos and a daily processing capacity of 4,300 tons of mineral as from 1974, resulting in an increase in blister copper.

Iron production will increase 23.6% during the period, rising to 14,229,000 tons in 1976, with an investment of 2.5 million escudos. The following projects are among the most important:

(a) The expansion of Romeral to attain a material-moving capacity of 24 million tons per year and the installation of a concentrating plant with a daily capacity of 13,600 tons. As a result, total output of the mine will increase 50%, reaching 4.5 million tons of mineral and concentrates.

(b) The Boquerón Chañar deposit will be developed and begin producing in 1974.

(c) The exploitation of big deposits in Atacama province. (Cerro Negro Norte and Santa Clara).

The nitrate expansion programme will permit an increase from the 1970 figure of 670,000 tons to over 1 million tons as from 1973, with an investment of 312 million escudos. Sodium sulphate and silicate plants in Antofagasta are among the projects which will help to develop chemical nitrate subproducts in substitution of imports. There are also plans to improve the supply of industrial water in order to rationalize production. The establishment of a chemical complex is programmed to complement nitrate mining, reviving the local economy. Two iodine plants will be built and iodine and borax deposits will be exploited.

4. ˙ Industry

The Government intends to substantially reorient the production structure in the industrial sector, breaking with the basic contradiction implied in redistribution policies which operate only on the side of demand while, on the supply side, production of non-essential goods is still given preference, nullifying redistribution efforts. This reorientation will be attained by breaking the control of industrial monopolistic power by establishing a dominant socially-owned sector, permitting a large part of the surplus to be channelled into investment. Real changes can be effected in the production relationship in this area through the effective participation of workers at all levels, without sacrificing or discarding rational administration principles. Worker participation, assisted by adequate technology, will facilitate the reorientation of production so that the great majority of the population may have access to a series of industrial goods that have so far been designed only to satisfy the requirements of wealthy groups.

However, since the socially-owned sector will encompass about one third of total output only, its main importance is qualitative. (The private sector will continue to be responsible for the greater part of the country's productive effort.)

The programme envisages the development of a sizeable mixed

area, preferably with state capital in majority control, which will ensure that social considerations determine production decisions, but in which national and foreign private managers have the opportunity to develop their initiative and management capacity, and to provide capital at a reasonable rate of return.

Alongside these two sectors a private sector will exist comprising medium and small enterprises, which will receive full guarantees for the security of their property and be freed from the monopolistic exploitation to which they were previously subject. In addition, they will enjoy full support from credit institutions and technical assistance to improve their output levels, productivity and efficiency, and they will be assured of supplies of inputs at reasonable prices.

With respect to foreign investment, some enterprises will be expropriated and others will be converted into mixed enterprises, in accordance with the agreed treatment of foreign capital in the Andean Group.

In the new economy there will be three different types of goods and services, subject to different policies. First, a number of essential mass consumption goods and services will require the provision of maximum facilities and encouragements to production in the private sector, and production and investment decisions in the social area. The main objective is to ensure very large supplies of these goods at reasonably stable prices. The demand for these products will become the most dynamic factor in the economy, substantially altering the historical trend in which these goods, known as 'traditional industrial products', grew less quickly than the durable ones known as 'dynamic goods'. The second important group of products is composed of a number of raw materials of widespread use such as steel, cement, wood, sulphuric acid, paper, electricity, fuels, glass, asbestos and other building inputs as well as capital goods, which can be manufactured domestically, and a number of industrial goods for export. The third group is composed of non-essential goods and services, which will only receive credit once the needs of the above groups are satisfied, to avoid serious unemployment. These goods will be less subject to price control, while special emphasis will be placed on maintaining the surplus generated, either directly, because they are produced in the social area, or through taxation, when they are produced in the private sector.

Another fundamental aspect of the new economic plan is increasing technological independence, which will lead to the new demand structure with emphasis on the production of basic goods.

The national policy will be one designed to select technologies which maximize the use of labour, consistent with previously fixed production levels. This does not imply a technological lag, but the selection of advanced techniques only in those phases of the production process where the quality of the product depends closely on specialized machinery. For all other phases, intermediate technology which helps to provide employment will be selected.

An increase in industrial production during this six-year period, and the adaptation of the productive framework to the new supply structure require a total investment of nearly 29 million escudos (at 1970 prices), or 23% of the country's total investment during this period.

The following are some of the projects in the plan:

(a) Nine milk plants including the milk plant in La Serena with a production of 7.3 million litres of pasteurized milk per year and 36,500 kilos of butter; the milk plant in Copalca which will produce 73 million litres of milk per year; the milk plant in Osorno (Calo) with 203 million litres per year.

(b) Four chicken slaughter-houses, among which is the slaughter and refrigeration house of Marchigue which will process and commercialize almost 4.5 million kilos of chicken.

(c) Sheep, cow and pig slaughter-houses, among the most important of which are the slaughter-house in Tierra del Fuego, which will process 3 million kilos of meat per year, and that in Castro which will process 4.5 million kilos.

(d) Industries connected with slaughter-houses such as those processing fats and suets, entrails, dried blood, wool, sausages etc.

(e) A national programme of refrigerating centres throughout the country. Three important freezing plants are presently being installed, one in San Antonio with an annual storage capacity of 200,000 boxes of apples and pears, 870,000 kilos of chilled meat and 2.7 million kilos of frozen meat. Another is in Valparaiso, with a storage capacity of 260,000 boxes of apples, and one in Los Lirios with a capacity for 1,150,000 kilos of lemons per year.

(f) Installation of plants to select and control the quality of agricultural products such as fruits and vegetables for immediate consumption.

(g) Installation of packing and canning plants including the fruit packing plant in Aconcagua which will process 2 million peaches a year and 3 million kilos of grapes; the fruit processing plant in Maipo which will have a processing capacity for 10 million kilos of fruit; an almond processing plant with an annual capacity of 1 million kilos; the fruit centre in Colchagua with a capacity to process 7 million kilos of fruit and to refrigerate 5 million kilos; a tomato concentrates factory with capacity to produce 7 million kilos a year, using 40 million kilos of tomatoes.

Among the most important agricultural projects are the plant for ploughs and harrows which will produce 2,400 units a year; a diesel motor plant with installed capacity for 15,000 units a year; and a power-saw factory, with a production of 6,000 units a year. There are projects for the installation of new superphosphates and fused phosphate plants with annual capacity for 2,600 tons and 60,000 tons respectively.

Among the projects considered in the construction plan is the enlargement of the Pacific Steel Company plant which will increase its production from 600,000 to 1 million tons per year; a cement factory in Antofagasta with a production of 130,000 tons per year: the enlargement of the Lirquén plate glass plant which will reach a production of 40,000 tons per year; and a mechanized brick factory.

There is also a copper processing programme which requires the expansion of the Copper Manufacturing Company (MADECO). Plants to elaborate plates, shapes and bars of copper alloys are being considered. There is also a plan to install a plant to produce precision parts for the electrical and electronics industry.

The main projects in the electricity and electronics programme are: a semi-conductor plant to produce transistors and small signal diodes using the 'flat silicon' technique and the single integrated circuits technique; expansion of the electric motor industry; production of telephones and automatic and semi-automatic plants in Chile; new factories to produce high-tension protection and manoeuvring equipment, electric traction equipment, condensers, potentiometers and carbon resistors, electric bulbs, domestic electrical products and others.

5. *Transport*

The Chilean transport system is anarchic and suffers from irrational competition. This applies even in state entities responsible for basic transport services. These entities have become centres of power whose ultimate aim, in many cases, has not been to provide good standard transport for the people but to promote the indiscriminate growth of the respective entity, by concentrating on the development of an immense infrastructure rather than efficient operation.

The source of this anarchy is the absence of policies, planning mechanisms, coordination and control. This has led to numerous simultaneous investments and tax exemptions granted to competing private groups resulting in a permanent deficit for the state transport services, or little more than a hidden subsidy to a series of private activities.

One of the most serious problems resulting from this lack of planning and coordination is in sea transport; there is a serious loss of foreign exchange arising from freight shipments,especially in the transport of minerals. Thus the central objectives for the transport sector within the framework of the overall development strategy will be:

● to support the policies set by the overall strategy;

● to support the policies of decentralization and a more rational regional development;

● to improve the transport system such that it no longer constitutes an obstacle to the development of numerous other activities.

The chief measures to attain these objectives are:

● creation of institutional mechanisms with sufficient means to set and regulate coordinated transportation policies;

● strengthening of the socially-owned sector in the different branches of transport by keeping or creating an operational specialization in accordance with the technological necessities of the different services;

● full rationalization of the various transport enterprises, improvement of their operating efficiency and internal techniques;

● general rationalization of price and tax policies in this area so as to promote the smooth development of the different means of transport.

The effective participation of workers in the planning, operation and control of the socially-owned sector is indispensable if the implementation of these policies is to be consistent with the substance of the Government's social objectives. Also important in this area is the workers' awareness and acceptance of the need to share the gains generated by the operation of highly productive enterprises.

The main projects in this area are:

Railroad Transport
Purchase and repair of locomotives: remodelling and construction of

carriages; equipping and reorganization of machine-shops; construction of detours and terminals and improvement of stretches where new or heavier traffic lines are expected; a freight station at Chena instead of Alameda, and completion of CTC between Talca and San Fernando; electricity and welded rails in the first zone; completion of the electricity and operation of signals to Concepción; a track renewal programme; a project for the reconstruction of the Transandean railway; new lines in the Concepción zone, and between Santiago and Valparaíso.

Road Transport
Production of 5,000 lorries a year for highway freight conveyance; production of 200 passenger buses a year for inter-urban transport; incorporation of 1,200 buses a year for urban, surburban and rural transport.

Road Investments
Hard-surfacing of 1,659 kilometres of roads a year, of 54.4 kilometres of bridges a year; construction of 200 kilometres of new routes a year; improvement of 775 kilometres a year; construction of 1,573 kilometres of roads extending within agricultural areas; connection of 26 international highways with neighbouring countries; a North to South motorway and a peripheral motorway, Americo Vespucio, in Santiago.

Air Transport
LAN Chile requires at least one plane for international service, a Boeing 727 for the national service, and a fleet of STOL planes to serve local traffic in the central area. As for infrastructure, projects include a General Airports Plan which includes Chacalluta Airport in Arica, Cerro Moreno in Antofagasta, Chañaral and Vallenar in Atacama, Mataveri on Easter Island, Pudahuel in Santiago, Bernard O'Higgins in Chillan, Manquehue in Temuco, El Tepual in Puerto Montt, Piruquina in Castro, Balmaceda and President Ibañez in Punta Arenas.

Sea Transport
'EMPREMAR' proposes to acquire ships for coastal service. For the international service there are plans to acquire eight second hand traditional 12 DWT freighters, two new 15-20,000 DWT bulkcarriers, four new 160,000 to 220,000 DWT oil and metal tankers. The investment programme in port infrastructure includes the reconstruction

of the Valparaíso bay, the construction of the port of San Vicente, complementary works in the port of Antofagasta, transformation of Punta Arenas into a centre for antarctic services, and enlargement of the port of San Antonio.

6. Energy

The overall strategy requires the full utilization and mass production of certain types of goods which, in turn, determine concrete lines of operation for the energy sector. In view of their strategic nature, it is necessary to incorporate the main entities in this sector into the socially-owned sector. This is favoured by the fact that the most important enterprises such as ENAP, ENDESA, SAESA, FRONTERA were already state institutions before the start of the Plan. Subsequently the area was further strengthened by the incorporation of CHILECTRA, Lota Schwager and other similar enterprises. This integration is necessary if decisions are to be taken in line with overall objectives rather than the particular interests of each enterprise.

Furthermore it is imperative to elaborate a system of relative prices for the set of products in this area so as to avoid unnecessary substitutions. Corfo, the parent company of most of these firms, has created an 'Energy Committee' which will be in charge of overall and specific policies for the sector.

To increase production it is necessary to continue making large investments. The main projects in the energy sector are: El Toro Central Station whose installed generating capacity will reach 400,000 KW; Colbun Project designed for irrigation and energy, with a generating capacity of 560,000 KW: Machicura Hydroelectric Central Station with a capacity of 180 MW; Antuco Central Station with 300 MW; improvement of ENDESA's transmission; improvement of interconnected systems; improvement of CHILECTRA's low-tension system; a popular electricity programme to supply 182,000 low-income homes with electricity; improvement of public lighting; a substitution programme for imported inputs, new oil field prospecting; the construction of the Vacuum Plant No. 2 in Concepción; the production of AUTUR kerosene in Concepción; the treatment of light distillates in Concon; the Topping Plant in Cabo Negro, Magallanes; the enlargement of Quintero Terminal; the construction of Maipu Terminal; the distribution of natural gas in Punta Arenas; enlargement of the liquid gas terminal in Antofagasta; the creation of a National Coal Company; an increase of 600,000 tons a year in Lota Schwager's coal production; the Rio Trongol Project with a yearly production of 150,000 tons of coal.

7. Construction

The overall strategy proposes a 92% increase in value added in construction in 1976 compared with 1970. Therefore there should be a rapid development of construction companies in the private, mixed and social areas.

Since most existing building companies belong to the private sector, measures will be taken to rationalize their operations, especially through cost-plus contractual arrangements, which will also reduce their risks. There will also be measures to develop building managers' cooperatives.

Mixed construction enterprises are practically non-existent. It is necessary to define policies relating to their creation, management, financing, lines of action, obligations and responsibilities.

It is also necessary to define the functions of state construction enterprises and to decide whether an integrated entity is desirable or whether a separate state enterprise in each fiscal organism is preferable. State enterprises will have to compete on equal terms with existing private enterprises in efficiency of negotiations, performance and costs, and show that they are at least at the same level as those which have attained a high degree of organizational efficiency in implementing the programmes and work assigned them. The magnitude of the role proposed for this sector will demand proper financing, a rather complex issue encompassing several aspects. In 1970 the public sector accounted for 53.6% of the gross value of construction output, hence it is clear that the construction sector cannot be expanded without proper financing of the state sector.

The performance of construction firms can be significantly improved since there is enough professional and technical capacity to increase output substantially, and capital is not considered a very significant limitation.

Plans exist for about 8 million square metres of constructions for public or social services, such as defence, police, the judiciary, civil administration, transport etc.

Among the projects are the Athletic Stadium; construction of swimming pools for low-income groups; building of approximately 700,000 square metres for shopping centres, nursery schools, social centres; 2.3 million square metres for new school buildings; buildings for clinics throughout the country and 315,000 square metres of hospital buildings.

8. Education

Education will no longer be a vehicle for providing certain social groups with a special status, while neglecting the real necessities of the population. It will become an effective tool for the country's social, cultural, political and economic improvement, and one of the fundamental agents of change in moulding the new society, whose characteristics can only be defined with the help of each of its members.

If education is seen as a permanent process of social improvement, then we confront a quantitative problem of unforeseen magnitude that can be coped with only by truly revolutionary methods. But we also face a more difficult qualitative problem, since we are proposing a society in which each citizen would always have the real opportunity to improve his cultural, educational and skill level — a goal clearly requiring extraordinary flexibility in the methods and contents of the educational process. The many transformations proposed by the Government for these six years assume the participation of the whole population in all kinds of decision-making including production decisions. For this it is at least necessary to have the capacity to understand written information and to acquire specific skills for particular tasks.

The educational efforts to be made in the next few years will be focused principally on the following tasks: ending of illiteracy; providing basic education for all children; the extension and diversification of secondary and professional education; strong emphasis on development of non-conventional educational systems; substantially improving efficiency at all levels of the education system.

By 1976, 4,457,000 people will be included in the Chilean educational system, or 40% of the population. This effort implies an ambitious plan of school building.

The education plan includes the following programmes:

1. Pre-school education. (This is the first educational level of the normal system, and is non-compulsory for children up to 5 years, 11 months old).

2. Basic education. This is the first compulsory educational level for children from 7 to 14 or 15 years old; in state institutions basic education is free.

3. Experimental basic education for children with mental deficiencies, physical handicaps, sensory limitations, and for the training of children in irregular social situations.

4. Middle level education offering two streams — humanities and sciences, or technical professions.

5. Higher education. This includes university education and training programme for advanced skills.

6. Adult education. This constitutes an additional form of education for those who have left school or have never entered the regular educational system.

7. Adult training. This is for persons who, having graduated from or having left the regular educational system at one point or another, need further teaching, training or specialization to perform a task, especially in industry and other production areas.

8. School assistance. Basically this programme provides food, clothing and funds through scholarships and loans.

9. *Public Health*

The health sector will extend its services to cover all the population, providing equal assistance for all social groups. It will cover preventative as well as curative services, offering adequate opportunities and efficiency so as to provide more humanitarian assistance.

Priority will be given to those age groups presenting the most serious health problems — mainly children and mothers, and to groups generally located in suburban and rural communities who, traditionally, have received little medical attention. Also, efforts will be made to decentralize medical services so as to attend to the needs of the whole population.

The improvement of sanitary and environmental conditions is especially important. This will be achieved through specific activities in the health sector or by promoting complementary activities in other sectors.

The present institutional situation in the public health sector gives rise to an inadequate distribution of resources between private and public groups and also within the latter. This maldistribution leads to discrimination among the different types of beneficiaries, and to a serious lack or complete absence of medical attention for some groups. To overcome these deficiencies, successive stages towards a unified health service are planned on the basis of the present National Health Service. Appropriate legal reforms will be made so as to ensure proper financing along with the reform of the Social Services System itself.

Many aspects of public health must be confronted by multisectoral programmes in nutrition, health education, basic sanitation, etc.

In addition to programmes of preventive medicine, it is necessary to rationalize the use of hospitals, and it is therefore necessary to expand medical attention at clinics, to relieve hospital congestion.

In short, health programmes are planned for children, adolescents, adults, the aged, maternity cases, mental health, occupational therapy, environmental sanitation, food control, hospitalization and clinics, milk delivery, and expansion and further training of health service personnel.

10. *Social Security*

Social Security in Chile is renowned as the most developed in Latin America. Its legal coverage is comparable to that of industrialized countries, but in practice it suffers from financial and administrative deficiencies and problems of internal coherence. The main deficiency, which the Six-Year Plan will try to overcome, is the discrimination between workers and employees, with respect to the extent of their coverage. It does not extend to the whole working population, and has unfavourable financial mechanisms and unequal distribution of benefits.

The social security development programme has the following goals: extension of social security to all the active population; uniformity in the requirements and services rendered; a further integration of the system; reform of the financing system; administrative decentralization through Regional Councils; planned utilization of the surplus from social service institutions.

11. *Low-income housing*

The Popular Unity Government inherited a deficit of 585,058 dwellings in 1971. For the 1971-1976 period, the construction of 594,125 housing units is proposed: 283,160 units to satisfy the normal population growth, the replacement and repair of 90,000 units, and finally, 220,965 to help cover the above deficit. The 594,125 units comprise 431,196 urban dwellings and 162,929 rural ones, spread throughout the country. The rural ones will all be single-storey buildings, whereas in urban areas both single and multi-storey housing will be constructed.

The public utilities programme includes supplying urban housing areas with pavements, sewage and drinking water systems. This would cover 42% of the paving deficit, 50% of sewers, and 64%

of drinking water requirements.

According to the house construction targets, an annual average of 99,020 units should be built, with a total of 6.2 million square metres. The private sector will not finance more than 15,000 units a year (approximately 15% of the area); therefore, the public sector will have to make a tremendous effort to finance annually nearly 5.2 million square meters.

The labour requirement for the construction of housing units would be 142.8 million man-days or 571,335 man-years over the entire six-year period. An average year would thus require 95,222 man-years of labour. This figure is equivalent to approximately 37% of the total employment in construction for the period, extrapolating from the yearly averages.

12. *Popular Holidays and Tourism*

The Popular Unity Government assigns high priority to the development of tourism. Tourism should be increasingly within the reach of the majority of the population. The plan aims at achieving opportunities for rest, recreation and entertainment for all Chileans. Furthermore, tourism is considered to be an effective instrument of national integration, through the workers' personal acquaintance with the whole of their country. This produces personal awareness of the challenge posed by development in every region and the magnitude of the task. The economic role of tourism should be understood in terms of the financial support it provides to other areas of economic activity. Eventually we expect the country to reach a level of development where the main importance of tourism will not be as a source of foreign exchange but rather a strictly social matter.

To achieve equal opportunities for rest, recreation, and social integration for the whole population, the following objectives are proposed:

● to allow workers' families the opportunity for leisure and communal recreation;

● to promote greater worker participation in developing their own recreation;

● to promote neighbourhood and work group integration;

● to create a class conscience that may lead to the strengthening of solidarity among the different groups in the community and a firm commitment to the process of change;

● to use popular holidays and tourism as a means of promoting and consolidating other community development programmes;

• to encourage workers' acquaintance with other national geographic, economic, labour and cultural realities;

• to facilitate contacts between workers from different branches of production in' order to enrich their cultural and social values.

Regional Development Strategy[3]

The Popular Unity Government assigns importance to the development of regional economies, based upon strictly rational economic utilization of the country's natural, technical and human resources. The Government proposes to move gradually from a pattern of 'concentrated', 'exclusive' regional activity to a 'decentralized' and 'integrated' one.

The basic objectives of regional development are: to readjust the country's structure to the needs of the planned production structure; to decentralize population growth; to create sources of productive employment in each region; to fully activate all idle or poorly used resources; to initiate a change in the regional structure itself; to increase the average productivity of each region; to create a social infrastructure that will assure the whole population of their right to health, education, recreation, housing, and to create mechanisms to promote cultural development in every region; to incorporate popular participation into all aspects of the development of a new society; to attain harmonious regional development.

Five planning zones have been drawn up for the purpose of regional analysis and planning — the Northern, Central, South-central, Southern and Austral zones.

Both the acceleration of the urbanization process as well as the incorporation of new areas into the national economy require the encouragement and consolidation of middle-sized centres which provide services for the regional economies.

Also it is necessary to exploit large marginal zones, such as a great part of the Southern zone, the Antarctic territory, Juan Fernández Island, Easter Island and the Andean foothills. The full development of sea transport is necessary as the principal means of integrating the country and as an outlet for exports which should increase in coming years.

Furthermore, an intensive and integral use of all sea resources is considered as a long-term strategy. Special attention should be paid to the development and consolidation of frontier areas and those

---

[3] In the original plan documents the strategic programmes and projects tor each region are set out in detail. (Editor)

parts of the country which are particularly depressed and suffer from economic and social instability, such as the provinces of Chiloé, Arauco, Malleco, Coquimbo and Cautín.

Over the longer term it is necessary to direct investment towards the creation of large industrial complexes capable of transforming regional economies.

1. *The Northern Zone*
This zone comprises the provinces of Tarapaca, Antofagasta, Atacama and Coquimbo. The development strategy for this zone will give special importance to the rational and efficient utilization of the area's natural resources. There are plans to develop an important industrial fishing centre in Iquique; in the Antofagasta-Calama-Tocopilla area the production of nitrates and copper by-products will be developed to support smaller-scale mining.

In Arica, Iquique and Antofagasta the traditional industries producing consumption goods will be developed to solve future supply problems.

Some dynamic industries with sophisticated technology might be located in Arica and in La Serena.

Substantial encouragement will be given to agriculture to improve supplies in this zone. In the Pampa of Tamarugal, forest and livestock activities will be developed, and in the Elqui and Limari valleys of the Coquimbo area there will be special emphasis on developing vineyards; fruit production in the Choapa area will be developed and also the cultivation of flowers.

Iquique and Arica will be important areas for tourism and the present infrastructure will be expanded for this purpose.

2. *Central Zone*
Valparaíso, Aconcagua, Santiago, O'Higgins and Colchagua comprise this zone. A development policy aiming at decentralization of the existing metropolitan centres must be formulated and the following strategic guidelines are proposed:

● decentralization of the industrial area within the zone to allow better use of the resource potential, and promoting real integration within the zone, improving the situation of those provinces and areas that so far have been dependent and lagging behind;

● reorientation of the growth and expansion of the regional productive structures, with emphasis on the production of goods necessary for the substantial rise in the standard of living in the masses;

● the achievement of a high degree of agricultural specialization in order to create and consolidate the necessary agriculture-based industries supplying both domestic and export demand;

● to achieve a restructuring of the existing distribution system so as to ensure supplies of basic goods for the majority of the people. This is of particular importance in the Central Zone, where there are large numbers of very poor. This will be achieved by incorporating the distribution monopolies into the social area and by creating an extensive supply network to prevent bottlenecks and shortages.

● a halting of the uncontrolled expansion of metropolitan areas and the consequent use of agricultural soil, and the reorganization of urban transport and services. It is thus hoped to attain a more balanced system of urban centres, and simultaneously to initiate the development of intermediate centres.

● rationalization of the port and transport system of the Central Zone in order to maximize the use of present capacity, achieving greater specialization and higher productivity;

● to achieve, to the maximum degree possible, the democratization and decentralization of education and health, reorienting them toward the satisfaction of the population's basic needs;

● the provision of the housing, urban services and social amenities to meet the backlog of demand along with a reordering of urban life to facilitate realization of new values and new forms of social and cultural organization;

● the encouragement of local entertainment and popular tourism by providing recreational facilities for metropolitan areas.

3. *South-Central Zone*

This zone consists of Ñuble, Linares, Curicó, Concepción, Maule, Bío-Bío, Arauco and Malleco provinces. The strategic guidelines for development of this zone indicate the need to settle the population in accordance with the possibilities of exploiting natural resources, improving access to all areas in the zone, and also with the aim of supporting the policy of metropolitan decentralization and diminishing rural-urban and urban-metropolitan migration. To accomplish this it is indispensable to construct all-weather roads along the coastal and the Andean foothill areas. The coastal area, in particular, is the most detached from the rest of the zone, and is not one of the most promising in terms of natural resources exploitation. In the Andean foothill region a longitudinal highway is urgently required, running parallel to the present one, to promote effective integration of the villages and hamlets in this area.

Temuco's industrial centre must be strengthened so as to achieve national importance. In the Concepción area, priority should be given to all aspects of agricultural, cattle and forest activities, especially by rendering services to development and industrialization activities and to the population.

In this zone there are critical areas in the provinces of Arauco, Malleco and Cautín. In order to renew and activate the present economic structure of these three provinces, a large industrial centre should be created that allows the incorporation of new industries and an intensive use of agricultural and cattle resources. Talca has a predominant role as a centre producing specialized farm implements. The areas of Curicó, Linares, Parral and Cauquenes are alternatives for the installation of food industries. Constitución should consolidate its present importance as a tourist and forestry centre.

4. *Southern Zone*

This zone encompasses the provinces of Valdivia, Osorno, Llanquihue and Chiloé which form a mainly agricultural area with emphasis on forestry and cattle. Therefore the strategic lines of development in this zone emphasize the development of land and cattle, and industries based on the latter. Since milk production is of special importance, an industrial milk programme for the provinces of Valdivia, Osorno and Llanquihue should be developed. The development of high quality forest products is also planned, encouraging the installation of important timber complexes. Fishing will also receive special attention. It will be necessary to invest in access roads which, besides having a social function and serving to integrate the area, will also promote tourism, another activity to be encouraged throughout this zone. With respect to maritime activity, the ports of Puerto Montt, Castro and Quellón should receive special attention.

Great encouragement should be given to the development of frontier valleys which are at present very dependent upon Argentinian sources of supply and marketing. Chiloé, one of the most critical areas in the country, also requires development.

5. *Austral Zone*

This zone consists of the provinces of Aysén and Magallanes. In view of the special characteristics of this zone, the development guidelines should be based upon two fundamental aspects: the intensified exploitation of natural resources, leading to industrialization, and the improvement of the transport system. At the same time, the social infrastructure should be improved and expanded, especially in Aysén.

Special attention should be focused on the province of Magallanes since the only natural route linking the Pacific and Atlantic Oceans runs through this zone and there is the political commitment to facilitate the return of 300,000 Chilean emigrants in Argentina. The possibility of creating two important industrial complexes based on timber and cattle is being considered. Another line of industrial development would be the enlargement of the refinery at Manantiales and the creation of petrochemical complexes.

In relation to the transport system, investment priority should be given to the Southern Airline (Linea Aerea Austral) a subsidiary of the National Airlines (LAN Chile), and at the same time the development of airports is required.

ANALYSIS OF THE ECONOMY IN 1971
National Planning Office, Republic of Chile

INTRODUCTION

The main achievement during the first year of the 'Popular Unity' Government has been the important advance made in pursuing each of the basic structural reforms proposed in its electoral programme. In fact, these transformations constitute a real confrontation with the inherent vices of the capitalist system, which is basically kept going by the monopolistic control of the means of production. This is expressed through the external economic dependency for important economic decisions; the outflow of income and resources from the country; and monopolistic concentrations of capital in the hands of the financial and large land-owning circles. It was mainly these factors which gave life to the acute inequalities among the population, and the irrational system in which population, machinery and natural resources remain unused or are misused.

The progress made on these fronts, even though achieving different speeds and degrees of profundity, has made it possible to eliminate some of the former persistent bottlenecks from the economy thereby facilitating vigorous economic expansion, a wider and better use of resources, and an essential re-organization of resources so as to increase the standard of living of the majority of the population.

In other words, in 1971 important increases in production and employment were achieved, exceeding that of any year of the last decade. This latter period covered two different political administrations during which large investments were made, relying mainly on foreign capital both in the form of direct foreign investments and credits. The 1971 results confirm the validity of a planned programme to confront rapidly and directly the vices of the capitalist system, and on the other hand, they firmly refute all the forecasts of economic catastrophe and chaos made by the reformist political movements.

These results also prove that, with a minimum social cost, it is possible to give a substantial proportion of production a social connotation and to put Chilean workers and technicians in charge of the administration of large enterprises in the field of agriculture, mining and industry. A significant expansion in economic activities can be achieved at the same time, even though in many cases severe technical and organizational problems arising from the resistance by groups whose interests were affected had to be overcome.

Preliminary estimates, based on concrete but still incomplete data given in this report, make it possible to estimate a growth of the gross domestic product of at least 8.5%, a change in income distribution which increased the participation of wage earners from 53.7% in 1970 to almost 59% in 1971, and an increase in employment of about 200 thousand persons, resulting in a drastic decrease of unemployment. In greater Santiago, unemployment dropped from 8.3% in December, 1970 to 3.8% by December, 1971.

The programme of drastic income distribution, despite the large increase in overall output, resulted in a slight decrease in real terms for those who derive their income from capital, and an extraordinary increase in that of the wage earners. This led to an absolute overall increase in family consumption, in which high-income families maintained their former consumption levels, thus reducing the margin of their savings, and the great majority favoured by the redistribution began to make a long awaited improvement in their consumption levels. Preliminary calculations indicate that total consumption increased on average by approximately 13%. Therefore, it is not at all unexpected that problems of relative scarcity have arisen in relation to some products, especially in the case of certain better foods such as beef, showing how inadequate the inherited production structure was to cope with the needs of the majority of our people.

These new demand levels resulted in great pressure to cover the deficits by increased imports, and this was done on a selective basis. Of course, this very large increase in family consumption, together with the subsequent reduction in their savings, is not an altogether desirable situation, and should not be maintained; however, the very special conditions within which the process developed in 1971 made it very difficult to attain any other results.

Economic policy in 1971 was based on these previous problems. It was foreseen that local private investment would continue to decrease as it had done during the preceding years, but that this decline would be partly offset by a substantial increase in public sector investment. In fact, investment in the public sector increased beyond the 1970 level, especially in housing and public works. However, this was not sufficient to compensate for the decrease in private investment which was greater than foreseen. This was due mainly to the cautious attitude of the private sector, exacerbated by a campaign waged by the opposition to discourage investment. This affected imports of capital goods and the local production of machinery and equipment, finally producing a decrease of approximately 8% in total investment from the level of 1970. The importance of this fact was minimized by the large margin of under-utilization of the existing installed capacity in the economy which will even be sufficient for maintaining production in 1972.

Foreign Trade

In 1971 a very difficult foreign trade situation began to emerge, mainly because of the false expectations which the large mining enterprises had fostered concerning the increased output resulting from investment in the previous period. According to the plans and official announcements of the former government in 1970, the investments were expected to render more in 1971, making it possible to double production in the principal copper mines. The 1971 plan which was prepared before the nationalized copper enterprises were taken over assumed a 44% physical increase of production, but it was impossible to attain this figure and the increase amounted to only 4%. Therefore, with better knowledge of the severe unsolved technical and technological problems existing in the mines it is now foreseen that it will only be possible to obtain a substantial increase in output as from 1975, for which additional investments amounting to about 100 million dollars will be necessary.

In addition, there has been a large fall in the copper price on the international market, from an average of 61 cents a pound in 1970 to approximately 49 cents a pound in 1971, and it can be foreseen that this situation will continue to affect the balance of payments during the coming years.

On the other hand, the reactivation of the economy and the large increase in consumption required a larger volume of intermediate and final imports. The restrictions on the capital goods imports by about 18% did not fully offset the increase of approximately 22% in these intermediate and final imports. Overall imports thus increased by a total of 5.6%.

One of the most important aspects of the struggle against monoplies — a struggle which has failed on other occasions when income redistribution only was attempted, is that of containing price levels. The most significant improvement in this respect is the drastic fall in the rate of increase of the general level of consumer prices. It has dropped from 29% and 35% during the years 1969 and 1970 to only 22% for the 12 months of 1971 (20.1% for the annual average). The wholesale price index reaffirms this decrease. During the 12 months up to November 1971 it amounted to 17.2% as against 33.7% in 1970 and 39.4% in 1969.

These figures, together with the total growth of nominal salaries and wages, amounting to about 50%, give an idea of the real growth in the purchasing power of wage earners, and explain the increase in the average level of real consumption per family, even after taking into account some items in the index which experienced a larger than the average increase, such as food and clothing.

The monetary aspects, which the opposition has pointed out as the weakest part of our economic policy, have been closely co-ordinated and have been drawn up to comply with the basic social and economic objectives. Substantial monetary expansion was necessary to facilitate a policy involving an increased public budget, which was necessary for the reactivation of the economy and the redistribution of income. These two last objectives were accomplished directly through a set of pump-priming investment programmes, created to solve urgent problems, such as increasing the availability of housing, sanitary services, schools, etc., and indirectly, by means of a policy of a differential increase in salaries and wages.

Had the same structural conditions in force in the past been maintained, it is true that the increase in the money supply would have had catastrophic effects. But this monetary expansion has played a different role in the framework of the previously mentioned structural changes.

First, in the face of increased demand it was possible to avoid price increases because the weakening of monopoly power and the existence of unused installed capacity facilitated an increase in production.

Second, greater state control of monetary and credit mechanisms, which had been dominated by monopolistic groups, made it possible to channel credits directly towards productive sectors rather than into the hands of speculative groups as had been common in the past. Third, a substantial change occurred in the procedures employed in these transactions, by significantly reducing the possibilities for payment by instalment, which require a larger volume of money circulation.

Finally, the decline in the inflationary expectations resulted in a greater preference for cash. In short, all these factors explain the important decrease in the velocity of monetary circulation, which in Chile was exceptionally high.

THE ECONOMY IN 1971

1. **The Economic situation in 1971** The programme of structural changes attained very significant advances during 1971. The large-scale copper, nitrate, iron, steel, coal and cement enterprises were nationalized, thus completing the control of the Chilean State over the country's basic industries, adding them to existing state owned activities such as oil, electricity etc. Sixteen private foreign and domestic commercial banks were nationalized, thus placing over 90% of credit in state hands.

Various industrial monopolies such as textiles, beer, copper manufactures, electronics, were brought under state control. A total of over 70 industrial firms were expropriated, requisitioned or put in the hands of an 'interventor'.* These form the basis of a socially-owned sector which will constitute the leading sector in national development. Likewise, a national distribution company was formed in order to rationalize wholesale trade.

The formation of a socially-owned sector, together with the elimination of foreign and national monopolies, and the transfer of control of the basic means of production to the people, are seen as means of furthering Chile's economic development and laying the foundations of an economic policy which will benefit the whole people. Without popular control of the principal means of production neither a higher growth rate in the medium term is possible nor is a short term economic policy favouring the people. Therefore, the principles governing the participation of workers in socially-owned and mixed firms have been laid down and plans for economic expansion have been implemented.

The copper mines have been nationalized and an investment programme to increase output in Chuquicamata and other mines has been started, with a production target for 1976 of approximately

---

* This 'interventor' is appointed by the Government as an interim manager when a firm is intervened by the government as a result of labour conflicts, non-compliance with the law, or in cases where production is interrupted due to economic problems. Until the enterprise is transferred to the socially-owned sector or, in some cases returned to its owners, the Government appointed manager has full responsibility for running the enterprise, even though legally it still belongs to the private owners.

1,130,000 tons* of fine copper. This will involve an additional investment of US$100 million.

Iron mining has been nationalized and an investment programme which will raise production to 14.2 million tons in 1976 is under way, providing Chile with an annual income of US$100 million and represents a 23.6% increase in mineral production over the six year period.

In relation to the nationalization of steel production a US$300 million expansion programme was begun and will permit an output of 1.2 million tons of steel in 1976, thereby doubling present output.

Nitrate production was nationalized and an expansion programme involving the investment of 312 million escudos has been commenced, to raise output from the 1970 level of 670,000 tons to more than 1 million tons in 1973.

Coal production has been nationalized and plans envisage an increase in output of 1 million tons, with a daily output of 7,000 tons. Cement production has also been nationalized and the expansion plans include the expansion of the El Melón cement plant, where a new cement kiln will increase the capacity by 350,000 tons a year. The construction of the Antofagasta and Magallanes plants should raise output to 2 million tons before 1976, as compared with 1.3 million tons in 1970.

The nationalized petroleum industry increased production by 30% from 1970 to 1971. Enap (National Petroleum Company) is undertaking exploration and drilling projects in Magallanes and on the coast, the construction of a No. 2 Vacuum Plant in Concepción, and the revamping of the topping plant in Concón.

Several projects have been initiated in the chemical and petrochemical industry in Concepción. These include an ammonia complex, a petrochemical complex (ethylene, polyethylene, polyvinyl chloride and polyvinyl chlorine), and plants for the production of triple sulphate, phosphoric acid, sodium chlorine (which complements the petrochemical and cellulose, detergent and rayon industries), and a sodium chlorate plant.

State electricity generation increased 15% from 4.99 billion Kwh in 1970 up to 5.76 billion in 1971.† Plans in progress will permit a continued expansion of production in the future. For example, the construction of El Toro Hydroelectric Station is progressing and will be operative by 1973, increasing by 30% the installed capacity in the national grid.

---

* Throughout the text tons should be taken as meaning metric tons.
† Throughout the text billion should be understood as a thousand million.

In 1971, the State Railway Company transported about 2.2 billion kilometre tons of cargo as compared with 2.09 billion in 1970, that is, an increase of 5%. Plans which have already been started will allow this service to be improved, and by 1976 3,600 railway wagons will have been constructed in Chile, and 26 locomotives will be purchased from Japan.

In 1971, the National Airline carried 11% more cargo than in 1970, reaching a figure of 32 million kilometre tons. Also, 1971 was notable for the 41% increase in passenger transport over 1970, registering the record of 1,126 million passenger kilometres.

Significant progress was also made in the industrial sector, in particular in the textiles firms which came under Government control, most of which increased output, with increases of more than 30% in some cases.

In the electronics industry, Corfo acquired the radio and television firms previously belonging to RCA. Production in this sector increased by more than 50% in 1971. A programme to produce 130,000 low cost television sets within 14 months for a retail price of 2,450 escudos is already in operation and 80% of the components will be national.

In the agricultural sector, the Development Corporation has acquired various integrated poultry businesses which include broiler houses, slaughterhouses, incubation plants and others. A National Poultry Company has been established which controls 40% of the output of chicken meat, which in 1971 stood at 2 million chickens a month. The present production of day old broiler chicks is over 4 million a month, a record level for Chile, and this year it is hoped to produce more than 70 million broilers in order to help compensate for the deficit in beef, pork, and lamb.

Significant advances were made in agrarian reform in 1971 with the expropriation of 1,300 *latifundia*, which covered an area of 2,300,000 hectares.

In foreign trade, the state assumed control of 85% of exports and 45% of imports in 1971.

Revolutionary transformation in the Chilean economy is therefore directly related to the momentum of national economic development which will both underwrite our economic independence and improve the welfare of the Chilean people, as provided for in the medium-term development plans drawn up by the Government.

2. The Principal achievements of economic policy in 1971

The economic policy implemented in 1971 was inspired by the Popular Unity Programme and the Annual Plan. The results achieved during the course of the year may be analysed in the light of the main lines of the economic policy adopted.

On the basis of increased popular demand the internal market became more buoyant, enabling an expansion of production.

Manufacturing industry, which accounts for almost one third of national output, grew by more than 12% in 1971. Copper output from the large mines, which were nationalized in July 1971 and are now run by Chilean technicians, reached 572,000 tons, an increase of about 6%.

It is also important to note that even with significant advances in agrarian reform, which in other countries normally involves a fall in output, agricultural production actually increased by about 6%, according to preliminary estimates by the Ministry of Agriculture. Crop production increased by 10%, while livestock production increased by 2%. Increased production of poultry, lamb, and pork offset the drop in beef.

Construction increased by 12% and construction of more than 90,000 houses was begun in 1971, as against 25,000 in 1970.

The policy pursued has led to a basic change in the level of popular consumption. In fact, the average level of consumption per family increased by 13.5% in 1971, with an even greater increase in the lower income strata.

The consumption of basic goods grew at almost the same rate as total consumption, which is in significant contrast to historical trends for consumption goods from different sectors. This growth would certainly have been greater if the supply of basic goods had responded more rapidly, and some of the bottlenecks had been dealt with earlier.

The production sectors with large accumulations of stocks and considerable margins of underutilized installed capacity also benefited from the boom in real purchasing power. This was the case for consumer durables, consumption of which increased by 12%, and the category 'other industrial products' where consumption increased by 28%. Consumption of domestically produced goods grew at twice the rate of consumption of imported goods.

The conversion of a depressed economy to an expanding one obviously entails problems of supply and this was particularly the case with products such as beef, chicken and certain fish.

Table I

INCREASES OF CONSUMPTION PER FAMILY BY MAIN COMPONENTS

(In percentages)

	Increases *(% over 1970)*
1. Agriculture and fishing	6.4
2. Mining	238.1
3. Basic consumption (a)	13.2
4. Consumer durables (b)	12.0
5. Other industrial products (c)	28.0
6. Rest of the economy (d)	7.5
TOTAL OVERALL:	12.9

(a) Comprises food, beverages, tobacco, textiles, clothing, leather and shoe sectors.

(b) Comprises mechanical and metallurgical sectors.

(c) Comprises wood, furniture, paper, printing and others, non-metallic mineral products, rubber, chemicals, oil and coal sectors.

(d) Comprises electricity, gas, water, transportation, storage and communications, various services, commerce and others.

During 1971, workers began to participate more fully in the management of the economic system. The National Development Council was set up with this purpose in mind, and includes six workers' representatives who join in these presidential level discussions of development policy. Regional Development Councils have also been organized and include regional workers' representatives. Models have been established for worker participation in firms in the socially-owned and mixed sectors, enabling them to assume responsibility for the direction and management of these firms, in accordance with the agreement signed between the Government and CUT.[1]

Educational services increased substantially in 1971, with primary enrolment up by 5.1%, the middle level 'humanities' by 21.1%, middle level professional by 37.1%,[2] and 28% in university enrolment.

In health, the infant mortality rate fell as a result of an overall improvement in living conditions for the mass of the people, and as a

---

[1] CUT: Central Unica de Trabajadores — The National Confederation of Unions, (Ed.).

[2] The basic level of education lasts 8 years, commencing at 6 years of age, and the middle level lasts 4 years, following completion of the basic level. (Ed.).

result of the Government's policy to provide a daily ration of half a litre of milk for each child and of the various health campaigns.

With regard to popular housing, before the end of the Government's first year in power 89,000 dwellings were contracted by the Ministry of Housing, 8,000 by Cora (the Agrarian Reform Corporation) and INDAP (The Agricultural and Livestock Development Institute), and 10,000 by the private sector. In addition, emergency housing was constructed in the areas affected by the earthquake. A beginning was made in developing popular tourism and providing beaches with facilities for workers and their families on holidays.

According to data showing the evolution of the main macro-economic variables, summarized in Table 2, the total output of the economy should show an increase of 8.5% over the level attained in 1970, though this figure may vary once definite calculations have been made.

Table 2

MAGNITUDE OF MACRO-ECONOMIC VARIABLES IN 1970 AND 1971

(In thousands of millions of escudos of 1970)

	1970	*1971 (a)*	*% Variation*
Gross domestic product	92.2	100.0	8.5
Personal consumption	64.9	72.3	12.9
Government consumption	12.5	13.1	4.6
Gross domestic investment	14.5	13.3	− 7.7
Exports	14.8	15.6	5.7
Imports	14.4	15.3	5.7

(a) Provisional figures.

Table 3

GROSS DOMESTIC INVESTMENT

(In thousands of millions of escudos of 1970)

	1970	*1971*	*% Variation*
1. Construction	7.6	8.6	12.5
2. Variations in stock and equipment (national)	1.7	.5	− 71.3
3. Imported machinery and equipment	5.2	4.3	− 16.8
TOTAL:	14.5	13.3	− 7.7

Table 4 indicates the growth of value added for the various sectors estimated on the basis of available production information.

Table 4

GROWTH OF VALUE ADDED BY SECTOR IN 1971

(In percentages)

	% Increase over 1970
1. Agriculture and fishing	6.0
2. Mining	5.7
3. Food, beverages, tobacco, textiles, clothing and leather	9.5
4. Wood, furniture, paper, printing, and others	19.9
5. Non-metallic minerals	12.6
6. Basic metals	6.7
5. Rubber, chemicals, oil and coal	23.0
8. Mechanical and metallurgy industries	5.1
Sub-total for industry (3 to 8):	12.1
9. Construction	12.2
10. Rest of the economy	8.0
11. Government	4.6
TOTAL:	8.5

There was a greater increase in the production of goods (sectors 1 to 9): than in services, with the first increasing by 9.5% and other sectors (11 and 12) by 7.1%. This represents a change from the historical patterns which indicated a greater increase in the services sectors.

Within the goods producing sectors the remarkable increase in industrial production (12.1%) stands out, with a growth rate that surpasses any attained during the last ten years (the next highest was in 1962, with 10.7%). In industry, those sectors linked with consumption increased at a higher rate than that of the overall economy, and those which had considerable margins of unused installed capacity grew in a spectacular manner, as, for example, rubber, chemicals, petroleum by-products and coal (23%), as well as wood, furniture, paper, printing and others (20%). Those industries which mainly produce essential goods expanded at the rate of 9.5%, which is extraordinarily high when compared with the rate of national output. This rate, in turn, would have been greater if there had not been problems relating to installed capacity and the supply of raw materials.

Basic metals and mechanical and metallurgic industries demonstrated the lowest rate of increase in output. The latter two industries increased by only 5.1% and were directly affected by the drop in investment. Copper smelting plants and production of iron and steel are among the highest, with a record production figure of 8% above the 1970 level reached by the Pacific Steel Company.

3. Employment

In order to better understand the implications for employment of economic revival in 1971, it is necessary to refer to the situation at the outset. The overall average level of employment in the country in 1970 reached 2,994,200 persons. The average unemployment for the year was 6.1%, which represents about 200,000 unemployed. In Santiago, the unemployment rate reached 8.3%, or 86,800 unemployed.

The employment level attained

Employment calculations are normally made on the basis of yearly averages, but this method does not show what happens in a rapid process of unemployment absorption, as occurred in 1971. Table 5 provides an estimate of the employment levels in the months of December 1970/71, based on more exact information for the years indicated, as well as on information for particular months for the city of Santiago.

Table 5

LABOUR FORCE, EMPLOYED AND UNEMPLOYED

	Annual average		December (a)	
	1970 (000's)	1971 (000's)	1970 (000's)	1971 (000's
Labour force	3,189	3,270	3,234	3,323
Employed population	2,994	3,140	3,000	3,194
Unemployment	195	138	234	129
Rate of unemployment	6.0%.	4.2%	7.2%	3.9%

(a) Estimated figures

During 1971 we succeeded in creating nearly 200,000 new jobs, completely absorbing the natural increase in the labour force which amounts to about 90,000 people, and also providing work for about another 100,000 formerly workless people. This is one of the most important concrete results of the Government's programme because it directly affects the improvement of workers' living conditions.

In general, in nearly every economic sector, the rate of increase in employment far exceeded the traditional rate. The construction

Table 6

EMPLOYMENT BY ECONOMIC SECTOR FOR THE FIVE YEAR PERIOD 1966-1970 AND FOR 1971

(Thousands of people and percentages*)

	1966	1967	1968	1969	1970	1971	Five year period average annual variation 1966-1970		Variation between 1970 and 1971	
							No. of people	Rate (%)	No. of people	Rate (%)
Agriculture	718	750	736	732	738	750	5	0.7	12	1.6
Mining	94	94	94	98	99	101	1	1.5	2	1.3
Industry	528	534	544	551	563	603	9	1.6	40	7.1
Construction	186	169	168	172	178	198	-2	-1.2	20	11.7
Electricity, gas and water	12	12	12	12	12	13	–	–	1	7.6
Commerce	351	375	404	429	452	470	25	6.5	18	4.2
Transportation	150	156	162	167	176	185	7	4.1	9	5.1
Services	665	721	758	761	778	818	28	4.0	40	5.1
TOTAL:	2,703	2,812	2,879	2,921	2,994	3,137	73	2.6	143	4.8

Note: Comparisons of one year to another are made taking the average of that year in relation to the former year's average. The figures are based on June of each year.

* Figures rounded to the nearest thousand.

and industrial sectors had a particularly strong impact on employment (see Table 2).

Furthermore, the socially-owned sector, provided permanent employment for 109,900 persons in 1970, or 3.7% of the total labour force. In 1971, due to the extension of the socially-owned sector through the incorporation of new enterprises, taking into account employment increases in firms already forming part of the social area, employment in this sector reached approximately 220,300 persons, or 7% of total national employment.

Analysis of the distribution of new employment created in 1970-1971 shows that the goods producing sectors provided the great majority of these jobs. This is quite a difference from the traditional tendency which can be observed during the 1966-1970 period (see Table 7).

Table 7

DISTRIBUTION OF NEW WORKERS INCORPORATED INTO THE LABOUR FORCE

(percentages)

	1966-1970	*1970-1971*
Agriculture	6.8	8.4
Mining	1.9	0.9
Industry	11.7	28.0
Construction	(*)	14.5
Electricity, gas and water	—	0.6
Transportation	8.7	6.3
Services	37.5	28.1
TOTAL:	100.0	100.0

(*) Negative value

During the period 1966-1970, the agricultural, mining, industrial and construction sectors annually provided about 20% of the new jobs created. In 1970-1971, these same sectors provided almost 52% of the new employment. Historically, these new sectors created about 15,000 new jobs yearly, whereas in 1970-1971 they created 53,000 new jobs.

The unemployment level

On the basis of data indicated above for sectoral employment, an average unemployment level of 4.3% is attained for the year 1971.

Considering that the growth of the labour force between 1970 and 1971 amounted to almost 90 thousand persons (population increase alone) and that employment grew by 143,000 persons, it is clear that a very significant decrease in the unemployment level was achieved in 1971.

This unemployment level of 4.3% is an average for the year and the highest levels were reached at the beginning of the year, when it was even higher than during the same period in 1970 and declining significantly by the end of the year. Moreover, even though during 1971 about 200,000 new jobs were created, the total number of unemployed decreased from 195,000 in 1970 to an average of 141,000 for 1971, because about 90,000 of the new jobs created during the year provided employment for workers newly entering the labour force, rather than absorbing the already unemployed.

The very significant decrease in the unemployment level in 1971 can be seen from the unemployment data by economic sector for greater Santiago, calculated by the Institute of Economics of the University of Chile (See Table 8). The decrease in unemployment by

Table 8

**MAGNITUDE OF UNEMPLOYMENT BY ECONOMIC ACTIVITY
IN SANTIAGO DURING 1971**

(Percentage unemployment in labour force)

	March	*June*	*September*	*December*
Agriculture	(*)	(*)	(*)	(*)
Mining	(*)	(*)	(*)	(*)
Industry	8.2	4.7	3.5	2.7
Construction	26.2	15.2	12.8	9.7
Goods producing activities	*11.4*	*6.9*	*5.3*	*4.1*
Commerce	2.5	3.4	3.2	2.1
Government and financial services	1.3	1.1	2.3	0.5
Personal services	5.5	1.6	2.2	2.6
Other services	3.7	3.0	2.9	2.8
Service producing activities	*3.5*	*2.4*	*2.7*	*2.2*
Transportation, storage and communications	5.8	4.4	3.6	1.7
Total unemployment	6.2	4.0	3.6	2.8
Unemployment	8.2	5.2	4.8	3.8

Source: Institute of Economics, University of Chile

(*) Insignificant values

economic activity is concentrated mainly in productive sectors such as manufacturing and construction.

In conclusion, the process of absorption of unemployment which started slowly at the beginning of the year grew remarkably faster during the second half, finally reaching a very low unemployment level. If this tendency is continued, an even lower unemployment level may be expected in 1972. The reduction of unemployment to a rather insignificant level does not imply complete elimination of all unemployment. There also exists a large group of working-aged people (such as women who are not part of the active labour force but who are willing to work) which must be considered as unemployed, and there is a high rate of under-employment concealed within those formally considered as gainfully employed.

4. Distribution of National Income
Variation in the structure of income distribution

Preliminary national income estimates for 1971 indicate a figure somewhat greater than 104 billion escudos.

Nominal wages and salaries rose 54% compared with 1970, signifying an extraordinary improvement in the real purchasing power of workers compared with the changes in the price indices. Thus the participation of wage-earners in the national income, including contributions from employers, increased from 53.7% to 58.6% in 1971.

It is important to point out that this large growth in real income of wage-earners was obtained mainly at the cost of the real growth of national income and not from the income of non wage-earners. This latter group grew 25% in nominal terms, which indicates that this income group more or less maintained its real purchasing power.

Table 9

NATIONAL INCOME BY TYPE OF COMPENSATION
(In thousands of millions of escudos of each year)

	1967	1968	1969	1970	1971(*)
Salaries	7.1	10.0	14.3	21.8	33.5
Wages	4.3	5.9	8.4	12.1	18.6
Contr. of employers	2.0	2.8	4.2	6.2	8.9
Remuneration for work	3.4	18.7	26.9	40.1	61.1
Other factors	13.1	17.0	25.6	34.5	43.2

(*) Estimated Figures

The purchasing power of wage-earners grew in 1971, partly due to greater employment opportunities and partly to the wage reajustments and a lower rate of inflation. If the indices for wages and salaries are deflated by the consumer price index, the greater purchasing power of July 1971, over October 1970, amounts to 28% (See Table 11).

Wage Adjustment and Minimum Legal Adjustments

The policy implemented in 1971 was the first step towards fulfilling the Government's plan to gradually equalize the minimum wage of workers and employees. In consultation with the workers, a general readjustment was set at 100% of the 1970 increase of consumer prices, which amounted to 34.9%. For the least paid groups differentiale readjustments were granted. The very high income brackets were also reduced, establishing a maximum level for net monthly income. This legal requirement, established in 1971, fixes a 100% tax on that part of net income over and above twenty times the monthly subsistence wage for active and retired public sector workers. Receipts from this tax are assigned to a retirement fund of the Social Security Service.

Minimum Legal Wage

Traditionally, the readjustment policy for the minimum legal wage is fixed according to the variations in the Consumer Price Index. This used to result in an erosion of purchasing power in previous years in periods of rapid inflation. The only exception to this loss of purchasing power was the agricultural sector which received special treatment regarding wage readjustments.

In converting minimum wage readjustments into indices based on 1962, the year in which the automatic readjustments policy was first established, the basic subsistence wage gradually loses its purchasing power over the five year period, finally reaching in 1970 the salary level set in the year 1962. The minimum industrial wage also underwent a deterioration up to 1969 but, commencing in 1970, on applying the first levelling stage for minimum wage readjustment for employees and workers, there was a very strong improvement, raising it above its real 1962 value. The minimum wage for agricultural workers, once equal with the minimum industrial wages, showed an increase of 50% in purchasing power over the 1962 base. In 1971, the second stage of the plan to reduce wage differentials was implemented by awarding considerably higher increases in workers' salaries than in the previous year, differentiated in such a way as to reduce differentials and on the whole benefit lower paid workers most.

Table 10

ANNUAL % INCREASE IN WAGES AND SALARIES

(% Variation)

12months to:	Index by sectors					Total Index		
	Public Utility Services	Mining	Manufac- turing Industry	Civil Service	Semi- Govt. Instit.	Salaries	Wages	Salaries and wages
1969 October	46.6	49.3	35.1	27.8	30.9	34.7	35.8	35.2
1970 October	34.9	68.9	43.2	61.6	58.2	54.4	50.9	52.7
1971 July	40.8	−9.4	97.3	46.3	55.7	49.0	39.0	44.0

Source: National Institute of Statistics

Table 11
PURCHASING POWER OF SALARIES AND WAGES

	Index of Salaries and wages 1968=100 (A)	Index of Consumer Prices 1968=100 (B)	Index of Purchasing Power of wages and salaries 1968=100 (C)*
1968 October	100	100	100
1969 October	135	127	106
1970 October	206	172	120
1971 October	297	192	154

Source: National Institute of Statistics; Index of Salaries and wages and consumer prices.

(*) $C = \dfrac{\text{Index 'A' } (1968=100)}{\text{Index 'B' } (1968=100)} \times 100$

Table 12
MINIMUM LEGAL MONTHLY WAGE READJUSTMENT

Year	Monthly subsistence wage (a)		Minimum daily wage for agriculture (b)		Minimum daily wage for industry	
	E° of each year	E° 1962 (*)	E° of each year	E° 1962 (*)	E° of each year	E° 1962 (*)
1962	81	81	1	1	1	1
1966	262	79	4	1	4	1
1967	306	78	5	1	5	1
1968	373	75	6	1	6	1
1969	478	73	7	1	7	1
1970	617	72	12	1	12	1
1971	833	80	20	2	20	2

All figures rounded to the nearest escudo
(*) Deflator: Index for average prices to the consumer
(a) Subsistence wage for the Province of Santiago
(b) Annual Average minimum agricultural wage.

The minimum wage increased 39% in real terms while the subsistence wage increased 12%. These improvements in the legal minimum favoured a large sector of the labour force, especially the least skilled and recently incorporated into the active labour force, and normally entering at the minimum wage level. This policy ended the absurd process by which each new generation entering the labour force at the minimum wage level entered at a lower real wage than the previous generation.

Table 13

INDEX OF REAL LEGAL MINIMUM WAGES *

	Subsistence wage[1]	Minimum agricultural wages	Minimum industrial wages
1962	100.0	100.0	100.0
1966	97.0	125.6	96.0
1967	96.1	131.1	95.8
1968	92.5	126.1	92.2
1969	90.6	123.4	90.3
1970	88.4	149.5	109.3
1971	99.3	207.4	151.7

Source: Table 12.

*   Deflator: Average index of consumer prices.

1   *Sueldo vital*

Figures rounded to first decimal point

5. Progress in Establishing the Socially Owned Sector

With the implementation in 1971 of the Government's basic programme, certain structural changes became necessary. One was the development of a dynamic and predominant state sector, which would permit the mobilization of economic surpluses in a rationally planned manner for the benefit of the whole nation. It was conceived of as a 'social sector' which would serve to stimulate production in key sectors and at the same time coordinate and orient productive efforts towards the people's essential and basic needs.

During 1971, firms were incorporated into the social sector either by expropriation or by state purchasing of shares. Another group of enterprises are now under state control, and some of them will most likely become state-owned in the near future. These are firms which have been requisitioned or intervened, the former being enterprises which the Government has taken control of in order to ensure the steady supply of goods and services, and the latter are firms which the Government intervened in order to solve labour or other conflicts.

A. General policies for the formation of the socially-owned sector

(1) **Nationalization of natural resources.** One of the first goals set by the Government was to recuperate the Chilean natural resources of copper, nitrate and iron. A Constitutional amendment, approved by Congress in July 1971, enabled the Government to nationalize the principal copper companies (El Teniente, Chuquicamata, El Salvador, La Exotica and Sociedad Minera Andina).

The nitrate corporation, Soquim, was acquired in the month of May. This enterprise had been formed by merging the companies Anglo-Lautaro and Salitrera Victoria, in which joint company the State maintained a 37.5% capital participation. The firm Alemania was placed under state management. The iron mines of Bethlehem Co.— were purchased by the state-owned Pacific Steel Company (CAP) between February and April. The firms of Santa Bárbara and Santa Fé were also purchased, thus bringing approximately 95% of iron production under state ownership, with the remaining 5% being in the hands of private national management (Atacama).

Thus, during the Government's first year, the initial stage of the process of creating the mixed and the socially-owned sectors was successfully completed.

(2) **Nationalization of monopolies or semi-monopolistic enterprises.** Monopolistic and oligopolistic enterprises are characterized by the use of largely mechanized technologies, under-utilization of installed capacity, by a high concentration of generated income, control of prices and supplies, and the use of policies discriminating quality and types of products etc. In order to avoid the damaging effects produced by monopolies usually linked with concentration of capital, the Government decided upon a policy of nationalization and/or direct intervention in all monopolies, and also in those enterprises with a capital of more than 14 million escudos.

In January 1971, this phase began with the nationalization of the Empresa Carbonífera Lota Schwager, which is responsible for about 80% of the national coal production. In the month of September the Company Cervecerías Unidas was intervened by the Government. The textile oligopolies were also expropriated or intervened, because in addition to being oligopolies, they are direct or indirect producers of mass consumption goods, for which the government wanted to ensure a normal, steady supply.

(3) **Nationalization of enterprises which produce strategic goods and services or influence the nation's economic development.** For the process of transformation being carried out by the Government, some sectors are considered vital. One of these is the financial one, in which formerly the most important private banks operated in close linkage with the industrial monopolies, directing credits only to this very limited sector.

During 1971 the Government began negotiations with all national and foreign banks regarding the purchase of their shares by the State Development Corporation   (Corfo),   through the intermediary of the Central Bank. These negotiations led to a majority state participation in 14 commercial banks   (11 national and 3 foreign), not including the State Bank, or the Central Bank or two other state-controlled banks. These sixteen banks are responsible for 90% of total loans, providing nearly complete control of credit. Credit was redirected toward small and medium industry, while lowering the interest rate at the same time.

Another key development sector is that producing materials and equipment for the construction industry, which is especially critical in view of the need to fulfil the Government's ambitious construction plan. During March, the Pacific Steel Company (CAP) came under social ownership, through purchase of its shares. Through CAP, negotiations were begun to purchase shares and establish production agreements with several firms, so as to create a major iron and steel complex. In this complex the following companies participate, to a greater or lesser degree — ARMCO, INDAC, ENDESA, PRODINSA, SOCOMETAL, INCHALAM, COMPAC, MADECO, NIBSA, SGM, EQUIT RM, AZA, and others. In May, El Melón and Cerro Blanco de Polpaico, two of the principal cement producing firms were intervened, in order to normalize cement production. Similarly Materiales de Construcción, El Volcán, Pizarreño, Vidrios Lirquén, Fanaloza, INDELCO, etc. were intervened.

Distribution and marketing is another of the main sectors to be transformed. This will not only eliminate supply problems in the poorer areas and permit a better price control, but also eliminate intermediaries, who only increase the prices of products without contributing any effective service.

In addition to strengthening the existing commercial firms owned by the State, other firms were created which then purchased or absorbed private enterprises. The most important of these is the creation of the National Distribution Corporation (Dinac). The agriculture Marketing Corporation (ECA) and the State Development Corporation (Corfo), absorbed the bankrupt company Weir Scott and purchased Duncan Fox, Williamson Balfour, the former import agents and retailers.

Also the National Poultry Firm (Enavi) was established for direct distribution of poultry, and the National Corporation for Fuel (Enadi) was created. Furthermore, the purchase of the shares of the Telephone Company of Chile began.

(4). **Nationalization of firms which produce goods and services for popular consumption.** In the textile sector, four enterprises were expropriated, and another nine were intervened, which represents over 50% of textile production. In the food sector there has been a great increase in fishing activities and approximately eight fisheries, as well as several poultry producing firms, were intervened so as to normalize supply of these products. The shares of Cecinas Loewer, producers of dried and smoked pork or beef, were purchased along with several other companies.

Finally, there are 90 other small enterprises which, because of abandonment by their owner, bankruptcy or other circumstances, made it necessary for the Government to intervene either directly in the interests of the workers, or to guarantee normal supplies to the population.

THE INTERNATIONAL CONTEXT OF *LA VIA CHILENA*

Clive Bell and David Lehmann*

A time of structural change must be a time of vulnerability — even, perhaps, of necessary confusion. It is a time of transition to a renewed political and economic order. The social forces which up-held the old order are still powerful, and by creating confusion seek to undermine the political leadership. At the same time the political support of the new leaders has yet to be consolidated and the un-questionable need for its immediate consolidation — to resist and defeat the forces of reaction and stagnation — may place severe con-straints on the pursuit of the ultimate ideals which inspire the mass movement. Time is of the essence in the politics of structural change. The process starts amid an abnormally intense constellation of con-flicting attacks and pressures for immediate action, few of which can be shelved with placatory measures. These forces, coming from all directions simultaneously, do not reduce each other's strength, but are mutually reinforcing. As the right moves from defensive to offensive action, so the left demands more firmness; when capitalists, lacking confidence or eager to provoke an economic crisis, 'go on strike', their workers demand nationalization; when landlords act likewise, pressures for land reform build up; whatever the offended, frightened or even indifferent imperialist power may do will be seized upon by some as justification for strong nationalist economic and political measures, and by others as a warning of dire sanctions to come.

Finding itself at the centre of the storm a government like the Popular Unity is in a position both enviable and unenviable. The prospect of success is as exhilarating as that of failure is daunting, while an uncertain external environment renders the consequences of its actions highly unpredictable. Although uncertainty is obviously a permanent feature of politics, it weighs with particular heaviness in

* Institute of Development Studies. We should like to thank Mary Kaldor for her very helpful comments on an earlier draft.

today's international situation, and is further enhanced for Chile by foreign reaction to the ideals and objectives of her government. We cannot totally explain present and past reactions to the Popular Unity, nor, *a fortiori*, can we safely predict them in the future. Nevertheless, it is important to set out realistic assumptions and the alternative courses of action they imply, in order to replace 'pure uncertainty' with 'ordered uncertainty'.

Most analyses of the relationship between developed and less developed countries which are based on the dominance-dependence thesis have a strongly absolute flavour. Crudely summarized, the options facing the dependent state are either total acquiescence in the relationship, including commercial and trading transactions, or a complete rupture. The response of the imperial power, anxious to preserve its hegemony over this and (by example) other client states, must necessarily be overwhelming, perhaps to the point of military intervention. In practice, of course, matters are more complicated — as the advocates of the thesis readily admit. This is not just because relationships, choices and responses are more finely graded than the above discrete description. More importantly, they are interrelated. How they are matched depends on the imperial power's perception of the implied threat to its interests and the cost of eliminating it. Both of these depend in turn, to some extent, on the position of the dominant power in relation to others wishing to compete for influence. Thus the concept of 'freedom to manoeuvre' in relation to external pressures cannot be established independently of the choices the dependent state seeks to exercise.

Such considerations affect three major areas of the Popular Unity's policy: land reform; nationalization of copper and other industries; and the redistribution of income. Although in 1971 agricultural output expanded faster than in previous years[1], the redistribution of income and price-fixing in the urban areas provoked an unprecedented rise in the demand for food. The result has been a surge in food imports, which are estimated at $153 million in 1971 and $237 million in 1972[2]. These rises may well continue, as the Agrarian Reform causes some dislocation to domestic supply over

---

[1] Some of the 5% may be attributable to premature slaughtering of cattle by landlords.

[2] Based on estimates (perhaps slightly exaggerated) of the *Sociedad de Fomento Fabril*, for the January — August periods of each year. Both Government and the *Sociedad Nacional de Agricultura* expect food imports to rise above $350 million in 1972. The SNA also estimated that imported wheat has risen from 19% of total consumption in 1969 to 27% in 1971. For other foodstuffs the proportions in 1971 were estimated thus: 54% for maize, 34% for milk, 62% for sugar. (*El Mercurio*, international edition, 27th December, 1970).

the short run. At the same time, copper prices have declined about 30% from their peak in 1970 and output targets have not been reached owing to certain technical difficulties — which would have arisen even in the absence of nationalization[3]. The upshot of these two developments is a precipitous fall in foreign exchange reserves. But the real point at issue here is not whether pursuing these policies is conducive to attaining more immediate goals, for they form indispensable political components of the transition to socialism. The paradox is that, all else being equal, carrying through these radical measures will increase the country's susceptibility to external pressures, in the short to medium run at least, by weakening the balance of payments position. If this is not to happen, then the growth of the real incomes of the masses will have to grow more slowly than planned.

This conclusion points to a rather delicate political-economic interaction. For although pushing on with land reform and income redistribution may result in rather smaller real benefits to the poorer half of Chilean society than anticipated, the fact of such redistribution, with its attendant erosion of the power and influence of the rich, may also serve to consolidate political support for the regime in the face of external constraints and pressures arising out of its policies. Important though this nexus is, it is however beyond the scope of this paper to explore in detail the probability that equality, austerity and cohesiveness can be long maintained.

In all this, the dominant power whose interests are threatened is clearly the United States. Thus we need to analyse the potential weapons at her disposal — principally those connected with aid and trade policy — and the likelihood that using them will damage Chile a great deal and the United States comparatively little.[4] But this is not simply a bilateral matter between the United States and Chile, since the efficacy of such weapons (and the chances of their being used) depends on the reactions of other major competitors for influence in the hemisphere. Thus we must first consider international relations in the large.

During the Cuban missile crisis in October 1962, Khrushchev is

---

[3] A further possibility is that the international copper companies might, in response to nationalization, take informal measures to weaken Chile's market position, even at a substantial cost to themselves.

[4] A detailed examination of the conditions leading to credible threat potential stemming from aid and trade policy may be found in: Michael Lipton and Clive Bell, *The Political Economy of Bilateralism*, mimeo, 1970.

alleged to have exclaimed: 'The Monroe Doctrine is dead and should be buried.' A State Department spokesman replied that the principles of the Doctrine were as valid as in 1823 when they had first been proclaimed.[5] As a long-term prediction, Khrushchev's statement may be valid; but in spite of changes the position today is not substantially different from what it was in 1962. The international relations of Latin American countries are still almost coterminous with their relations with the United States.

The Soviet Union is the only power capable of matching the United States politically and her support of Cuba is a permanent ideological challenge. The missile crisis of 1962 carried with it a double and not unambiguous lesson. It showed that the United States Government was prepared to go to extreme lengths in removing Soviet-controlled missiles from the Western Hemisphere, above all in the Caribbean. But it also showed that there were limits on her capacity to remove Soviet military and economic protection of other kinds from a socialist regime which enjoyed the whole-hearted support of the people. Today, competition between the United States and the Soviet Union is modified by the dangers of direct confrontation. However, the force of this statement depends on circumstances. Outside the traditional spheres of influence, it is limited to aid, investment and the sale or grant of arms; it never takes the form of direct intervention. But within the spheres of influence, closer military ties in the form of defence and security pacts bring with them dangers of a more direct kind. Just as the United States restrained its response to the Czech events of 1968, so it is unlikely that the Soviet Union would again accept a military involvement which contradicts the Monroe Doctrine — in spite of Mr. Khrushchev's remarks. This said, however, an anti-imperialist government in Latin America could well benefit from the second part of the lesson mentioned above, while the first part would be of little relevance to its security and well-being. Such a government has also the added advantage of knowing the internal difficulties which a foreign adventure would today create for any United States government.

Events in Cuba in those years give us strong indications as to the definition, for practical purposes, of 'spheres of influence'. When Cuba first signed trade agreements of a very substantial kind with the Soviet Union and received economic aid, the United States reaction

5 Gordon Connell-Smith, *The Interamerican System,* London, 1966, p. 171.

— the Bay of Pigs, for example, though it was a response to a host of other actions as well — was not directed against the Soviet Union. (Similarly, the delivery of Czechoslovak small arms to the Guatemalan Government in 1954 was used to justify intervention against Guatemala, not against Czechoslovakia!) But the reaction was different when Soviet-controlled missiles were installed within range of American cities.

Speculations on United States reaction to a new revolution in the hemisphere are, by their very nature, of limited reliability. Past events would lead us to suppose that the Soviet Union and her allies would agree to provide substantial aid to Chile if requested, so long as such aid does not alter the existing military structure in the region— and there is no reason why Chile should seek to achieve such an end. But the aid requested by Chile will no doubt depend on the reactions and threatened reactions of the United States Government. Since 1970, United States aid has become negligible, and is likely to remain so, on account of the nationalization of the copper mines. Other sanctions, such as the restriction of trade credit or the unilateral imposition of trade sanctions, are available however.

Apart from great power politics, we must also consider the implications of the present international monetary crisis for Chile and Latin America as a whole. Here, the two salient tendencies are the declining capacity (reinforced by internal political objections) of the United States to engage in foreign military adventures, and the remote likelihood of further expansion of the aid programme. If aid declines, the United States will lose many opportunities to influence the actions of recipient governments. Aid, of course, does not necessarily have a direct and visible independent impact on a *society* or an *economy,* but its 'fungible' character, and its opportune arrival, may save *governments* from difficult situations. Hence a decline in the capacity to influence such governments implies a reduction of the 'political superstructure' of empire.

In the long term, the United States disposes of only limited economic weapons to defend what she sees as her interests in the Third World. But we speak here of the very long term, for the United States will remain for many years to come the richest country in the world. However, actions as drastic as trade blockades are now unlikely to occur in the Western Hemisphere, because the necessary cooperation of Latin American governments is no longer forthcoming.[6] As economic and military dependence on the United States declines, albeit slowly, they are less easily brought to heel.

In this context the emergence of CECLA[7] is significant, though its importance should not be exaggerated. This is the only forum where representatives from all the Latin American and Caribbean governments (except Cuba) meet without a representative of the United States, which has manifested some unhappiness over this situation. CECLA has recently placed special emphasis on trade with Europe and has initiated collective contacts with the EEC, a field in which there is a fair amount of consensus among its membership.[8] These developments, however, do not imply that many Latin American governments would find common ground in actively supporting a government engaged in deep conflict with the United States or any other capitalist power, nor in taking collective anti-imperialist action against the United States.

Clearly it is hoped that a diversification of trade and aid flows will reduce dependence on the United States. Table I shows just how far has to be gone before such aims are achieved for Latin America as a whole, while tables II and III show, for Chile, how far changes in aid-flows lag behind trade-flows. It is possible however, that in the name of 'burden sharing', the European countries will propose to take over some of the United States aid 'burden'. This would offer them wider export markets and, in the case of Latin America, might turn Western Europe's present trade deficit into a surplus. Latin America comes low on the European list of vested interests — lower than the Mediterranean, Africa and probably Asia — but precisely because of the consequent absence of conflicting interests in the area among EEC members, some coordination of aid policies towards

[6] It was not forthcoming at Punta del Este either, in 1961, when the Alliance for Progress was signed. OAS rules allow such decisions to be taken by majority vote and make them obligatory on all members. However, compliance depends more on other sanctions from the United States than on rules which the United States herself has declared she would violate (c.f. the speech by Kennedy in which he said that his country would act unilaterally if her security was threatened, irrespective of the OAS and of the non-intervention doctrine. Connell-Smith, *op. cit.* p. 24) And the United States is slowly losing her capacity to apply such sanctions. By the decline of military dependence on the United States, we mean the growing expansion of Latin American arms purchases in Western Europe.

[7] The Latin American Economic Coordination Committee. It was formed originally in 1963 to work out a common policy for the first UNCTAD Conference, but it now holds fairly regular meetings to discuss matters of common concern, especially in the field of trade.

[8] See the *Declaration of Buenos Aires*, 29 July 1970.

Latin America, as well as an increase in the volume of aid, may occur during the coming years. Certainly, this prospect flows logically from present trends, but it is doubtful whether the outcome would be beneficial to social groups in Latin America other than those which already gain from external dependence, or whether indeed it would lead to a reduced dependence on the advanced capitalist world in general.

Table I

Latin America; Trading Patterns 1958 — 1968* (in millions of US dollars)

	Exports to Latin America (f.o.b.) 1958		1968		Exports from Latin America (f.o.b.) 1958		1968	
	Total	Proportion	Total	Proportion	Total	Proportion	Total	Proportion
US	4030	49.4	4515	37.2	3725	44.3	3980	31.7
Western Europe	2455	30.1	3680	30.4	2560	30.4	4120	32.8
Comecon	110	1.3	880	7.2	140	1.6	675	5.3
Japan	190	2.3	635	5.2	230	2.7	665	5.3
World	8145	100	12105	100	8395	100	12545	100

Source: UN, *Yearbook of International Trade Statistics*, New York, 1961 and 1969.
* Midpoints of three year averages.

Table II

Chile's Main Developed Trading Partners in 1968* (in millions of US dollars)

	Imports (c.i.f.)		Exports (f.o.b.)	
	Total	Proportion	Total	Proportion
US	297.5	41.3	188.8	19.4
UK	46.4	6.4	140.0	14.4
France	21.7	3.0	49.7	5.1
German Fed. Rep.	89.5	12.4	82.0	8.4
Italy	19.5	2.7	74.3	7.6
Japan	13.5	1.8	123.8	12.7
World	719.3	100	970.5	100

Source: UN, *Yearbook of International Trade Statistics*, New York, 1969.
* Midpoint of three year average.

Table III

Net Aid to Chile From Market Economies and Multilateral Sources*

(in millions of US dollars)

	1961	1962	1963	1964	1965	1966	1967	1968	1969	1970
Total	121	138	147	134	120	151	105	180	118	97
of which: US			111	97	102	88	50	151	104	56

Sources: UN, *Statistical Yearbooks*, 1965 and 1971.

US Department of Commerce, *Statistical Abstract of the United States, 1970 and 1971.*

* Aid flows from Comecon were negligible in this period.

European governments and businessmen probably have an even more traditional, though less self-deluding, concept of aid and foreign investment. Apart from seeking out new markets, they see their role, if anything, as bringers of capital and modern technology. However, considering that social reform and 'democracy' are the province of the United States,[9] they may engage in less political interference.

Similar observations would apply to Japanese penetration which is far more vigorous than that of Europe at the moment, but is limited to private investment.

What kind of support could governments pursuing structural change hope to obtain from these other capitalist sources, even if we ignore the doubtful benefits to be gained therefrom? In answering this question we must remember that Western Europe and Japan also have interests to defend and are as unlikely as the United States to go out of their way to support programmes of structural change, even though they may not actually withdraw aid and investment from a country unless their own interests are adversely affected. Their political interests, after all, are not so different from those of the United States as far as the Third World is concerned. So long as the United States takes responsibility for keeping the hemisphere strategically and politically 'safe', Europeans and Japanese need not concern themselves overmuch with such matters, and can even take marginal advantage of the situation, for example, by building fertilizer complexes in Cuba. In the same way, the Japanese require no substantial political and military superstructure so long as American

[9] European business opinion is unlikely to find the new Andean Pact regulations concerning foreign investment any more attractive than its American counterpart. On the other hand, they may eventually come round to the view that it is better to have stable rules – which could be far worse than they are – than no rules at all.

forces protect their reborn 'Co-Prosperity Sphere' in East and South-East Asia. It will not be easy for governments seeking to carry out structural changes to 'play off' the various capitalist powers against each other, except in a very limited framework of competition for markets. Once the rules of such competition are unacceptable or unstable, capitalist corporations and powers will be wary of committing themselves.

Within the rules of the game Latin American governments may be able to achieve two general but limited objectives: they may succeed in improving to their advantage the terms on which foreign private capital is invested, and they will certainly diversify further their trade relations. But there will be no special benefits — if anything, the contrary — for those engaged in programmes of social and economic transformation.

These, then, are the outlines of the emerging political economy of Latin America's relationship with the world, assuming the absence of major upheavals, or of a world-wide depression. They do not offer much hope for improvement of the situation of the workers and peasants of the continent. Indeed, they hold out rosy propects for the landed and industrial bourgeoisie, which can count on a continuation of the conditions which have permitted them to benefit from the fruits of economic growth without the political risks of an expanding internal market and without the austerity of a high rate of saving. European and Japanese capital will bring more advanced industries, but have little apparent interest in a modification of the terms of trade between primary and manufactured products, or in the balanced industrial development of the continent. The aid policies of European governments all rely heavily on tied aid, and there would be little interest in granting aid to a government concerned with less capital-intensive technologies, or whose greatest need was balance of payments or budget support for egalitarian policies. The best a reforming government could hope for would be for them to tolerate selective nationalization or compensation for nationalized assets; but this game also carries serious risks. Insofar as they owe the maintenance of their position to external economic relations, the ruling classes are likely to maintain it in the long run — if anything on more favourable terms. The 'retreat from empire' of the United States will not affect their interests unduly. This means that, for some time to come, governments seeking to reduce economic dependence on capitalist powers and the inequalities which it reinforces, are likely to find active support only in socialist countries.

Before going on to examine the relationship between North and South America, we should consider the relationships among the states of Latin America themselves — relationships which declined in importance during the first half of this century, but which have now again become the object of interest and concern.

A number of Latin American countries appear at present to be engaged in a search for influence and shifts in alignments which are difficult to interpret. Some speak of the competition for influence between Argentina and Brazil, but it is not at all clear what factors divide these two countries, unless it is a very abstract conception of national pride or an equally abstract Metternichian search for a 'balance of power'. The one conceivable rationale for this conflict is the need to expand on the basis of foreign markets on account of the political difficulties their governments would face in the expansion of the internal market. Whatever the rationale, the cordiality of recent meetings between Presidents Lanusse and Allende would be explained by the former's desire to counteract the influence of Brazil.

The experience of CECLA shows that Latin American governments are capable of uniting on limited issues when they feel that their individual interests are served thereby. When viewed in a global context, their internal conflicts emerge as possessing limited intensity. Thus Brazilian and Argentinian policies towards the United States and towards foreign investments have been strikingly similar in recent years. In the same way, it has been said that Venezuela's refusal to sign the Pact of Cartagena[10] was not unwelcome to the other member countries because they feared the possibility of her being used as a Trojan horse for United States capital in the region. Yet Colombian policy has also been favourable to foreign capital, indeed more so than Venezuela's in recent years, and Colombia is a member of the Andean Pact. In short, there seems little reason to emphasize intra-Latin American conflicts or alignments. The truth of the matter — uninteresting as it may sound — is probably that most governments in Latin America seek to avoid confrontation or even minor difficulties in their relations, and therefore all seek multiple alignments but still subordinated to their links with the United States. The armed forces have gradually turned their attention away from external threats towards those of internal subversion without any marked increase in crises of identity or pride, and the social and political situation within most countries is such as to make the

[10] Signed by Chile, Peru, Colombia, Ecuador and Bolivia, 26 May 1969.

prosecution of an international war highly impracticable and dangerous for the internal *status quo*.

Tension will only arise within Latin America when one country — perhaps Brazil — becomes economically so powerful that it begins to penetrate the economies of the others. However, the dangers involved in a vigorous pursuit of such a course are likely to be overwhelming — so long as the economic strength of the country concerned is not backed by a large measure of political order and widespread consensus. Such factors might be less important in colonial situations, where the imperial power is at a safe distance, and unperturbed by prospects of invasion, but they do apply in a 'crowded' continent like Latin America. Of course, the rise of nationalism and of socialist forces in Peru and Chile perturbs some of their neighbours, but there is little that they can do apart from imposing censorship in the (vain) hope that news will not filter through. The prospect of two rival ideological blocs facing each other across the Andes finds little support — at least in an examination of existing trends. Rather, the Andean Pact has succeeded where a wider agreement failed because of the higher stages of industrial development reached by various countries, especially Brazil, Mexico and Argentina.

In outlining future trends at the global level, we made a number of assumptions about the present situation. We have taken for granted the predominant role of United States capital investment in, and trade with, Latin America. Perhaps more controversially, we have assumed an interdependence between that external factor and the inequalities which prevail within Latin America — though it should be noted that we do not see this as a unilinear, casual relationship.

More subtle, but by no means negligible, are the mechanisms of political, military and cultural dependence, whose importance may in the long term be reduced by the changes outlined above. A decline in United States economic dominance means a reduced capacity not only to give aid, but also to send out the ubiquitous economic advisers, professors and overseers who, form the apanage of empire.[11] Even CIA operations may decline, unless it is considered that they offer a cheaper means of intervention than the marines.[12]

---

[11] For an illustration of 'prying' and 'pressuring' by an AID mission, see Philip O'Brien, 'The Alliance for Progress and Programme Budgeting in Chile', *Estudios Internacionales*, II, 4 January, 1969.

[12] See Richard Barnet, 'The New CIA', *The New York Review of Books*, December, 1971.

How far training courses at Fort Gulick and Fort Bragg for Latin American soldiers will decline is another matter, for, as we shall see, the one definition of American 'interest' in the southern hemisphere which may still be viable is the strategic and military one.[13] Similarly, United States arms supplies to Latin America are not an overwhelming expense, yet they create strong dependence. Consisting mostly of intentionally unsophisticated equipment[14] for external use by armies, with more modern equipment for 'counter-insurgency', 'special' forces and the police, arms assistance still supplements local military expenditure by an average of 50 per cent. On the other hand, the size of military missions is being reduced on the grounds that they constitute too exposed a symbol of American presence,[15] as Governor Rockefeller remarked in his report. In general, in the military sphere, it would appear that the United States can retain substantial leverage at relatively low cost, so long as Congress and the Executive do not place such tight restrictions on purchase under their own programme that Latin Americans are obliged to seek arms elsewhere, as has been occurring in the past five years.

In politics, intervention has been permanent and multifaceted, but it is becoming clear to the United States government that it can also be risky, counter-productive or just frustrating. Ventures such as

---

[13] Almost 25,000 Latin American soldiers were trained under the United States Military Assistance Programme, 1950 — 69, at a cost of $90 million up to 1967. See Stockholm International Peace Research Institute, *The Arms Trade with the Third World*, Stockholm, 1971, pp. 166-7.

[14] With some exceptions. For general information see Stockholm International Peace Research Institute, *op. cit.*, Chapter 21, and pp. 175 — 179. Sophisticated equipment seems to become available only when a government threatens to purchase it elsewhere. Congress has been paring down military arms sales in recent years, imposing a ceiling of $75 million. United States Government sales of military equipment averaged only $38 million 1966 — 70, declining from $81 million in 1966 to a record low of $21.4 million in 1970, but are estimated to rise to $72 million in 1972, while the President has requested the ceiling be raised to $150 million. *Letter* from Assistant Secretary of State to Congressman D. Pascell, May 26, 1971 reprinted in *Interamerican Economic Affairs*, XXV, Autumn, 1971. See also *Hearings* of the Senate Sub-Committee on Western Hemisphere Affairs, 8 July 1969.

[15] *Hearings, ibid.* The figure of 50% was given in a report to the Committee by Dr. Henry Lieuwen. Mission personnel in Latin America have already been reduced from 800 in 1967 to 505 in 1970. *Hearings, ibid.*

IADEL,[16] the International Development Foundation,[17] or the massive financing of the 1964 Christian Democratic election campaign in Chile have not yielded the desired fruits, and have often rebounded. Project Camelot was a classic instance. This particular kind of activity by the CIA and the Pentagon may be on the decline,[18] except perhaps in countries like Brazil where there is little danger of exposure.

In diplomacy the exclusion of Cuba represented the zenith, but also the beginning of the decline, of exclusive dominance by the United States. Although six countries abstained from voting on the measure in the OAS, the United States was able to pressure all but Mexico into abiding by the decision, and even Mexico's relations with the island are largely symbolic.[19] The invasion of Santo Domingo met with strong disapproval in the OAS, but enough client states voted with the United States and sent troops to the island to save her face.[20] Yet today, we find that even countries with no ideological quarrel with the United States participate in CECLA and recognize or intend to recognize China and Cuba.[21] Many countries now have diplomatic relations with the Soviet Union and the State Department barely raises its eyebrows at such ties.

Although these changes represent a reduction in United States hegemony, no in-built dynamic assures us that the process will continue indefinitely. The changes so far have been consonant with the development of peaceful coexistence between Great Powers. Moreover, with the evidence that if revolution is to come to the

---

[16] American Institute for Free Labour Development, run by AFL-CIO but 90% financed by AID, devoted to the promotion of anticommunist unions. The AIFLD received $28 million out of a total income of $31 million from AID between 1962 and 1968. Its efforts do not seem to have met with spectacular success. For data see House of Representatives, *Hearings* of the Sub-Committee on Interamerican Affairs, 6 May, 1969. For Senate criticism see *Hearings* of the Foreign Relations Committee, 1 August, 1969. According to the latter, the 1970 AID contribution was $5.8 million.

[17] Almost certainly a CIA front organization, see Eduardo Labarca: *Chile Invadido*, Santiago, 1969.

[18] See Barnet, *op. cit.*

[19] Connell-Smith, *op. cit.*, p. 178.

[20] *Ibid.* pp. 337 – 339.

[21] Apart from Chile, Peru intends to establish relations with Cuba, and Argentina has already done so with China.

continent, it will find channels other than Soviet embassies, United States governments may feel that they can spare themselves the embarrassment of interfering in petty matters, while acting unilaterally where their interests are gravely threatened. It has become increasingly difficult for the United States to obtain hemispheric consensus on any issue, perhaps because within the OAS, for example, discussions have shifted away from issues of hemispheric security and anti-Communism towards those of aid and trade, over which there are real differences between the ruling classes of north and south. Important strategic matters are generally to be resolved bilaterally between the Great Powers themselves, while interventions such as that in Santo Domingo are, as always, essentially unilateral. The United States Government may feel that window-dressing exercises in the OAS are of little usefulness, knowing that, despite the changes we have described, there is little that Latin America can do if unilateral intervention is decided upon by Washington.

Thus we can conclude that United States power to initiate collective action in the hemisphere, or to stimulate governments to adopt policies (internal and external) of her own choosing, has suffered a decline; but she retains the power to deny resources to, or prevent the adoption of certain policies by, her southern neighbours. This, of course, contrasts with the continued inability of Latin American governments to bring strong pressure, positive or negative, to bear on Washington.

How then, does Washington define its 'interest' in Latin America? The question almost certainly has no precise answer, because of the combination of confusion and neglect which surrounds the subject. But the present situation of flux with respect to the totality of American foreign policy has a number of implications for the region.

One can offer, broadly speaking, two rationales for imperialism. One is essentially economic: the control of raw materials, the search for markets, the international division of labour and the usefulness of balancing profits and losses in different countries with different tax laws so as to maximize global profits. The other rationale is political and strategic, and speaks of balance of power, spheres of influence and so on. The two parts are in part complementary, for the political apparatus of empire is necessary to secure its economic benefits; but if the economic benefits are outweighed by 'maintenance' costs, the empire may lose its *raison d'être*. It is not clear that this situation has been reached yet by the United States, and if we separate the interests of multinational corporations from those supported by the

United States Government the issue becomes even more unclear. But there is evidence that the costs of ensuring a stable political framework for private foreign investment in Latin America are running very high and some influential voices in the United States have recently been arguing for withdrawal,[22] or in the face of what is seen as deterioration in the United States' political leverage, against attempts to re-establish political pre-eminence.[23] The extent to which Latin America is 'essential to the health of the United States economy', is now an open question. The only conceivable 'essential' might possibly be Venezuelan oil. A different perspective would point to the need for markets to forestall declining rate of profit, but this also involves a political superstructure which the Government is expected to finance, and it is not clear whether the United States economy can do so any longer.

Another definition of United States interest in the hemisphere is in terms of security, and here again the scope of that word is being narrowed down. The only powers which can effectively threaten United States security (strictly construed) are nuclear powers: the Soviet Union and eventually, perhaps, China. A security threat in the hemisphere, in Washington's eyes, would consist of bases for missiles or, perhaps more crucially, for naval purposes. Both great powers already have enough missile capacity to destroy each other many times over, but there is a constant rivalry on the high seas. Thus Washington would probably wish to ensure that no Latin American country offers base facilities to the Soviet Union, and in pursuing this objective the military assistance programme can provide a bargaining counter. From this point of view the ongoing battle between Congress and the Executive over the level of arms sales is of particular relevance.

If the definition of the United States interest in Latin America is now so narrow, not only objectively, but also in the minds of decision-makers, this implies a search for new 'deals', new con-

---

[22] Albert Hirshman 'How to Divest in Latin America, and Why', Princeton Univ. International Finance Section, *Essays in International Finance*, No. 76 November 1969. Governor Rockefeller thought very differently about private investment, but his ideas about a 'hemispheric division of labour', with capital-intensive industries in the US and labour-intensive ones in the South, is perhaps a means of partly limiting foreign private involvement while retaining dependence in an accentuated form.

[23] John N. Plank, in leaked proceedings of the Council of Foreign Relations (NACLA's *Latin America and Empire Report* V.7 November 1971) suspects that Henry Kissinger thinks: (a) that confrontations with Latin American governments are counter-productive, and (b) that he has 'persuaded' the President that protection of US private interests in Latin America must not be permitted to assume an overriding priority.

ciliations, new bottles for old wine, and the sacrifice of some sacred but useless cows. The handling of the IPC in Peru illustrates the diversity of situations which can now be constructed as 'in the United States interest'.

The Peruvian Government managed to bring little thunder upon itself as a result of the confiscation of the oilwells and refinery of the International Petroleum Company. These represented but a tiny fraction of the global turnover of Standard Oil, but the cool reaction of an American government bent upon avoiding confrontation was probably independent of such considerations. The IPC affair was the end-result of a particular long-standing grievance whose removal was also an occasion for making political capital out of nationalist excitement. It was an isolated incident: the government wished to attract foreign capital, and wished to do so on a contract basis which would ensure foreign companies a guaranteed return and stable rules of the game, while sparing them the embarrassment of a conspicuous presence. Finally, it emerged as a very stable and strongly non-Communist government. The Agrarian Reform did not affect substantial American interests. Those which were affected seemed not unhappy to be rid of somewhat unprofitable sugar estates, while preserving control of the profitable chemical and paper industries based on sugar by-products. The reform promised to create a conservative class of peasants who would not unleash a rebellion in the future.

The possibly crucial importance of the ideological question in the response to the Peruvian Government leads us to ask whether, in the Western Hemisphere, ideology is not a touchstone of American reactions. If this is true, as it was to a large extent in the Cuban case,[24] then the United States reaction is far more difficult to predict both at the level of policy or doctrine, and at the level of practical judgement.

For the Chilean challenge must be seen in Washington as predominantly ideological, which means that it is advanced at all the levels on which United States interest might be defined. It involves the global rivalry of capitalism and socialism — and it involves a weakening (hopefully) of the traditional institutions and channels of foreign political leverage. Above all, ideology travels, and its routes

---

[24] Was not the crux of the problem the fact that the Cuban leadership, for ideological reasons, refused to be bought off, refused to play the traditional game of Caribbean politics?

are more difficult to control than those of armies or cargo ships, and therein lies the greatest source of uncertainty.

Expropriations in themselves, even of copper mines, barely affect the United States economy, but they might do if they provoked many imitations within Latin America and elsewhere. An isolated socialist society in Chile could not represent a security threat to the United States, and it is probably not perceived as such by most influential people there; but would United States interests be harmed by a 'spreading' of socialism to other countries? The conditions under which these fears could be confirmed are far from clear.

The United States Government cannot, on some assumptions, put a step right. If it helps Chile, it is promoting the cause of socialism, and letting others think they will 'get away with it'; if it remains aloof and indifferent by neither helping nor hindering, it is already accused of economic agression;[25] and if sanctions are applied some will say 'we are driving them into the arms of the Communists'. Speaking to so many 'publics' at once, there is little hope of satisfying them all. More fundamentally, it is not clear whether socialism spreads like a contagious disease, nor is it clear whether nationalism does so. Since the massive Cuban expropriation, only Peru and Chile have expropriated without paying the expected compensation, and each on only one occasion,[26] hardly the alarming 'wave' of nationalism so commonly proclaimed in Congressional Hearings! Cuba has soldiered on, but has found no imitators. Similarly, it is far from clear that Chile will become totally dependent on the Socialist countries as soon as the United States commits a 'blunder'. In other words, the empirical relationships on which an anti-Communist Latin American policy might be based are simply unknown and unpredictable. Ten years ago the assumptions were no more realistic, but at least they were widely shared. Today, new assumptions are not available, but old ones are undergoing 'agonizing reappraisal', and in the consequent lack of sureness and confidence lies the main danger for Chile. An unpredictable negotiating partner is an unhappy lot,

---

25 Refusal to give aid to a nationalizing government is, after all, a perfectly rational economic decision, since there is reasonable doubt whether loans will be repaid. Whether this is 'just' or not is a complex problem in moral philosophy, for one would have to establish that there exists a moral obligation to give aid — and one would also have to show that, in the light of certain values, aid is not in fact harmful to some social classes in the receiving country.

26 The case of Gulf Oil in Bolivia is complex, but has been in the end resolved in a manner agreeable to the company involved.

but a partner who does not himself know what he is seeking is even worse. For, together with the empirical assumptions, the value judgements underlying American policy are also undergoing revision. The difference between a 'low profile' and 'no profile' is hard indeed to detect at the moment.

Having engaged in a general and long-term survey of the international relations of Latin America, we must end by returning to the pressing and immediate problems facing the Popular Unity. We mentioned at the beginning of this paper the difficulties liable to face the political leaders of any revolutionary process in the Third World today, and especially in Latin America, and the tables presented here bear out these suspicions. Despite the limited reliability of some of the most recent figures, the trend is surely unmistakable: reserves have declined drastically since the third quarter of 1970, and the balance of payments position also shows an unfavourable trend. The proportion of food in imports is rising and promises to rise further if the estimates quoted earlier are to be believed, while that of capital goods and spares declines. Moreover, the proportion of food imports is dramatically high when compared to the position in the late sixties. As we said earlier, these trends reflect the beneficial effects of government policies on the standard of living of the masses — the urban poor have more to spend, and spend much of it on food, while the beneficiaries of the land reform consume more of the food they produce than before. Nevertheless, this creates difficulties. The crucial question is: how will different measures taken to deal with these short-term problems affect the medium and long-term course of Chilean development?

The balance of payments position in the past few years has been shored up, it would appear, by short-term loans permitting a high level of imports. But one result is an enormous public foreign debt: $3,700 million according to the most recent estimates, of which $1,200 million are owed to the United States. This has come home to roost in the early years of the new government. The price of copper reached 70 cents per pound in April 1970, having been high during the entire Frei administration. It seems now to have stabilized at around 50 cents per pound, but the copper companies do not expect it to rise above that figure for at least one or two years. This means that a 40% increase in copper exports is required over that achieved in 1970 simply in order to achieve the 1970 level of earnings. Since imports of food in 1972 are estimated to be three times their value in 1970, and since aid in support of the country's balance of payments is unlikely to be forthcoming, there must surely be a decline in imports of capital and intermediate goods.

Table IV

Chile: Balance of Payments (in millions of US dollars)

	1964	*1965*	*1966*	*1967*	*1968*	*1969*
Goods and services	-143	-52	-108	-142	-151	-13
Trade balance c.i.f.	-30	67	80	102	112	247
Investment income	-103	-128	-201	-232	-227	-228
Other	-10	9	13	-12	-36	-32

Source: IMF: *International Finance Statistics*, XXV, 1 and 10,
January and September, 1972.

Table V

Chile: Public External Debt (in millions of US dollars).

	Total Debt	*Total Debt Service*
1955	320	38
1960	457	78
1966	1,020	125
1968	1,392[1]	
1970	1,478[1]	
1972		409*

Sources: IBRD: *World Tables*, various years.
[1] Chile: *Presidential Message*, 1971.
*Assuming no renegotations.

Table VI

Chile: Gold and Foreign Exchange Reserves (End of period: in millions of US dollars)

1966	*1967*	*1968*	*1969*	*1970*	*1971*			
					I	II	III	IV
172	126	208	344	367	341	299	239	221

Source: IMF: *International Financial Statistics, loc. cit.*

Table VII

Chile: Food and Live Animal Imports as Proportion of Total Imports, 1961—69

	Total Imports (A)	Food & Live Animals (B)	A as a percentage of B
1962	2513.43	443.31	17.6
1963	3093.96	581.84	18.8
1966	875.5	123.3	14.1
1967	907.7	107.4	11.8
1968	935.9	112.8	12.1
1969	1067.9	137.0	12.8
1970			16.2[1]
1971			23.1[1]

Sources: UN *Yearbooks of International Trade Statistics*, New York, 1965 & 1969. Comparable data not available from this source 1963-66.

[1] Chile: Presidential Message, 1972.

Table VIII

Chile: Capital Goods and Foodstuffs as Proportion of Total Imports, 1968—71.

	1968 $US million	%	1969 $US million	%	1970 $US million	%	1971 $US million	%
Capital Goods & Spares	426	53.1	405	44.5	177	26.8	144	19.2
Foodstuffs	64	8.0	65	7.1	115	17.4	178	23.7
Total Imports	802	100	911	100	660	100	750	100

Source: EIU: *Quarterly Reports*

Note: These series are included because they are the only ones available to the authors at present which give data for 1971. It is recognized that they are inconsistent with other sources for 1968, 1969 and 1970, but it is felt that the trends manifested are of interest. The definition of foodstuffs is obviously different from that of agricultural products in Table VII.

The negotiations with creditor governments at present taking place in Paris may relieve this situation. But it should be noted that, even if a moratorium is granted, this will in the long term further increase the debt burden with added interest and amortization charges. In the short term, taking nationalizations into account, the 'Investment Income' deficit should at least not deteriorate further (it has been above the $200 million mark since 1966). The crucial question then will be whether the new agrarian system is firmly entrenched at the end of the moratorium period, so that food imports do not continue to eat into the resources available for importing capital goods.

All this points to a crucial role for the agricultural sector in solving the external problems of the economy during the coming years. Dependence on food imports has for long been denounced as one of the worst ills of the Chilean economy, but its elimination acquires greater importance in the light of the outside world's unwillingness or inability to provide an easy solution today. The Soviet Union, being herself an importer of agricultural products for many years, is not in a position to ease this particular situation, and the aid she customarily gives is not of the kind that would liberate much 'hard' currency for the purchase of food.

An alternative approach to these problems would place far more emphasis on self-reliance. One could envisage agricultural expansion being based to a far larger extent than in the past on domestic resources and labour-using inputs. One could argue also that technological dependence on the United States has had such harmful effects that it would be best to break it once and for all, and to generate local invention and innovation instead. If, for example, self-sufficiency in food production (or at least a surplus in agricultural trade) is not feasible in the breathing space afforded by a moratorium, so that continued reliance on foreign aid is necessary in order to keep industry supplied with spare parts and capital goods, then the difference — in the long term — between reneging and accepting a moratorium appears relatively narrow. From this standpoint, the continued availability of commercial credit in the Western world offers relatively few benefits compared to those of being relieved of debts and of engaging in a truly independent path of development.[27]

Independence, of course, has its costs as well as its benefits. It means a long and hard path of development. But it also leaves fewer

[27] The Government might of course have to consider the effects of its actions on the possibilities for borrowing by other countries engaged in structural change.

hostages to the future. It would probably involve, in the early years, institutions such as rationing and a strong central planning organization, leaving little autonomy to decision-makers at the enterprise level. But it is not impossible that rationing, at least, can be avoided. Moreover, it has the merit of being a highly egalitarian measure, which would prevent sacrifices from being unequally distributed, so long as it could be effectively administered. It would continue and consolidate the already substantial redistribution carried out by the Popular Unity, and would ensure that the gains from the redistribution were not eroded by price inflation. Finally, as has already been implied, the choice of an essentially agricultural strategy in the early years and the postponement of further industrialization might allow the country to abandon the present path of industrial development.

Apart from these considerations, what pressures are likely to be exerted from outside in the present situation? Assuming that its reaction is based primarily on political considerations, it is conceivable that the United States Government will refuse a moratorium, or that it will insist on unacceptable conditions, such as a revision of the terms of the nationalization of the copper companies. In this case, the Chilean Government would have little alternative but to renege, thereby foregoing most Western credit for at least a year or two, as well as all aid. It would also be forced to reorient much industrial technology if unilateral measures were taken by the United States. The extent to which some multinational corporations would nevertheless continue to trade with Chile through foreign subsidiaries is impossible to guess, but there is a danger that even those wishing to continue to trade with the country will be swept away in the flood. However, such provocative action by the United States seems inconsistent with present efforts to avoid confrontation in Latin America.

A more realistic prediction is that the moratorium will be granted, but that aid from the United States will continue at its present near-zero level. As our earlier analysis implies, European governments are unlikely to give aid to the level hitherto given by the United States, while aid from the socialist countries would have little effect on the food problem, and would in some cases involve a substantial change in industrial technology. Under this hypothesis the Government will be walking the tightrope described above.

A final alternative would be for the United States to resume aid flows in exchange for political concessions. These would certainly involve some form of compensation for the copper companies. Other possible demands are an end to the process of mass mobilization and political education, and, on the external front, some kind of loosening of ties with socialist countries, especially Cuba. None of these is likely to be acceptable to the Popular Unity.

In the final analysis, resistance to all these forms of external pressure depends for its effectiveness on the political support for the revolution inside the country, and therefore on the political education, consciousness and participation of the masses. Although there may be an initial period of expanding consumer demand, the process of development must surely be a painful one at some stage, as must the transition to socialism. Even now the Government is asking the population to contribute voluntary labour, and to participate in the *batalla de la producción,* though as yet these are not very painful sacrifices. The leaders of revolutions in the past have always found it necessary to preserve power while the population suffers the unpleasant effects of economic warfare and structural change. The sadness is that, from a long-term point of view, these unpleasantnesses may be necessary for the achievement of socialism, while compromise and concession may push the ideal even further into the future, despite making present burdens less onerous.

HUNGARY: THE EXPERIENCE OF MARKET SOCIALISM

Richard D. Portes*

The history of Hungarian economic policy and the means by which it has been implemented during the postwar period falls into clearly defined periods. Nationalization was virtually complete by 1950. From then until the end of 1956, the direction of production was highly centralized. All-embracing central physical allocation of commodities, centrally determined and highly detailed current production plans, and total central control over investment guided the economy *in natura*. All this was in the service of a few simple policy goals: the maximum rate of growth of industry, with primary emphasis on heavy industry, and a correspondingly high savings ratio; and an attempt at a form of autarchy, which in practice meant import substitution for a wide range of basic industrial goods, as well as large increases in output of the few domestically available raw materials (mainly coal). The development strategy and planning methods were fundamentally those which had been used in the Soviet Union since the late 1920s.

Although these policies brought quantitative results, they were carried to extremes, and towards the end of the period their disadvantages and unsuitability to Hungarian conditions became increasingly apparent. In early 1957, many steps were taken to correct the major faults of the system, introducing what may be called partial decentralization of the command economy mechanism. Binding plan targets, fixed prices, and central physical allocation remained, but all were more or less rationalized, and many decisions which had previously been taken by the ministries were left to the enterprises. At the same time, there was some effort to move towards a more balanced growth path, with a greater role for foreign trade.

Gradual recentralization began only a few years later, however, and by the mid-1960s the economy was facing serious problems. The leadership took the basic decision to reform in 1965, and after three

* Princeton University and University College, London.

years of careful preparation, in January 1968 the Hungarian economy switched from administrative to market socialism. There were relatively minor modifications in 1968-70, and although the changes of January 1971 and a few recent measures are more important, on the whole they confirm the broad directions of the reforms.

In size and level of development Hungary is not so dissimilar to Chile as to exclude analogies. Hungary's pre-1968 experience with nationalization and running a command economy might be instructive, but the standard Soviet-type system and its application in developing countries is quite fully discussed in the literature. What is especially interesting for our purposes is that Hungary chose, after twenty years, to change to a new system, which is itself unique: regulated market socialism, without workers' control, in a semi-industrialized country. I shall therefore discuss the reasons why Hungary undertook these reforms and some aspects of the system they created. I shall not give a general assessment of the reforms, nor an analysis of the interesting set of problems involved in switching from administrative to market allocation (the *process* of decentralization).[1] Rather, I shall consider three areas which are particularly relevant to the policy choices now facing Chile:

1. The organization and control of the public sector — its administrative structure, the distribution of decision-making authority, the determinants of economic decisions, and the policy tools used by planners.

2. Incomes policies. This is one key to the viability of the Hungarian reforms, and a long history of inflation makes it especially interesting for Chile. Here I include profit-sharing, control over wage levels, effects on the labour market, and the economic and political implications of distributional questions.

3. Workers' control — why Hungary rejected it, and what has been done instead through the trade unions to promote industrial democracy.

Throughout, I shall deal only with the industrial sector, although there have, of course, been significant changes in other branches.

---

[1] On these issues, see R.D. Portes, 'Economic Reforms in Hungary', *American Economic Review* May 1970; 'The Strategy and Tactics of Economic Decentralization', *Soviet Studies* April 1972; and *Economic Reforms in Hungarian Industry* Oxford University Press, forthcoming. See also B. Balassa, 'The Economic Reform in Hungary', *Economica* February 1970, and Balassa's paper presented to the Research Conference on Economic Reforms in Eastern Europe, Ann Arbor, Michigan, November 1970.

I. Background to the 1968 Reforms

By the mid-1960s, the planners found that the rate of growth of national income was falling, and they were unable to raise living standards at the rate they thought necessary. Plans were over-optimistic, and the planners themselves were so overwhelmed by details that they could not properly plan structural changes. More specifically, we may stress five related groups of problems facing the economy.

1. Foreign trade. Hungary is a small country, poor in raw materials. The early attempts at autarchy had merely increased the economy's dependence on imported materials. It was therefore necessary to move towards an export-oriented, transforming economy. But the structure of trade was unsatisfactory – Hungarian machinery was of poor quality, acceptable only to other Comecon countries, and Hungarian trade with the West was mainly an exchange of agricultural goods for raw materials. The balance of trade deficit was rising steadily throughout the period 1962-64, especially with hard currency countries. Thus Hungary could not import enough of the advanced Western machinery she needed, nor could competition from imports be used to prod domestic producers into improving quality. Exports were insufficiently specialized, so there was no opportunity for long production runs and economies of scale. The distorted domestic price system made it impossible rationally to choose commodities for export and import.

2. The labour market and productivity. Hungary was running out of labour to transfer from agriculture into industry and exhausting the possibilities for increasing participation rates. To compensate for falling growth rates of industrial employment by increasing capital inputs even faster would quickly run into diminishing returns, so more rapid technical progress was essential. The planners thought also of stimulating productivity by improving incentives, and they were unhappy with the existing wage, premium and profit-sharing systems because of their apparent inability to promote productivity growth.

3. Matching the structure of supply to that of demand at the disaggregated level was particularly difficult for the Hungarian economy in the early 1960s. This was evident in foreign trade, on consumer goods markets and in inter-enterprise relationships. The quality and variety of output were poor. More fundamentally, the objective of satisfying demand was neglected in the enterprises' choice of production programmes, and the planners were unable to

solve the problem with directives from above. One manifestation of the problem was excessive stockbuilding, and even with large and rapidly growing stocks, there were still shortages of material inputs (often disrupting production) and of consumer goods. Although deliberate enterprise hoarding of inputs accounted for much of the excessive inventory accumulation, a good part occurred because enterprises produced goods for which there were no customers. And so, at a more aggregative level, did the economy itself. Throughout the production structure there was evidence of the planners' poor choices of industries to expand and goods to produce. Structural change was required, but there were no meaningful prices to guide it.

4. Investment. The investment market was characterized by excess demand from 1959 on, with consequent dispersal of resources and delayed completions. Projects were poorly prepared and executed, so incorrect technical choices and large cost overruns were common. Replacement and modernization were neglected in favour of new plants.

5. Innovation and technical progress. The planners tended to think of dynamic inefficiency in terms of rising incremental capital-output ratios and slow growth of labour productivity. Recent studies using the conceptually more satisfactory measure of total factor productivity confirm that dynamic efficiency was indeed worse in the period 1960-65 than it had been during the 1950s.

The authorities attributed these problems to the weaknesses of the highly centralized command system. Changes in the structure of the economy and the goals of economic policy required changes in the economic mechanism: better planning; a more flexible system of short-run management of the economy; better incentives, information and criteria for choice; and more direct relationships between foreign trade and domestic production. As the major desired structural shifts were achieved, the major indivisibilities and externalities exploited, the planners felt that the weaknesses of the market and market prices became less important. Concern for the uses of output, especially consumption and exports, was replacing the previous emphasis on growth of output.

The reformers were not renouncing planning. They were trying to adjust the nature of planning to new circumstances, and thereby to increase efficiency, put the economy on a more balanced growth path, and improve its capacity to satisfy consumer needs and to compete in foreign markets. They wanted to decentralize decision-making, in the sense of transferring decision authority to appropriate levels, while improving the information available for decisions at all levels. It was hoped that the planners would then be free to deal with the important issues of structural change, macro-economic balance, etc., where their information was best. Correspondingly, enterprises would be able to take a much broader range of allocative decisions, with improved price and incentive systems to guide them. Moreover, decentralization was expected to release initiative and innovation, much broader participation, and better motivation.

Socialism, in the sense of state ownership, was unquestioned — indeed, not even workers' self-management was considered (see section IV). A regulated socialist market system was chosen because the other alternatives seemed unsatisfactory. Partial decentralization in the framework of the old command system had already been tried in 1957. The use of mathematical planning techniques to guide the command system or substitute for a market mechanism did not seem realistic, although, (or because) Hungary had pioneered in developing large-scale programming models for planning.[2]

As well as providing a background to the following sections, the discussion so far may offer some lessons. Hungarian experience suggests that in a small country, although the command system may be useful in the early period of forced-draft industrialization, its advantages diminish and its disadvantages increase as growth proceeds. The economy becomes more sophisticated, the relative priority given to present consumption increases, and allocative choices (especially in foreign trade) become more important. To some extent this experience has parallels elsewhere in Eastern Europe, but for various reasons other countries have chosen different responses. Czechoslovakia had started on the Hungarian route, roughly simultaneously (but with some important differences, especially workers' control); the German Democratic Republic, on the other hand, is attempting to rationalize the command system. Whatever their current policies, however, all the Eastern European Sociallist countries are watching the Hungarian experiment very closely.

II. Organization and Control of the Public Sector

The reforms have brought little change in the administrative structure of the economy, but significant transfers of decision-making authority and changes in the policy tools used by the planners have taken place. There were only minor alterations in the structure of

2 For a discussion of the obstacles to practical application of such techniques in centrally planned economies, see R.D. Portes, 'Decentralized Planning Procedures and Centrally Planned Economies', *American Economic Review* May 1971.

industry. As before 1968, there are about 800 state-owned enterprises and 800 industrial cooperatives, the former producing 93% of industrial output. The state enterprises are quite large; they average almost 2000 employees per enterprise, and at the beginning of the reforms, almost fifty enterprises had over 5000 employees each. There are no industrial associations interposed between the enterprises and industrial ministries, in contrast with other Eastern European countries. The closest Hungarian equivalent is the trust, of which only a few remain under the reforms. There are some 'associations' which are not state administrative bodies, but rather service organizations subordinate to their constituent enterprises. Anything closer to cartels was thought to be incompatible with market pricing, and in any case a superfluous (because enterprises were already so large) administrative layer between the enterprises and the ministries. Indeed, the existing degree of concentration is often criticized because of the market power it creates, but it is tolerated in the hope that competition from imports can eventually be given free rein.

Since there is no worker's control (see section IV), the industrial branch ministries still exercise the 'ownership' rights of the State: appointing managers, setting their remuneration, determining the fields in which enterprises may operate, etc. The responsibilities, broadly defined, of the various state administrative bodies changed hardly at all in 1968. But their actual executive authority, the kinds of decisions with which they are concerned, and the policy instruments they use are considerably different. Previously, current production decisions were controlled in detail by annual plan targets for inputs, outputs, costs, short-term credit, exports, imports, inventories, etc. These targets were set by the National Planning Office and ministries for enterprises and enforced through a complex system of sanctions and rewards. Such plan targets were eliminated in 1968. Central physical allocation (rationing of producer goods) was severely restricted, and has since been further cut back until it now affects only a few commodities. The distribution of inputs and outputs now takes place through free trade between enterprises. The formerly unlimited authority of industrial ministries to give direct operative instructions to the enterprises they supervise was confined to exceptional circumstances. Industrial producer prices were completely revised (the first time since 1959), so they more closely reflected full costs. More important, a large proportion of these prices, as well as of consumer prices, were free to vary according to market forces. The turnover tax structure which had effectively divorced producer and consumer prices was made more uniform, so consumer price ratios are now much closer to producer price ratios. Foreign prices were converted to domestic prices by separate uniform exchange rates for the dollar and rouble, and although extensive tariffs and subsidies were applied, at least domestic prices were to vary directly with foreign prices. Since the foreign trade enterprises were put on a commission basis (so they no longer implemented detailed import and export plans fixed by the Planning Office and Ministry of Foreign Trade), this meant reuniting foreign and domestic markets.

Thus current production decisions were almost completely decentralized and left to enterprise choices in the market – a highly regulated market, of course. At the same time, a significant share of investment in industry was also put under enterprise control, to be financed by funds created from profits. This included all capital replacement and modernization within the enterprise, as well as smaller expansion projects. Larger projects are usually jointly financed by the enterprise and the budget, although the largest – major new plants, etc. – may be entirely initiated, financed and controlled by the central authorities.

The basic guide for all these decisions put under enterprise control is the profit motive. Incentives, as we discuss below, are based on the total annual profit of the enterprise. But the planners do not just sit back, make a few major investment decisions, and otherwise just observe how things go. They have a wide range of policy instruments which they use to influence enterprise decisions.

First, they do still plan. Annual and five-year plans are issued as before, but somewhat less disaggregated, and organized on a sectoral rather than an 'addressee' basis. For the enterprises, these plans are now only 'indicative,' intended to serve as a comprehensive source of information which will help to coordinate decentralized decisions and thereby generate planned outcomes.

This is not to say, however, that when evaluating the performance of an enterprise director, the supervising ministry would not consider whether the activities of his enterprise were guided by the priorities and broad principles expressed in the plans. But more important is that the plans are binding directives for the state administrative bodies, which are charged with devising and applying policies which will promote plan fulfilment, using the tools available to them. An interdepartmental committee works out the principles of credit policy, which the banks must apply: the total amounts of working capital and investment credit to be offered during the year, a broad division by sectors, and the terms on which it is to be extended, including some preferential conditions for individual industries and purposes. Two other interdepartmental committees administer the wide-ranging system of export subsidies. A further interdepartmental committee formulates the principles of pricing and material allocation policy for the year, to be implemented by the National Materials and Price Office: any major changes in centrally fixed prices and other forms of price control, the commodities which are to be subject to allocation controls, etc. The Ministry of Finance annually fixes subsidies and tax concessions for some enterprises, and for longer periods it sets profit and income tax rates and regulations. It also cooperates with the Price Office for changes in indirect taxes and with the Ministry of Foreign Trade for tariffs and subsidies on imports (and, until 1971, administering the import deposit scheme). The Ministry of Foreign Trade and the Planning Office preside over negotiation of annual and five-year bilateral trade agreements, and the Ministry of Foreign Trade administers the system of import and export licences. The Ministry of Labour fixes basic wage tariffs and from time to time adjusts the provisions of the incentive system and average wage control (see below).

While the functional bodies apply this far-reaching, often highly specific and differentiated set of financial ('parametric') controls, the industrial branch ministries manage to keep busy: working out long-term policies and investigating technological alternatives for their branches; planning major investment projects and advising on projects for which enterprises seek state financial aid; offering advice and occasionally intervening more forcefully when particular problems arise in their branches; and, of course, evaluating the performance and determining the remuneration of top-level enterprise executives.

It should now be clear that we are talking about a *highly regulated* socialist market system, which is still guided by 'planning', on any reasonable definition of the term. There are two basic motives behind the use of the formidable array of 'economic regulators'. One is precisely that the authorities only trust the unregulated market, working through the profit motive, within rather narrow limits. They *plan* not merely to deal with classical causes of market failure — externalities, increasing returns, imperfect knowledge — but also to retain central control over the broad features of structural change, foreign economic relations, income distribution, the allocation between public and private needs, and macro-economic equilibrium. The objectives of the reforms were to bring greater efficiency, more innovation and initiative, and the like, but not at the cost of surrendering any significant degree of central authority in these areas.

To the extent that this first motive requires the various interventionist measures discussed, the Hungarian experience in controlled decentralization under socialism may be directly relevant to Chilean problems. Unfortunately, however, it is difficult to separate these ends and their consequential means from a second, rather different set of problems. These were created by the need to cushion the economy and individuals from the shock of transition to a market after twenty years of administrative allocation and the distortions it bequeathed, while satisfying certain domestic and foreign political constraints on the scope and effects of the reforms. I have discussed these problems at length elsewhere.[3] Here we may simply note that many of the specific forms and instances of central intervention are regarded by the Hungarian authorities themselves as 'brakes' limiting the full effectiveness of the reforms, essential in the short run but to be discarded as soon as possible. They have found it quite difficult, however, to apply uniform conditions for granting short-term credit where this will endanger the liquidity of financially weak firms; to reduce export subsidies and make them more uniform where this will impose painful adjustments, possibly entailing closure of plants or liquidation of entire enterprises; to loosen the foreign trade licensing system if this will threaten the achievement of bilateral balancing with other Comecon countries; to relax price and wage controls, etc. When evaluating decentralization in Hungary and its relevance to other countries, one must try to keep in mind that many of the 'brakes' might be unnecessary outside the Hungarian historical, political and socio-economic context – although analogous measures might be required elsewhere.

Despite the 'brakes', observation of the reform period suggests that decentralization has on balance brought some allocative improvement over the old command system. Four years is too short a time to expect a major advance. On the other hand, it is long enough to say with some confidence that the reforms are firmly installed, the basic system is viable, and only a major, exogenously determined political change could bring significant recentralization. This is in itself impressive, given the history of other attempts at decentralization in Eastern Europe since 1956.

On the available evidence, one can go further. Although industrial output is growing somewhat more slowly since 1968, national income originating in industry is growing at the same rate as before,

---

[3] 'Strategy and Tactics...', *op.cit.*

and the latter is now slightly faster than the former. As this suggests, the share of intermediate use in total output has fallen, and in particular, inventory accumulation is somewhat less shocking than before. Prices have risen quite slowly, although consumers complain nevertheless. Material supply conditions for producers are much better, and this has allowed progressive relaxation of the remaining allocation controls. The structure of output has improved at the product level. Producers are more responsive to consumer demand, and this is reflected in the quality and assortment of consumer goods. There has been some improvement in the structure of foreign trade, and there is promise for the future in the many technical cooperation agreements with Western firms. There are some signs of more initiative from below — but this is more apparent in the cooperative and private sectors than in the state sector, and more in services and agriculture than in industry. Overall, there is no reason to think that plan fulfilment is any poorer, and the plans themselves seem somewhat more realistic and better prepared than before.

On the micro side, therefore, market allocation does seem to have brought some of the greater flexibility and responsiveness to demand which had been anticipated, without any sacrifice of quantitative growth. Any index growth of output which allowed fully for quality change and the correspondence of the pattern of output to demand would, we suspect, show a considerable improvement, and in this respect market socialism is performing better than the command economy which it replaced. It seems, however, that there are two major, interrelated problems here which are important for any country which might consider an economic mechanism operating along the lines we have sketched.

First, it has been claimed on various grounds[4] that only part of the putative informational advantages of the market are being used, and that the information which guides producer choices may in fact be poorer overall than it was under the command system. Horizontal dealings between buyers and sellers are indeed faster, less cumbersome, and more likely to result in the satisfaction of perceived needs than was the bureaucratic planning system relying on the vertical communication of information (often distorted from below) and commands. But the prices now setting the terms for producers' and users' choices are heavily distorted by subsidies, indirect taxes, and central price controls, all of which also obscure the differences between high-cost and low-cost producers and industries. Efficiency

---

[4] Most recently in an unpublished paper by D. Granick 'The Hungarian Economic Reform'.

considerations are at best secondary in determining the pattern of this extensive central interference with the price mechanism. The various 'parametric' controls are worked out in many different committees and ministry offices, often with only nominal coordination between them. To the extent that prices are formed 'in the market', the market itself is highly oligopolistic and suffers from chronic excess demand (see below), so often the only limitation to price increases is the enterprise director's judgment of how far he can go without provoking ministerial or public wrath — circumstances which are unlikely to yield a 'rational' price structure. Finally, it is not only enterprise pricing decisions which are taken on criteria other than profit maximization. Many input, output, sales and investment decisions are influenced by 'social' considerations, ministry and trade union pressure, and objectives (for example, the growth of sales) other than profits. The role of such factors is increased by conditions which diminish the incentive force of profits: high marginal rates of taxation; the dependence of executive remuneration and promotion on an overall ministry assessment of performance as well as on the enterprise's profit record; and the recognition that a large proportion of the profit is a consequence of subsidies determined individually for each enterprise.

This is a strong but not entirely convincing case. To evaluate it properly would require more space than would be justified here. Without producing evidence, therefore, my own views are the following:

1. Despite the subsidies, taxes, and controls, the price system is a better guide to allocation than before 1968. The 1968 price reform improved it tremendously, and perhaps more important, it does now respond to supply, demand, and foreign market prices, however imperfectly. But I should stress that this view is the more defensible, the finer the level of commodity disaggregation one is considering. When one looks at relative prices of broad product groups or industrial sub-branches and branches, the picture is *much* less clear, the distortions much more important and harder to sort out. There is, however, some gradual improvement taking place (except perhaps for import prices), as the categories to which subsidies and taxes apply are made progressively broader and the rates more uniform.

2. On the other hand, individual high-cost producer enterprises are still being protected, and while there has been some shake-out of the production structure within enterprises, there have been only *very*

limited moves towards shutting down uneconomical plants and enterprises.

3. I suspect that the coordination of the 'economic regulators' is
rather better than appears to the casual observer. The committees
overlap, the functional bodies responsible for administering the
regulators are probably better run than the industrial branch ministries, and their cooperation is likely to be more effective than was
the National Planning Office's coordination of the industrial ministries before 1968.

4. In so far as the comparison is relevant, I should guess that profit
is at least as heavily weighted in the Hungarian manager's utility
function as in that of his Western counterpart, with two qualifications: his horizons are probably shorter — or, if one prefers, his
discount rate higher; and he need not fear take-over bids.

The second micro-economic problem is the capital market. In
part, the difficulties here are simply a consequence of the un-
reliability of prices and profits as guides to resource allocation at the
broad product groups, enterprise, and industrial branch levels. No
mechanism for the allocation of capital can operate with tolerable
efficiency until the price system more accurately reflects opportunity costs. Within each enterprise, the choice of products and processes to develop and techniques to use may not be too bad, but the
inter-enterprise and inter-branch allocation of capital can have little
rational basis. Even if relative prices were more helpful here, the
heavy predominance of internal financing in decentralized investment and the limitations imposed by the ministries on enterprise
diversification would seriously hinder the proper use of investment
resources. But these problems are also aspects of a major unresolved
institutional question which, in the long run, may prove the deepest
and most difficult issue raised by the Hungarian economic reforms:
how to set up an efficient, flexible, and dynamic capital market in a
system of state ownership. This was foreshadowed by the 'socialist
debate' of the 1930s and remains a fundamental obstacle to any
attempt to run a socialist market system. The structural transformation of the economy cannot proceed very far without diversification, mergers and liquidations in response to profit opportunities
or their absence. If the ministries retain control here, enterprise
'independence' is compromised, and the initiative from below,
characteristic of a market system, will be sacrificed. But the reformers have not yet devised institutions which will permit such

initiative without involving any basic changes in the form of state ownership — and this may indeed be impossible.

Finally, the major macro-economic problems facing the Hungarian system are also related to the capital market complex of issues, in so far as they are primarily attributable to excess investment demand. Starting from an already high base in 1968-69, the investment boom of 1970-71 has led to considerable disorganization in the execution of projects, and it has been the main force generating disequilibria in the labour market and balance of trade. Capacity in construction is severely over-stretched, while building material and machinery imports have risen rapidly. Although the reformers recognized that they would have to reduce 'planners' tension', they succeeded in doing so only in 1968-69, and the pressure on the economy has again risen. Hungarian economic policy is still excessively influenced by the biases towards maximum investment and maximum quantitative growth inherited from the pre-reform period. These attitudes are reinforced by the authorities' concern for their position in the Comecon 'league tables' of economic growth. Thence a dilemma: rapid growth is necessary to 'vindicate' the reforms — yet a slow-down may be essential to preserve them.

Moreover, when investment booms went too far in the past, the planners were able to take direct measures both to cut back investment itself and to protect the balance of trade. Now they are in principle limited to fiscal and monetary policy, however. To encroach on the enterprises' freedom to use their development funds as they like or to reimpose import quotas would clearly not be in harmony with the reforms. The power of monetary policy to reduce investment directly is limited, because less than 20% of investment is financed by credit, but a more restrictive credit policy for working capital could force enterprises to use more of their development funds for this purpose. The planners could argue that the ministries were allowed to go too far in getting their pet investment projects into the fourth five-year plan, and try to cut back state-financed investment accordingly. But this would require both difficult political decisions and giving the Naional Planning Office enough authority over the ministries to implement them.

III. Incomes Policy

By one criterion — and perhaps the most important one — Hungarian incomes policy has been extraordinarily successful. Although enterprise managers have wide discretion in setting wages, average money earnings in state industry have risen at roughly the same rate as industrial productivity (about 4% a year) over the four years since the reforms. The key policy instrument here has been 'average wage control', a form of tax on wage increases.

This performance has been essential to the survival of the new system. Public opinion is *extremely* sensitive to price increases. Hungary had hyper-inflations after both World Wars, and another bout of severe inflation in the early 1950s (in 1950-52, the consumer price index for workers and employees rose 69%, and real wages fell 19%). This was followed by over a decade of virtually constant prices. This historical sequence seems to have generated a 'perverse' money illusion — in 1966, price increases which were *over*compensated by decreases in other prices and increases in money incomes were perceived as an overall *cut* in real incomes and generated considerable hostility. Subsequent increases in consumer prices have been very moderate (slightly under 2% a year since 1968, while per capita *real* income of workers and employees has risen by 6% a year). Yet even this has been a constant source of complaint and is clearly close to the limit of public tolerance. Had unit labour costs in industry not been constant, but instead risen sharply, they would inevitably have been passed on and the resulting consumer price increases would have been politically insupportable.

The contrast here with the Chilean acceptance of secular inflation is quite striking. If one gives high priority, however, to moderation of this inflation, the Hungarian case may be very instructive.

'Incomes policy' is not simply a matter of slowing the rate of increase of money wages. The Hungarian authorities have had other policy objectives, but they have been rather less successful with some of these than in controlling wage inflation, and some of the problems here may ultimately threaten their major achievement. The further goals of Hungarian incomes policy have been the obvious ones: distributional equity; eliciting desirable incentive effects from wages and other forms of remuneration; promoting macro-economic equilibrium, by keeping aggregate personal consumption to planned limits; and creating labour market equilibrium, with efficient allocation of the labour force.

The relative emphasis which the planners have given these objectives is not obvious, however. By the mid-1960s, the planners were convinced they had gone too far with the policy, pursued steadily since 1950, of narrowing wage differentials in the name of socialist principles.[5] Thus the reforms stressed greater differentiation between enterprises and individuals for incentive purposes. Enterprise performance and individual initiative were to be rewarded, the former through a profit-sharing system for employees, the latter by managers exercising greater freedom in wage-setting. The authorities hoped that average wage control and the profit taxation system would together control aggregate personal incomes, while labour market equilibrium would improve because market forces would have much wider scope than before. They paid relatively little attention to distributional equity, except for some social measures to improve the situation of those with very low per capita family incomes (increased family allowances and pensions, fixed prices for basic wage goods).

The two basic tools, average wage control and profit sharing, are variants of policy instruments introduced in 1957 and used throughout the following decade. The enterprise's annual plan prescribed the percentage by which it could raise its average wage (total wage bill divided by number of workers and employees) over the preceding year; this was rigidly enforced, and it did not vary with the level of fulfilment of the output or productivity plan. Since this limited the scope of incentive pay schemes, a profit sharing system for workers and employees was simultaneously established. Average wage control achieved its purpose: the rate of increase of average money earnings in state industry fell from 11% a year in 1950-1957 to 2% a year in 1958-1967. It did, however, give an artificial stimulus to employment of low-wage workers (so as to reduce the average wage, thus giving room for increases all round), and it was some hindrance to productivity increases.

Profit sharing was no help here. For several reasons, the scheme had little incentive force. It was paid at year end, based on the increase of the enterprise's profit-sales ratio during the year. In response to the pressure from employees for 'egalitarianism', shares were usually paid at the same percentage of basic pay for all employees of the enterprise; it was seldom over 5%, even in the early years when amounts were highest. Each year, the ministry would *ex*

---

[5] For the background of 1950-67 on, some of these issues, as well as estimates of equations describing the labour market behaviour of workers and planners, see D.S. Hamermesh and R.D. Portes, 'The Labour Market under Central Planning: The Case of Hungary', forthcoming in *Oxford Economic Papers.* The paper suggests an explanation of why the planners' labour market policies appeared unsuccessful by the mid-1960s, and why any centrally planned economy might eventually find itself in a similar situation. Labour market problems were in fact a significant impetus for the reforms (see Sec. I), in other Eastern European countries as well as in Hungary.

ante set an 'adjustment factor' for each enterprise, based on the possibilities for increased profit, as shown by its cost reduction plan. This was meant to give all enterprises the same opportunity to earn the average profit share planned for the year. Thus the scheme was tied to plan indices, and therefore subject to the normal 'plan bargaining', 'ratchet effect', etc. Finally, it was hard to take the system seriously as an incentive to better enterprise performance, since profit was measured using prices which everyone knew to be totally misleading as indicators of any sort of trade-off between goods.

The 1968 reforms combined average wage control and profit sharing in an ingenious way intended to mitigate the weaknesses of both. I describe the system used until 1971, with certain inessential simplifications; new regulations have operated during the past year, but it is too early to evaluate them, although they seem to have roughly the same effect as the previous system. When the enterprise draws up its annual balance sheet, its total actual profit is augmented by the product of its total labour force and the amount by which its average wage during the year exceeds the average wage paid in 1967. This 'accounting profit' is divided (in proportions which are a function of the enterprise capital-labour ratio) into a 'development portion' and a 'sharing portion'. The two are then taxed separately, the former at a constant rate, the latter on a progressive scale, to give the development and sharing funds. (Marginal rates of taxation are high, to aid macro stabilization policy and to avoid excessive inter-enterprise differentials in profit shares.) Finally, from its post-tax sharing fund the enterprise pays the state a sum equal to the amount added to actual profit in the first step. The remainder is then available for distribution among employees.

In effect, profit is calculated, divided up, and taxed *as if* the enterprise had not increased its average wage since 1967; then, a sum corresponding to that part of the increase in its wage bill over 1967 attributable to the increase in average wage is paid as a tax on the sharing fund. Thus all increases in earnings attributable to increases in the average wage are paid out of the post-tax sharing fund.

This in itself is a considerable deterrent to wage increases; in fact, for given revenues and non-wage costs, an enterprise *could not* increase the average remuneration (wage plus profit share) of its employees by raising their wages and salaries. In the first year (1968), however, a further twist made managers even less inclined to raise wages, since some of any wage increase would inevitably come out of their own pockets. This was the consequence of the 'category system'. Each employee was classed in one of the three groups, supposedly depending on his capacity to affect enterprise profit. Group I would include the director and several other top-level executives; Group II would include other executives and most technical workers; and Group III the rest, among whom were all manual workers. Consider now the aggregate of total annual wages and salaries (excluding profit shares) for each group, calculated separately. The sharing fund available for distribution was divided into three parts in proportion to these totals, but giving that for Group I a weight of 80, for Group II a weight of 50, and for Group III a weight of 15. These weights also served as maxima to the amounts which could be distributed to each of the groups in a given year: members of Group I could get in total no more than 80% of their combined basic annual salaries; 50% and 15% were the respective limits for others. Thus, if the sharing funds came to half the maximum total amount distributable under this regulation, members of Group I would get on average 40% of their basic pay, the others receiving 25% and 7½% respectively. The distribution within the groups was, in principle, entirely flexible, with the rules to be established by the enterprise employees in their annual collective contract; in practice, everyone in a given group received the same percentage, except for minor allowances for length of service.

Since any rise in the average wage would reduce the distributable sharing fund, and this would affect managers most, workers least, this set up a straightforward and important conflict of interests, and it did not take the workers long to realize why managers were so tight-fisted. Moreover, when the time came for distribution of the shares, and manual workers saw executives getting shares fifteen to twenty times their own (80/15 times 3, say, if the executive's base pay were three times that of the worker), their sharply hostile reaction assured the demise of the categories. Workers were unconvinced by arguments that, because managers were no longer receiving separate bonuses, total managerial incomes had in fact increased only slightly while becoming more variable. The categories were abolished at the end of 1969, retroactively covering the distribution of that year's sharing fund. This was despite a blanket pledge (otherwise observed pretty faithfully) at the beginning of the reforms that all major provisions would remain unchanged until 1971, and, in the unlikely event that something were to be altered, the change would never have retro-active effect.

I have discussed average wage control in rather technical detail because it seems a measure of potentially wide applicability.[6] The category system and its fate, on the other hand, illustrate two very important points: the extreme public sensitivity to distributional issues; and the extent of the planners' concern to construct a *powerful* profit-based incentive which would automatically give large rewards for good enterprise performance to those most responsible for it. This would give some of the desired differentiation of incomes, and at the same time would eliminate the supervising ministries from any role in giving large executive bonuses—a powerful stroke for enterprise independence. That the reformers' otherwise good political judgement was so wrong here testifies to the importance they attached to these desiderata.

In the event, the category system was replaced by a scheme of 'profit premia' for top management, for which the conditions of award are determined *ex ante* by the ministries. This does, I think, maintain the primacy of profit as a managerial objective, but it involves the ministries in an undesirable way. All employees still receive profit shares usually in the same percentage of their base pay (with some adjustment for length of service) — although the authorities continually urge differentiation, social pressure will not allow it. Nor do any but the most courageous enterprise managers follow the authorities' exhortations to differentiate wages and salaries according to merit, as well as the customary grades of age, training, experience etc.

As mentioned above, the system of average wage control introduced in 1968 was subsequently somewhat modified, then replaced in 1971 by a rather different form of tax on wage increases. Output per worker in industry was virtually constant in 1968-69, and there has been considerable excess demand in the labour market (with high rates of labour turnover) for several years. The authorities blamed these phenomena on the inducement given by average wage control to hire excessive numbers of unskilled workers, and they hope that the new tax will restrict wage increases with less undesirable side-effects than the previous version. In my own view, they would be unwise to risk any weakening of their control over wage inflation, especially since the trade unions are becoming increasingly assertive (see below). The stagnation of productivity in 1968-69 was partly due to special factors operating in the labour market at that time[7], and partly a consequence of a cyclical slow-down in output growth;

[6] A related idea is discussed by S. Weintraub in *Lloyds Bank Review* January 1971.

[7] See Portes, 'Economic Reforms in Hungary', *op,cit.* p. 312.

the renewed rapid expansion in 1970-71 has been accompanied by substantial productivity increases. As for labour market disequilibrium, this is surely as much the result of excess demand in product markets (fed by the investment boom) as of wage restriction; and in any case, the planners have always exaggerated the scope and harmful effects of labour turnover. Average wage control does inhibit 'productivity deals', but whatever misallocation it may cause seems a worthwhile price to pay for the system's advantages.

The authorities in a socialist economy must pay the greatest attention to the whole range of distributional issues — not merely because ideology so requires, nor just as ends in themselves, but also because they interact in complex ways with so many political and economic variables. And their importance is automatically greater under socialism, because people are generally more jealous of disparities in earned income than in incomes from accumulated wealth. The basic issue in incomes policy is jealousy. The Hungarian reformers may have underestimated its strength and the forces released by their call for differentiation, incentives, initiative in seeking profits, and the like.

Industrial workers have reacted very sharply to what they regard as distributional inequities generated by the reforms, and the trade unions have effectively expressed their resentment. Its sources are manifold. The workers are highly conscious of the relative increase in peasant incomes over the past several years, as well as the increase in food prices which is its primary cause, and they overestimate the expansion of the ancillary industrial activities of the agricultural cooperatives. Private artisans (mainly in services) and traders have been quick to take advantage of the greater scope given them in the reforms, and their higher incomes are quite visible. Managers, too, are thought to be doing much better out of the reforms than their employees — not just with higher earnings from bonuses and profit-sharing, but also through exploiting new opportunities for shady activities. Moonlighting, real estate speculation, country houses at Balaton, 'profiteering', 'moneygrubbing', 'materialism', — innumerable examples are cited as evidence of a *petit bourgeois* morality associated with the reforms. More substantively, perhaps, inter-enterprise and inter-industry earnings differentials are seen not as justified by performance, but rather as consequences of distortions in the price system, unequal conditions facing different enterprises, etc. Finally, these conflicts and tensions are exacerbated by the rising expectations created by unaccustomed rapid increases in living standards since the mid 1960s. The reforms

themselves explicitly embodied some shift in priorities towards satisfaction of consumer needs, and many workers believe they are not
getting their rightful share of the benefits.

Although willing to condemn 'abuses', the authorities have
clearly been reluctant to respond to these complaints in ways which
they feel might contravene the spirit of the reforms. They firmly
believe that incentives and wider differentials are compatible with
socialism, indeed necessary for their model of a socialist system to
function more effectively in delivering the goods which the workers
want. They have belatedly recognized, however, that political
support for the reforms requires a substantial share of the goods to
be seen to go to the working class, and that profits become more
closely identified with social benefit, both in appearance and in
fact.

Recent measures in this area, while not objectionable in themselves, are directed primarily towards appearances rather than any of
the underlying economic issues. As we have stressed, however, here
form is at least as important as substance. Moonlighting and the
ancillary industrial activities of agricultural cooperatives have been
restricted; there are new limits on real estate ownership and new
taxes on speculative land transactions and private rentals; and taxation of private artisans and traders has been made more progressive.
One may nevertheless doubt whether this will allow more than a
temporary respite. The fight over income shares seems endemic in
moderately decentralized industrial societies, socialist or not, and the
Hungarian authorities have only begun to come to terms with it.

IV. Workers' Control
Since the beginning of the discussion of reforms, any form of
'workers' self-management' has been explicitly ruled out from the
highest political level. To the south was the Yugoslavian example; to
the north, the Czechoslovakian reformers first discussed the idea in
theory, then found it spontaneously but briefly realized in practice.
In Hungary, both foreign and domestic political considerations made
it completely unacceptable, even if anyone had thought it socially or
economically desirable. The Hungarian reformers knew that it would
be unpalatable to their Comecon partners, who would in any case be
apprehensive about the repercussions of the Hungarian reforms on
their own countries. Moreover, in Hungary workers' control was
historically associated with the 1956 uprising. Workers' councils had
sprung up in November-December 1956, and the government was
compelled to legitimize them and grant them considerable powers in

the management of enterprises. But the implications of the councils were inevitably as much political as economic, and they were a clear challenge to Party authority. As political consolidation proceeded, it was made clear that the councils could not be reconciled with central direction and 'one-man responsibility', a cardinal tenet of administrative practice in Soviet-type economies. They never became firmly implanted; by mid-1957 they were already being downgraded, and they were soon replaced by 'factory councils' of little importance. In 1966, even these were eliminated in all but small enterprises, and their functions were assumed by the trade unions.

In the 1968 reforms, therefore, efforts to promote industrial democracy took the form of strengthening the trade unions, while the only attempt to modify state ownership (as implemented through ministerial supervision of enterprises) was a limited experiment with enterprise 'supervision committees'. The latter was in principle the more interesting innovation, but the former has in practice been much more important.

Indeed, although the new trade union powers were a key element in a conscious process of interest group articulation accompanying the reforms, the authorities may not have expected that the trade unions would so quickly and effectively come to speak for the economic interests of the working class. Their emergence in this role is of course related to the prominence of the distributional issues discussed above. This explains why, so far, their main impact has been at the national rather than the local level, which seems the reverse of what had been intended.

Originally, the expansion of trade union responsibilities emphasized their potential contribution to greater enterprise democracy. The new Labour Code laid out broad principles which were to be specified in detail in the collective contracts negotiated with enterprise managements. These contracts cover conditions of hiring and dismissal, procedures for setting norms, the distribution of fringe benefits and profit shares, the principles of enterprise wage policy, and other similar matters. The contracts also set the framework within which the trade unions exercise certain new prerogatives: to decide on the allocation of enterprise social and cultural funds; to require that management obtain their consent to certain decisions (e.g., on child care arrangements, canteen meals, etc.); to check on working conditions and the observance of the contract itself; and to veto certain actions of management (e.g., norm revision). The veto is not absolute. It simply holds the matter in abeyance by referring it to the joint consideration of the supervising ministry and the branch trade union body, which together decide the dispute.

In addition to prescribing these rights at the enterprise level, the Labour Code also required in general terms that ministries and other government bodies consult the appropriate national or branch trade union body in questions affecting wages, employment and working conditions. In practice, the National Council of Trade Unions has taken the initiative in dealing with the government, while its branch and enterprise bodies have been relatively weak. At the enterprise level, trade unions officials are apparently often either intimidated by management (despite a new regulation intended to protect them from reprisals) or not as well briefed as they should be. The veto is used very seldom, and there are frequent criticisms that the collective contracts are virtually written by management. At the branch level, the ministries often simply bypass the trade union bodies which they are supposed to consult. The National Council of Trade Unions, on the other hand, has emerged as an effective advocate of worker interests, dealing directly with the Council of Ministers and the functional ministries. It openly criticizes price, wage and social policies, and it proposes various policy measures to the government, which in turn must defend and justify its policies to the National Council of Trade Unions. Indeed, recent reports of such meetings have often made them sound like negotiations — the government might promise a given degree of price stability, for example, in exchange for trade union cooperation in reducing labour turnover.

All this is a considerable departure from the time when the trade unions were merely a 'transmission belt', another vehicle through which centrally determined policies were implemented. It is, nevertheless, nothing like workers' self-management, and, as yet, there is little evidence even of greater 'enterprise democracy'. Meanwhile, the ministries continue to exercise the functions of state ownership. In this role, they are advised by newly created 'supervision committees' for large enterprises. Each committee has from five to nine members and is chaired by a delegate from the supervising ministry. Its 'external' character is emphasized by the requirement that the majority of members come from outside the enterprise, while not more than one-third of the membership may be ministry employees. The committee prepares (at least annually) a report for the supervising ministry on the work of the enterprise. It has the right to examine documents and consult persons inside and outside the enterprise, but it has no power to take operative measures or to interfere in enterprise affairs in any way. Its reports are to serve as an independent evaluation which the ministry considers when deciding on managerial promotions and remuneration, and whether to let the enterprise deversify into new lines of production, etc.

The concept is new and interesting. Its natural extension would be to make the committees into boards of directors representing the public interest — that is, to vest ownership rights in them. The branch ministries could then be merged into a single industrial ministry, responsible for industrial policy but not the supervision of industrial enterprises. There is no sign whatsoever of this kind of development, however, and there is little indication that the supervision committees in their present form have had much influence. They certainly do not seem to have given the enterprises any greater independence from the ministries.

The relevance of the Hungarian experience to Chilean socialism is, of course, less a matter for an outside observer than for Chileans themselves to determine. In our judgment, there is a great deal to learn from the Hungarian case. But the strenghts and weaknesses of Hungary's new economic system are in part a function of specific historical, political, and economic circumstances, and one can never expect to transfer institutions successfully from one country to another without modifications to take account of such circumstances. Indeed, this is a lesson which Hungary itself discovered and to which the Hungarian economic reforms are in part a response.

ECONOMIC ORGANIZATION AND SOCIAL CONSCIENCE:
SOME DILEMMAS OF CUBAN SOCIALISM

Bertram Silverman*

Introduction

The confrontation between the past and the future is never more visible than in periods of revolutionary transition. During the revolutionary phase what is possible seems unlimited as the weight of oppression and tradition is lifted, and in the euphoria of newly-discovered power the present appears as an unbounded future. But the morning after is not too long in coming. As Marx so aptly wrote, "the tradition of all the dead generations weighs like a nightmare on the brain of the living. And just when they seem engaged in revolutionizing themselves and things, in creating something that has never yet existed, precisely in such periods of revolutionary crisis they anxiously conjure up the spirits of the past.."[1]

This tension between revolutionary will and historical constraint has been an on-going dialectic of the Cuban revolution. In response to the economic difficulties through which Cuba is now passing, the advocates of greater conformity to tradition are again raising their voices inside and outside Cuba. Declining worker productivity[2] is seen as a product of romantic attempts to radically alter social consciousness and to develop new systems of motivation based on social (socialistic) rather than material (capitalistic) incentives. Recently Professor Leontief argued that:

"In Cuba as in other socialist countries such moral incentives failed in their effectiveness to measure up to more conventional individualistic self-

---

* Hofstra University New York

[1] Karl Marx, *The Eighteenth Brumaire of Louis Bonaparte,* New World paperback, p. 15. The same tension between revolutionary will (voluntarism) and recognition of historic constraints are exhibited in the Eighteenth Brumaire. A few pages after this citation Marx writes: "The social revolution of the nineteenth century cannot draw its poetry from the past, but only from the future. It cannot begin with itself before it has stripped off all supersitition in regard to the past. Earlier revolutions required recollections of past world history in order to drug themselves concerning their own content. In order to arrive at its own content the revolution of the nineteenth century must let the dead bury their dead. There the phrase went beyond the content; here the content goes beyond the phrase."

[2] Cuba named 1971 the 'Year of Productivity'.

interest...[3] In prompting an average labourer, sales clerk, manager or technician to exert himself day in and day out in steady purposeful, i.e. productive, work nothing seems as effective as a steady flow of material benefits closely commensurate with the results of his individual effort... this is not to imply however that human nature cannot change in the long run."[4]

Yet, there is no evidence presented to show the correlation between moral incentives, *per se,* and declining worker productivity. Indeed, material incentives were used extensively through 1965 and worker productivity declined during this period. Certainly one would not conclude from this evidence that material incentives are ineffective. The relationship between moral incentives and worker productivity is more complex, and cannot be disassociated from the economic organization of which it is a part.[5] This paper is primarily concerned with examining how pragmatic responses to the problems of the Cuban transition to socialism influenced economic organization and the ideological commitment to moral incentives.[6]

Marxian analysis suggests two fundamental criteria in the transformation of economic organization within a socialist society. On the one hand economic organization must be consistent with the stage of development of the social forces of production, that is, technology, skills, education, work habits, etc. On the other hand economic organization must also be consistent with the formation of socialist values and behaviour. Since all socialist revolutions have occurred in relatively backward economies, an inevitable contradiction exists between the organizational forms held to be most consistent with communist goals and the capacity to establish such an economic organization. Generally, traditional economic analysis has tended to obscure the relationship between economic organization and social character. The rationality of economic organization has been defined primarily in terms of an efficiency criterion (e.g., the rational allocation of scarce resources among competing ends). And the market and

---

[3] Leontief, W., 'The Trouble with Cuban Socialism', *The New York Review of Books.* January 7, 1971, p. 22.

[4] *Ibid.* For a similar view see the writings of Carmelo Mesa-Lago. Inside Cuba the view is expressed by those who were supporters of the system of self-management.

[5] See Benjamin Ward, *The Socialist Economy,* Random House, 1967, pp. 36-37, who argues that questions of incentives within the socialist context have hardly been explored.

[6] In this paper I have not considered the many important political factors influencing policy (e.g. U.S. imperialism) nor have I attempted to describe in any detail the changes in the structure of economic organization and planning. For the latter see Juceplan, *La planificación económica en Cuba,* Santiago de Chile, 1968.

mercantile relations were the most effective means of achieving those ends.[7]

Cuba's rejection, after 1966, of an economic organization based on the money motive reflects strong commitment to revolutionary principles and socialist ethics. Further, Cuba's revolutionary ethics do not mean an end to ideology in the Marxian sense. Cuban economic organization and developmental strategy have been closely tied to Cuban praxis, and ideology has frequently served to rationalize practice and economic policy goals. While ideology has played an important role in mobilizing mass commitment to social and economic goals, it has also had the effect of obscuring real underlying forces. Unravelling the *actual* social and economic relationships that have governed the development of economic organization may help to 'demystify' Cuban ideology: to bring theory and practice into a more conscious harmonious correspondence, i.e. to comprehend socialism in the way that Marx comprehended capitalism.[8]

From Praxis to Principle:
The Development of Cuban Economic Organization

The evolution of socialist economic organization, in this period of the transition to socialism, has historically been the dynamic result of a previously adopted socialist ideology and a pragmatic

---

[7] This is particularly evident in the discussion about the economic rationality of socialist economy. In dealing with the Mises-Lange *et al.* controversy Professor Dobb argued that "most of the socialist critics of Professor Mises have argued, in one key or another, that a socialist economy can escape the irrationality which is predicted of it if, but only if, it closely imitates the mechanism of the competitive market and consents to be ruled by the *values which this market affirms.*"(my emphasis). Maurice Dobb, *Political Economy and Capitalism,* International Publishers, 1945, p. 273. Of course, there have been outstanding social scientists who have seen this relationship, e.g., Marx, Weber, Polanyi, Fromm, Riesman to name just a few.

[8] Marx's analysis of ideology is illustrated in the following passage: "In considering such transformations (social revolutions) the distinction should always be made between the material transformation of the economic conditions of production, which can be determined with the precision of natural science, and the legal, political, religious, aesthetic or philosophic — in short, ideological forms in which men become conscious of this conflict and fight it out. Just as our opinion of an individual is not based on what he thinks of himself, so can we not judge such a period of transformation by its own consciousness; on the contrary, this consciousness must rather be explained from the contradictions of material life, from the existing conflict between the social forces of production and the relations of production."
Karl Marx, *A Contribution to the Critique of Political Economy,* in Feuer (ed.) *Marx & Engels,* Anchor, p. 44. Marx's approach was evident in his earlier writing, thus: "The immediate task of philosophy, which is at the service of history, once the saintly form (religion) of human self-alienation has been unmasked, is to unmask self-alienation in its unholy forms (ideology)."
Karl Marx, Toward the Critique of Hegel's Philosophy of Right, in *ibid.,* p. 263.

response to experience. Consequently, the theory of a particular experience has frequently served as the ideological veil to justify or rationalize that experience. Ideology has been an *ex post* response to experience as well as an *ex ante* guide to practice.

Cuba's pragmatic style has been a recognized characteristic.[9] "But an absence of theory 'lends an air of crisis' to the present situation in socialist countries. The apologetic nature of the pragmatic theory of economic practice obscured many fundamental problems that today have become paramount."[10] No doubt Alberto Mora, the former Minister of Foreign Trade, had Cuba in mind when he wrote this comment in 1965. Cuba began her economic experiment without a well-developed theory of economic organization.

During this first phase (1959-1961), the rapid nationalization of the strategic sectors of the Cuban economy presented the Government with serious problems of economic control and planning. The rapid nationalization[11] began with the first Agrarian Reform that led to confiscation of the *latifundia* and sugar *centrales*. This was followed by a confrontation with the United States that resulted in the confiscation of United States holdings. Simultaneously, the nationalization process was accelerated by the confiscation of domestic enterprises that had openly collaborated with Batista or who were resisting the economic programmes of the regime. At this time many owners simply abandoned their businesses. Spontaneous action by workers, led by an aggressive trade union leadership demanding immediate changes in the distribution of income and privilege, resulted in increased labour conflict. These early struggles frequently led to government intervention. According to Luis Alvarez Rom, the former Treasury Minister:[12]

> Toward the end of 1960, the revolutionary government had to confront its first practical economic and financial problem. The problem had to do with the need to take charge of the administration and conrol of nationalized enterprises that had been recuperated or intervened.

---

[9] C. Richard Fagen, "Continuities in the Style and Strategies of Cuban Revolutionary Politics" (mimeographed) 1970.

[10] Alberto Mora, "On Certain Problems of Building Socialism", in Betram Silverman (ed.), *Man and Socialism in Cuba*, Atheneum, 1971, p. 329.

[11] For a description of the nationalization process see: Dudley Seers (ed.), *Cuba: The Economic and Social Revolution*, The University of North Carolina Press, 1964. James O'Connor, *The Origin of Socialism in Cuba*, Cornell, 1970, chs. 5 and 6.

[12] Luis Alvarez Rom, "Finance and Political Development", in Silverman (ed.) *op. cit.*, p. 271.

The Industrial Administration Department of INRA (National Agrarian Reform Institute), headed by Che Guevara, had to deal immediately with problems of financing the production of economic units as complex as petroleum refining or as simple as shoe workshops. The centralization of financial control, the keystone of Cuba's organizational model, emerged from a number of related experiences and problems.[13] First, during the initial phase of nationalization the banking system was still in private hands. Credit restrictions were frequently used as a method of opposing government policies. Moreover, the state sector still had to pay interest on loans to finance a growing government deficit. Second, there existed in Cuba highly advanced forms of cost accounting which gradually emerged as a model for the Ministry of Industry (that was subsequently established in 1962). There was (and still is) a strong bias toward adopting the latest administrative techniques.[14] Third, central control provided a method of integrating and controlling small and medium sized workshops, gradually eliminating inefficent shops and relocating labour to other sectors. Fourth, centralization of financing permitted the State to confront the enormous demands for funds associated with the sugar harvest without total dependence on a private banking system. Fifth, the centralization of finance permitted production units to focus their attention on physical output rather than on financial matters.[15]

Finally, the revolution had unleashed dramatic shifts in the administrative structure. The old managerial and staff personnel began leaving as the revolutionary process accelerated. Accountants and financial experts who were trained in the latest United States techniques left the country with transferable skill. Consequently those with the most specialized skills, *and who were committed to*

---

[13] Many of these observations are based on conversations with Cuban economists during the period 1968-1969 in Cuba and on JUCEPLAN, *Notas sobre el nuevo sistema de dirección* (mimeographed) 1968, hereafter, noted as *Junta Report*. For additional evidence that the initial development of central finance did not arise out of the need to develop the worker's conscience see Alexis Codina, "Experiences of Control under the Budgetary System", in Silverman (ed.), *op. cit.*, pp. 204-206.

[14] Ernesto Che Guevara, "On the Budgetary Finance System", in Silverman (ed.), *op. cit.*, p. 130. "From a technological standpoint, we should borrow the most advanced forms of economic administration available, from whatever source, so long as they can be adopted for use in the new society... the same rule applies with regard to technical standards in production control and administration... We might say, then, that as a technique the predecessor of the budgetary finance system was imperialist monopoly as it existed in Cuba...".

[15] Interestingly Cuban planners cite ECLA advisors for influencing their bias toward physical and structural rather than financial analysis.— see *Junta Report*.

the revolution, assumed staff positions at higher administrative levels. Therefore, managerial functions, particularly at the production level, were increasingly left in the hands of more reliable political cadres. Initially, the actual transfer of power to workers and peasants with relatively little formal training symbolized the dramatic transformation of the social structure. This process of permitting the free emigration of old civil servants, and the managerial and administrative strata, is a distinctive feature of the Cuban revolution. It permitted a relatively peaceful transformation of the social structure and at the same time avoided the dominance of the State by the old bureaucracy.[16] But despite their political reliability, the cadres did not fully understand economic problems and the need for a rational distribution of scarce resources that required economic controls and measurement. Thus, central finance and accounting also provided a method of economic control over 'over-enthusiastic' cadres. There were also innumerable problems due to the inconsistency of the budget programme and poor record keeping. Initially many concrete operational problems made it difficult for enterprises to follow the budget programme and as a consequence many enterprises accumulated large unplanned deficits.[17] The standardization of the system of central budgeting did not take place until 1961.

During this initial period specific events and problems transformed conflicts about the development of organizational forms into central issues of principle. This occurred after 1961 when Cuba entered its socialist phase.

The 'Great Economic Debate' over Economic Organization. Phase II

The ideological and theoretical controversy over market socialism versus centralized planning began in Cuba with the formulation of the first economic plan in 1962. Economists from socialist countries, particularly Czechoslovakia, were invited to aid Cuban planners. Many advisors placed considerable importance on financial planning and particularly on 'profitability' as a measure of economic efficiency.[18] But these suggestions were in conflict with the methods

---

[16] See Moche Lewin, *Lenin's Last Struggle,* Vintage, 1970, for discussion of these problems in the Soviet Union.

[17] Codina, *op. cit.,* pp. 206-208.

[18] Junta Report, *op. cit.,* p. 2. See also comments by outside observers such as René Dumont, *Cuba: Socialism and Development,* Grove, 1970.

that were developing in Che's Ministry of Industry.

The economic crisis in that year also raised questions about Cuba's organizational methods and economic development. In August 1961, the Minister of Economy, Regino Boti, predicted that in ten years Cuban living standards would be comparable to those of any European country.[19] But, instead of increasing, Cuban national output may have declined by 10 per cent between 1962 and 1963.[20] It is likely that, initially, declining productivity may be an inevitable phase of socialist development in an underdeveloped society. Still, Cuba had rapidly transformed her important economic institutions. However, individuals without previous experience, technical know-how, or reliable information were directing an economic system. In part, Cuba's difficulty stemmed from an initial economic strategy. The regulated national and international market had made the co-existence of idle land and labour rational from the viewpoint of the large-scale capitalist farmer. By abolishing capitalist production these constraints on land and labour utilization were exploded. It was now argued that an expanded and diversified agriculture could increase and stabilize employment while providing foreign exchange for expanded industrial development. This in turn would absorb a high and rising proportion of urban unemployment. The theory broke down, however, as the import content of the new industries turned out to be higher and their productivity lower than expected, while agricultural productivity in the new crops were disappointingly low and suguar production dropped precipitously. As a result a growth strategy, designed to reduce Cuban dependency, resulted in a tendency toward 'economic stagnation via a growing strangulation of foreign trade.'[21]

As a consequence production bottlenecks arose with greater frequency and other economic problems became apparent: A serious supply problem led to rationing in 1962; shortages increased the political and economic resistance of the peasants, which in turn led to the Second Agrarian Reform in 1963 that nationalized all land-holding above 165 acres; the re-emergence of bureaucratic in-

19 *Obra Revolucionaria*, No. 30, 1961.

20 These were Charles Bettelheim's estimates. See Carmelo Mesa-Lago, *Availability and Reliability of Statistics in Socialist Cuba*, University of Pittsburgh, 1970, p. 50.

21 Based on B. Pollitt, "Employment Plans, Performance and Future Prospects in Cuba", Overseas Studies Committee Conference, 1970 University of Cambridge, 1970, pp. 11-12. Also C. Romeo, "Acerca del desarrollo económico de Cuba", *Cuba Socialista*, December, 1965.

efficiency led to a breakdown in economic coordination. As a result, the economy seemed to be running *por la libre,* that is without effective controls.[22] The first response to these problems was an abrupt revision of Cuba's developmental strategy — a return to agriculture and sugar as the turnpike to development, a turn that was to have serious implications for Cuban economic organization.

Some Cuban leaders and foreign advisors began to argue that Cuba's economic difficulties were rooted in Cuban economic organization. What began as a response to circumstances was transformed into 'the Great Debate' over fundamental issues of ideology and revolutionary principles.[23] The participants included most of the members of the Council of Ministers.[24]

In opposition to central direction and control in the industrial sector, another system of economic organization was emerging in agriculture under the direction of Carlos Rafael Rodriguez, and in foreign trade under Alberto Mora. This system of self-finance or self-management was given official sanction in 1962. In order to understand the basic differences between the two systems it is necessary to distinguish between them in their ideal form.[25]

Under the system of self-management enterprises are juridically independent. They trade their products with different enterprises through the market and profitability is the basic measure of their success. Although each enterprise has considerable financial independence, it has to cover its current expenses through banks that provide interest bearing credits. Bank loans are closely supervised so that the banks play a critical role in evaluating and contolling the enterprise. Basic output and investment decisions are set by the Central Planning Agency, but within the aggregate constraints enterprises have independent decision-making functions. Most significantly, managerial incentives and labour income are based primarily on material incentives.

[22] For a description of this earlier period see Edward Boorstein, *The Economic Transformation of Cuba,* Monthly Review Press, 1968.

[23] For a compilation and discussion of the Debate, see Silverman (ed.), *op. cit.*

[24] See Dumont, *op. cit.,* esp. pp. 115-133. The debate included some outside observers, and Dumont was one of the first to criticize centralization.

[25] For a good description of the two systems see Sergio de Santis,"The Economic Debate in Cuba", *International Socialist Review,* August 1965. Neither system ever functioned in this ideal form. Nor did the system of self-finance become operational except in a restricted form during the 1963-1965 period.

Under the system of central budgeting, enterprises are more seriously circumscribed by the national plan. Rather than being legally independent, each firm is considered a part of a larger productive unit — the public sector as a whole. Therefore, the movement of products from one enterprise to another is an intermediary step, and products acquire the characteristics of commodities only when they leave the socialized sector and are sold in the market (i.e., in the private sector, to consumers or to other countries). Profitability plays no role in the evaluation of the enterprise, and all net income is deposited with the Treasury, which centrally allocates funds to various enterprises. Each enterprise is directed by the central plan, and, as its function, fulfills the targets set by the plan. Rigorous financial control is established through a central organization, *Empresas Consolidades,* that coordinates the accounts of enterprises in a particular sector (e.g. textiles). Finally, moral rather than material incentive is emphasized as the prime form of motivation. Thus, in the system of central budgeting, the 'administration of things' provides greater possiblility for eliminating mercantile and economic incentives. In 1963, two systems of economic organization and ideology were emerging, representing different sectors of the Cuban economy. A confrontation was inevitable. The central issue was the viability of market socialism as an organizational model during the transition to communism.

The Great Debate over economic organization represented two divergent views concerning the transition to socialism. While each group accepted comprehensive planning, they disagreed about the economic laws regulating the socialist transition and the institutional forms that best correspond to those laws.[26]

Supporters of a great reliance on the market, decentralized economic organization and decision-making and material incentives, argued that the law of value operated in all sectors of the Cuban economy. In their view, so long as the productive forces were unable to provide for the distribution of consumer goods according to need, the stage of commodity production could not be willed away through changes in juridical forms. Centralized organization designed to circumvent the market were beyond Cuba's current level of technological and administrative capacity. Consequently centralization would result in the misallocation of resources, inefficiency, bureaucracy and ultimately in the breakdown of planning. Economic

---

[26] For a more complete discussion of the debate see my introduction to *Man and Socialism in Cuba: The Great Debate, op. cit.*

organization was an aspect of the relationship to production and could not be 'higher' than the historically determined level of the productive forces.

The Guevarist opposition rejected both the 'economism' of their argument as well as the applicability of the law of value to the transition to socialism. The basic elements of their argument were: First, the law of value was not merely an expression of a universal problem of relative scarcity but an historical phenomenon that reached its fullest development under the capitalist mode of production. Therefore, changes in juridical relationships that resulted from the socialization of the means of production did affect the law of value. Second, the pursuit of socialist values required interference with the law of value and the implicit ethics of the market-place Once the law of value was distorted through planning, how could you determine what it was? Third, the ethics of communism based on non-market relationships could only be realized under a centralized system of administration. But Guevara never fully explored the connection between centralization and worker-participation in decision-making. Fourth, contradictions between the relationship to production and the forces of production were inevitable during the transitional phase. But they could be overcome by the development of administrative and technical skills and through the growth of revolutionary consciousness. Thus, Guevara's aim was to consciously use the process of socialist economic development as a force to create a new socialist morality.

Fidel never formally entered the debate, although in 1965 he seemed to display impatience with the controversy when he argued "our obligation as revolutionaries is not to theorize in the fields of philosophy." Moreover, in the same speech, his support of material incentives seemed to suggest opposition to Guevara.[27] Nevertheless, beginning in 1966, Cuba moved decisively to adopt Che's organizational model and by 1967 all *organismos* were operating under radicalized versions of central budgeting. Fidel not only adopted Guevara's ideas but carried them forward more rapidly and in ways that went beyond the arguments of his comrade.

[27] See Fidel Castro's speech "Criterios de Nuestra Revolución", *Cuba Socialista*, September 1965. In this speech Castro reveals a pronounced long-term commitment to moral incentives that probably accounts for Gerassi's suggestion that Fidel supported Che's position (see *Venceremos* Clarion, 1968, p. 20.) But Fidel's pragmatic approach strongly suggested the need to use material incentives. In the same speech he argued that it would be idealistic to assume that the large majority of workers cut cane from a sense of duty Therefore, it is logical to use economic incentives for work that is of critical importance. As a consequence Mesa-Lago in his book, *The Labour Sector and Socialist Distribution in Cuba*, Praeger, 1968, p. 124, suggests that Fidel rejected Che's thesis.

The Radicalization of Economic Organization: Phase III

1966 marked the beginning of a new phase in the evolution of economic _ organization. During the earlier period, economic organization was linked to the practical problems of nationalization, social justice and the transition to socialism. The new period seemed to signal a conscious effort to develop a communist society and create *el hombre nuevo* (The New Man).

During this phase the transformation of social consciousness (social character) was linked very closely to organizational forms. Market socialism was regarded not merely as a contradiction in terms, but a road to capitalism. Thus Fidel argued:[28]

> The problem is not in equalizing salaries and placing emphasis on the distribution of incomes. If one limits oneself to that, one does not yet break with the conception of a society founded on money. What we wish is to demystify money and not rehabilitate it. We propose to abolish it totally.
>
> Man will liberate himself completely from his lust for money only when his necessities are able to be satisfied outside his wages. But it is not possible to prepare the advent of this period of communism of abundance while continuing to apply the method of the old society.

The emphasis upon the money motive has had special consequences for economic organization.

1. The New System of Economic Management:[29]

The introduction of the new system of economic management in 1967 radically extended Che's system of central budgeting. The new system of economic management eliminated transactions between *unidades* within the socialized sector. Under the guidelines set by the annual plan, firms entered into direct contractual relations but no monetary or credit relations were involved. Records of receipt and transfer of goods were kept but no payments were required. Mercantile relations still occurred in foreign trade, in final sales to consumers, in wage payment,and in the private sector but in the latter three cases they were, as we shall see, seriously limited. Since *unidades* received materials for production without monetary exchange, a major function of banks and the Treasury was eliminated. Domestically, the major purpose of financial planning was keeping the wage fund in balance with the value of consumer goods — a task

---

[28] Junta Central de Planificación, *Sobre el Salario y la Organización del Trabajo*, Havana, 1968. See also R.S. Karol, *Guerrillas in Power*, Hill & Wang, 1970, pp. 342-345.

[29] Based on Junta Report, *op. cit.*, Juceplan, *La planificación en Cuba*, *op. cit.*, and interviews with Cuban economists.

made exceedingly difficult because all taxes were eliminated under the new model. Moreover, the de-emphasis of money undermined consciousness of financial controls.

The new system of direction raised significant problems for economic control and measurement. Under this system traditional economic measures became obsolete. Thus, analyses based on production costs and revenues were useless and misleading. This was due to two related factors. First, the price freeze and rationing had destroyed any real relationship between value and price. Moreover, the value of final goods was designed to reflect social rather than market factors. Second, labour policy called for the separation of the relationship between wages and output (work). Thus, the new system of economic management had to confront the complex problem of devising new economic measures that were applicable to this economic model (an exceedingly complex task that has not yet been achieved).

The immediate consequence has been to place prime importance on physical rather than value measures. As a consequence, Cuba's reliance on accounting, including cost accounting, has been virtually eliminated, and in its place the system has turned logically to statistical analysis of data, such as delivered output, consumption of raw materials, inventories, etc., expressed in physical units. The goal is to develop a statistical system that would facilitate highly centralized planning.

The new system of economic direction is a logical extension of centralization of economic planning. Therefore, Cuba has moved rapidly to introduce advanced mathematical techniques into its planning apparatus. The latest computer technology is planned to process information and coordinate decisions. Indeed, a visit to the top levels of the planning hierarchy leaves an impression of a relatively technically advanced system. Yet, even on this level contradictions are apparent. By 1968, Cuba had not yet codified her principal products and activities, essential elements of input-output analysis. But, more significantly, a unit of account of economic cost, which makes aggregation and comparison possible, had not been developed. In practice, monetary measures are still used to estimate costs, and shadow prices are employed to calculate the 'actual' cost of production, particularly to account for changes in the price of imported materials that play such an important role in Cuban production costs. But even this procedure is still in its infancy and is only employed for selected goods. Ultimately, Cuba's organizational model is leading economists to experiment with a non-monetary measure of relative costs such as man hours of labour time. Cuban economists have begun experimenting with a unit of account that would translate all output in terms of a unit of simple labour necessary to produce a given quantity of sugar — a commodity that accounts for approximately 85 per cent of export earnings.

Ideologically, Fidel has argued that the commodity myth must be exploded if man is to fully appreciate the social and community implications of productive relationships. Human labour would then be expressed in real terms, rather than in money, its fetished commodity form. But monetary measures still remain the simplest way to deal with the complexities of modern economic relations. And, more significantly, the real test of demystification lies in the real relationship to production that the new system has introduced. And to this we shall shortly turn.

2. Technical versus Political Cadres

The new system of management had special significance for administrators and technicians, particularly at the *unidad* level. On the one hand, the leadership placed increasing emphasis on revolutionary and political commitment. President Dorticos argued:[30]

> We don't conceive...the possible usefulness of an economist that is not absolutely and fully identified with the objectives of this revolution and with its defined conception...
> And consequently, it is just and valid to affirm that we don't think an economist is either useful or usable if in addition to being a good technician he is not, *above all*, a good revolutionary in theory and in practice...
> It. is a task that can be understood not only with an adequate technical preparation but moreover with an attitude and a positive presence before the difficulties that can only be developed by an independence from personal temperaments with the presence of revolutionary faith and of an absolute conviction in the correctness of the Cuban revolution.

On the other hand, the Cuban revolution has stressed the importance of technical development and education. The shortage of technical and administrative cadres has always been singled out by Fidel and Che as the major constraint on economic development. Of course, the ideal administrator should be technically competent as well as a revolutionary. Yet, at this time Cuba's model places special importance on political rather than technical criteria in the management of the production unit.[31] Thus, in 1969, it became obvious that little economic analysis took place at the work place.

30 Unpublished speech presented at Economic Institute in Havana 1969.

31 For a recent discussion see *Cuba Internacional,* February, 1970, p. 30.

Statistical data were sent to the *Empresa,* or regional level, for analysis, comparison, aggregation. Thus, economic control and responsibility were removed from the production units and transferred to technicians who were less likely to be militants.

This procedure was consistent with the functional requirements of the model. Since material incentives no longer guided managerial and worker behaviour, the major function of management was to mobilize worker participation in the major economic efforts of the regime; freed from 'paper work' and 'money illusions', the manager can concentrate on the problems of work and social consciousness.

But there is a relationship between social consciousness and economic control and responsibility, a factor that has not been fully appreciated in the development of Cuban economic organization.

3. Moral versus Material Incentives

A motivational system based on economic rewards and penalties was inconsistent with the new system of economic management and centralized planning. As a result, Cuba moved rapidly to eliminate many of the remaining material incentives that had been part of Che's central budgeting system. The separation between work and wages was rapidly introduced. Thus, bonuses or penalties for fulfilment or non-fulfilment of work norms were eliminated. Piece rates were rapidly phased out and, where they were part of traditional seasonal work patterns, attempts were made to develop steady year-round employment. Income differentials were narrowed through efforts to reduce the high salaries for new entrants in the labour force and to raise the income of the lowest groups.[32] There were strong tendencies to reduce the use of economic penalties to enforce labour discipline, and the system of work norms, while still in effect, seemed, at least in 1969, to be loosely enforced. How could one norm a worker's conscience? Organized efforts in 1969 led to the virtual renunciation of overtime pay. The salary scale developed prior to 1966 providing differentials was still in effect, but restrictions on personal consumption reduced their motivational significance.

Conscience or moral incentives were the means through which work and sacrifice would be induced and economic development fostered. Essentially moral incentives have been used as a lever for mass mobilization and to convey the idea that work is a social duty rather than a means of personal advancement. In Cuba, the 'moralization of work' has replaced the carrot of material incentives as the

[32] The highest salary cited was 300 pesos for engineers.

means of modernization. Thus economic development would grow simultaneously with social consciousness, social commitment and egalitarianism; essential elements in constructing communism.

The renewed emphasis on moral incentives, particularly in 1968, was reflected in new experiments with socialist emulation. The emulation system that had emerged after 1962 was suddenly abandoned in 1966. Bureaucratic and complicated regulations had provided few possibilities for worker participation or recognition of particular problems within individual enterprises. Moreover, the Stakhanovite aspect of the system led to competition among managers for prizes and status, and motivated them to falsify reports.

The transition to a new system began in 1966 and 1967 with the development of industrial efficiency plans. General goals were set up by individual ministries. These general targets were then translated into concrete plans by individual firms. After six months of experimentation, a decision was made to tie the efficiency plans to socialist emulation. The previous bureaucratic structure and complicated point system was abandoned. Although competition between plants· was still occasionally practised, the central idea was self-emulation where individual workers and *unidades* set their own *compromisos* (goals) and tried to fulfill them. In 1968 emulation plans were connected to historic periods in Cuban history, culminating, on July 26; with the possibility of winning the Moncada flag. Thus, theoretically, every enterprise could win a flag. Winning did not mean being better, but rather, fulfilling one's *compromisos* (i.e. efficiency plans).

The role of Cuban trade unions (CTC-R) seemed unclear in 1969. They were assigned a major task of fulfilling socialist emulation goals. But their bureaucratic structure and limited function in the plant seriously undermined their effectiveness. There was considerable speculation that Cuba would soon eliminate or replace the trade unions whose function seemed unclear under the new·system of management. Experimentation was underway to establish an Advanced Workers Movement that would replace the older system of selecting vanguard workers. In 1969 the Advanced Workers Movement had replaced the local trade union in some factories. These experiments were aimed partly at revitalizing mass participation in the work centre. But in general these efforts were mainly concerned with mass mobilization and increasing work efficiency rather than worker participation in social and economic decisions.

But moral incentives have radically extended the original commitment to social equality and ruralism. First, rationing reduced the consumption patterns that had separated upper income groups from lower income groups. While, paradoxically, scarcity tended to magnify small differences, in general, shared austerity also reduced the disparities in the distribution of consumption and guaranteed minimum standards of living for the entire population. Second, the new orientation de-emphasized private consumption and expanded collective goods and services made available free or with slight charges. This included the continued extension of education, medical and health care as well as free local public telephones, transportation for funerals, weddings, recreation and sporting events. Collective meals were served at work centres and schools. Rent, which was already abolished for many consumers, was eliminated for all families with *per capita* incomes under twenty-five pesos per month. Fourth, mass mobilization has significantly affected the Cuban social structure and re-emphasized the rural bias of the revolution. Large 'armies' of volunteer labour participate in the *Zafra* and in thousands of micro-projects. Youth and communist brigades have been created. Mass education has been increasingly concerned with problems of economic and technological development and students, teachers, intellectuals, and urban workers have been intimately involved in rural development; thus reducing occupational and regional distinctions. The plans to bring the schools to the country, and, more recently, to remove the university from its urban base and connect more closely to the work environment, are all part of the same pattern.

But these policies are not seen as ends in themselves. Thus education, economic and technological change are essential prerequisites for a communist society. Only in the technologically and economically advanced society would the 'moralization of work' end. The work ethic — work as a social duty — would be replaced by the identification with work as a creative activity.

4. Revolutionary Offensive: The Death of the Private Sector

It is inconceivable that Cuba's organizational model could operate effectively within an economy having a significant private sector. Yet in 1966, the beginning of the radicalization process, a considerable private sector existed. (See Table No. 1) Thus a large proportion of the labour force was not only outside the economic organizational model but working in the private-sector, either in retail trade, service, light industry or agriculture. This not only undermined the centralized planning system but provided an ideological alternative to

Cuba's radical model. Indeed, under the condition of severe shortages, the private sector provided an illegal source of consumer goods and was competing successfully for scarce resources and labour. Thus, the prototype of the 'consumer goods society' worked within the heart of the Cuban system, playing on the inherent contradictions and inefficiences within the socialized sector.

On March 13, 1968 the Revolutionary Offensive was launched to eliminate the remaining private sector,[33] and to significantly limit

TABLE No. 1

Distribution of the Labour Force between the Private and Public Sectors

January, 1965

Total Labour Force		2,492,919
	Unemployed	376,293
	Employed	2,116,626
	Public	1,355,259
	Private	761,367
By Sector		
	Industry	
	Public	281,755
	Private	105,425
	Construction	
	Public	93,404
	Private	20,247
	Transport	
	Public	71,585
	Private	10,987
	Communications	
	Public	11,690
	Private	979
	Commerce	
	Public	208,661
	Private	53,606
	Agriculture	
	Public	364,508
	Private	304,299
	Other Productive Activities	
	Public	8,608
	Private	70,238
	Services	
	Public	287,085
	Private	202,516

Source: Ministry of Labour, *Balance de los Recursos Laborales,* January, 1965.

[33] "La Nacionalización de los Establecimientos Privados en la Ofensiva", *El Militante Comunista,* June, 1968. See also *Granma* Weekly Review, March 31, 1968.

the role of private enterprise in agriculture as well as to intensify the ideological campaign for revolutionary commitment. It demonstrated Fidel's commitment to radicalize the revolution despite serious economic difficulties. Thus, he rejected the NEP alternative, that is, market socialism. But the Government added to its difficult organizational problems the necessity of planning and managing the many small enterprises in services and retail trade.[34] In many cases this simply meant the reduction or termination of neighbourhood stores.

The move to end private enterprise in agriculture has also become part of the Revolutionary Offensive — but this has proceeded more cautiously and less publicly. In 1968 the Cuban Government revealed that private agricultural production was supervised by and included in the nationwide development plans; what Dumont has called the Third Agrarian Reform. Dumont summarized the process as follows:[35]

> Until 1967 a controller of ANAP (National Association of Small Farmers) asked peasants their forecasts with respect to planting. In the year 1967 the ANAP suggested modifications that seemed desirable. In 1968 he gave them orders established by the regional agricultural plan. In 1968 there began a campaign of exclusive-delivery to the State of all available production. First presented as purely voluntary, it was then made obligatory with the publication of sanctions against those who did not participate.

Moreover, peasants were forbidden to hire their own labour. In effect, peasant land-holdings were incorporated within the large *granjas*. In exchange, the State provided labour, machinery, and technical advice. A campaign was initiated during this period for peasants to voluntarily sell their land to the State. Model projects such as San Andres were also given considerable publicity. They have been held up as examples of the voluntary integration of the *campesino* into socialist agriculture. But, rural workers are permitted one hectare of land for subsistence, which has influenced their effort.

As a result of the Revolutionary Offensive, Cuba could report that in less than a decade it had become the socialist country with the highest percentage of state-owned property. Yet, the Revolutionary Offensive and its strong ideological undertones reflected deeper underlying social and economic forces, to which Cuban economic organization was a response.

---

[34] For a critical view of this approach see Mandel, *op. cit.*, p. 81.

[35] René Dumont, *Cuba: Est-il Socialiste?*, Paris, 1970, p. 92.

Ideology and Reality

1. Economic Organization and Socialist Accumulation

In part, the radicalization of Cuban economic organization was a response to problems immanent in the Cuban model: the spontaneous growth of the private sector and the corresponding rise of the black market; the exposure of corruption at the highest levels of the army and trade unions; the persistent growth of bureaucracy as well as the apparent contradiction between demands of the accounting procedures of Central Budgeting and the available cadres at the base. These problems were not unrelated to the growth of criticism among some members of the old Communist Party within and outside Cuba, who saw both Cuba's domestic and foreign policies as romantic and naive. But in particular, response to economic problems was necessary as GNP in 1966 declined by more than four per cent.[36] The radicalization of Cuban economic organization was closely linked to the decision to intensify the rate of economic development. The unfolding economic strategy of the post-1966 period reflected a determined effort to confront the persistent problem of economic stagnation and inefficiency.

The new strategy originated in 1963, when a deepening balance of payments crisis forced a shift away from industry to agriculture as the leading economic sector. Essentially, the strategy called for capital accumulation through sugar exports. This would provide needed foreign reserves — first, to develop agriculture in which Cuba had a comparative advantage, and later, after increasing agricultural productivity, to transfer this surplus to industrial development. The greater potential yield in agricultural investment was explained primarily in 'terms of the productivity-increasing potential of applying advanced techniques to activities such as cane and animal husbandry, where previously considerable long-term practical experience coexisted with a traditional primitive technology.'[37] The post-1966 period marked a rapid increase in the rate of capital accumulation, leading symbolically to the production of ten million tons of sugar in 1970.

The most significant effect of the policy was to rapidly convert Cuba's labour surplus into labour shortage. The unemployment problem disappeared and a new problem of discovering sources of labour reserves emerged. This was particularly troublesome because

[36] Mesa-Lago, *op. cit.*, p. 51.

[37] Based on Pollitt. *op. cit.*, pp. 12-13.

the initial income policy of the Government had set in motion a large migration of labour from rural to urban employment, particularly services. In part, this was the result of the growth of small towns and state farms in the interior of the country where social and educational services were rapidly expanding. The reduction in the number and productivity of the traditional cane cutter — a seasonal worker — was particularly troublesome. Thus the rural poor were either moving to the higher income centres of the towns or taking part of their increased income and economic security in additional leisure. The rapid expansion of the service sector from one quarter to one third of the labour force, a sector with considerable disguised unemployment, reflected the rapid expansion of the bureaucratic apparatus, as well as the expansion of social services. (See Table No. 2)

Moreover, the increase in the rate of gross investment from an average 18 per cent in the period 1961-1963 to 31 per cent of GNP in 1968 required a reduction in personal consumption. As a result, rationing—established in 1962—was extended to include virtually all consumer goods, as well as a reduction in the variety and quantity of commodities available for personal consumption. By 1969 personal consumption of durable goods virtually disappeared and most non-food items, such as clothing, were distributed irregularly. Thus, Cuba's strategy implied a rapid expansion in employment co-existing with a planned reduction in *per capita* personal consumption. It was this apparent contradiction — the need to increase work, expand and shift the labour force while reducing personal consumption — that set the stage for Cuba's distinctive growth strategy: economic development with moral incentives.

TABLE No. 2

Active Population by Productive Sector in Cuba, 1958-1965
(000's)

	1958/59	1960/61	1965
Agriculture	813.0	862.0	838.0
Industry and Mining	378.5	411.8	390.0
Construction	82.8	71.7	123.0
Transport	80.6	86.5	90.1
Commerce	284.3	265.5	258.8
Services and Others	558.3	572.7	846.1
TOTAL	2,197.5	2,270.2	2,546.0

Source: Republic of Cuba, JUCEPLAN, Central Statistics Department.
Resumen de Estadísticas de Población, No. 2, Havana, 1966, p. 120.

First, in 1966 Cuba was faced with a decline in agricultural labour at a time when extensive growth of this sector was planned. Reversing rural-urban migration through a programme of resettlement made little sense since economic plans called for a technological revolution in agriculture that would shortly reduce agricultural labour requirements. Therefore, the short-run solution required the redeployment of urban labour to agriculture, particularly during planting and harvesting. The type of labour required was the most menial and unskilled. Material incentives would have had to be unusually high to induce urban labour into these occupations. Moreover, the use of wage differentials made little sense because the transfer was frequently of workers from more skilled and productive activities to less skilled, that is, from industry to agriculture. The moralization of work under these circumstances is quite rational and reliance on unpaid voluntary labour is reasonable. Since 1962 Cuba has increasingly relied on this method to mobilize labour for agriculture. In 1968 perhaps 15-20 per cent of the agricultural labour force was made up of non-agricultural labour.[38] Such a transfer of labour could only make economic sense if it was based on moral rather than material incentives. Moreover, such a transfer of labour inevitably disrupted other sectors of the economy. Under these circumstances of extremely tight factor supply, market socialism was untenable.

Second, the planned reduction in personal consumption made expansion of employment possible, only through the worker's heightened sense of social commitment and conscience. Furthermore, the already low level of available consumer goods made increased capital accumulation possible primarily through the expansion of unpaid labour. Therefore, Cuba seemed to be in a stage where the dangers of 'primitive accumulation' — a period in capitalist development where force was used to extract the economic surplus — was possible.

Yet, if additional labour can be supplied voluntarily, that may be a more consistent translation of the concept of primitive accumulation in a socialist society than that used in the Soviet experience. The translation of primitve accumulation to socialist accumulation was an essential element of the organizational model. But if moral incentives fail then the ominous necessity of coercion must be faced. While the commitment of the Cuban population to the revolution has reduced the reliance upon force, *conciencia* is also a scarce resource and the

---

[38] More than fifty percent of the labour force was working in agriculture in 1969. See *Granma*, April 1, 1969.

failure to use it efficiently may be one of Cuba's fundamental problems.

Finally, the sharp decline in personal consumption made reliance on material incentives politically dangerous. An emphasis on material incentives during a period when workers were asked to increase hours worked, and to reduce personal consumption, would merely serve to heighten the sense of economic sacrifice and exaggerate economic distinctions and privileges. Politically, under these circumstances an emphasis on collective efforts toward social goals was more reasonable.

2. Cost of Social Conscience

The ideological preoccupation with the commodity fetishism problem and its relationship to economic organization becomes comprehensible when related to Cuba's economic strategy. But it is precisely the contradictions between Cuba's economic strategy and economic ·organization that have challenged Cuba's ideological goals. Conversely, ideology has frequently become a rationalization for economic and social policy. In order to fully understand these contradictions, as Charles Bettelheim has suggested, "it is necessary...to bring to light the real social relations that are revealed and hidden, at the same time, by the forms of representation and the elaborated ideological notions based on them." [39]

Cuba's economic strategy made the reliance on material incentives and market relations inoperable. In a system of organization based on moral incentives which eliminates the direct connection between individual performance and reward, the individual's motivation for increasing his economic performance must come from a heightened identification with the goals of the nation (internalization of social goals). Paradoxically, over-zealous political leaders can undermine this commitment. This had become in 1968-1969 a serious problem since economic decisions at the base were politically rather than economically motivated. This problem had been compounded by an over-ambitious economic strategy associated with the ten million ton goal which overburdened Cuba's fragile economic controls and planning structure.

Economic controls, through a system of planning, must serve as a substitute for the market and economic incentives. Yet, if national output and efficiency do not increase, a cynical attitude may develop which undermines the worker's identification with the system — an

[39]   Charles Bettelheim,"The Transition to Socialism",*Monthly Review* December, 1970, p.5.

essential ingredient of the model. As of the moment, effective planning and economic controls are extremely weak in Cuba. Economic decisions depend on a bureaucratic planning structure that must translate information about physical output collected from the base into operational instructions. Managers under this system are seriously circumscribed from making independent decisions based on economic analysis (nor do they often have the skills to do this). As a result, the data collected have little meaning to management and are therefore frequently inaccurate and under-utilized. This is reflected in the hostility sometimes expressed about the useless information that is sent up to the *Empresas* or Ministries that, the managers felt, is rarely used. On the other hand, instructions from above are frequently beyond the competence and skills that exist at the local level. Moreover, Havana-based administrators have no real knowledge of local problems. Despite romantic feelings, a man with a sixth grade education has difficulty collecting and using the simplest statistical data. This is particularly problematic in such critical sectors as agriculture where large-scale state farms have become the basic organizational unit. As a result, success is frequently measured simply by fulfilment of gross output targets expressed in physical terms and by the conservation of scarce raw materials. The fragile planning is further undermined by 'overcommitment' of resources, frequently a product of revolutionary enthusiasm and the uncertainty of foreign supplies. The inevitable has occurred: first, shortages and bottlenecks have reduced industrial capacity and worker productivity; second, the decision-making process has been plagued by bureaucracy, so that a parallel planning apparatus that bypasses the existing bureaucratic structure has been created to ensure the fulfilment of special or urgent strategic economic goals; these special plans are under Fidel's personal direction. Third, there has been a large turnover of managerial and administrative personnel. Problems similar to 1962 have re-emerged.

To meet these inefficiencies, managers have frequently called upon the worker's conscience, that is, labour's willingness to work overtime without pay. Thus, moral incentives have served to compensate for the inefficiencies and irrationalities of the economic organization. Indeed, moral incentives often foster the irrational uses of labour and capital, since managers do not feel compelled to complete tasks that could be done during the normal work day. Nor do they feel compelled to explore sources of inefficiency. Administrators frequently considered overtime or voluntary work costless, and were often perplexed when asked whether they had wasted *conciencia* in fulfilling their goals. The same attitude was prevalent in agriculture. Since no production unit assumed the cost of voluntary work, more labour was freqently demanded than was needed in order to guarantee results. Often, the irrational use of moral incentives results in problems of worker apathy and discontent. The cost of *conciencia* (Cuba's most precious resource) needs to be considered.

3. Conscience and Compulsion: Some Dilemmas of the Cuban Model

In the face of these difficulties Cuban economic organization has undergone some significant changes. First, the search for organizational efficiency has led to some imitation of the military model. The military is the most efficient organization in Cuba and considerable talent has been shifted to this sector. Recently, military techniques have been used in organizing large production units and directing large units of labour. Command Posts have been set up throughout Cuba that resemble the operational headquarters of an army. These techniques should not be confused with regimentation. Their purpose is to establish more effective controls over the organization and deployment of labour and capital, particularly in agriculture. Moreover, labour brigades have frequently employed military techniques and schedules. However, the model has not effectively dealt with the problems of bureaucracy, particularly in developing greater responsibility and self-reliance at the production level. Nor has it effectively helped foster real participation in the decision-making process. Inefficiency and the absence of effective control still plague Cuban economic organization.

A second response to inefficiency is reflected in labour force controls. According to Risquet, the Labour Minister, previous labour legislation that penalized workers with discharge and loss of salary had become outmoded.[40] At first, increased moral pressures were to be used. A labour file was created for each worker where merits and demerits are to be entered after his work record has been discussed at semi-annual assemblies. The second phase was the promulgation, in 1971, of an anti-loafing law aimed at dealing with absenteeism and bringing all able-bodied men between the ages of 17 and 60 into the labour force. The penalties for absenteeism ranged from working under the vigilance of other workers and revolutionary organizations,

[40]   *Verde Olivo,* August 17, 1969, pp. 12-13.

to working in a rehabilitation centre for up to one year.[41] Thus Cuba's economic model posed the serious issue of using coercion in pursuing economic development.

In an interview in Havana, Regino Boti argued that after a socialist revolution a period of primitive accumulation may be inevitable. A socialist revolution inevitably leads workers to reduce their efforts because they think that the end of employer control means less work. Therefore, he argued, all socialist revolutions face the inevitable dilemma between economic development and consent. In Cuba this problem has been complicated because the initial welfare and redistribution policies of the Government had retarded the rate of investment and created illusions about the relationship between work and economic development. The question therefore, Boti argued, then becomes how do you get workers to increase their efforts and discipline. Thus Boti's analysis raised some critical questions: Does Cuba's experiment suggest that compulsive work requirements are the inevitable consequences of an organizational model based on socialist values? Is low worker productivity and absenteeism functionally related to Cuba's radical efforts to eliminate material incentives? The economic problems that were admitted in a remarkably candid speech by Fidel in 1970 have reopened these questions.

Our analysis suggests that the roots of Cuba's economic problems must be found in deeper sources than moral incentives. In the first place Cuba's economic strategy required massive increases and deployment of labour. This created an overcommitment of available labour resources. Part of the difficulty can be explained by the particular nature of surplus labour in pre-revolutionary Cuba. In large measure under-utilization of labour was a seasonal problem. Thus, during the months of peak labour requirements, the 'reserve army of labour' was sharply reduced or disappeared. The revolution over-estimated the labour surplus.[42] Consequently, increasing numbers of outside workers, students, and the military, are needed to fulfil agricultural targets, disrupting production schedules in the industrial and service sectors. One of the results is the need to exhort workers to work longer hours or move, when needed, to critical sectors. But these efforts are frequently frustrated because of bottlenecks of poor planning. Thus, workers may spend many hours in the factory or in agriculture but considerable time is wasted or

---

[41] For complete text see *Granma*, Weekly Review, March 28, 1971, p.2.
[42] Pollitt, *op. cit.*, p.20.

misused. And despite the large increase in land cultivation, "season after season,....the administrators of numerous state farms were obliged to decide which harvests should be sacrificed entirely, or, at least, which crops should be harvested outside their optimal time-period at the cost of a decline in their volume and/or value."[43] Such pressures on labour resources lead to uneconomical hoarding of labour and a work ethic that may contradict the goals of the revolution. It creates a cynical attitude on the part of workers toward the Government's exhortations about labour discipline. The process of primitive accumulation is not a 'law' of social development but rather a function of policy decisions.

A second aspect of the strategy required a reduction in personal consumption while expanding (relatively) employment. Under these circumstances it is quite logical for workers to take part of their real income in the form of reduced effort and increased leisure. Increasing aggregate personal consumption has nothing to do with a system of differential economic incentives. As Ernest Mandel, a defender of moral incentives, has argued, "raising the producer's standard of living is a major way to stimulate output and raise labour productivity."[44] Ideological pre-occupation with the disappearance of money is, to a degree then, a rationalization of austerity.

The decline in money as a medium of exchange reflects a decline in real personal income, that is, shortages of consumer goods. Its consequences show up in worker resistance and cynicism.Thus, shortages tend to undermine the system of moral incentives by undermining social conscience.

Moreover, rather than diminishing in importance, scarcity reinforces the desire for material goods. True, rationing does provide a more equitable distribution of subsistence than would exist under a free market and many basic services are virtually free. But under conditions of severe shortages, small decreases and additions to consumption assume great importance. As a result informal markets exist where goods are bartered or traded at unofficial prices. The decline in consumption is related to the high rate of planned investment. Unlike the shortages that emerged in 1962, Cuba claims that the present phase of austerity has been planned. But there is a relationship between rate of capital accumulation and the rate of compulsion.

Third, Cuba's development strategy required a highly centralized organizational model where material incentives were

---

[43] *Ibid.*
[44] Mandel, in Silverman (ed.), *op. cit.*, p.81.

inappropriate. Economic incentives could not move hundreds of thousands of workers into the *Zafra*. Political rather than technical cadres direct the productive process under the new system of economic management. Thus far, the results have seriously undermined effective economic control. There is considerable evidence that a highly centralized economic organization is beyond Cuba's present administrative capacity. Political enthusiasm is no substitute for technical and organizational knowledge. This is reflected in the high rate of turnover of politically-committed administrators. Nor does the winning of the Moncada flag necessarily imply economic efficiency.

But what types of economic controls are compatible with moral incentives? The issue becomes apparent when confronting the problem of labour discipline. Economic planning depends on a reliable labour force. High labour turnover and absenteeism are inimical to planning and efficiency. But since economic rewards and penalties have been rejected, only social pressures, and ultimately compulsion, remain as methods to deal with these problems. Policies that lead to premature controls and direction of the labour market may lead to unnecessary compulsion. A supporter of Che's defence of moral incentives cautioned that "to abolish the private ownership of labour power before the society can assure the satisfaction of all its people's basic needs would actually introduce forced labour."[45]

In the face of these contradictions there is a natural tendency for the Government to increase the use of ideological instruments to develop greater expression of social commitment. This is the basis of the Revolutionary Offensive and the 'radicalization' of Cuban ideology which has virtually declared a moratorium on public debate over economic and social policies. These developments have resulted in the externalization of revolutionary ethics. But a system of incentives that relies on directives from above becomes just another form of repression. As Alberto Mora, a participant in the debate over moral incentives warned:[46]

> We must at the same time assure that the superstructure is so organized as to prevent the substitution of the money motive by the power motive.

Thus, worker-resistance is also reflected in the absence of real participation in decision-making. While mass organizations such as the Committee for the Defence of the Revolution and the Federation of Cuban Women have recruited large numbers of para-professionals

[45] *Ibid.*
[46] Mora, in Silverman (ed.), *op. cit.*, p.334.

in the extensive dissemination of health, welfare and child-care services, these organizations remain primarily transmission belts for centralized party decisions. Mass meetings are used primarily to gain support for policy decisions already made. Fidel seemed to understand this shortcoming when he recently said:[47]

> We have been able to unleash the energy, interest and will of millions. Now we must channel this energy into greater participation in decisions that affect their lives.

The economic crisis of 1970 has opened a new phase in the discussion about economic organization. Castro's speeches, since July 1970, have revealed considerable frankness about economic and social problems. These initial problems are, after all, part of an early process of experimentation; Cuba's organizational model is only five years old. Certainly an insignificant period to test its efficacy; nor do productivity statistics include the large investment in training and education. Nevertheless, if our analysis is correct, Cuba faces a serious dilemma in the immediate future. Some modification in Cuba's ambitious economic strategy and organization to provide greater local responsibility will be necessary, if the link between socialist consciousness and economic development are to be encouraged and the connection between economic development and compulsion dissolved. This will also require a greater concordance between ideology and reality.

There are some indications that the demystification process has already begun as *praxis* once again triumphs over ideology. Thus, 1970 seems to 'mark the beginning of a new phase in the relationship between moral incentives, economic organization and economic development. This new chapter will have much to instruct us about the relationship between socialist economic development and *conciencia*.

[47] Fidel Castro Speech in *Granma*, Weekly Review, August 25, 1971.

PROBLEMS OF SOCIALISM IN TANZANIA

Brian Van Arkadie*

Introduction[1]

It is appropriate that Tanzania should receive attention at a conference in Chile, not because there are specific lessons to be learnt — probably the political and the economic structures of the two countries vary too widely for that to be true — but because in the larger sense it is desirable for there to be more communication, understanding and solidarity between Africa, Latin America and Asia, and particularly between those countries currently at the forefront of the struggle to end dependence.[2]

During the past five years (1967-72) Tanzania has been moving in a socialist direction. This has been a period of decisive change and impressive achievements; however, despite this, the society remains at the early stages of a process of transition, during which the outcome will remain highly uncertain. The inherited economic and social situation at the time of the shift in a socialist direction was such that while great changes were implemented smoothly with remarkably little opposition, it was in the nature of the underlying structure that quite enormous tasks for subsequent socialist transformation remained.

1. Economic Structure before the Arusha Declaration[3]

As a starting point in explaining why this is so, it will be useful to outline the main features of the Tanzanian economy in 1967. This

---

* University of Cambridge.

[1] Within the limits of a short paper, it has been necessary to summarise to an extreme degree. Inevitably much of the space is taken up with actual or potential difficulties; this is not because I am pessimistic about the overall situation, but because the difficulties require discussion and analysis if they are to be overcome.

[2] Chile and Tanzania did in fact establish diplomatic relations in 1971.

[3] February 1967. The Declaration firmly committed Tanzania to a path of self-reliance and socialism.

need not be done in great detail, because many of the features will be familiar as typical of underdevelopment elsewhere.

Rural preponderance

Tanzania is a predominantly rural society. In this respect the extremely limited degree of urbanization contrasts with some other underdeveloped regions where even without successful industrialization, the demographic balance has been shifted decisively to urban areas. At the time of the last census (1967) only 5.7% of the population of mainland Tanzania lived in urban areas.

In the rural areas, the characteristic form of economic activity is small-holder farming. In many parts of the country much, if not most, of the productive effort still goes into subsistence production.

Export Agriculture

At the beginning of the 1960's export agriculture had been divided roughly evenly between the non-African owned sector consisting of plantations and mixed farming, and African small-holder production. By 1967 the process of decline in the leading plantation crop, sisal, had already set in as the world market for hard fibres contracted. With the fast expansion of a number of small-holder crops, the balance of the export sector was shifting increasingly to small-holder farming.

The impact of small-holder export development on rural society varied greatly from region to region. Some areas, particularly those where coffee had been established since before the Second World War, were highly committed to commercial export production. In other areas, export production impinged only marginally on an economy still predominantly based on subsistence production.

In national terms, both short-term economic performance and medium term growth prospects depended largely on the performance of this small-holder agriculture.

The degree of overall dependence on export earnings is indicated by the fact that overseas exports equalled some 38% of estimated marketed GDP in 1967, and this ratio had been even higher in some previous years. Except for diamonds (10-15% of exports), export earnings consist virtually entirely of the unprocessed products of agriculture.

The major economic activities outside agriculture were still the provision of commercial, transporting and other services (including those of the state), which played an essentially intermediary role between the agricultural export economy and world markets.

Another characteristic of the Tanzanian economy was the very low degree of social differentiation among the African population. During the colonial period, economic and social divisions had been drawn predominantly along racial lines. Of course, within African society there were localised instances of semi-feudal social arrangements (e.g. West of Lake Victoria) and in those areas with the most prolonged and successful participation in export agriculture the economic basis for rural class formation could be identified. Also, by 1967, the displacement of expatriates by citizens in bureaucratic postitions was creating a possible basis for new social and economic distinctions in African society. Nevertheless, an urban proletariat was only in its infancy, there was no substantial group of landlords (although a significant area of land had been alienated and was being used for estate agriculture), and no coherently defined African bourgeoisie.

Although class formation in African society was limited, it should be noted that in similar settings elsewhere in Africa, the social situation has changed dramatically over quite short periods, the liquidation of the colonial presence being associated with an accelerated process of class formation.

Managerial and technical dependence
Even by standards of African colonies, Tanganyika came to independence with an extraordinary limited cadre of trained manpower. The manpower survey for the First Five Year Plan indicated that in 1964/65 only 13% of high level manpower requirements (i.e. those jobs normally requiring university training) were filled by Africans. The situation was particularly dismal in relation to technical skills — of the 481 engineers only 34 were African.

Needless to say, all capital equipment was imported. Furthermore not only was there no domestic capacity to produce equipment, there was also very little indigenous basis for a capacity to make informed choices about the purchase of foreign capital equipment or to operate projects once created.

T.A.N.U.
To complete a highly schematic summary of the Tanzanian background, it is necessary to say something about the party — T.A.N.U.[4] Tanzania became a one party state following an almost total domination by T.A.N.U. of the electoral politics of the country. The party is

[4] Tanzanian African National Union.

a broadly-based mass organization, it is not an exclusive, tightly disciplined vanguard party, but is open, inclusive and probably reflects the actual composition of African society.

Since becoming a one-party state, political arrangements have allowed for public elections of parliamentary representatives from a number of party candidates (in a two-stage election). However, in the absence of open factions and caucussing, the outcome of such elections seem to reflect local popular standing or the registration of generalised discontents (for example, when a sitting member, most notably a minister, is defeated) rather than ideological choices. While the party is apparently decisive in determining major shifts in direction, the political forces at work within it remain obscure to the outside observer (at least to this one!) Because of the somewhat amorphous nature of the party there is a tendency to ascribe decisive political shifts, and the style of politics in general, to the personality of the President, Julius Nyerere. Evidently, he is a figure of some substance and he is the origin of much that happens in Tanzania. However, his own freedom of manoeuvre results from the unchallenged position of T.A.N.U. and the acceptability of the political line adopted within the Party.

2. Arusha and after

Typical development programmes in Africa have attempted to attack the problem of dependence by changing the commodity composition of production, through import-substitution industrialization, agricultural diversification, and 'Africanization' of the staffing of the bureaucracy. This has sometimes been combined with displacement of immigrant groups (e.g. European settlers, and Asian traders). At the same time, there has been an acceptance of existing salary structures, an encouragement of private foreign investment and an emphasis on external finance for the public development budget.

Although such policies have engendered, in some instances, quite buoyant growth, they have also been associated with the fast emergence of a privileged African bureaucratic class, often associated with, or actually engaged in, small-scale capitalist economic activities. While this class displaces the old colonial civil servant and encroaches on the interests of settlers (where these exist) and traders, it is willing to accept the larger-scale foreign corporation as a natural ally.

Broadly, until 1967 this pattern had been adopted in practice in Tanzania. Although there had been a distinctive quality in Tanzanian rhetoric, there was little in actual performance which significantly distinguished the economic path followed.

The change in direction came dramatically in February 1967, with the Arusha Declaration. At this time T.A.N.U. leadership publicly recognised that their past policies were resulting in a drift in the direction of a class society and of new forms of foreign dependence, while the special problems and possibilities of development in a predominantly peasant society had been neglected.

Therefore, there was a sharp change in direction involving:-

i   nationalization of larger-scale economic activity (predominantly foreign owned interests);

ii   steps to check the growth of an African capitalist class, including the trimming of salaries and benefits at the upper reaches of the bureaucracy, and the exclusion of the political or bureaucratic leadership from ownership for profit or from playing the role of private employer;

iii a commitment to self-reliant development patterns, de-emphasizing external finance, concentrating attention on means of development utilizing local (and therefore rural) resources;

iv   a recognition that the characteristic Tanzanian way of life would be rural for some generations and that therefore development must not only be based on the rural sector but must also respond to its needs.

In the period following Arusha, remarkable success was achieved in implementing those parts of the Declaration which could be translated into immediate legislation and institutional changes. The financial system was nationalized immediately, most manufacturing and large-scale agricultural processing enterprises were taken into full or majority public ownership and more than half of the largest plantation industry (sisal) was taken over. Public utilities and railways were already publicly owned.

The distribution sector was taken over less dramatically. Crop marketing was already handled by a system of co-operatives and public marketing boards. Following Arusha, part of the wholesale and import-export trade handled by the larger trading companies was taken under control by the State Trading Corporation. The range of state trading has been progressively expanded since 1967. Retail trade and a diminishing proportion of wholesale trade is still in private hands.

During 1971 an important additional step was taken when real property holdings were taken into public ownership. This step has apparently acted as a final warning to the Asian community that any future private commercial or property owning possibilities in

Tanzania would be extremely circumscribed, leading to an increased interest in emigration by members of that community.

The shift to public ownership over the period 1967-71 was carried out remarkably smoothly. Despite the abrupt withdrawal of management personnel in 1967 for example, the commercial banks were taken over with little disturbance of business and the new National Bank of Commerce subsequently carried through a successful programme of reorganisation and rationalization. Similarly, the creation of the Tanzanian Sisal Corporation at the end of 1967 put a large part of a decaying industry on a much more effective organizational footing than before. In other cases, such as the creation of the Milling Corporation, nationalization was implemented in co-operation with local private businessmen. In the case of a number of manufacturing enterprises, as with the publicly owned hotels (which had been developed publicly from the start of the First Plan and had not been nationalized), management was arranged through agreements with foreign firms, in some cases the previous owners (who in some instances maintained a minority interest).

The implementation of this first stage involved the transfer of a small number of the most able civil servants to the new or expanded state corporations. In some instances the management problem was eased by rapid promotion of personnel already employed in the enterprises. Friendly powers co-operated in supplying personnel (e.g. the Danes helped with the nationalization of the banks). Negotiation of the compensation arrangements and management agreements were undertaken by a very small group of officials, including a number of foreign officials with a strong commitment to the Tanzanian Government.

A number of points can be made about the ease with which Tanzania carried out the extension of public ownership:

i   While the interests taken over during this period were of importance to the Tanzanian economy, they were not of great international significance. The extreme poverty of Tanzania, the lack of great mining developments, and the secular decline of the sisal industry, meant that from the point of view of foreign capital, nationalization presented no great challenge. There were no significant U.S. interests involved. The British whose interests were most affected, were in a weak position to exercise leverage as relations were already at an extremely low ebb — diplomatic relations had been broken after the failure of the British Government to take effective action following the Rhodesian Unilateral Declaration of Independence (in 1965), and U.K.

capital aid had been frozen.

ii   Although Tanzania had a scarcity of trained nationals, the very limited development of the economy meant that the existing operations taken over posed no insurmountable technical complexities. Operations such as banking, while large-scale, are fairly bureaucratic in character; it is not difficult to transfer civil servants effectively to their management. Possibly the most difficult managerial tasks of state take-over were posed by state trading, where the activities of a large number of enterprises were involved and where the system of organization being displaced was highly informal in character.

iii   Although the steps taken after Arusha to eliminate the possibilities of bureaucrats or politicians becoming capitalists may have worked against the interests of a few individuals, the measures did not pose a threat to the existing interest of any sizeable group in African society. Five years later the situation might already have been very different. Moreover, for the current generation of civil servants, even if some potential avenues were closed, many more immediate possibilities were opened up by the expansion of posts in state economic enterprises. Even if the upper salary scales were squeezed and fringe benefits trimmed, for many civil servants the fast promotion prospects outweighed such effects.

The fact that Tanzania negotiated compensation agreements with the owners of the nationalized activities also limited the external pressures. (Just at this moment, however, the U.K. Government is attempting to bring pressure to bear through the World Bank, to block agricultural development loans, as it claims that the compensation arrangements for the recent take-over of buildings are unsatisfactory. One may surmise that the U.K.'s interest here arises as much from the dangers of a demonstration effect elsewhere as from the value of the assets involved.)

Although that part of the Arusha Declaration relating to public ownership of larger-scale economic activities was carried out with remarkable effectiveness, only the sisal nationalization had a substantial immediate impact in the countryside. True, various fiscal measures favourable to the rural sector were introduced. A commitment was made to restructure the educational system to adapt it to rural needs, but the effective implementation of such an intention requires sustained and detailed innovations; this cannot be achieved simply through legislation, but will require a creative effort over some years. The difficulties of developing satisfactory methods of providing rural mass health services are probably even greater. While there is no reason to suppose that the rhetorical commitment to rural development is not genuine, the means of delivery are not readily available.

At the most fundamental level, it was seen to be unsatisfactory to leave the productive basis of rural development to the efforts of individual peasant farmers. A commitment was made to displace individual small-holding by co-operative production (in 'Ujamaa Villages'), supplemented by state farms, where these are appropriate on technical grounds. The basic objective was spelt out in a number of public documents, and a commitment to move vigorously towards the desired system was made in the Second Five Year Plan (1969-74).

The desire to move towards 'ujamaa' as a basis for rural development did not arise from any pressing economic crisis of the kind which provided a prelude to Soviet collectivization, nor was there any widespread tendency for a landlord or a kulak class to emerge. True, in some of the more successful farming areas there were successful African farmers employing labour and beginning to invest in expensive capital equipment, but this did not present an immediate challenge to the social and political objectives of the government.

The desire to introduce 'ujamaa' rested both on the disbelief in the efficiency of the existing forms of agricultural organization as a basis for accelerated rural mobilization — a concern which had pre-dated Arusha and had been reflected in earlier settlement pro-grammes — and on a belief that co-operative systems would be readily acceptable in communities with long traditions of collective productive effort.

The move toward 'ujamaa' was to be a voluntary one — incentive and encouragement was to be provided, but acceptance by the farmers themselves was needed. Since the introduction of the Second Five Year Plan in 1969 considerable political and administrative weight has been thrown behind the campaign for 'ujamaa'. Because of the nature of the exercise it is very difficult to assess progress — and possibly inappropriate to try. Before the introduction of the publicly-sponsored campaign there had been a local initiative for 'ujamaa' in Ruvuma in the Southern poorer part of the country. The organization which emerged (the Ruvuma Development Association) was dissolved, however, following conflicts with the party leadership. Since 1969 the most publicized progress in the government campaign has been in Dodoma, again in one of the poorest parts of the country.[5]

By mid-1971 the Government estimated that 6.3% of the total population lived in 'ujamaa villages'[6] but these were admitted to be in varying stages of development.The estimate is offered that about a quarter of the population will be living in 'ujamaa villages' within a decade.[7] Meanwhile, Tanzania remains predominantly a society of small-holder farmers.

3. The Nature of the Economic System

At first sight it would seem that a solid foundation has been laid for further development in the transition to a socialist system in Tanzania. The State itself, various state corporations, marketing boards, and co-operatives, together dominate a large part of the economic terrain, particularly outside agriculture, and there are not clearly identifiable social forces to back a counter-revolution.

However, further consideration gives rise to more cautious assessment. The State, the financial and marketing institutions, and the limited industrial sector, remain in an essentially intermediary position in a continuing structure of economic dependence. On one side — the world market, still providing markets for agricultural primary products, still the source of supply for all capital equipment, many consumer goods and for intermediate goods on which the new industries depend. On the other side — the mass of small-holder producers, who supply products for export and are therefore the ultimate domestic source of finance for investment. No matter what long-term economic objectives are espoused, in the short term there seems little alternative to encouraging the maximum response by farmers to existing export possibilities.

Thus, although the State can pursue structural transformation and seek to mould the character of a society, freedom of manoeuvre is more limited than is immediately apparent. The achievement of fundamental structural change is itself likely to require a long struggle. It is not surprising that even the State itself, as elsewhere in Africa, sometimes appears to be superficial in character — not impinging deeply on the lives of much of the populace, and changing

---

[5] It has recently been reported that a leading government official was assassinated by a prosperous farmer during a campaign promoting ujamaa villages. The circumstances surrounding this incident are obscure.

[6] Annual Plan for 1971/72, p. 57.

[7] *ibid*. p. 71.

hands as a result of the casual initiatives of a battalion or two.

The fundamental question which might be posed is whether it will be possible at all to build a socialist mode of production on such a fragile foundation. However, such a question, whilst understandable, in another sense is not helpful. It is of no use to a current generation of Tanzanian socialists to say, in effect, 'the objective conditions are not ripe, it must be the task for some future generation.' Certainly there are favourable aspects inherent in the situation we describe — the very underdevelopment of Tanzania which poses very real problems also has meant that indigenous bases for opposition have been limited. Similarly, although the possibility of accumulation is constrained by foreign exchange availability, given the limited industrial base, the limited degree of industrialization and urbanization leaves a wider range of choices of the future economic structure.

4. Tasks for transition

The perspective, then, is that a basis has been created for the transition towards socialism but that the period of struggle must be a long one fraught with uncertainties. We need to examine questions which may arise in this period of transition, not expecting that there is a set of ready-made answers on which we can draw — in most cases we can merely hope to illuminate the areas in which choices will have to be made.

Agriculture

The dilemma here is fairly clear. Although there is some basis in pre-colonial social formations for collective economic activity, the source of output growth, particularly of exports, has been the expansion of individualistic petty commodity production.

This poses two problems. Over any medium-term planning period the macro-constraint on the growth of the economy is likely to be the availability of foreign exchange, which for some time is likely to be dependent upon the buoyancy of the output performance of individualistic small-holder agriculture. Also, where these cash income opportunities have developed, a stake has been created in the individualistic organization of production, albeit in general still on a small scale.

For some time potential dilemmas can be postponed by concentrating the efforts to introduce collective agricultural systems in those parts of the country where cash crop agriculture has been more limited in its development. In such areas possible public incentives (e.g. provision of services) will be of greater relative impact, tradi-tional bases for collective action will be less eroded, and the costs of collective action will be less than elsewhere.

However, if collective agricultural systems are to become the characteristic form of rural productive organization they must also be viable in those areas which have experienced the greatest growth.

One possible line of advance lies in a calculated response to the limitations in the successful small-holder systems. For example, where population densities have become excessive, settlement of new areas provides an opportunity for social innovation. Also, although small-holder crop systems experience very high growth rates for extended periods they also reach a too early maturity. This is because growth is often based on the introduction of a new crop or the bringing of new land into cultivation, or the fuller utilization of available labour power. These all have a limit, beyond which growth must be based on new technology or the use of more capital. At this point further growth will often require a larger unit of production than the existing small-holder. This could become a basis for further social differentiation by the growth of larger private units or again it could be an occasion for a move in a collective direction.

State Corporations

Since 1967 State Corporations (or *parastatals* as they are known in Tanzania) have expanded dramatically, and are now a strategic ele-ment in the pattern of state influence on the direction of economic development. The capital budget of these corporations was set at shs.370 million for 1971/72, compared to a development budget of shs.594 million for the Government itself, and a declining level of private fixed capital formation (which probably now runs at about half the parastatal total).[8] Moreover, state ownership of the financial system and expanding state control of the trading system is of strategic importance not revealed by investment figures as such. The effectiveness of decisions in this sector will be decisive for overall economic performance, and its social character will be decisive in determining the direction of future development.

One danger which has been identified arises from the dependent character of the underlying structure which even despite the changes in ownership could foster new and dangerous forms of exploitation. Equipment is still purchased entirely abroad, processes imported, foreign managerial personnel employed.

---

[8] There are approximately 17 Tanzanian shillings to the sterling pound.

There are three obvious sources of danger. Through inexperience and inadequate planning capacity, decisions can be made more to the benefit of foreign promoters — that is, machinery salesmen, participants in joint ventures etc. — than to the successful development of the local economy. Also, the bureaucracy at the higher reaches of this sector, in considerable contact with external influences might be unduly influenced (either subtly, by assimilating the values of the international business milieu, or more crudely through outright corruption). Finally, in a more general sense, through a mixture of inefficiency and privilege it is only too easy for the state bureaucracy to become a heavy burden on the rest of the society.

These arguments are by now familiar enough and they are aired, not from any undue alarm about specific developments in recent Tanzanian experience, but in order to note the dangers inherent in this general situation.

The ways to be pursued in avoiding these dangers have been sought in three directions:

i   There has been a continuing concern for the improvement of the technical efficiency of the state sector. It is not easy to identify effective methods to achieve desired managerial improvement. So far the approach has been eclectic — a number of young Tanzanians have been sent overseas to acquire business skills, and steps have been taken to expand local training facilities — but obviously it is neither evident that appropriate training is available nor is it clear what is the best training capacity to create. The Tanzanians have made extensive use of the American management consultants, McKinsey, to advise; this degree of pragmatism has been viewed with alarm by some observers on the left, but must be understood in the light of the poor results achieved by using other sources, such as available technical assistance facilities.

ii   There has been experimentation to achieve the right system of control. At the time of the formulation of the Second Plan it seemed necessary to bring the various parastatals under more systematic central control. It seemed possible, for example, that individual parastatals were in danger of making investment decisions which were neither consistent with the Government's overall policy, nor even very sensible from the standpoint of the firm. Since then, while there has apparently been a continuing effort to create a more systematic foundation to decision-making — e.g. in the area of project evaluation — there has also been some concern that too tight a central bureaucratic control will check the proper development of responsibility and initiative within the parastatals.

iii The question of the role of the state bureaucracy must ultimately be a *political* as much as a *technical efficiency* issue. A number of steps have already been taken to prevent the isolation of the bureaucracy. National Service involves those who have received higher education in a brief experience of rural labour. Trimming of fringe benefits has reduced some economic privileges. Involvement of some of the bureaucracy in the Party, and the Party in the bureaucracy has broken down some of the excessive and explicit isolation of the bureaucracy from political life — although the effect of this should not be over-emphasized, as the Party itself remains somewhat amorphous.

Two developments since the publication of the Second Plan (1969), with which the author of this essay is not directly familiar, have been the introduction of an element of workers control in the State Corporations, and the generation of a degree of open discussion and criticism of their policies and administration in the Dar es Salaam press.

The development of workers' participation in the management of state enterprise will be of fundamental importance, but so far there is little evidence that its impact has been great.

The problem of the bureaucracy will always be a sensitive one. The relatively small elite amongst the higher paid workforce and the bureaucracy are needed, and the maintenance of their morale, efficiency and support is probably, in the short-run at least, a necessary condition of survival.

Yet, as John Saul has argued, commenting on Tanzania: "popular participation is not merely good because it provides the population with a sense of involvement and consequent enthusiasm, but also because it may be the means, increasingly, to *force* the leadership to sustain their dedication to the popular cause and to the quest for economic independence.."[9]

If we look outside Tanzania we see that the failure of a number of experiments in state-directed development have come when the bureaucratic elites, who were managing the system, became disaffected, and passively resisted or moved against the political regime,

[9] John S. Saul 'The Political Aspects of Independence' Regional African Meeting of Development Training and Research Institutes, Nairobi 1971.

and such moves have been acquiesced in by the mass of the populace, with understandable cynicism. The rhetoric of the regime was addressed to the masses, but its practice alienated them.

Industrial strategy

While Tanzanian rhetoric has emphasized rural development as the focus for economic strategy, over the long term the identification and implementation of a successful strategy for industrial growth will be as crucial for successful development as in any other under-developed economy. Indeed, the very possibility of rural development on a basis other than export crops is contingent on success in the industrial sphere.

Such industrial projects as have so far occurred have been in the obvious first stage of import substitution activities — textiles, cement and other simple building materials, food processing and a small petroleum refinery. Industrial growth has been at a high rate from a small base, with production for a heavily protected market. As a result of a high degree of integration in the East African Common Market (with Uganda and Kenya), Tanzania has also provided a market for simple manufactures from her partners.

So far, most industrial expansion has come in East Africa as a piecemeal reaction to obvious market opportunities, often at the instigation of private promoters (even in the case of ostensibly public projects or joint projects). The potential limitations of such a growth pattern are by now well known from experience elsewhere, but the alternative possibilities are not immediately apparent.

Tanzania by itself provides a small market for capital goods; even the East African market as a whole will remain small in relation to viable size for a steel industry or an integrated transport equipment industry in the near future. The Tanzanian import bill for transport equipment and capital goods has been of the order of $100 million annually in recent years; imports of iron and steel manufactures (excluding transport equipment) in the range of $15-20 million.

While the existence of a common market offers one avenue for easing the limitations resulting from the small size of market, it should also be recognized that in addition to the usual tensions which characterize common markets in underdeveloped regions, there are contradictions which can arise from the co-existence of two alternative modes of production within such a market — the market provides opportunities but poses problems at the same time.

Thinking about industrialization is now under way, in the

context of the formulation of a long-term industrial strategy. The Second Plan was admittedly *ad hoc* in this regard, but it did include a commitment to a systematic examination of the long-term strategy in this plan period.

Within the scope of this short essay, it would not be possible to outline an appropriate strategy, even if there was one easily available. All that can be done is briefly to suggest useful lines of discussion.

An appropriate strategy must be consistent both with technical possibilities and political objectives. Political objectives:

i   aim for an egalitarian income distribution;

ii   place limits on the degree to which the rural masses can be expected to finance an industrialization effort;

iii emphasize a strong element of self-help mass participation and rural mobilization.

It is difficult to think of an industrialization model from elsewhere which fits these criteria. The most obvious example might be the People's Republic of China. However, there are two important distinctions: China has a continental economy which is able to combine large-scale industrialization with small-scale self-help, and the possibilities of rural mobilization have arisen from the specific Chinese historical experience, which has contributed both to the effectiveness of cadres and to the consciousness of the mass of the people. Nevertheless, it is in that direction that Tanzania might most usefully look, rather than to the experience of Western Europe, the United States, or, for that matter, the Soviet Union.

Some fragmentary thoughts which might be offered are as follows:

i   by expanding national income through a strategy in which the mass of the population participates in small increases, rather than the more usual patterns in which the minority participates in large increases, it may be possible to concentrate consumer demand upon simple consumer goods, many of which could be produced domestically;

ii   this could be reinforced by the use of both political persuasion and economic tools to shift consumer preferences — an organized counter-demonstration effect — in favour of those goods which can be potentially produced;

iii in thinking of what goods these might be, it will be appropriate to consider the possibilities of improving the quality of life through *collective* consumption (some problems are insoluble on the individualistic basis of the past, e.g. transport);

iv   consideration of consumption expansion should be concerned not only with *manufactured commodities* (existing methods of measurement and discussion have a heavy bias in that direction) but also with the provision of *services* — which often meet high priority needs (e.g. health);

v   in considering the provision of services in particular, and methods of production in general, an emphasis on simple labour-intensive techniques seems appropriate, for political as well as economic reasons. Industry must not become an isolated, high income sector.

vi   In considering labour-intensive developments, special attention might be addressed to the possibilities of labour mobilization for capital projects — using labour directly to expand the capital stock.

At the same time there must be concern for a number of conventional programming problems. Even if one of the objectives of the industrial strategy is, in essence, to create an expanded internal market which can be supplied by an increased utilization of domestic resources, the need to participate successfully in the international market is unavoidable for a long intermediate period. In one respect the pursuit of a radical strategy increases the need for adequate reserves since international credit will be less freely available.

The question of the role of heavier industry will arise specifically with reference to a set of interrelated projects now being investigated which may be on the agenda for the 1980's — the study of iron and coal deposits in the southern part of the country and a major new hydro-electric power source in Stiegler's Gorge. The problem will be to place such developments in the context of an overall strategy which is concerned with the possibilities mentioned above.

In formulating an industrial strategy and translating it into a programme, the Tanzanians will have to overcome the problems posed by their limited industrial experience, continuing dependence on imported equipment, and lack of an available model. The appeal to labour-intensive methods, simple products and provision of mass services should not be taken to imply that Tanzania should turn her back on modern science and technology. Quite the reverse. Modern science and technology has predominantly worked in the interest, and to meet the needs, of the large industrial powers — the real problem is that access to modern technology comes in practice through the mediation of the large corporations. In the longer term, a choice of strategy must be based upon an expanding scientific and technical capacity in the periphery, operating in tune with local conditions. In practice this means increasing local technical cadres, and ensuring that they adjust their thinking to local realities rather than professional cosmopolitan conceptions of standards and methods.

At the moment, professional training involves considerable exposure to social attitudes, technical approaches and ideologies which are irrelevant to Tanzanian needs — much technical training is still received in Western universities, and the curriculum of local higher education, despite serious efforts to adapt, is still predominantly a Western product. The managerial elite in the State Corporations is inevitably the most cosmopolitan group in society, necessarily so because of the structure of external dependence, and undertakes frequent transactions with foreign business; it is therefore not difficult to understand the fears of critics on the left who have identified the managerial and technical elites as a potential threat.

There is a danger that foreign technology will operate as a Trojan horse. However, isolation is no solution since it is from modern scientific knowledge that solutions to the problem of poverty and underdevelopment are to be found.

Conclusions

The overall perspective is that the struggle for development and economic change will require the mobilization of the rural population for both agricultural development and for building rural infrastructure, and the adjustment of industry and the service sector to the needs of this rural population.

The degree of existing dependence, the low levels of income and the small size of the economy suggest that the period of transition will be long and precarious. During that transition there will be a continuing tension between political and technical criteria in seeking solutions. The possibilities of success will increase if there are revolutionary changes in neighbouring African countries over the coming two decades — revolutionary changes which Tanzania cannot herself promote, but which may emerge from the logic of African history.

Population (1967)

	Thousands	*Urban as % of total*
Mainland	11877	5.7
Zanzibar and Pemba	354	23.5
TOTAL	122131	6.2

Wage Employment (1970)

TOTAL	375,000
Estate Agriculture	107,000
Non-agriculture	267 000

Total G.D.P.:

8232 million East African Shillings.
($1 = 7 E.A. shillings)

Per capita G.D.P.: US $88

Composition of G.D.P. (1970)

	Percentage
Subsistence	28.7
Monetary	71.3
	100%

Agriculture	40.1
Mining and Quarrying	1.8
Manufacture and Handicrafts	7.9
Construction	4.8
Services	45.4
	100%

Fixed Capital Formation (1970)

Monetary *TOTAL*	*Million Shillings*
	1535
of which: Central Government	472
State enterprises	584
Other public (including East African community)	202
Total Public	1258
Private (including co-operatives)	277

Trade (1970)

Million Shillings

	Exports	Imports
Kenya and Uganda	147	335
Rest of world	1689	1939
TOTAL	1852*	2274

* Includes re-exports

Composition of Exports (1970)

(Outside East Africa)	*Million Shillings*
Coffee	312
Cotton	247
Sisal	179
Diamonds	161
Cashew nuts	115
Cloves	109
Tobacco	45
Tea	42
Petroleum products*	111
Other	368
TOTAL	1689

* Sales from Dar es Salaam refinery, i.e. mainly to Zambia

APPRAISING YUGOSLAV SOCIALISM

Benjamin Ward*

The transition to socialism is probably a permanent state of affairs. The course of world events imposes its constraints on socialist development and the process of learning through experience has its various subtle and not-so-subtle effects on the very concept of socialism. Consequently in asking the question: What has the Yugoslav experience to offer in the way of guidance through the transition?, there seems to be no reason to concentrate attention on the first few years, and a good deal of picking and choosing from many parts of Yugoslavia's quarter century of socialist experience will occur in this paper.

There are three background ingredients to the Yugoslav transition which are of overwhelming importance in appraising the transfer value of her experience. The first is that an early political revolution stripped the urban capitalist class of its power, and this group has not exercised any significant political power since the first year or two of the revolution. The second is that on the morrow of the revolution there was in place a communist party which was well organized and integrated by several years of intense guerilla warfare. This force was able to provide reliable cadres for the mobilization of the population, and especially the urban one, for the tasks of economic reconstruction and growth and the building of a new society. Third, and closely related to the above two factors, for the first fifteen years of its history Yugoslav socialism faced a number of crises, but none entailed anything like a serious domestic challenge to the leadership. Taken together, these three factors substantially opened the range of options which could be selected in the pursuit of socialist development.

A paper of this kind cannot avoid making value judgments, when simply deciding what to include and what to exclude and what to qualify as 'successes' and 'failures'. A simple criterion is needed which is morally appealing and at the same time sufficiently

* University of California, Berkeley, California.

specific to have some reasonably clearcut empirical consequences. All too often output per capita serves this role, perhaps accompanied by side comments on other relevant matters.[1]

At the cost of a brief digression, an alternative performance concept will be discussed now and later applied in a rough and ready way to aspects of the Yugoslav experience.

The primary obligation of an organized society, a nation, is to provide for the 'integrity' of its members, meaning a basic level of physical and mental health, and of freedom from coercive restraint, which is necessary for the individual to be able to represent himself, so to speak, in his behaviour. A society is not doing its job to the extent that avoidable failures of integrity are occurring. An economic appraisal of a society should concentrate on those integrity failures that are correctable through the reallocation of resources.

What sorts of phenomena constitute integrity failure? There are many strong cases which hardly need defence. A society that allows many of its children to die of malnutrition or of infectious diseases brought on by malnutrition and inadequate water supply and sewage disposal systems is, unless it is very poor indeed, *producing* integrity failures. A society that allows a significant fraction of its children to be raised in the lassitude, growth-stunting and possible mental retardation of under-nourishment, even though they live, is producing integrity failures. A society that permits an inordinate number of accidents in the workplace, through inadequate use of safety equipment and training, is producing integrity failures. A society that finds it necessary to incarcerate large numbers of its citizens in brutalizing prisons and camps is producing integrity failures. In all of these cases resource reallocations would clearly play a vital role in the correction of failure.[2]

---

[1] This is not because researchers are unaware of the deficiencies of output concepts as measures of welfare. Many bourgeois and socialist writers comment on the failure of such measures to consider distribution, nonmarketed goods, and the failure of market prices to reflect social costs. But, having made their obeisances to principle, writers all too often return to *de facto* measurement of performance in terms of output per capita simply because it is the most easily available overall measure.

[2] Of course, not every case is easy to decide. Not all deaths are avoidable, and avoidability is sometimes a controversial matter, as with the use of kidney machines or transplants. And some deaths occur in avoidable activities such as motor racing where the risk of death is an important part of the attractiveness of the activity. The margin between low-energy normality and low-energy integrity failure is no doubt between detention and non-detention (Swedish prisoners in a work-furlough system, 'free' intellectuals in a dictatorship with tight press controls and jailing of dissidents), but the strong cases do not cause such doubts, and there are plenty of them in most societies.

In this paper no serious attempt to measure the proportion of the Yugoslav population possessing integrity in the above sense will be made. Nevertheless, the criterion will be used in judging some basic economic strategies chosen by the Yugoslav leadership, and therefore some notion of the extent of success using this criterion, however vague, must be obtained. Several approaches have been used in the past to get essentially at the extent of integrity failure. Probably the most familiar is the poverty line, where an attempt is made to determine the proportion of the population which has the minimum support, in terms of goods and services available to it, for full membership in the normal life of the society. Some aspects of integrity have been measured traditionally in terms of inputs to the system of necessary services, such as doctors per capita. Attempts to identify lack of integrity in terms of attitudes, the 'culture of poverty', have also been made, as have estimates of the opportunities open to the citizenry, measured in such terms as the probability that a member of one 'deprived' socio-economic group will move into another and 'undeprived' group. Finally, there are measures of direct failures which are available in the statistics on mortality, illness and detention. Unfortunately, for all societies the primary data in these areas is meagre, unreliable and unstandardized, and integrity as a concept is itself underdeveloped. Consequently, the judgments of performance that occur in this paper are highly subjective, and, in addition, are not based on extensive investigation but hopefully they provide a correct qualitative appraisal of performance in terms of the integrity criterion.

To be more precise our criterion is a multi-stage lexicographic[3] ordering, of which only the first two stages are of relevance here. The first, which, to give it a name, is called LEP-1 (for Levels of Economic Performance), measures the proportion of the population possessing integrity, and is the basic criterion for measuring the performance of the economy. However, as an economy improves on this measure it will begin to approach that proportion which exhausts economically correctable integrity failure and a new criterion takes over as the measure of success. LEP-2 measures the proportion of the population which has adequate goods support for the practice of acceptable identities.

The goods and services which must be adequate to support identities under LEP-2 include the labour services provided by the

---

3 The measure is called lexicographic in that no substitutions are possible between higher and lower stages; for example, no increase on the LEP-2 measure can compensate a small decrease in LEP-1.

individual. A job of deadly routine pursued without alternative for many years, such as those held by many assembly-line workers, is, for many such workers, inadequate to support a healthy identity. A worker who makes enough to survive but not enough to support a family and who has no prospects for higher income may also be a LEP-2 failure. The basic notion is the existence of the opportunity for a decent life, the term 'decent' no doubt being in part culturally and socially determined.

The measurement of the LEP-2 dichotomy poses more serious problems than LEP-1. Attempts have been made to estimate 'moderate' or 'decent' family budgets in various societies, and such measures can capture a substantial portion of the LEP-2 concept. Attitude studies can provide some indices of the discrepancy between aspiration levels and prospects. More fundamentally, measures of alienation and anxiety come fairly close to capturing the extent to which an individual feels secure and content in his identity. The most direct measurement procedure would require the specification of types of identities in terms which would permit their appraisal, including instruments for correcting defects. There is far less to go on here than there is even with LEP-1, and our appraisals must be even more speculative.

This has been a very brief sketch of a way of appraising the economic performance of a society. It has tried to capture the essential ingredients that should, morally speaking, go into such an appraisal. Does it succeed? That question can only be answered by trying cases to see if, in fact, it gives one a good rough guide, and to see if there is anything approaching consensus regarding the resulting judgments. If such a standard exists in usable form, those engaged in the task of building a good society could certainly make use of it in choosing among broader strategies for socio-economic development.

Coming to power in a war-devastated country, Yugoslav communists had to begin their political tenure with a major effort of reconstruction. Assisted by substantial UNRRA aid this effort was carried out with great energy and success. It should be noted that the LEP-1 criterion captures a basic idea of the Yugoslav reconstruction very well, namely the restoration of the population to reasonable health and energy through provision of food, medical care and shelter. The point of LEP-1 is that it does not stop at some socially-conventional notion of restoration but continues as the primary goal until essentially all the correctable integrity failures have been 'restored'.

With the reconstruction effort under control, in their eyes, the Yugoslavs quickly came to a basic development-strategy choice, which was to dominate their policy for almost two decades. This strategy was the 'Soviet way', rapid growth with a high investment ratio and with investment overwhelmingly concentrated in industry, and within industry on heavy industry and producer goods. This is the first of the key issues regarding the Yugoslav transition to socialism that requires appraisal.

This kind of concentration on industry implies relative inattention to agriculture. One might argue that the leadership planned to provide ample resources to agriculture as well, and the official first five year plan of 1946-47 testifies to that intention. But it is clear enough from policy decisions then, and later, that the possibility that resources would not be available to do everything in the plan was recognized, and that agriculture was to be the major victim of plan cutbacks. This agricultural policy had a number of important costs:

1. It probably meant acquiescence in the existing structure of land-holdings with their small size, the tremendous fragmentation of farms in many areas, the limited ability to use modern machinery, and the continued unusually sharp peak labour-demand problem caused by the backward technology under a dominant winter wheat-corn cropping pattern. There were of course political and social factors operating here as well, such as the unwillingness to collectivize by force, Soviet style (this latter being an exceptionally costly LEP-1 failure). But, with that alternative excluded, the resources were simply not available for a policy of collectivizing by attempting to demonstrate its benefits to the peasantry. Yugoslavia already had a primarily peasant freehold agriculture before World War II and the actual tenure reforms of the early socialist period were modest in scope, providing additional land for a good many of the poorest peasants. There has been no essential tenure change in the last twenty years.

2. As a result of the split with the Cominform countries, the Yugoslavs became especially concerned with the preservation of national sovereignty. Having traditionally possessed an agriculture capable of feeding its own population and of providing the major share of export income, some development of agriculture was of course essential, though American P.L. 480 grain was a tempting substitute for many years. It was a decade after Tito came to power before Yugoslavia even reached prewar levels of agricultural output. Certainly by the later fifties this policy did not entail a substantial

loss of sovereignty, and the American grain meant that the cost of the policy in foreign exchange earnings foregone was probably substantially less than the cost in agricultural output foregone. Nevertheless the policy did give the American government some blue chips to bring with it to the bargaining table.

3.   Relative social neglect in the countryside is a rather direct consequence of economic neglect. Systematic access to medical care came late to the countryside and remains spotty. Infant mortality rates still hover around 100 in Macedonia and Kossovo, or three to four times these rates in other parts of the country. Abysmal poverty can still be found, extensively in the less developed areas, but by no means absent from the Slovenian countryside, the richest of Yugoslav republics.

4.   Contributing to all this, the urban/rural lifestyle split makes most active youngsters long for city life, a fact which compounds agricultural problems over the longer run. Primary education was effectively spread throughout the countryside but seems overwhelmingly to have promoted urban values, and also to have generated far less than its share of secondary and higher level students. And the political consequences of this strong social and economic dichotomy have no doubt been substantial. For example it may have exacerbated the current inter-ethnic conflicts. The peasantry no doubt provide a strong reservoir of support for such things as Croatian nationalism, based in part on distrust of the central government and on their semi-exclusion from nearly all governmental processes.

5.   A major argument in favour of the extensive growth strategy is that after the early big push it is possible to do more for everyone, so that the benefits of modernization will then trickle down to all segments of the population. This process has in fact occurred in many parts of the countryside but, as noted, has also, two decades later, still left out a substantial fraction of the rural population. One of the big hopes for extensive growth has been that by very rapid expansion of urban employment the rural overpopulation will be eliminated, thus making rural modernization that much easier. The Yugoslav experience with this policy does not bear out that hope. It is true that the active agricultural population declined by ten per cent between the 1953 and 1961 censuses. But this was mainly due to an almost doubling of the active population in industry. I have not seen the latest census data, but employment in industry has grown by only twenty per cent in the last decade and there do not appear to be prospects for further massive transfers from agriculture to basic

urban pursuits. Close to half of Yugoslavia's population remains essentially rural; two decades of extensive growth did not do its job in this area.

Industry-based extensive growth, more or less along Soviet-inspired lines, has been the Yugoslav way down to 1965. Very substantial benefits have been generated by this strategy. Already mentioned was the substantial agricultural population absorption during the first decade. Industry has grown at rates exceeding ten percent a year resulting in a tremendous increase in the availability of domestically produced consumer and producer goods. Growth in both the quality and sophistication of output has also been outstanding with the result, among others, that the manufactured-goods component of exports has increased several fold and now constitutes the major share of exports. A necessary concomitant of this has been a dramatic increase in the skill and education levels of the Yugoslav population. Yugoslavia is in a sense already the Sweden of the Balkans, and in a couple of decades she may have become another of Europe's Swedens.

Socialism has greatly benefited the urban population in the relatively equitable distribution of medical care and housing, in the provision of family allowances that form a very substantial proportion of the incomes of workers' families containing several children, and in the availability of post-primary education. But there are gaps here to which, as with the incidence of access to unemployment compensation, tend to be concentrated on recent arrivals to the city. Neither town nor country has, after a quarter century of socialism, passed out of the LEP-1 stage of socio-economic development.

What modifications in the Yugoslav development strategy would the LEP-1 criterion have dictated? Of course no difinitive answer to that question can be given, even in a much more extended appraisal than the present one. But a few comments are in order which, though they reflect the author's views, should be taken as no more than suggestions for discussion.

It is quite possible that the extensive growth strategy was inefficient for Yugoslavia; perhaps she could have had more of everything by adopting a policy of more balanced growth of industry and agriculture. True, Yugoslavia was relatively well-endowed for the strategy she chose, with her good mineral and energy base and a population large enough potentially to provide a substantial domestic market. Even so the Yugoslavs were forced to break early with one hallowed tenet of the strategy, namely autarchy, and to follow what has looked very like an export-led pattern of growth.

However there seems to be a worldwide tendency to at least modify the extensive strategy and so our question is really: given an efficiently-balanced strategy which remains, as far as is consistent with efficiency, on the extensive, big-industrial-push side, what happens to the integrity of the population? If one believes the complementarity version of the extensive growth thesis, then it will seem unlikely that marginal adjustments of the level of the push are really feasible; that is, if modern industry comes in large, inter-dependent, indivisible chunks, then '95 per cent' of a modern industry may generate only '50 per cent' of a modern industry's output. Whatever the truth of that position may be, remarks of the last few pages suggest that there is a similar complementarity problems with respect to the integrity of the population. By far the largest numbers of integrity failures existed in the Yugoslav country-side, scattered through hundreds of villages isolated by custom and poor roads from the centres of power and national life. The terrible poverty, energy-sapping illness and early death that they suffered could not be ended by the application of such 'cool' instruments as inoculation programmes and the occasional delivery of a cart full of goods over those rutted roads. What was needed was warm instru-ments, the introduction of skills in both the arts of living and of working, which could only be done by cadres bringing to the village both the approriate knowledge and the human qualities necessary to obtain the peasants' trust. The provision of such cadres is a big order in itself; but in addition they need a certain amount of goods support, in the form of medical supplies, implements, construction materials, and the like. Much of such an effort would involve building infrastructure in the countryside with at best a modest return even in the medium run, and of course much of the effort would have to be concentrated in areas whose productive potential was not of the highest. Given simultaneous need for increased agricultural output, this begins to look very like a big-push thesis shifted from town to country.

My task here is not to design programmes but to appraise the Yugoslav experience. These last comments, which are purely specu-lative, suggest that if the LEP-1 criterion of integrity is a good, humane, socialist criterion for evaluating economic performance, then there may well have been a substantially better alternative economic path than that chosen by the Yugoslavs a quarter century ago. If this is at all plausible then later comers should look very carefully before they leap into an extensive growth strategy.

Yugoslavia's income-distribution figures being of a quality and scope comparable to those of other countries, no very definitive judgments on the goods aspects of Yugoslavia's LEP-2 performance is possible. However, there are some general considerations which give good if rough qualitative guidance. First is the by now institutionalized absence of a class of the very rich receiving, as in many developing countries, a third of the personal income and consuming heavily, particularly imported luxury goods. Secondly among the employed population there is a relatively very high level of egalitarianism in income structure, brought about partly by the absence of private *latifundia*, partly by a deliberate policy of modest wage and salary differentials in the city. And finally there is the effect of these two factors on the structure of consumption goods: there is a broad range of consumer goods suitable and necessary for low-income consumption available at often astonishingly low prices. One should not gloss over too lightly some problems, such as the low consumption ratio out of GNP caused by the extensive growth policy, the weak supply of services to the consumer sector, especially in the fifties, and the growing income opportunities for private entrepreneurship in the sixties. But these difficulties are strongly dominated by the successes noted above, and one should certainly add to the success column the very widespread availability of social services, especially in secondary and higher education, but also in medical care and the propagation of the arts.

A substantial portion of the Yugoslav population, surely more than half, supports a standard of living significantly above even a social definition of subsistence, as is suggested by the fact that an average urban worker's family of four spends only a third of its income on food and drink, an average peasant family less than half (including self-produced food and drink on both sides of the ledger). It is also clear that a large fraction of the active population is willing to work very long hours, including moonlighting at home and short-period emigration abroad, to increase the goods support for its life-styles. In some gross sense this sounds like a high level of LEP-2 success for a country that a quarter century ago could have been in serious competition for the title: Poorest in Europe.

As for the other side of LEP-2, the quality of identities, it is fruitless for an outsider to try and penetrate seriously into the subjective aspects of life under Yugoslav socialism. But there is one particular feature of the Yugoslav experience that requires some comment, namely workers' management. It is often advocated as a cure for fundamental social ills, providing higher productivity incentives through direct sharing of the enterprise's income, higher efficiency through common concern in the performance of the enterprise, and higher levels of solidarity and individual satisfaction through worker participation in the basic decisions that affect his working life. How has the Yugoslav self-management system performed over its twenty-year life?

Worker management came to Yugoslavia as a revolution from above. In the early days there was very little for the councils to do, since all major decisions during the administrative system were made at a level above that of the firm. After the switch to a market system of short-run resource allocation in the early fifties, the workers' councils began to come into their own, but even then party and government kept a close watch on enterprise behaviour and the enterprise manager, essentially an outside appointee, had considerable power to override council decisions that were not liked. In the years since then there has been some backing and filling, but the general trend has been toward increasing the power of the workers' councils to make basic policy for the firm and to control more effectively the implementation of policy. Nowadays, it is clear, there are many factories in Yugoslavia in which the workers' council is both representative of the workers in the factory and the dominant force in the making of basic enterprise decisions. In some general sense this situation was reached in short hops, with revision of relevant laws and statements of government policy playing a leading role in the process.

The effects on gross productivity of the workers' management system seem to have been, very roughly, neutral. Neither the enthusiasts nor the Cassandras were right. In industrial growth terms Yugoslavia is one of the world's most notable success stories. Much of this was achieved through a rapid increase in capital stock but support for the programme in terms of worker effort was, to say the least, clearly adequate. However the aggregate statistics do not suggest any release of great stocks of human energy, and this despite the high propensity to moonlight. It seems reasonable to conclude from this that, in its Yugoslav form, worker self-management can support adequately a high-growth rate effort.

One area in which participation served to reveal worker preferences clearly was in the area of work rules and hiring and firing. One result is an apparently exceptionally low industrial accident rate. Short-term layoffs seem virtually to have disappeared in worker-managed factories as the workers have decided to spread short work over the whole staff instead. There has also been a tendency to substitute straight time pay for piece-work. Perhaps most important in LEP-2 terms has been the general recognition that, given the more or less permanent existence of unemployment in the cities, a permanent layoff is a social decision, and that there is a general obligation of the factory to try to retain the worker until his and his family's economic condition is secured, and a general obligation of local and regional authorities to generate alternative employments. Given the agricultural surplus population and generally higher wages in the city, these outcomes have not been the result of deliberate central government policy so much as a response to the clearly expressed desires of the workers themselves in that surplus-labour environment. The required adjustments do not seem to have had any serious effect on factory productivity, at least when appraised in terms of the general performance of the urban economy.

As a system of participation Yugoslav self-management has clearly left something to be desired. Perhaps most important, they did not succeed in abolishing the 'iron law of oligarchy', which states that the very nature of organized human interactions decrees that real decision-making power inevitably devolves on a small group. In the Yugoslav case, as in industry around the world, there is a strong tendency for management to co-opt most technicians into a coalition which controls much of the information-flow into and out of the enterprise and most of the skills required for the design of alternatives for choice-making. This weakens, even destroys, the effectiveness of worker representatives in many firms and, as survey data have shown, leads many Yugoslav workers to view their work environment in much the same terms as do workers in capitalist and bureaucratic socialist firms.

The Yugoslavs of course started with some severe constraints on their organizational reforms. Both the average educational and skill levels of workers were very low at the start, the former averaging well below primary school completion; also the rapid expansion of employment in the fifties brought large numbers of peasants into the factories, whose ability to make reasonable judgments on an alien environment surely takes some time to develop. During much of the fifties, and the sixties as well, Yugoslavs were engaged in learning how to operate the unique new kind of economic system they had created, and this process of getting technical control of the operation probably enhanced the relative influence of the technicos. And the fact that this was a revolution from above, introduced in modest jumps from an initial situation in which enterprises were under the control of a technical-administrative elite, gave the technicos an initial advantage which *de facto* they were often able to preserve despite the trends in laws and political exhortations. Finally, Yugoslavia's extensive involvement in foreign trade has tended to put technicos to the fore in order to provide comparable negotiating talent with foreign business and government, a factor also in enterprise-Yugoslav government relations.

Nevertheless, the self-management system offers many advantages when compared with either corporate capitalism or bureaucratic socialism. Even in enterprises where the council does not seem terribly strong, there is very strong worker interest in work rules and these have been adapted to the needs and wishes of the work force in an atmosphere that is not fraught with the bureaucratized bargaining of union-management relations. Yugoslav workers are often surprisingly well informed as to the economic situation of their enterprise, and the system of worker-council-appointed technical commissions has provided a substantial counter to technocratic information hoarding. And, most important of all, Yugoslav factory work forces, unlike those in any other country, have the genuine ability to offer serious challenge to the making of unwanted major decisions through a variety of instruments varying from the right to strike (sometimes against their own unrepresentative workers council) to the right to dismiss management. These rights, introduced slowly and tentatively but steadily expanded, provide a check on the technocratic-bureaucratic coalition that is far greater than an examination of worker-participation in day-to-day decisions would suggest, for it stems from genuine power which has acquired full legal status and over the years has become institutionalized through actual use in a great many individual instances. It seems quite plausible to argue that the dignity, the self-respect of workers is greatly enhanced by their awareness of this collectively exercisable power.

At least a very brief comment on a very complex subject, the role of the market, is in order. Since the reforms of the early fifties there have been essentially two types of market regimes in Yugoslavia. For the first decade the market was allowed primary influence on short term allocations within the socialist sector, but the central government continued to control most investment decisions in considerable detail. In the mid sixties, however, the government dropped out of much of this investment activity and has allowed basic investment allocation decisions to be taken at a more decentralized level by such bodies as enterprises, banks, local governments and republican governments. The initial scheme was based on the argument that a socialist government should prescribe the basic trajectory for a socialist society, and this required centralization of the investment decision, while short-run allocation decisions were too many in number and too unimportant to be made effectively at the centre, with the quality of the market-based goods as perhaps the principal evidence for the latter case. A decade of experience with this system convinced most Yugoslavs that much the same argument could be made against centralized investment decisions as against short-run allocation decisions, with hosts of 'political' factories requiring substantial operating subsidies to survive at all being the principal evidence for this case.

If the argument for the market is based primarily on efficiency — and quality — considerations, the argument against is usually made on social grounds. Operating in a market, it is argued, is too distorting an educational experience. The participant has his choices structured so that, each time he comes on the market, he finds that what he does is of considerable importance to him but of little importance to others. Secondary effects of a purchase or sale on others can almost always be ignored without apparent cost to anyone. Thus the market teaches egotism. This is true if the markets are competitive; if it is not true then the participant has monopoly power, and that is not exactly a social blessing.

I think there is no denying this argument, but the efficiency argument seems good too; at least there is a very high level of agreement among Yugoslavs that their own history supports the efficiency case. So this is a genuine dilemma. Workers management is supposed to promote feelings of solidarity but the market on which their enterprises are forced to operate keeps teaching the workers just the opposite. A more hierarchic solution, such as the Cubans or Chinese have been trying, sharply reduces the range of market-like interactions, but at the cost of raising the level at which decisions are made, with the consequent reduction in influence that comes with increasing the number of participants in a decision. It seems that a socialist society is forced to make a specific choice of one or other horn of this dilemma.

One might have thought that LEP-1 was not a socialism-sensitive criterion, that all policy makers with any serious claim to being socialist would recognize the elimination of correctable failures of integrity as the primary and minimal goal of all such regimes. Certainly the Yugoslavs, like most other socialist regimes, have made great progress in correcting integrity failure. However, it is no less true that a great many clear cases of correctable failure have gone uncorrected down to the present day. One might even argue that the net effect of the reforms of the mid sixties may even have had the effect of causing a net retrogression on the LEP-1 criterion because of the deterioration of resource availability for social services in the poorer republics.

As for LEP-2 the Yugoslavs have accomplished great things in the proportion of their citizenry who have been brought up to some sort of 'minimum-decent' level of supply of goods and services, and in the scope they have offered the urban population for participation in many of the decisions that affect their daily lives. But the reforms of the mid-sixties on this criterion as well may turn out to have been retrogressive, especially in terms of the impact of the continued inflation on the real consumption standards of the poorer urban citizenry, and the possibly increased variability of agricultural incomes.

The basic problem seems to be the quite general tendency for markets to push towards increasing inequality of income distribution. Yugoslavia has, through socialization of major means of production and other egalitarian measures, generated a market system whose absolute level of inequality is, relatively speaking, very low, but the direction of change remains, even under socialism, toward greater inequality. The reforms of the mid-sixties were intended to increase freedom of self-realization through further withering away of the central state government, but the major substitute for that body was increased marketization. Without as yet possessing a firmly fixed and institutional LEP-1 floor these reforms, designed to increase the autonomy of individuals and smaller groups, can easily be retrogressive in terms of both criteria.

Much, perhaps most, of the problem can be traced to the failure to deal effectively with two of the three great adversary relationships of Yugoslav society: that between capitalist and worker, between town and country, and between one ethnic group and another. We are ignoring the last of these problems; the first was solved early and has not been a serious issue since; the second was and is unresolved and has distorted policies and outcomes throughout Yugoslavia's socialist history. It is perhaps not too strong to say that a solution to this problem which is compatible with socialist values must be found or the other adversary relationships will return in a progressively intensifying form.

The early years of a revolution are crucial, since they structure the society and its leadership for the taking of later decisions. This structure is not irreversible, but it seems clear that major changes of course become more difficult as time goes on. For even revolutions became institutionalized. Options are narrowed, partly because people have got used to the framework, maybe even believe in it and want to work within it, partly too no doubt because the leadership identifies with its earlier policies, and perhaps as they become older the leaders also become tired of turmoil. The Yugoslav leaders made basic choices in the mid-forties and modified them fundamentally in the early fifties, perhaps before such stabilizing forces became very strong. The agricultural decision was one of the most important of the decisions which was taken at that time. *The* most important decision of that time, and one that has been followed since to the point of thoroughgoing institutionalization, was the decision to go essentially for the creation of a liberal socialist society.

Like all societies, of whatever political and social hue Yugoslavia is neither perfection incarnate nor evil incarnate. Unlike the situation in many societies, the Yugoslav experience is oriented toward a utopian view of man and society. It is a view in which the dignity of the individual is to be sustained through freedom and autonomy for individuals and smaller groupings in the society, in which the role of solidarity is to emerge from the needs of these groupings rather than from the pressures of some centralized cadre. But it is also a view in which the interaction, even the need for some compatibility for interaction, between Yugoslavs and the rest of the world, is recognized as a right, and one that may at times conflict with other socialist values. The resulting pragmatic struggle for socialism does not appeal to purists, but it may well be the nearest thing to socialism that is feasible in the world today. That it has astonishing successes to its credit in comparison with developing capitalist countries must be apparent to every visitor who has a basis for comparison. In comparing the Yugoslav Way with other forms of socialism, judgment must depend in the final analysis on the strength of one's 'taste for solidarity' and of one's willingness to control other humans in the service of that solidary conception of humanity.

457

BIBLIOGRAPHY*

The literature on the Chilean road to socialism is not plentiful — particularly in English — but the following brief list may be found useful.

1. Philosophy of the *'via chilena'*.

An essential political text is the collection of Salvador Allende's speeches, edited by Joán Garcés, *Nuestro Camino al Socialismo*, Buenos Aires, Ediciones Papiro, 1971. (An English translation is to be published in the Pelican Latin American Library in 1973.) Equally important is its economic counterpart, edited by Gonzalo Martner, *El Pensamiento Económico del Gobierno de Allende*, Santiago, Editorial Universitaria, 1971. Regis Debray's *Conversations with Allende: Socialism in Chile*, London, New Left Books, 1971, remains the best introduction to the thinking of the Chilean President and to the ideological problems confronting the Popular Unity Government.

2. Chilean official documents

The extensive publications of the *Oficina de Planificación Nacional* (ODEPLAN) include the fourteen volumes of the Six-Year Plan, *Plan de la Economía Nacional, 1971-76*, Santiago, ODEPLAN, October 1971. A preliminary volume, *Antecedentes sobre el Desarrollo Chileno 1960-70*, provides a useful summary of the economic situation in the previous decade, while the first volume, *La Estrategia del Plan*, discusses the Plan's fundamental strategy. ODEPLAN also publishes the *Plan Anual* in March each year as well as an economic survey, *Informe Económico Anual*, which is an indispensable source of information. Late in 1971, ODEPLAN sponsored the production of a quarterly review, *Nueva Economía*, Santiago, Editorial Universitaria. Its first number, September-December 1971, included articles by Pedro Vuskovic and Gonzalo Martner, as well as documents,

* Thanks are due to the library Staff of the Institute of Development Studies and to Richard Gott for help in compiling this bibliography.

communications, and the texts of various decrees. Essential for grasping both the political atmosphere in Chile and the nature and extent of United States involvement are the *Documentos Secretos de la ITT*, Santiago, Quimantú, 1972. (Published in English under the title, *Subversion in Chile: a case study in US corporate intrigue in the Third World*, Nottingham, Bertrand Russell Peace Foundation, 1972.)

3. Comment and analysis in Chile

The most significant debate on Chile's road to socialism takes place within the covers of the quarterly review, *Cuadernos de la Realidad Nacional*, published by the *Centro de Estudios de la Realidad Nacional* (CEREN) of the *Universidad Católica de Chile*. Among the many interesting articles to have appeared recently are: Jacques Chonchol, 'Elementos para una discusión sobre el camino chileno hacia el socialismo', March 1971; Lucio Geller, 'Algunas preguntas sobre la construcción del socialismo en Chile', September 1971; Julio Lopez, 'La estrategia económica del gobierno de la Unidad Popular', September 1971; James Petras, 'Nacionalización, transformaciones socio-económicas y participación popular en Chile', January 1972; Sergio Bitar and Eduardo Mogano, 'Redistribución del consumo y transición al socialismo', January 1972; Rene Billaz and Eugenio Maffei, 'La Reforma Agraria y el camino hacia el socialismo: algunas consideraciones', January 1972.

Another university institute, equally committed politically as CEREN, the *Centro de Estudios Socio-Económicos* (CESO) of the *Universidad de Chile*, has recently published a new quarterly, *Sociedad y Desarrollo*, edited by Theotonio dos Santos. Its first issue, January-March 1972, includes: Sergio Ramos, 'La situación de transición: características de la coyuntura chilena'; and Pio Garcia, 'La política económica del gobierno popular: consideraciones políticas'.

In October 1971, CESO and CEREN joined forces to sponsor an international conference whose proceedings were published under the title *La Transición al Socialismo y la Experiencia Chilena*, Ediciones PLA, 1972. Contributors included Lelio Basso, Rossana Rossanda, Paul Sweezy, and Michael Gutelman, as well Pedro Vuskovic and Jacques Chonchol. CESO was also responsible for producing *Chile Hoy*, Mexico, Siglo Veintiuno, 1970, a collection of serious analytical essays by Anibal Pinto and others covering most aspects of the political and economic development of contemporary Chile as seen on the eve of Allende's presidential victory.

Allende's Chile, edited by Kenneth Medhurst, London, Hart-Davis MacGibbon, 1972, contains a number of essays by Chilean authors on political and economic topics, and will prove useful to those with no Spanish. It concludes with the summary of a conference held in Manchester in March 1972 discussing the implications of the Chilean experience for France and Italy.

The *Instituto de Economía* of the *Universidad de Chile* has produced a sizeable volume, *La Economía Chilena en 1971,* with competent contributions from those of its research staff broadly sympathetic to the aspirations of the Popular Unity. A rival group from the *Departamento de Economía* of the same university has printed three semestral volumes in 1971 and 1972 entitled, *Comentarios sobre la situación económica,* which are more critical of the Government's performance and less penetrating.

For a frankly hostile view of the Popular Unity's policies and actions, see *Itinerario de una crisis,* Santiago, Editorial del Pacifico, 1972, which contains contributions from Christian Democrat politicians and economists, including Alvaro Bardon, Jorge Cauas, and Sergio Molina.

4. Reportage in Chile

For sharp topical comment on Chilean economic affairs, there is the monthly review *Panorama Económico,* published by the Editorial Universitaria on behalf of a group of independent economists. The monthly Jesuit magazine, *Mensaje,* is also often worth looking at. More popular is the weekly magazine, *Chile Hoy* (Avenida Italia 654, Santiago), edited by Marta Harnecka.

The views of the various components of the Popular Unity can be found in their journals: *Principios* (Communist Party), *Posición* (Socialist Party), *De Frente* (MAPU). Further to the left, *Punto Final* (fortnightly) and *Causa Marxista-Leninista* (monthly) favour the MIR and the pro-Chinese Communist Party respectively.

5. Foreign Observers

Two accounts in French, both appearing in 1972, give a good, professional summary of the problems and achievements of the Popular Unity Government. Alain Labrousse, *L'Expérience Chilienne,* Paris, Editions du Seuil, is marginally more profound than Catherine Lamour, *Le Pari Chilien,* Paris, Stock. But both are good. Alistair Horne's trivial diary, *Small Earthquake in Chile,* London, Macmillan, 1972, is not in the same category.

6. Foreign reportage and comment

The weekly *Latin America* (Latin American Newsletters Ltd., 69 Cannon Street, London) provides succint up-to-the-minute economic and political comment on events in Chile in English. *BOLSA Review*, the monthly magazine of the old Bank of London and South America, has useful information in its News Review, while the *Quarterly Review: Chile* of the Economist Intelligence Unit is usually well-supplied with the most recent statistics.

7. Foreign comment and analysis

New Chile, North American Congress on Latin America, California, NACLA, 1972, is the best brief introduction to the aspirations and achievements of Allende's government, produced with the style and attention to detail that characterizes NACLA's work. Yves Goussault, in 'La réforme agraire chilienne: hésitations ou impasse,' *Tiers Monde*, July-September 1972, has looked at the agrarian reform, while Dudley Seers in the *World Today*, May 1972, asks 'Is the road to socialism blocked?' A more hostile analysis on the same topic, probably written by a Christian Democrat politician, is 'Chile's economic reforms: what kind of revolution?' *World Today*, November 1972.

For some light on the international implications of Allende's policies, the following articles are worth considering: Claudio Veliz, 'The Chilean Experiment', *Foreign Affairs*, April 1971; Theodore H. Morgan, 'The Alliance for Progress and "the foreign copper companies and their local conservative allies" in Chile 1955-1970', *Inter-American Economic Affairs*, Spring 1972: 'The Kennecott White Paper on Chile's expropriation of the El Teniente copper mines', *Inter-American Economic Affairs*, Spring 1972; James Petras and Robert Laporte, 'Can we do business with radical nationalists?' *Foreign Policy*, Summer 1972.

The American Marxist *Monthly Review* has taken considerable interest in the Chilean experience and the articles by the editor, Paul Sweezy, reflect a view-point that is somewhat to the left of the Popular Unity: 'Peaceful transition to socialism', *Monthly Review*, January 1971; and 'Chile: advance or retreat?' *Monthly Review*, January 1972. Also see, James Petras, 'The transition to socialism in Chile: perspectives and problems', *Monthly Review*, October 1971.

Some useful insights can be found in Alan Angell, 'Allende's first year in Chile', *Current History*, February 1972; Harold Blakemore, 'Continuity and change on the road to socialism', *BOLSA*

Review, January 1972; Robert Myhr, 'Chile's path to socialism: observations on Allende's first year' (Special Study No. 9), Centre for Latin American Studies, Arizona State University, 1972.

LIST OF PARTICIPANTS*

Clodomiro Almeyda	*Minister of Foreign Affairs, Chile.*
Sergio Aranda	*Regional Deputy Director, National Planning Office (ODEPLAN), Santiago, Chile.*
Jorge Arrate	*Executive Vice-President, Copper Corporation, Santiago, Chile.*
Aleksander Bajt	*Economist, Institute of Economics, Faculty of Law, University of Ljubljana, Yugoslavia.*
Lord Balogh	*Economist, Balliol College, Oxford, England.*
Jorge Bertini	*Adviser, Ministry of Economic Affairs, Chile.*
Solon Barraclough	*Economist, FAO International Director, Institute for Training and Research in Agrarian Reform (ICIRA), Santiago, Chile.*
Jorge Cauas	*Economist, Institute of Economics, Catholic University, Santiago, Chile.*
Hollis B. Chenery	*Economic Adviser to the President, International Bank for Reconstruction and Development, Washington D.C., U.S.A.*
Jacques Chonchol	*Minister of Agriculture, Chile.*
Antonio De Barros C.	*Latin-American Institute for Economic and Social Planning (ILPES), United Nations, Santiago, Chile.*
Emanuel De Kadt	*Sociologist, Institute of Development Studies (I.D.S.), Brighton, Sussex, England.*
Dag Ehrenpreis	*Latin American Department, Swedish International Development Authority, Stockholm, Sweden.*
Academician N.P. Fedorenko	*Director, Central Institute of Mathematical Economics, Moscow, U.S.S.R.*
Luis Figueroa	*President, CUT (Central Trades Union Confederation), Santiago, Chile.*
Alejandro Foxley	*Economist, Planning Centre (CEPLAN), Catholic University, Santiago, Chile.*
Roberto Frenkel	*Adviser, Ministry of Economic Affairs, Santiago, Chile.*
Hernan Frigolett	*Economist, National Planning Office (ODEPLAN), Santiago, Chile.*
Istvan Friss	*Director, Institute of Economics, Hungarian Academy of Sciences, Budapest, Hungary.*

* The positions listed here are as they were at the time of the Conference in March 1972.

Celso Furtado	*Economist, Faculté de Droit et de Sciences Economiques, Sorbonne, Paris, France.*
Joán Garcés	*Political Scientist, National Planning Office (ODEPLAN), Santiago, Chile.*
Eduardo Garcia	*Economist, Institute of Economics, Catholic University, Santiago, Chile.*
Pio Garcia	*Adviser, Ministry of Economic Affairs, Chile.*
Oscar Garreton	*Under-Secretary, Ministry of Economic Affairs, Chile.*
Manuel Garreton	*Director, Centro de Estudios de la Realidad Nacional (CEREN), Catholic University, Santiago, Chile.*
Marcos Gomez	*Economist, National Planning Office (ODEPLAN), Santiago, Chile.*
Joseph Grunwald	*Coordinator, Programme of Joint Studies on Latin American Development, The Brookings' Institution, Washington D.C., U.S.A.*
Eberhardt Hackethal	*Economic Historian, History Department, Karl-Marx University, Leipzig, German Democratic Republic.*
Jose Ibarra	*Deputy National Director, National Planning Office (ODEPLAN), Santiago, Chile.*
Academician Boris L. Isaev	*Central Institute of Mathematical Economics, Moscow, U.S.S.R.*
Lal Jayawardena	*Additional Permanent Secretary, Ministry of Planning and Employment, Colombo, Ceylon.*
Alain Joxe	*Political Scientist, Centre d'Etudes de Politique Etrangère, Paris, France.*
Ricardo Lagos	*Economist, Interim Secretary General, Latin American Faculty of Social Sciences (FLACSO), Santiago, Chile.*
Bernardo Leighton	*Deputy, Christian Democrat Party, Santiago, Chile.*
David Lehmann	*Sociologist, Institute of Development Studies (I.D.S.), Brighton, Sussex, England.*
Julio Lopez	*Economist, Institute of Economics, University of Chile, Santiago.*
Flavio Machicao	*Economist, FAO, Santiago, Chile.*
Alberto Martinez	*Adviser, Ministry of Economic Affairs, Santiago, Chile.*
Gonzalo Martner	*Minister of Planning, National Planning Office (ODEPLAN), Santiago, Chile.*
Ajit Mozoomdar	*Minister at the High Commission for India, London, England.*
Dominic Mulaisho	*Managing Director, State Mining Development Corporation, Lusaka, Zambia.*
Oscar Muñoz	*Economist, Planning Centre (CEPLAN), Catholic University, Santiago, Chile.*

Urs Muller-Plantenburg	*Economist, Centre of Latin American Studies, Free University of Berlin, Berlin, Federal Republic of Germany.*
Ifigenia Navarrete	*Economist, Autonomous National University of Mexico, Mexico City, Mexico.*
Eduardo Novoa	*President, National Defence Council, Chile.*
Anibal Palma	*Under-Secretary of Foreign Affairs, Chile.*
Gabriel Palma	*Economist, National Planning Office (ODEPLAN), Santiago, Chile.*
James Petras	*Political Scientist, Department of Political Science, Pennsylvania State University, Pennsylvania, U.S.A.*
Richard Portes	*Economist, Department of Economics, University of Princeton, U.S.A. and University College, London, England.*
Clark W. Reynolds	*Economist, Department of Economics, Food Research Institute, Stanford University, Stanford, California, U.S.A.*
Darcy Ribeiro	*University of Chile, Santiago, Chile.*
Alejandro Schejtman	*Adviser, Ministry of Economic Affairs, Santiago, Chile.*
Salvatore Sechi	*Economic Historian, Institute of Historical Studies, University of Venice, Venice, Italy.*
Dudley Seers	*Director, Institute of Development Studies (I.D.S.), Brighton, Sussex, England.*
Francis Seton	*Economist, Nuffield College, Oxford, England.*
Jose A. Silva Michelena	*Sociologist, Centre for Economic and Social Development Studies (CENDES), Central University, Caracas, Venezuela.*
Julio Silva Solar	*Deputy, Party of the Christian Left, Chile.*
Bertram Silverman	*Economist, Department of Economics, Hofstra University, New York, U.S.A.*
Osvaldo Sunkel	*Economist, Institute of Economics, Catholic University, Santiago, Chile.*
Volodia Teitelboim	*Senator, Communist Party, Chile.*
Radomiro Tomic	*Professor, Catholic University, Chile.*
Brian Van Arkadie	*Director of Development Studies, Faculty of Economics, University of Cambridge, Cambridge, England.*
Pedro Vuskovic	*Minister of Economic Affairs, Chile.*
Benjamin Ward	*Economist, Department of Economics, University of California, Berkeley, California, U.S.A.*
Adam Watson	*Former British Ambassador in Cuba.*
J. Ann Zammit	*Economist, Institute of Development Studies (I.D.S.), Brighton, Sussex, England.*
Rene Zavaleta	*Sociologist, National Planning Office (ODEPLAN), Santiago Chile.*